Conflict Between
People and Groups

Nelson-Hall Series in Psychology
Consulting Editor: **Stephen Worchel**
Texas A&M University

Conflict Between People and Groups

Causes, Processes, and Resolutions

Edited by

Stephen Worchel *and* Jeffry A. Simpson
Texas A&M University

Nelson-Hall Publishers
Chicago

Library of Congress Cataloging-in-Publication Data

Conflict between people and groups : causes, processes, and
   resolutions / edited by Stephen Worchel and Jeffry A. Simpson.
        p.   cm.
   Includes bibliographical references and index.
   ISBN 0-8304-1307-3
   1. Social conflict—Congresses.   2. Conflict management—
Congresses.   I. Worchel, Stephen.   II. Simpson, Jeffry A.
HM136.C668   1993
303.6—dc20   92-36418
                                                                        CIP

Manufactured in the United States of America

10   9   8   7   6   5   4   3   2   1

TM   The paper used in this book meets the
     minimum requirements of American
     National Standard for Information
     Sciences—Permanence of Paper for
     Printed Library Materials, ANSI
     Z39.48-1984.

Contents

Part III
INTERNATIONAL CONFLICT

Acknowledgments

This book emerged from the proceedings of the 1990 Symposium on Group Conflict held by the Department of Psychology at Texas A&M University. Financial support for the symposium and production of the book was provided by a grant from the College of Liberal Arts at Texas A&M University. We would like to thank Daniel Fallon, Dean of the College, for his assistance in making the symposium and book a reality. Thanks also go to Vicki Corrington, who oversaw the coordination of the symposium, and to faculty members in the Department of Psychology—especially William Graziano, Charles Samuelson, and Wendy Wood—for their invaluable help with the symposium. Finally, we would like to extend a special thanks to all of the graduate students in the Department of Psychology who spent countless hours planning, organizing, and facilitating the operation of the symposium. These individuals include Robert Agans, Michael Biek, Tami Blackstone, Dawna Coutant-Sassic, Michelle Grossman, Kathy Hannula, Betty Harris, Stephen Jenner, Laurie Jensen, Sharon Lundgren, Eric Olson, Nancy Rhodes, and Brian Young.

1 Introduction: Multidisciplinary Perspectives on Conflict

Jeffry A. Simpson and Stephen Worchel

The history of research in much of the social sciences reads like a description of tides in the ocean. Hot topics or central themes dominate for a period of time and then slowly recede as a new topic crashes onto the research shores (cf. Meehl, 1978). This pattern of events often instigates articles that sound much like the popular song of the 1960s, ''Where Have All the Flowers Gone?'' Every decade or so, investigators lament about what has happened to research in areas such as groups (Steiner, 1974), leadership (Hollander, 1985), and dissonance theory (Cooper & Fazio, 1984). While this pattern of ebb and flow characterizes many research topics, some tend to buck the trend. One such area is *conflict*.

Whether one examines sociology, psychology, anthropology, business, organizational psychology, political science, clinical psychology, philosophy, or a host of other disciplines, conflict is never far from the empirical and theoretical limelight. Indeed, the multidisciplinary focus on conflict is evident in theory, research, and application across all of these disciplines. It is interesting to speculate about why conflict has continued to dominate the horizon.

The most optimistic explanation is that we suffer from a universal Zeigarnik effect. We simply do not have closure in our understanding of the causes of conflict and ways to manage it. A more likely explanation, however, is that conflict plays a central role at all levels of our lives. At the intrapersonal level, we typically experience conflict each time we make a decision. Over time, these experiences are thought to serve as a foundation of our personalities and self-concepts (Rogers, 1961). Conflict also shadows all of our interpersonal contacts, whether they involve work, play, or love (Peterson, 1983). And as the scope of our interactions expands to include small and large groups, so too does the potential role of conflict expand (Deutsch, 1973).

In addition to conflict's pervasive presence, two other features heighten

1

its importance. One feature is its enormous potential to destroy everything with which it comes in contact. There is more than ample evidence showing that conflict can be the downfall of the psyche, dyadic relationships, small groups of every nature, nations, political systems, and civilizations (see Worchel & Austin, 1986). Such a villain demands attention, whether that attention be aimed at removing conflict, resolving it, managing it, or converting it from an evil force into a constructive one.

A second feature of conflict that adds urgency to its investigation is the growing presence of conflict in the world. While modern advances in science have increased our options for travel, lengthened the days of our lives, and given us more leisure time than ever before, each of these gains has also provided greater opportunities for conflict to emerge at all levels of our lives.

As evidenced by the escalating divorce rate (Norton & Glick, 1976), the potential for conflict and discord in marital and romantic relationships has risen dramatically in recent decades. Although a variety of factors may be responsible for this situation, three factors stand out as major culprits. First, general expectations and aspirations for what one can and should get out of romantic relationships have risen rapidly (Berscheid & Campbell, 1981) without concomitant increases in understanding how to manage the conflict that arises when aspirations do not match reality. Second, because of recent advances in the social, economic, and legal status of women within most Western countries, women have become less dependent and more "coequal" partners in many dyadic relationships. Greater equality, however, can exacerbate overt conflict, particularly when neither partner in a relationship is highly dependent on its continuation (see Kelley & Thibaut, 1978). And third, given the rise in dual career families, coupled with recent reductions in the amount of available leisure time (Marney, 1991), individuals are experiencing more stress in their daily lives than ever before. This has placed a tremendous strain on dyadic relationships, heightening the potential for dissension and strife.

Prospects for conflict also have increased for various types of small groups, particularly those in work settings. In addition to increased stress in their personal lives, American workers are experiencing more stress than ever before at the workplace (Dewe, 1989), due in large part to greater economic competition from abroad. Based on the success of the Japanese, many businesses and organizations are now utilizing small work groups to increase employee satisfaction and company profits. These groups, however, now must operate in an economic and social climate characterized by increasingly greater pressures and demands. As a result, the potential for conflict in the workplace has risen in the last decade.

Finally, despite better relations between the superpowers in recent years, the prospects for conflict between nations and larger collectives of people continue to pose serious threats to world peace. Technological advances, democratic reforms in Eastern Europe and what once was the Soviet

Union, and worldwide environmental concerns have fostered more frequent and closer contact among various nations. Yet tremendous economic disparities still exist between technologically advanced countries and third world countries. Since close contact does not reduce intergroup conflict unless groups have equal status on important dimensions (Amir, 1969), the potential for conflict among nations is not likely to abate—and might actually intensify—in the coming years.

Viewed together, these societal changes have produced an environment in which conflict can more easily emerge and escalate. Given this somber reality, new insights into the origins, nature, and management of conflict are needed.

THE PRESENT VOLUME

During the spring of 1990, we convened a conference on intragroup and intergroup conflict at Texas A&M University, bringing together a diverse array of leading scholars who have made significant contributions to the conflict literature. This book reflects the deliberations and discussions that took place at that conference.

Contributors to this volume represent a number of different academic disciplines, including clinical psychology, sociology, industrial/organizational psychology, business, political science, and social psychology. Their research interests include the perceptual origins of intergroup conflict, conflict mediation, conflict in romantic relationships, interracial conflict, political conflict, international conflict, and conflict within and between small groups. Instead of being organized around traditional academic disciplines, the book is divided into three major sections: dyadic conflict, conflict within and between small groups, and conflict within and between larger collectives.

The objectives of this book and the conference on which it was based were threefold. First, we wanted to showcase state-of-the-art theory and research on conflict that currently is being conducted in several different academic fields by scholars possessing diverse theoretical perspectives. Second, we wanted to highlight new ideas and theoretical approaches to understanding conflict, including how and why it originates, how and why it is maintained, and how and why it oftentimes becomes amplified over time. Finally, we wanted to stimulate new ways of thinking about conflict management, including how conflict can be reduced, channeled into more constructive actions, and used to promote positive changes in people, work groups, and society.

When we planned the conference and the present volume, one issue continually arose: Should we cast a wide net and attempt to include a variety of different perspectives and fields, or should we narrow our focus to include investigators who represent a single approach or discipline? Clearly, there are several advantages to the latter approach. Investigators from a common discipline already share a perspective, they speak a common language, and they generally agree on the major issues of importance within the field. On the other hand, increasing the diversity of participants opens up new vistas, invites consideration of broader issues, and may set the stage for collaborative research efforts. Conflict is not the exclusive domain of any single area or discipline, and we felt that there was much to be gained by sharing and incorporating diverse perspectives.

With this view in mind, we chose the path of greater diversity. Our hope is that the present volume will demonstrate that there are common themes in these diverse approaches. We also hope that the diverse perspectives advocated in this volume will encourage interdisciplinary research geared toward achieving goals common to *all* disciplines—namely, understanding conflict and developing theories and applications to reduce and manage it.

Part I
INTERPERSONAL CONFLICT

2 Conflict in Marriage: A Cognitive/Behavioral Formulation

Donald H. Baucom, Norman Epstein,
Charles K. Burnett, and Lynn Rankin

In order to understand conflict within groups, it is important to investigate one of the most common and important types of groups that exist across societies: the married couple. The continuing high divorce rate indicates that a high proportion of married couples experience significant relationship distress. Furthermore, marital conflict appears to have a major impact on individual well-being. For example, the Life Events Survey (Holmes & Rahe, 1967) includes a variety of events that might occur in an individual's life, along with empirically derived ratings of how stressful the events are likely to be to the person experiencing them. The three events rated as most stressful all relate to the termination of marriage.

Furthermore, the research to date indicates that in most instances, marital distress is marked by overt conflict between the partners. (In the current context, "conflict" refers to the expression of negative behaviors, thoughts, and emotions that result from differing goals and values or a dislike between the spouses involved.) Whereas this statement about the relation between marital distress and conflict might at first appear to be obvious or even tautological, it is not. Spouses engage in both (a) positive, or rewarding, behaviors and (b) negative, or punishing, behaviors with their partners. It is a pertinent question to ask whether marital distress is related to the absence of positive behaviors between spouses and/or to an excess of negative behaviors between partners. Both types of behaviors appear to be of importance, but as will be demonstrated in the remainder of this chapter, the presence of excess negative behaviors appears to be more closely related to marital distress. Snyder's (1979) work on the Marital Satisfaction Inventory (MSI) provides one demonstration of this finding. Snyder and Regts (1982) factor-analyzed this 280-item inventory and derived two broad-band factor scales: disharmony and disaffection. They found that within the general population, marital distress was more closely correlated with the factor scale that assessed overt discord, perceived disharmony, or conflict between the spouses. Thus to a large extent, the study of marital distress involves the investigation of conflict between two persons in an intimate, ongoing relationship.

THE ROLES OF BEHAVIORS, COGNITIONS, AND EMOTIONS IN MARITAL CONFLICT

A cognitive/behavioral formulation of marital conflict asserts that behaviors, cognitions, and emotions are all important and interrelated in marital functioning (Baucom & Epstein, 1990). Thus, a change in one of these domains is likely to result in changes in the other two domains. However, to a large extent, a cognitive/behavioral formulation focuses on the ways that spouses' behaviors and cognitions (e.g., thoughts about the relationship) influence the spouses' emotions about the marriage. For example, if the two spouses engage in a large number of negative behaviors toward each other, then they are likely to be unhappy in the relationship. Similarly, if a husband interprets his wife's long hours at work as resulting from her desire to avoid him, then he is likely to become distressed. Since the late 1960s, investigators have conducted a large number of studies to elucidate the role of behaviors and cognitions in marital discord.

BEHAVIORS IN MARITAL DISCORD

Behavioral researchers have differentiated between two major categories of marital behavior: communication and noncommunication behavior. Couples' communication (i.e., the exchange of information) has been focused upon for several reasons. First, communication problems are the most frequent presenting complaint of maritally distressed couples (Geiss & O'Leary, 1981). Second, not only are communication difficulties common, but they seem to be almost synonymous with marital discord; for example, self-report measures of communication problems often correlate above .80 with the couples' self-reports of marital satisfaction. These communication difficulties include frequent arguments, not feeling understood by the partner, infrequent conversations among partners, etc. Third, effective communication seems to be essential for other aspects of marital relationships to proceed adaptively. That is, good communication helps spouses resolve conflicts and reach decisions about the many issues confronting all couples. Similarly, clear communication assists couples in understanding each other and feeling closer to each other (Baucom & Adams, 1987). Without effective communication, the couple is at high risk for conflict whenever they have to confront the many problems inherent in married life.

However, not all behaviors between spouses consist of attempts at communication. Spouses engage in a wide variety of behaviors on a daily basis that have the potential to create conflict between them. The ways in which finances are handled, the quality and variety of meals that are prepared, the degree to which the home is kept clean and orderly, and how the work load is distributed, all can contribute to, or become the forum for, a couple's conflict. Thus, to come to a clearer understanding of the role of behaviors in marital distress and conflict, one must take into account both communication and noncommunication behaviors.

Communication

Although there is an almost unlimited number of specific types of marital communications that could be investigated, for data analytic purposes most investigators have differentiated between broad categories of positive communication (including such behaviors as making eye contact and offering solutions to problems) and negative communication (such as blaming, denying personal responsibility). Whereas the terms *positive* and *negative* are opposite in valence and seem to imply opposite ends of a single bipolar dimension, it is important to recognize that they do not necessarily operate in a bipolar fashion in marital interaction. For example, the fact that a husband does not criticize his wife (absence of a negative) does not mean that he necessarily compliments her (presence of a positive). Consequently, the relation of both positive and negative communication to marital conflict must be explored.

Two different data analytic strategies have been employed in investigating the role of positive and negative communication in marital interaction, and these two strategies provide different types of information. First, investigators have explored the frequencies or base rates with which distressed and nondistressed couples demonstrate various communications. Whereas this approach can provide the needed information to address issues such as differences between distressed and nondistressed couples in how often they employ various communications, this strategy provides no information about the *patterns* or sequences of communications that occur during an interaction. That is, are there any regularities regarding what types of communications tend to follow each other when a couple interacts? To investigate these issues, sequential analytic strategies have been employed.

Communication Frequencies. Although the results are not totally consistent (see Margolin & Wampold, 1981, for an exception), most investigations demonstrate that maritally distressed couples exhibit significantly more negative communication than do nondistressed couples (e.g., Birchler, Weiss, & Vincent, 1975). However, when the frequency of positive communication is considered, the findings are not as consistent. Some studies have found that nondistressed couples exhibit more frequent positive communications than do distressed couples (e.g., Vincent, Friedman, Nugent, & Messerly, 1979), whereas other investigations demonstrate no difference between the two groups on frequency of positive communications (e.g., Robinson & Price, 1980). Thus, distressed couples appear to be distinguished primarily by a surplus of negative communication that is experienced as overt conflict.

Gottman and his associates have assessed verbal and nonverbal communication separately. Employing this approach, they have found that distressed and nondistressed couples could be better differentiated using nonverbal communication (e.g., facial expression and body language) than verbal codes (Gottman, 1979; Gottman, Markman, & Notarius, 1977). When both verbal and nonverbal communication were considered together, Gottman et al. found that when positive nonverbal communication was exhibited, the two groups did not differ on verbal codes. However, the two groups of couples did differ on the frequency of verbal codes expressed with neutral and negative nonverbal communication. These findings reinforce the relative importance of negative communication as a discriminator between distressed and nondistressed couples, as well as pointing to the utility of assessing nonverbal as well as verbal communication. Thus, conflict in communication involves not only what is said verbally but also the bodily gestures and facial expressions used to convey these negative messages.

Communication Sequences. Current space does not allow for a discussion of the many issues that can be addressed regarding sequences of communication between spouses (see Baucom & Adams, 1987, for a review). However, one issue of central importance in understanding conflictual interaction involves the notion of *reciprocity*. Broadly stated, reciprocity involves a communication pattern in which a particular type of communication from one spouse leads to a similar response from the partner. Thus in negative reciprocity, a negative communication from one spouse is followed by a negative communication from the partner, creating and perpetuating a chain of negative interactions. This is a conflictual style of interaction that is experienced as an escalation of negative communication. Similarly, in positive reciprocity, a positive communication from one person is followed by a positive communication by the other. In order to investigate the presence of reciprocity, researchers have operationally defined it in a manner that remains independent of overall frequencies of positive and negative communication. Reciprocity is examined in terms of conditional and unconditional probabilities, evaluating the extent to which knowing one partner's communication improves the ability to predict the other partner's subsequent communication.

As expected, maritally distressed couples exhibit higher rates of negative reciprocity than do nondistressed couples (e.g., Billings, 1979; Margolin & Wampold, 1981). That is, in a maritally distressed couple, if one spouse says something negative, it greatly increases the likelihood that the partner will respond with a negative statement. For example, in one of our recent studies of maritally distressed couples, the likelihood that distressed wives would respond with a negative statement increased 270 percent if their husbands' immediately previous statement was negative, compared to the wives' responses when the husband had not been negative. Similarly, if the wives had just communicated negatively, the likelihood that their husbands would respond negatively increased 300 percent, compared to when the wives had not been negative (Sayers, Baucom, & Sher, 1989). These findings deal only with two-sequence patterns. However, other investigations demonstrate not only that distressed couples exhibit greater levels of negative reciprocity, but also that the negative reciprocity continues for a greater number of sequences than occurs among nondistressed couples (Gottman et al., 1977). These findings corroborate the complaints of distressed couples that once they begin interacting in negative ways, the negative interaction continues and escalates—perhaps the sine qua non of conflict between spouses.

Positive reciprocity also appears to exist for both distressed and nondistressed couples (Gottman et al., 1976; Margolin & Wampold, 1981). However, the two groups demonstrate the reciprocity with different timing. Among distressed couples, there is a tendency to reciprocate with positive responses immediately, whereas nondistressed couples respond with positive communications after longer lags in the conversation following the initial positive communication (Gottman, 1979). Other interpretations of this finding are feasible, but one possibility is that nondistressed couples have a sense of trust and security in the relationship, and there is not the pressure to respond immediately to a positive with a positive. However, among distressed couples, the positive interaction is more tenuous and uncertain, and the partners may feel that they must respond immediately with a positive to acknowledge the other person's behavior and/or to maintain the positive interaction.

Gender and Sex-Role Differences. Not only are there differences between distressed and nondistressed couples regarding both frequency and sequences of communication, there are gender differences as well. Wives in distressed relationships engage in higher overall frequencies of negative communication behaviors than do their husbands (Notarius, Benson, Sloane, Vanzetti, & Hornyak, 1989). Especially in situations in which the potential for conflict is high, wives are more likely than their husbands to interpret messages as negative, to feel less positive affect, and to be more critical of their partners. Distressed wives, generally, tend to exhibit high levels of anger, noncompliance, disapproval, complaints, and commands (Gottman & Krokoff, 1989).

Gender differences also appear to play a major role in moderating the intensity of negative reciprocity. Women in distressed relationships are much more likely to provide a negative response to a negative partner statement than are women in nondistressed marriages or distressed or nondistressed men (Notarius et al., 1989). However, wives in nondistressed relationships are more likely to respond to a negative statement from their partner with a nonnegative statement than are distressed wives, distressed husbands, or nondistressed husbands (Gottman et al., 1977). This feature of nondistressed communication is often referred to as "editing" and is likely to reduce the amount of negative reciprocity in a relationship. Thus, the research to date suggests that wives are more likely to play the critical role in determining the extent of negative reciprocity that occurs in the couples' interactions. One clinical implication of this finding is that there needs to be an increased emphasis on teaching husbands to learn the editing role in couples' negative interactions, so that both partners share the responsibility for ending negative interaction cycles.

Another gender-related feature of couples' communication is a dimension of *engagement-disengagement* (Baucom, Notarius, Burnett, & Haefner, 1990). In both distressed and nondistressed couples, many wives tend to seek increased communication in problem situations, whereas many husbands tend to withdraw from potentially conflictual situations, especially as problem intensity increases. One interpretation is that in these situations wives are concerned with maintaining engagement with their husbands in an effort to resolve problems. Many husbands, on the other hand, often find their wives' efforts to continue discussions aversive and attempt to avoid dealing with the problem (Gottman & Levenson, 1988). This kind of engagement-disengagement behavior is predictive of a decline in marital satisfaction over time (Gottman & Krokoff, 1989). Thus, discussing areas of conflict appears at times to be necessary so that problem areas are not avoided. Teaching couples constructive engagement strategies is likely to be necessary in order to terminate this engagement-disengagement cycle.

Whereas the above investigations have focused on gender differences in communication, gender per se might not be the critical variable. Instead, sex roles might be the important factor, and the two genders may differ in the frequency of sex roles displayed. In order to begin addressing this issue, Sayers and Baucom (in press) assessed the communication sequences of distressed couples and obtained a measure of their sex-role identities. On these measures, masculinity involves a sense of leadership, assertiveness, and focus on achievement; femininity incorporates being emotionally attuned and interpersonally sensitive and behaving in a socially acceptable manner (Baucom, 1980). The findings demonstrated that sex-role identity is an important factor in spouses' communication. For example, couples in which the wives scored high on a measure of femininity (Baucom, 1976) demonstrated a significantly greater frequency of negative communication sequences, and the negative sequences were longer. In addition, when the distressed wives scored high on femininity, they were unlikely to terminate the negative communication sequences in which they were involved with their husbands. More directly, the wives' femininity correlated significantly with an index of negative reciprocity.

On the sex-role scales employed, masculinity and femininity are statistically independent of each other; therefore, the role of masculinity in communication must be evaluated separately. The findings indicated that distressed couples including wives high on masculinity exhibited shorter negative communication sequences. Overall, the findings indicate that the sex-role identities of distressed wives (but not husbands) are correlated with the couples' communication patterns. At present it is unclear how to interpret these findings. Do these distressed wives create conflict for the couple through their interaction style, or does their negative interaction reflect their attempt to force their husbands to address the serious difficulties the couple is experiencing? Findings from other investigations suggest that although high femininity among distressed wives is related to negative communication, there is something potentially adaptive about high levels of femininity among distressed wives. That is, findings indicate that distressed couples respond significantly better to behavioral marital therapy (BMT) when the wives have a high level of femininity prior to treatment (Baucom & Aiken, 1984). At first, (a) feminine wives being involved in more negative interactions and (b) feminine wives being predictive of response to BMT might seem contradictory. However, these two sets of findings can be reconciled if the role of highly feminine, distressed wives is seen as forcing the couple to confront conflictual issues that must be addressed for the couple's relationship to improve. More detailed analyses of couples' interaction patterns will be needed to clarify these issues, and the relation of sex-role identity to communication patterns among nondistressed couples is yet to be explored.

Noncommunication Behavior

Couples' interactions are not made up entirely of their attempts to communicate with each other. In fact, a great number of maritally distressed spouses report that they spend little time talking with their partners. What role, then, do these noncommunication behaviors play in marital adjustment and conflict between the spouses? In addressing this question, cognitive/behavior investigators have relied heavily upon the Spouse Observation Checklist (SOC) developed by Weiss and his associates (Weiss, Hops, & Patterson, 1973; Weiss & Perry, 1983). The SOC asks each spouse to record which of 408 behaviors he or she received from the partner during the past twenty-four hours. Each behavior also is rated by the respondent as pleasing, displeasing, or neutral. Finally, the respondent rates how satisfied or dissatisfied he or she has been with the relationship during the same twenty-four-hour period. Typically, each spouse completes an SOC for fourteen consecutive days. Several studies have employed the SOC and have demonstrated that distressed couples report significantly more displeasing and significantly fewer pleasing behaviors than nondistressed couples (e.g., Jacobson, Follette, & McDonald, 1982; Margolin, 1981). In addition, the ratings of daily relationship satisfaction are predictable from the daily frequencies of pleasing and displeasing behaviors (e.g., Christensen & Nies, 1980; Jacobson, Waldron, & Moore, 1980). For example, Baucom, Wheeler, and Bell (1984) found that daily relationship satisfaction was significantly correlated with the frequency of pleasing and displeasing behaviors for both husbands and wives, among both clinic and nonclinic samples (Rs ranged from .41 to .49).

Clinical Implications of Behavioral Differences among Distressed and Nondistressed Couples

The above findings indicate that there are significant differences between distressed and nondistressed couples with regard to both communication and noncommunication behaviors. An important issue becomes whether effective strategies can be developed to help maritally distressed couples alter these behaviors and whether these behavioral strategies result in a decrease in conflict and an increase in marital adjustment among the spouses. In recent years, behavioral marital therapists have developed a number of communication/problem-solving and behavior change strategies to assist maritally distressed couples (see Baucom & Epstein, 1990, and Jacobson & Margolin, 1979, for a detailed description of these clinical interventions). Briefly stated, BMT is an approach that focuses primarily on the couple's current behavior patterns, with an effort to teach the couple new skills in interacting with each other. Thus, couples are taught new communication skills along with strategies for engaging in more positive noncommunication behaviors, such as going out together to activities they both enjoy.

The results from various controlled outcome investigations indicate that distressed couples who receive training in these conflict-management skills do decrease their negative communication, become more satisfied with their partners' noncommunication behavior, and increase in their overall levels of marital adjustment from pretreatment to posttreatment (Baucom, 1982; Baucom & Lester, 1986; Baucom, Sayers, & Sher, 1990; Mehlman, Baucom, & Anderson, 1983). In addition, these changes appear to be maintained for at least six months posttherapy. These findings are consistent with those of other investigators in the field (e.g., Jacobson, 1978; Snyder & Wills, 1989).

The communication results discussed above reflect the frequencies of positive and negative communications that the couples displayed. The changes in communication patterns also are of interest. The findings from a recent outcome investigation indicated that the frequency of negative communication sequences decreased from 1.7 per minute before therapy to 1.0 per minute after therapy (Sayers et al., 1989). Similarly, the length of negative sequences decreased significantly in response to therapy. Thus, BMT was successful in decreasing negative communication sequences as well as decreasing the frequency of negative communications. Stated differently, BMT appeared to be effective in decreasing the conflict exhibited between spouses as they attempted to resolve difficult issues in their relationships.

Another way of examining the effectiveness of BMT is to compare it to a wait-list group, as well as to other nonspecific control groups. In studies comparing the two, BMT has been found to decrease negative communication (in a clinical setting), decrease problem areas and requests for behavior change, and correlate with an increase in marital adjustment (e.g., Baucom, Sayers, & Sher, 1990). BMT has not been found to increase positive communication consistently, which is a source of concern to behavioral marital therapists. This lack of consistent change in positive communication might occur for at least two reasons. First, because negative communication is so apparent and seems to have such immediate negative effects on the couple, therapists might focus upon it more than upon positive communication. Also, when distressed spouses first arrive for treatment, they often are very angry with each other. In such a context, it might be difficult for therapists to convince them to say positive things to each other. Finally, increasing positive communications might be more difficult because for many positive communications to be *viewed* as positive, they need to be offered spontaneously by the partner. Therefore, for the therapist to instruct one spouse to say something complimentary to the partner at a given time can be artificial. However, the therapist can almost always ask the couple to refrain from negative communications.

Because BMT typically consists of more than one treatment procedure (e.g., teaching communication and problem-solving skills, contracting), it is appropriate to examine each of the components more carefully to ascertain whether particular treatment procedures are responsible for a couple's treatment gains. This has been approached in different ways, with the results showing that no one component was superior to the others or to a multitreatment method (e.g., Baucom, Sayers, & Sher, 1990). The clinical implication of these findings is that therapists should probably consider all behavioral components (e.g., communication and problem-solving skills, contracting) as possible intervention strategies. It is likely that the needs of each particular couple differ and might suggest which components would be most useful for them in reducing conflict and increasing relationship satisfaction.

Other parameters of BMT also have been explored. For example, Mehlman et al. (1983) investigated whether there was any differential effectiveness in employing cotherapists in working with distressed couples compared to a single therapist. The findings indicated that the two approaches were equally effective. Even though the presence of two therapists does not seem to improve the overall effectiveness of BMT, a study by Epstein, Jayne-Lazarus, and DeGiovanni (1979) indicated that verbal dominance patterns modeled by cotherapist teams can have an impact on client couples' communication patterns. Couples in the study received communication training from male-female cotherapist teams who intentionally modeled a pattern of verbal dominance by either the female therapist or the male therapist. Although couples were not informed about the systematic patterns in cotherapist behavior, the spouses' verbal dominance patterns shifted from pre- to posttherapy in the directions modeled by their therapists. These results suggest that cotherapy teams may have utility in providing distressed couples with models of alternative interaction patterns. However, there is a need for considerably more research to identify the degree to which behaviors by cotherapist teams can contribute to constructive outcomes in BMT.

Results reported to this point suggest that BMT is effective in changing various aspects of marital discord (requests for behavior change, decreasing negative communication, increasing marital adjustment), but the traditional inferential statistics used have not provided useful information regarding the magnitude of BMT's effects. Several ways of doing so have been suggested and carried out. Hahlweg and Markman (1988) employed a meta-analysis to evaluate the effect size of seventeen different BMT outcome studies. They found that an average couple receiving BMT was "better off" than 82 percent of couples on a wait list or who received nonspecific treatment. However, other investigators questioned whether this effect size was clinically meaningful and proposed a different way of examining the magnitude of BMT's effects. This strategy involved evaluating whether couples move from the distressed to the nondistressed range on the variable of interest (Jacobson, Follette, & Revenstorf, 1984). Results from these investigations indicate that many couples (approximately 60 percent) still experience some notable distress after short-term BMT (Jacobson, Follette, Revenstorf, Baucom, et al., 1984). These findings suggest that the format of BMT may need to be altered (increase the average number of sessions, broaden the focus to include more cognitive and affective factors, etc.).

BMT also has been compared with other theoretical orientations to marital therapy, including (a) communication training (which emphasizes emotional expressiveness and listening skills); (b) cognitive restructuring alone and cognitive restructuring plus BMT; (c) a systems approach; (d) a group interaction approach; (e) a group analytic approach with a present focus and an insight-oriented approach; and (f) an experiential approach. Although there are exceptions (Hahlweg, Revenstorf, & Schindler, 1982; O'Farrell, Cutter, & Floyd, 1983; Johnson & Greenberg, 1985), few differences have been found between BMT and the other approaches. It is important to recognize that although no one particular marital therapy has been shown to be significantly more effective than the others, this does not mean that particular therapies do not work better with particular couples. The above studies have been conducted while assigning couples randomly to treatment, without taking individual couple differences into account. Indeed, there are almost no studies that attempt to match couples with treatment.

For example, although the interventions in BMT have recently been broadened, BMT as implemented in the majority of studies discussed above has had a very instrumental, problem-solving focus. Such interventions might be particularly well suited to couples who have had difficulty structuring their roles in marriage (such as couples early in marriage) or who have difficulty reaching solutions to everyday problems that all couples confront. From the opposite perspective, BMT as implemented in the above studies might not be optimal for addressing issues of passion, play, and other concerns not easily negotiated (Margolin, 1978). Commensurate with these speculations, Bennun (1985a, 1985b) found that BMT was more effective in alleviating presenting complaints that involved instrumental tasks than in providing relief from complaints involving care, concern, and ways of demonstrating feelings between spouses. These findings and observations have led theoreticians and investigators to broaden their conceptualization of marriage and marital intervention to include greater focus on cognitions and emotions in marriage (e.g., Baucom & Epstein, 1990).

COGNITIONS IN MARITAL INTERACTION AND CONFLICT

Although there is a substantial body of empirical evidence that behavioral exchanges between members of couples have significant impacts on relationship satisfaction and conflict, theoreticians and researchers in the field have come to recognize that understanding relationship dysfunction also requires attention to couples' cognitions about their behavioral interactions. Spouses' interpretations and evaluations of each other's actions influence their emotional and behavioral responses to those actions. In the past decade, theoretical and clinical literature emerged that described cognitive factors that can produce or maintain marital distress. For example, Doherty (1981a, 1981b) applied attribution theory and the reformulated attributional model of learned helplessness to the development of marital and family conflict, and clinically oriented publications (e.g., Ellis, 1976; Epstein, 1982, 1986) described the use of cognitive therapies to treat marital problems. In recent years, empirical investigations, both in the United States and abroad, have focused increasingly on identifying the roles that cognitions play in couples' relationships. Among the major tasks facing researchers have been (a) the identification of the *types* of cognitions that can influence marital conflict and distress, (b) identification of *casual relationships* among cognitions, behaviors, and emotions in marital interactions, and (c) investigations of the *efficacy of cognitive treatments* for relationship problems, alone and in combination with behavioral interventions.

TYPES OF COGNITIONS

Baucom, Epstein, Sayers, and Sher (1989) proposed a taxonomy of couples' cognitions that can influence levels of marital conflict and satisfaction. The five types of cognitions identified in the taxonomy are (a) spouses' *selective attention* about what events occur in their relationship, (b) their *attributions* or explanations for why those events occur, (c) their *expectancies* about probabilities that particular events will occur in the future, (d) their *assumptions* about the characteristics of intimate relationships, and (e) their *standards* about characteristics that relationships "should" have. To date, marital theorists and researchers have devoted most of their attention to spouses' attributions concerning determinants of their positive and negative behavioral interactions. Doherty (1981a) proposed that certain types of attributions can contribute to relationship conflict, particularly by fostering blaming attitudes and behavior (e.g., punitive actions), by generalizing such responses to other areas of the relationship, and by decreasing the spouses' sense of efficacy in resolving their conflicts. Most theoretical and empirical work on marital attributions has examined the inferences that spouses make about the causes of relationship events along the dimensions of global-specific, stable-unstable, and internal-external, although marital attribution research increasingly has investigated a variety of other types of attributions (e.g., how intentional a partner's behavior was). The emphasis on these three dimensions was derived from Abramson, Seligman, and Teasdale's (1978) attributional learned helplessness model of depression. Bradbury and Fincham (1990) and Thompson and Snyder (1986) have provided excellent reviews of the marital attribution literature. The only other notable work on marital cognitions has focused on potentially unrealistic relationship beliefs (assumptions and standards).

Research on Marital Attributions

The previously mentioned study by Baucom et al. (1984) provides an example of how knowledge of spouses' attributions accounts for levels of marital distress above and beyond the impact of the couple's behavioral interactions. In addition to listing their partners' behaviors daily for two weeks and reporting their relationship satisfaction each day, spouses were asked to provide an explanation (i.e., casual attribution) for each of the partner's behaviors, using five ratings based on learned helpless theory. First, the cause of the partner's behavior was rated on the *locus* dimensions of self, partner, and outside factors (categorized as such because, in a couple, "internal" might be interpreted as referring to either within the individual or within the relationship). Next, the cause of the behavior was rated on stable-unstable (likely to continue in the future) and global-specific (extent to which the cause affects many situations or is circumscribed) dimensions. Results of the study already had demonstrated that fluctuations in daily satisfaction could be predicted from the frequencies of spouses' behaviors. When spouses' attributions about causes of their partners' behaviors also were taken into account in the analyses, the proportion of variance in marital satisfaction accounted for more than doubled.

In another study, Baucom, Sayers, and Duhe (1989) developed a self-report measure of attributions that asks respondents to explain causes of their partners' behaviors. A sample of eighty-three distressed and nondistressed couples completed this instrument and Spanier's (1976) Dyadic Adjustment Scale, a global measure of marital satisfaction. Baucom et al. found that the correlations between attributional dimensions and marital satisfaction were almost identical for males and females, with members of happier couples attributing negative partner behaviors to outside circumstances (rather than to themselves or their partners) and to unstable, specific causes. Thus, happier couples tend to discount the significance of negative events in their interactions. In fact, on other rating scales, happier couples rated negative events as less important and less upsetting than did distressed couples. These findings were consistent with those found by other investigators (see reviews by Bradbury & Fincham, 1990; Thompson & Snyder, 1986).

The Baucom, Sayers, and Duhe (1989) study also afforded an opportunity to examine whether individuals have consistent attributional *styles* when making inferences about causes of events in their relationships. Based on the five attributional rating dimensions, the investigators developed sixteen different patterns that couples may use to explain relationship events; for example "not due to me," "due to my partner," "not due to factors outside the relationship," "due to a stable cause," and "due to a global cause" reflect one pattern of explanation. In explaining twelve different events, men on the average used six different attributional patterns (range from two to ten), and women averaged seven different patterns (range from three to ten). Thus, some people exhibited a consistent style or pattern in attributing negative relationship events to particular causes, whereas other individuals did not. Furthermore, among men, use of more patterns was associated with significantly higher marital satisfaction ($r = .30$). Among women, use of any single pattern of explanation was associated with significantly lower satisfaction ($r = -.23$). Thus, it appears that lack of flexibility in identifying sources of relationship problems is associated with marital discord.

In contrast to research focusing on attributional *dimensions* derived from learned helplessness theory, there has been increasing attention to the *content* of spouses' attributions. For example, Fincham (1985) proposed that spouses' distress may be associated more with the degree to which they attribute negative partner behaviors to negative motivation than with attributions along dimensions such as global-specific. In a number of studies by Fincham and his colleagues (e.g., Fincham, Beach, & Nelson, 1987; Fincham & Bradbury, 1987b), spouses' attributions about their partners' negative intent, blameworthiness, and selfish motivation were equally or more strongly associated with distress than were attributions involving causal dimensions such as global-specific. Fincham and Bradbury (1987a) generally found empirical support for Doherty's (1981a) attribution-conflict model but have extended it to differentiate among attributions concerning locus of an event's cause, attributions concerning responsibility for the event (e.g., how voluntary and intentional the actor's behavior was), and judgments concerning the actor's capacities to behave responsibly. The increasing refinement of theoretical and empirical work on couples' attributions is a good example of the trend toward a multidimensional approach to the study of cognitive and behavioral factors affecting marriage.

Pretzer, Epstein, and Fleming (in press) developed a self-report measure that focuses on the content of spouses' attributions concerning relationship problems. Rather than asking respondents to rate causes of events on dimensions such as global-specific, the Marital Attitude Survey (MAS) items describe causes of problems in terms of concepts such as "due to my partner's personality." In addition to the MAS subscales assessing attributions to the partner's personality, the partner's behavior, one's own personality, and one's own behavior, there are motivation-oriented subscales tapping the degrees to which the individual sees relationship problems as due to the partner's malicious intent and lack of love. In a sample of eighty-two females and seventy-four males ranging in level of marital satisfaction, the more that individuals attributed relationship problems to the partner's personality and behavior, one's own personality, and to the partner's malicious intent and lack of love, the more distressed they were. In multiple regression analyses, attributions to the partner's personality, behavior, and lack of love each added significantly to the prediction of marital distress. Furthermore, Epstein, Pretzer, and Fleming (1987) found that the commonly demonstrated correlation between marital satisfaction and spouses' ratings of the communication in their relationships can be mediated by the attributions assessed by the MAS. Although both the measure of marital communication and the MAS accounted for unique variance in marital satisfaction scores, the correlation between perceived communication and satisfaction was reduced significantly when variance due to spouses' attributions about relationship problems was partialed out. In other words, it appears that spouses' perceptions of their communication are likely to be influenced by the degree to which their cognitions about their relationship are positive or negative.

In summary, the findings of research on attributions for marital events consistently indicate that they are an important aspect of marital interaction and that taking both actual behaviors and attributions concerning those actions into account increases our understanding of a couple's happiness or distress.

Research on Relationship Assumptions and Standards

In addition to the substantial amount of work that has been devoted to the study of couples' attributions, marital researchers have examined some of the assumptions and standards that individuals hold about the characteristics of intimate relationships. Based on clinical literature and a survey of marital therapists, Eidelson and Epstein (1982) identified a set of five potentially unrealistic "beliefs" about relationships that can lead to conflict and dissatisfaction between partners. They developed the Relationship Belief Inventory (RBI), which has subscales assessing the beliefs that (a) disagreement between partners is destructive to their relationship, (b) partners should be able to mind-read each other's thoughts, emotions, and needs, (c) partners cannot change themselves or their relationship, (d) one should be a perfect sexual partner, and (e) problems between men and women are due to basic inborn sex differences in personality and needs. Initial validation studies with the RBI (Eidelson & Epstein, 1982; Epstein & Eidelson, 1981) indicated that higher scores on the RBI subscales differentiated clinical from nonclinical couples, were associated with self-reported marital distress, and were better predictors of marital distress than a measure of irrational beliefs focused on individual rather than relationship issues. Subsequent studies (e.g., Epstein et al., 1987; Fincham & Bradbury, 1987b; Jones & Stanton, 1988) have provided more evidence that the beliefs tapped by the RBI are associated with marital dysfunction.

As noted by Baucom, Epstein, et al. (1989), the RBI subscales assessing the beliefs that disagreement is destructive, that partners cannot change their relationship, and that the sexes are different measure assumptions, whereas the expected mind-reading and sexual perfectionism subscales measure standards. Consequently, use of RBI total scores in research and clinical practice may mask important differences in couples' assumptions and standards. At present little is known about the relative importance of assumptions versus standards in producing marital conflict and distress, although work by rational-emotive therapists (e.g., Ellis, Sichel, Yeager, DiMattia, & DiGiuseppe, 1989) emphasizes the evaluative component of unrealistic standards as the source of relationship dysfunction.

Even though the RBI has a good record as a measure of problematic cognitions, its five subscales necessarily assess a limited number of the potentially dysfunctional relationship assumptions and standards that may be held by members of couples. Therefore, we are in the process of developing a new set of cognitive measures that differentiate assumptions from standards and cover a broader range of each type of relationship belief. The following is a description of the initial development of a questionnaire assessing couples' standards for their intimate relationships.

Development of a New Measure of Relationship Standards. Although there is an unlimited number of specific standards that couples may hold concerning an intimate relationship, we have attempted to organize the assessment of marital standards by focusing on important *content areas* and *dimensions* of relationships where standards have the potential to elicit or maintain conflict. First, it seemed important to examine whether spouses' standards vary from one content area of their relationship to another (e.g., handling finances versus expressing affection) and to investigate whether standards in particular content areas have different impacts on relationship conflict and satisfaction. Therefore, twelve content areas were identified as major aspects of marital functioning, based on a review of clinical and research literature, as well as existing inventories that assess marital adjustment, such as Spanier's (1976) Dyadic Adjustment Scale, Snyder's (1981) Marital Satisfaction Inventory, and Burnett, Egolf, Solon, and Sullivan's (1984) Premarital Inventory PROFILE.

Next, based on a review of the marital literature, we identified three major dimensions of marital functioning that cut across the twelve content areas: (a) the *boundaries* within the relationship, (b) *power/control*, and (c) *relationship investment*. The boundary dimension involves the degree to which partners (a) share personal information (thoughts, emotions, fantasies) with each other, (b) participate in activities together, and (c) have similar thoughts and emotions. The power/control dimension includes both (a) the process by which partners attempt to influence each other and (b) the degree to which the outcomes of joint decisions reflect each partner's preferences. Investment in the relationship consists of each spouse's efforts to (a) maintain or enhance the quality of the marriage and (b) make the partner happy.

By writing items that reflect standards concerning each of the above dimensions within each of the twelve relationship content areas described previously, we constructed the Inventory of Specific Relationship Standards (ISRS; Baucom, Epstein, Rankin, & Burnett, 1990). For example, there are items that ask about the respondents' standards concerning boundaries in the couple's use of leisure time, their standards concerning relative control over decisions about leisure time, and their standards about the degree of relationship investment that partners should demonstrate through use of leisure time. Spouses indicate their standards by responding to items such as "My partner and I should take part in our leisure activities (for example, hobbies, recreation, free time) with each other," using a five-point frequency scale ranging from "never" to "always." They also indicate how important for their relationship they consider the subjects described in the items, using a three-point response scale (important, somewhat important, unimportant).

Initial data derived from 101 community couples who completed the ISRS and Spanier's (1976) Dyadic Adjustment Scale demonstrate that relationship standards are correlated with marital adjustment for females. Females who believe that there should be fewer boundaries between spouses are more satisfied than other females (their husbands also are happier with the marriages). In addition, females who believe that there should be equal decision-making power between the spouses are more satisfied; also, compared to other females, the females who believe that both partners should be more invested or give more to the relationship have higher levels of marital adjustment. Combining these findings, the results suggest that females who believe that the partners should have more of a "relationship focus" in their marriage are more satisfied with the marriage. It is unclear why husbands' standards appear to bear less of a relationship to marital adjustment, but written comments from some of the males suggest one possibility. Some of the males provided comments asking why we would be interested in how the relationship "should be"; it is what actually happens that is important. Although it is speculative at this time, at least some males may find the cognitive aspects of marriage to be less important in their relationship. Instead they may be more concerned with how the two persons behave toward each other. This is consistent with our clinical observation that a number of males in distressed marriages express concern that their wives spend too much time thinking about the relationship; they encourage their wives to "relax" and not to make "such a big deal" out of what happens. In essence, they might be asking their wives to decrease the amount of cognitive processing that they engage in relative to the marriage.

Research on Relationship Expectancies

Doherty (1981b) proposed that spouses' expectancies of efficacy in resolving their relationship conflicts and problems can influence the degree to which they will engage in problem-solving efforts rather than exhibit learned helplessness responses. He also hypothesized that efficacy expectancies would be lower when spouses attributed relationship problems to factors in their partners that were seen as global, stable, and involving negative intent. Until recently, however, the role of expectancies in marital conflict and problem solving has received little attention in empirical studies. Pretzer et al. (in press) found support for Doherty's views with subscales of their Marital Attitude Survey that assess expectancies. The more that spouses reported expectancies that the couple (a) had the ability to change their relationship and (b) actually would change their relationship, the more they reported marital satisfaction and good communication in their relationships, and the less they attributed relationship problems to their partner's behavior, personality, malicious intent, and lack of love. Among wives, but not husbands, lower efficacy expectations concerning marital problem solving were associated with higher depression.

Fincham and Bradbury (1987a) assessed spouses' efficacy expectancies with self-report items focused on perceived overall ability to perform behaviors needed to resolve relationship conflicts. They found that such global efficacy ratings had a significant but lower inverse correlation with spouses' reports of helplessness responses (giving up efforts to resolve conflicts). Although this finding was consistent with Doherty's (1981b) conceptual model, Fincham and Bradbury (1987a) suggested that future research on expectancies will benefit from a distinction between efficacy and outcome expectancies (Bandura, 1977) as well as consideration of spouses' *motivation* to engage in behaviors that can resolve conflicts.

Weiss (1984) found evidence that spouses' expectancies of efficacy in resolving conflicts were related significantly not only to their levels of marital satisfaction and commitment to their relationship, but also to the process of their behavioral interactions when discussing conflictual issues. When the spouses were asked to review a videotape of their conflict-resolution discussion and rate the impact (helpfulness) of their partner's responses, their prior reports of efficacy expectancies predicted 44 percent of the variance in their positive impact ratings and 33 percent of the variance in their negative impact ratings. Furthermore, the efficacy expectancy scores significantly predicted positive behavioral interactions during the taped discussions, as coded by an independent observer, using the Marital Interaction Coding System (MICS; Hops, Wills, Patterson, & Weiss, 1972). The relationship between efficacy expectancies and subsequent positive behaviors (particularly nonverbal) during the conflict-resolution discussion held up even when variance due to spouses' marital satisfaction scores was partialed out of the analysis. Similarly, Bradbury and Fincham (1989) found that spouses' efficacy expectancies were correlated with marital satisfaction, and (for wives only) they were associated with higher quality approaches to problem resolution during videotaped problem-solving discussions. Thus, initial studies indicate that couples' expectancies concerning resolution of their conflicts play an important role in conflict behavior, and they should be a focus of future marital research.

Research on Couples' Selective Perceptions of Relationship Events

Behavioral marital therapists commonly have observed systematic biases in distressed spouses' perceptions of events in their relationships, including the process of "negative tracking," in which an individual focuses attention on the partner's negative behaviors but overlooks positive acts (Jacobson & Margolin, 1979). A number of studies have demonstrated that members of a couple commonly have low rates of agreement about the occurrence of specific behaviors in their marital interactions, and that spouses' perceptions of marital behaviors often do not agree with those of trained outside observers (e.g., Christensen, Sullaway, & King, 1983; Elwood & Jacobson, 1982; Floyd & Markman, 1983). Floyd and Markman's (1983) findings suggested that such perceptual discrepancies are due to biases in the spouses' perceptions. Marital therapists commonly are faced with the task of sorting through spouses' divergent views of behaviors that are sources of distress and conflict (Baucom & Epstein, 1990). However, at present there is a lack of research investigating the effects that perceptual discrepancies and biases have on the development and maintenance of marital conflict. Markman (1984) found that closer correspondence between the valences (positive, neutral, or negative) of intended messages and the impacts of those messages on the partner was correlated significantly with relationship satisfaction five and a half years later, but the small sample size (twelve couples) indicates a need for replication.

Given the pervasiveness of selective perception in interpersonal relationships and the frequency with which it becomes an issue in marital therapy, spouses' perceptions should receive more attention in future investigations of marital cognition. Marital researchers may have "selectively attended" to other types of cognitions due to the difficulty of measuring moment-to-moment perceptual *processes*, but studies of spouses' perceptions during ongoing dyadic interactions will be necessary for the advancement of knowledge about the roles of cognitions in marital conflict.

The Causal Role of Marital Cognitions

The clinical and theoretical literature on marital cognitions generally has reflected an assumption that spouses' cognitions mediate their affective and behavioral responses to each other's actions (cf., Baucom & Epstein, 1990). However, almost all of the existing empirical studies have been correlational, and the consistent links found among cognitions such as attributions and indices of marital distress and conflict do not necessarily indicate that they play such causal roles. Longitudinal studies in which cognitions, behaviors, and affects all are assessed at multiple points in time are needed to identify causal sequences. The initial longitudinal studies that have been conducted have provided support for the idea that cognitions have an influence on later marital conflict and distress, although more extensive studies will be required to clarify the causal direction.

Fincham and Bradbury (1987b) found that, for wives but not husbands, attributions for marital problems and negative partner behavior predicted levels of marital satisfaction twelve months later, with initial levels of satisfaction controlled statistically. In contrast, initial satisfaction did not predict later attributions. Fincham and Bradbury also found that spouses' initial responses to Eidelson and Epstein's (1982) Relationship Belief Inventory (which were correlated with their attribution scores) did not predict their later marital satisfaction. Fincham and Bradbury interpret this finding as consistent with a causal model in which relationship "expectations" (i.e., standards and assumptions) give rise to attributions, which then influence satisfaction. In a second longitudinal study, Bradbury and Fincham (1989) found that wives' (but not husbands') efficacy expectancies predicted their marital satisfaction twelve months later.

Markman (1984) conducted a longitudinal study in which couples' communication was assessed in terms of the degree to which a speaker's intended impact for each message sent (positive, neutral, or negative) corresponded to the listener's report of each message's impact. Markman found that in a sample of premarital couples, the impact ratings, rather than either the intent ratings or the level of relationship satisfaction, significantly predicted satisfaction two and a half and five and a half years later. This longitudinal study is relevant to our understanding of cognitive factors in relationships, because it was the spouses' subjective perceptions of each other's communication behavior that were associated with later satisfaction. As noted earlier, a further indication that cognitive factors may influence relationship development can be found in Markman's finding that perceptual agreement between partners concerning the valence of messages was correlated with satisfaction five and a half years later.

At present, longitudinal studies of marital cognitions may be constrained by the limited cognitive measures available. Baucom, Epstein, et al. (1989) argued that further advancement of knowledge concerning the role of cognitions in the development of relationship problems will require the expansion and refinement of instruments for assessing various types of spouses' cognitions. For example, as more refined measures of couples' cognitions become available, it will be possible to investigate whether extremity or husband-wife discrepancy in particular assumptions and standards about relationships shapes later communication patterns and areas of conflict.

THE EFFICACY OF COGNITIVE RESTRUCTURING

As described above, there is a growing body of empirical evidence that various types of cognitions are associated with marital distress and predict the development of marital conflict over time. However, the question remains whether specific therapeutic interventions can be used to alter these cognitions and improve marital adjustment. Beginning in the 1980s a number of marital therapy outcome studies have been conducted to examine the impact of cognitive restructuring procedures, in combination with behavioral interventions and alone. Given the limited number of studies to date, the findings must be considered preliminary, but they are encouraging.

Two of the outcome studies (Baucom & Lester, 1986; Baucom, Sayers, & Sher, 1990) examined whether the effectiveness of behavioral marital therapy could be increased by adding a cognitive restructuring component that focused on spouses' negative attributions and extreme standards concerning their relationships. Three other studies (Emmelkamp et al., 1988; Epstein et al., 1982; Huber & Milstein, 1985) investigated the impact of cognitive restructuring alone. Most of the studies have focused on attributions and standards, although Epstein et al. (1982) examined distorted and unrealistic cognitions more broadly, within a standard approach to cognitive therapy (Beck, Rush, Shaw, & Emery, 1979).

Overall, the results of these studies indicate that cognitive interventions do produce meaningful decreases in couples' problematic cognitions, as well as increases in marital satisfaction. However, most of the studies used only the Relationship Belief Inventory (Eidelson & Epstein, 1982) as the outcome measure of cognitions, so it is unknown whether the cognitive restructuring altered other types of cognitions, such as attributions. One exception was Huber and Milstein's (1985) finding that couples who received brief cognitive restructuring had increased expectancies that therapy would benefit them, as well as increased marital satisfaction and desire to improve their relationships, compared to couples on a waiting list for therapy.

Although Epstein et al. (1982) found that cognitive restructuring reduced couples' extreme relationship standards more than communication training did, other studies found that cognitive and behavioral interventions produced comparable cognitive changes.

In the largest study to date examining the effectiveness of cognitive restructuring for maritally distressed couples, Baucom, Sayers, & Sher (1990) investigated whether the effectiveness of behavioral marital therapy (BMT) alone could be improved upon by adding cognitive restructuring (CR) and/or teaching the couples to express emotions more adaptively—emotional expressiveness training (EET). Thus, sixty maritally distressed couples were randomly assigned to one of five treatment conditions—(a) BMT alone; (b) CR + BMT; (c) BMT + EET; (d) CR + BMT + EET; or (e) wait list. The results indicated that all four of the active treatment conditions were more effective than no treatment, but there were no significant differences among the four active treatments. However, more detailed analyses indicated that the couples receiving CR were the only couples who demonstrated consistent cognitive changes in response to treatment. Consequently, the findings from this study and the others noted above indicate that we have now developed intervention strategies that are effective in altering cognitions that have been shown to be related to marital discord.

The question arises, then, why these treatments including CR have not been more effective in increasing marital satisfaction than BMT alone. In large part, the findings might have resulted from the way that these studies were conducted. In initial efforts to explore the effectiveness of CR techniques, distressed couples have been randomly assigned to treatments. However, in no investigations have the couples' specific presenting complaints been taken into account in assigning them to treatment. There is no assumption that all marital distress results from cognitive factors; thus, the lack of optimal fit between couples' specific needs and treatment assignment could contribute to the current set of findings. Consequently, future treatment studies must evaluate whether matching couples' needs to treatment results in an increase in treatment effectiveness. In addition, in order to include CR along with behavioral interventions in a fixed number of sessions, the number of sessions specifically devoted to CR was relatively small (either three or six sessions). Helping spouses change their beliefs about their partners and their relationships might require much more time and effort.

CONCLUSIONS

In the past twenty years, a great deal of basic research has substantiated the importance of spouses' behaviors and cognitions in marital discord. As a result of these investigations, there is a much clearer understanding of the role of (a) positive and negative behaviors, (b) communication and noncommunication behaviors, and (c) frequencies and sequences of behaviors in marital distress and conflict. More recently, a delineation of the important cognitions in marriage has been introduced, and findings to date document the role of these cognitions in marital discord. In response to these empirical findings, cognitive/behavioral marital therapists have developed interventions to assist distressed couples, and over thirty well-controlled studies demonstrate the effectiveness of these intervention techniques in assisting couples. Yet, clearly not all couples respond to these interventions.

What then is the next step in this attempt to understand and alleviate marital conflict? To date, most investigations have focused upon the role of a single type of behavior or a given class of cognitions in relation to marital distress. There have been a few studies that have sought to understand the interplay among various behaviors and cognitions. In part this has resulted from the lack of a meaningful, yet comprehensive, model of marital functioning that considers the interactions among behavior, cognition, and emotion in marital conflict. Clearly such models are needed in order to guide future research. Such models should also take gender differences into account (cf. Baucom, Notarius, et al., 1990). For example, many of the gender differences noted in the current paper seem to indicate that females are more likely than males to focus on, evaluate, and attempt to discuss problematic aspects of the marital relationship. With such models available, increasingly sophisticated research investigations can be conducted to substantiate portions of the model. Such findings can then be used to develop new and more enlightened intervention techniques that can be empirically validated with couples. Thus, if this field is to progress as it has during the past two decades, it must continue to demonstrate an integrated perspective based on theory, basic research, and empirically validated interventions within the context of a more comprehensive model of marital functioning.

3 Understanding Responses to Dissatisfaction in Close Relationships: The Exit-Voice-Loyalty-Neglect Model

Caryl E. Rusbult

No close relationship maintains uniformly high satisfaction, irrespective of how idyllic it may appear. All relationships move through both happy times *and* times that are not so happy. Accordingly, one of the more important themes in the study of relationships concerns the manner in which partners react to periodic dissatisfaction. Indeed, over the past several decades the field has witnessed an explosion of research designed to extend our theoretical understanding of the manner in which couples deal with problems in their relationships (for reviews, see Berscheid, 1985; Clark & Reis, 1988; Holmes & Boon, 1990).

Traditionally, social scientists have examined relatively specific responses to dissatisfaction, such as divorce and breakups (e.g., Baxter, 1984; Buunk, 1987; Levinger & Moles, 1979; Simpson, 1987), conflict-resolution style (e.g., Braiker & Kelley, 1979; Buss, 1989; Gottman, 1979; Jacobson, Follette, & McDonald, 1982; Levenson & Gottman, 1985), cognitions and attributions regarding relationship problems (e.g., Baucom, Sayers, & Duhe, 1989; Bradbury & Fincham, 1990; Eidelson & Epstein, 1982; Holtzworth-Munroe & Jacobson, 1985), avoidance behaviors (e.g., Birchler, Weiss, & Vincent, 1975; Kelley et al., 1978; Schaap, 1984), relationship violence (e.g., Daly & Wilson, 1988; Gelles, 1980; Snyder & Fruchtman, 1981; Strube, 1988), and extrarelationship sexual involvements (e.g., Buunk, 1981; Reiss, Anderson, & Sponaugle, 1980; Wachowiak & Bragg, 1980). Unfortunately, this literature is limited in at least three respects.

CRITIQUE OF THE LITERATURE

One limitation of this literature is that a good deal of the extant research and theory is designed to describe the manner in which relationships ultimately terminate (e.g., Baxter, 1984; Levinger, 1979; Miller & Parks, 1982). That is, the implicit assumption in much of the existing work is that understanding the road to breakup will inform us about more general responses to dissatisfaction. This emphasis on the steps that precede actual dissolution has tended to obscure the diversity of available reactions to dyadic problems, including both destructive *and* constructive reactions (e.g., couples on the road to dissolution may not react to dissatisfaction with a sincere and mutually affirming heart-to-heart talk). Such an approach may well lead to an inaccurate description of the manner in which couples react to periodic, potentially reparable declines in relationship quality.

A second problem with prior research is that much of this work explores responses to dissatisfaction within the context of relationship conflict (e.g., Gottman, 1979; Jacobson et al., 1982; Margolin & Wampold, 1981). That is, couple response patterns are frequently examined during the course of specific conflicted interactions (e.g., a ten-minute simulated argument). However, many dissatisfying incidents do not involve overt disagreement between partners and accordingly are unlikely to emerge in the context of simulated conflicts (e.g., "My partner doesn't love me enough"; "We don't make love as often as I'd like"). Also, many problems cannot be characterized as discrete "conflicts" per se, in that dissatisfaction frequently spans an extended period of time and involves pervasive, long-term problems rather than specific disagreements. Furthermore, many responses to dissatisfaction are unlikely to emerge in the context of a simulated conversation, in that they do not involve talk (e.g., silently walking out of the room). Finally, partners on occasion react passively rather than allowing problems to erupt into overt conflict (e.g., working long hours rather than going home to face an argument with the partner). A related point is that many problems in relationships are unilateral—an individual may not necessarily even be aware of the partner's dissatisfaction. Thus, studying responses to dissatisfaction in the context of conflicted interactions is likely to yield an incomplete and possibly inaccurate theoretical account of responses to dissatisfaction.

A third problem with the extant literature is that researchers by and large have examined single modes of response—avoidance *or* breakup *or* extrarelationship sexual involvement *or* couple violence—rather than simultaneously exploring multiple reactions to dissatisfaction. That is, few authors have developed or studied systematic taxonomies of this domain of behaviors. Although we may learn much about particular responses by studying them in isolation from one another, a broader, typological approach has much to recommend it. The existence of a more general typology would enable researchers to study a broader range of reactions, recognizing that a given response is but one option out of the full range of available reactions. Also, the existence of a general typology would encourage researchers to study a wider range of phenomena, including the relationships among various reactions to decline, temporal patterns of individual responding, and interdependent patterns of partner response. In short, identifying a more general typology of responses to dissatisfaction is an important first step toward developing a comprehensive theoretical understanding of reactions to dissatisfaction.

Thus, there are a number of good reasons to believe that it may be fruitful to extend the more traditional approaches to the study of response to dissatisfaction. Specifically, we may learn much about how couples deal with problems by expanding our orientation in two important respects: First, it may be useful to explore the entire domain of responses to dissatisfaction, not merely those behaviors that emerge in the context of conflicted interactions, and not merely those behaviors that precede the termination of relationships. Second, it may be beneficial to develop a more general, comprehensive model of responses to dissatisfaction, attempting to capture the full range of available reactions.

TYPOLOGIES OF RESPONSE TO DISSATISFACTION

In response to concerns such as these, three typologies of response to dissatisfaction have been proffered in recent years—the exit-voice-loyalty-neglect model (Rusbult, Zembrodt, & Gunn, 1982; Rusbult & Zembrodt, 1983), the interpersonal conflict model (yielding, compromising, withdrawal, integrating, dominating; Rahim, 1983), and the dual concern model (yielding, inaction, problem solving, contending; Pruitt & Rubin, 1986). Discussing the similarities and differences among these approaches is beyond the scope of the current chapter, although readers familiar with the three approaches will no doubt note parallels among the models (e.g., all three include several categories of response that differ in terms of positivity and activity).

This chapter describes theory and research on the exit-voice-loyalty-neglect model, a comprehensive typology of responses to dissatisfaction that describes a broad range of reactions to periodic decline in close relationships. Like the interpersonal conflict and dual concern models, the exit-voice-loyalty-neglect typology is intended to serve an integrative theoretical function by identifying the systematic links among the full range of responses to dissatisfaction. Specifically, this typology represents responses to *all* forms of dissatisfaction, including both constructive and destructive reactions, including both overt and passive responses, and including reactions to a wide range of dissatisfying incidents—the typology not only deals with behaviors preceding termination and interactions during conflict, but also is capable of handling less frequently studied phenomena such as the character of silent despair.

The chapter begins with a description of the typology itself, including a brief discussion of research designed to assess the validity and comprehensiveness of the model. Rather than presenting the details of each piece of research we have conducted using the exit-voice-loyalty-neglect model, the chapter includes a general review of appropriate research strategies and methods for studying responses to dissatisfaction. This is followed by a discussion of research that examines the determinants of exit, voice, loyalty, and neglect. This body of research is based on the interdependence theory concept of dependence (Thibaut & Kelley, 1959)—a construct that appears to powerfully account for the manner in which individuals react to dissatisfying incidents in their relationships. Research on the consequences of each category of response is then reviewed, and one very important interdependent pattern of response is identified—a pattern of couple responding termed "accommodation." Interdependence theory constructs are employed as a means of understanding the accommodative situation, and a program of research on willingness to accommodate is briefly discussed. Finally, directions for future research are considered, and several applications of the model are outlined.

A Typology of Responses to Dissatisfaction

Four Responses: Exit, Voice, Loyalty, and Neglect

The current typology emerged from Hirschman's (1970) classic work, *Exit, Voice, and Loyalty: Responses to Decline in Firms, Organizations, and States*. Hirschman's goal was to identify the primary categories of reaction to decline in formal organizations. According to this model, there are three characteristic modes of response to decline: exit—ending, or threatening to end, a relationship; voice—actively and constructively expressing dissatisfaction; and loyalty—passively but optimistically waiting for conditions to improve. This typology appeared on the face of it to capture a diverse range of reactions to deterioration and therefore seemed to be an excellent starting point in our attempt to understand responses to dissatisfaction in close relationships.

Two multidimensional scaling studies were conducted to determine whether Hirschman's (1970) model effectively described the domain of responses to dissatisfaction in close relationships (Rusbult & Zembrodt, 1983). One of these studies examined responses to decline in undergraduates' dating relationships, and a second study examined responses in more long-standing adult relationships. Both studies demonstrated that Hirschman's three categories characterize responses to decline in romantic relationships. However, both studies also revealed a fourth important category of response: neglect—passively allowing a relationship to atrophy. The following examples delineate the sorts of responses that fall in each category, including illustrative verbatim descriptions from participants in our research:

> Exit—actively harming the relationship (e.g., separating, moving out of a joint residence, actively abusing one's partner, getting a divorce, threatening to leave, screaming shrewishly at one's partner):
>
> "I told him I couldn't take it any more, and that it was over."
> "I slapped her around a bit, I'm ashamed to say."
> "It drove me crazy, so I left."

> Voice—actively and constructively attempting to improve conditions (e.g., discussing problems, compromising, seeking help from a friend or therapist, suggesting solutions, changing oneself or one's partner):
>
> "We talked things over and worked things out."
> "I wrote him a letter to find out what was going on."
> "I tried my hardest to make things better."

> Loyalty—passively but optimistically waiting for conditions to improve (e.g., supporting the partner when others criticize him or her, continuing to wear symbols of the relationship [a ring, a locket], praying for improvement):
>
> "I loved her so much that I ignored her faults."
> "I just waited to see if things would get better, and went out with him when he asked me."
> "I prayed a lot and left things in God's hands."

> Neglect—passively allowing conditions to deteriorate (e.g., ignoring the partner or spending less time together, refusing to discuss problems, treating the partner badly, insulting the partner or criticizing him or her for things unrelated to the real problem, just letting things fall apart):
>
> "Mostly my response was silence to anything he might say, ignoring him if we were around other people, etc."
> "We seemed to drift apart; we might have exchanged five to ten words in a week."
> "I didn't really care whether the relationship ended or got better. I think I just kind of coped. I played duplicate bridge and read a lot."

Two Dimensions: Constructiveness/Destructiveness and Activity/Passivity

Exit, voice, loyalty, and neglect differ from one another along two important dimensions, as displayed in figure 3.1. First, the responses differ in terms of constructiveness versus destructiveness. Voice and loyalty are constructive responses that are intended to revive or maintain a

Figure 3.1: A typology of responses to dissatisfaction

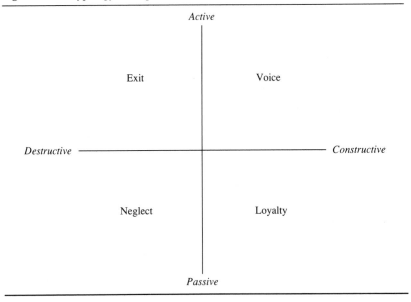

relationship. In contrast, exit and neglect are relatively more destructive to the well-being of a relationship. It should be noted that ''constructiveness/ destructiveness'' refers to the impact of a behavior on the relationship, not to its impact on the individual. For example, an exit response such as separation is clearly destructive to the future of a *relationship*, although this might be a constructive reaction for an *individual* who is involved in an abusive relationship.

The responses also differ on a second dimension, activity versus passivity. Exit and voice are active behaviors, wherein the individual takes direct action with respect to the problem at hand (i.e., ''shape up or ship out''). In contrast, loyalty and neglect are relatively more passive with respect to the dissatisfying incident—the individual fairly passively allows the relationship to take its own course, either waiting for it to improve or allowing it to deteriorate. It should be clear that ''activity/passivity'' refers to the impact of a reaction on the immediate problem, not to the character of the behavior itself. For example, it involves overt activity to walk to a local bar so as to avoid discussing things, yet this behavior is passively neglectful in regard to the couple's problem.

Before moving on, several additional comments are in order. First, the category labels are symbols for a broad range of related reactions and should not be interpreted literally. For example, ''voice'' refers to all active and constructive reactions, not necessarily to all behaviors that involve vocalization. Screaming ''I don't know why I married you'' involves vocalization but is clearly an example of exit rather than voice. Similarly, the "exit" category encompasses not only overtly terminating a relationship, but also other actively destructive behaviors such as screaming at one another or hitting the partner.

Second, it should be clear that since the primary dimensions of the model are continua, the behaviors within each of the four categories likewise differ along two continua—they differ in degree of constructiveness/destructiveness and in degree of activity/passivity. For example, the neglect category includes exceptionally passive behaviors, such as spending long hours at work instead of with the partner, as well as moderately passive reactions, such as nagging the partner about issues that are unrelated to the problem at hand. Similarly, responses within the exit category range from mildly destructive to exceptionally destructive and from mildly active to exceptionally active.

Third, an individual's response to a specific problem may sometimes be a blend of two or more categories. For example, the response "I swallowed my pride and asked for another chance" combines voice and loyalty. A related point is that during the course of an extended period of dissatisfaction, an individual may engage in a sequence of responses. For example, a common sequence might involve beginning with loyalty, attempting to maintain the relationship; moving to voice when such a stance fails to improve conditions; reacting with neglect when attempts at voice are frustrated; and eventually resolving the problem with exit.

And finally, the exit-voice-loyalty-neglect typology can be utilized in at least two ways. First, the model can obviously be employed as a means of describing specific reactions in discrete interactions or problem situations. Employing the model in this context, one might anticipate that tendencies toward each category of reaction might be influenced by such factors as the nature of the dissatisfying incident (e.g., how severe is the problem?), the quality of the partners' broader relationship with one another (e.g., are one or both partners dependent on one another and on their relationship?), and more general dispositions that might color partner response preferences (e.g., is the individual inclined to engage in partner perspective-talking?). Alternatively, the typology can be used as a means of characterizing generalized response tendencies across a wide range of dissatisfying incidents. The latter approach is likely to be more desirable in attempts to understand the relationship between responses to dissatisfaction and healthy couple functioning, and may be a fruitful way of characterizing the nature of partner interdependence in long-standing, ongoing close relationships.

Measuring Responses to Dissatisfaction: Reliability and Validity Issues

Prior research on the exit-voice-loyalty-neglect typology has provided good support for the validity of this model. Importantly, we have obtained evidence regarding the convergent and discriminant validity of measures designed to tap the four categories of the typology (e.g., Rusbult et al., 1982; Rusbult, Johnson, & Morrow, 1986a; Rusbult, Zembrodt, & Iwaniszek, 1986): First, items tend to correlate more strongly with other items from their response category than with items from other response categories (range from .50 to .90 or so); second, measures of opposing categories tend to be moderately negatively correlated with one another (range from −.30 to −.50 or so; e.g., voice and neglect behaviors are negatively correlated); and third, measures of adjacent categories tend to be weakly correlated with one another (range from −.30 to +.30 or so; e.g., exit and neglect tendencies are weakly positively correlated).

Also, alpha coefficients for items within categories are of moderate magnitude, typically ranging from .60 to .90 or so. Furthermore, self-report measures of each response are related to alternative means of measuring each response category. For example, structured self-report measures have been shown to be related to reactions coded from open-ended descriptions of behavior in specific dissatisfying incidents as well as to reactions coded from audiotaped or videotaped recordings of partners' interactions (e.g., Rusbult et al., 1982; Rusbult, Verette, Whitney, Slovik, & Lipkus, 1991). Finally, measures of exit, voice, loyalty, and neglect are only minimally related to individuals' tendencies to describe themselves in a socially desirable manner (e.g., Rusbult, Johnson, & Morrow, 1986b).

METHODS FOR EXPLORING RESPONSES TO DISSATISFACTION

Rather than including the methodological details of each of the studies mentioned in this chapter, the broad approach employed in this program of research will be described in terms of four "methodological commitments." First, our research makes use of the concept of converging operations. We cannot "create" long-standing close relationships or strongly manipulate features of existing relationships in the context of a laboratory experiment. Therefore, many issues in this program of research have been explored using a variety of methods, including laboratory experimentation on nonromantic relationships, role-playing research on "make believe" close relationships, cross-sectional surveys, and longitudinal research. Considered individually, none of these methods are ideal, but when employed together in tests of specific predictions, these methods provide good, complementary evidence regarding the validity of theoretical predictions.

Second, this program of research studies responses to dissatisfaction across diverse subject populations. For example, we have conducted research on both college students and adults residing in the local community (e.g., Rusbult et al., 1986a), we have studied both heterosexual and homosexual relationships (e.g., Rusbult et al., 1986), and we have examined the relationships of young adults residing in both the United States and Taiwan (e.g., Lin & Rusbult, 1991). Thus, our findings appear to be relatively generalizable, not limited to a single category of participant or a single type of close relationship.

Third, as noted earlier, many of our studies utilize multiple modes of measurement—structured Likert-type items, coded open-ended responses, ratings of videotaped interactions, and so on (e.g., Rusbult et al., 1991). We have observed good convergence across multiple measures of a construct and have obtained fairly consistent support for theoretical predictions using diverse measures of exit, voice, loyalty, and neglect. Thus, our findings do not appear to be colored by response artifacts produced by use of a single measurement technique.

Fourth, this program of research has been used to understand multiple domains of social behavior. The model not only has been applied to the study of responses to dissatisfaction in close relationships, but also has been used as a means of understanding responses to job dissatisfaction (e.g., Rusbult, Farrell, Rogers, & Mainous, 1988). Thus, many of the propositions explored in this research program appear to be very general interpersonal phenomena, applying to a wide range of social relationships.

DETERMINANTS OF EXIT, VOICE, LOYALTY, AND NEGLECT

Degree of Dependence: Satisfaction, Investments, and Alternatives

In the search for powerful predictors of the four responses, our first step was to determine what it is about interdependent relationships that leads to a greater or lesser probability of engaging in each category of response. Initially, we studied three qualities of interdependent relationships: degree of satisfaction with the relationship (i.e., passionate love, respect for partner, positive feelings about a relationship); magnitude of investments in the relationship (i.e., the resources that are directly or indirectly linked to a relationship and would be "lost" if the relationship were to end); and quality of alternatives to the relationship (i.e., CL-alt, or the quality of the best available alternative, including a specific alternative partner, dating around, or noninvolvement). Why should we expect that these three variables would powerfully influence responses to dissatisfaction?

According to interdependence theory (Kelley & Thibaut, 1978), one of the more important features of interdependence concerns the degree to which one or both partners are dependent upon their relationship. Dependence can be defined in a variety of ways, but for the present purposes it is convenient to adopt a relatively global definition—a definition that characterizes relation-ships as a whole rather than focusing on dependence within the context of specific interactions. Interdependence theory suggests that dependence on a relationship is greater to the degree that satisfaction with that relationship is greater and the quality of available alternatives is poorer: "As outcomes in a relationship exceed CL-alt by larger and larger degrees the participant be-comes progressively more dependent on the relationship" (Kelley & Thibaut, 1978, 9). Rusbult (1980) extended this definition, proposing that dependence is also increased to the extent that the individual has invested numerous or sizable resources in a relationship. Thus, dependence can be formally represented as follows:

$$\text{Dependence} = (\text{Satisfaction} - \text{Alternatives}) + \text{Investments}$$

Level of dependence affects a wide range of events in relationships, including such diverse issues as the nature and extent of partners' power over one another, the odds that one or both partners will wish to maintain a relationship, the cognitions and attributions that are likely to be formed for partners' behaviors, and so on (e.g., Johnson & Rusbult, 1989; Rusbult, 1980, 1983; Rusbult, Johnson, & Morrow, 1986c). Accordingly, it seemed quite reasonable to predict that the three basic components of dependence—satisfaction, investments, and alternatives—might affect responses to dissatis-faction in ongoing close relationships.

We reasoned that individuals should be more strongly motivated to react constructively to relationship problems (i.e., should be more likely to engage in voice or loyalty) to the degree that they had previously been more satisfied with their relationships and to the degree that they had invested heavily in the relationship. With lower satisfaction and lesser investments, concern with maintaining the relationship should be weaker and exit and neglect should be more probable. In contrast, we reasoned that quality of alternatives should affect response tendencies along the activity/passivity dimension. That is, we expected that good alternatives would serve as a source of power and motiva-tion for bringing about change—to "shape [the relationship] up or ship out" (i.e., to engage in voice or to exit). Thus, we predicted that individuals with higher quality alternatives would be more likely to react to dissatisfaction with exit or voice and would be less likely to engage in loyalty or neglect.

These predictions were tested in five separate studies—two cross-sectional surveys of dating relationships, two role-playing experiments, and one cross-sectional survey study using a more diverse sample of adults residing in the local community (Rusbult et al., 1982; Rusbult et al., 1986a). A summary of the results of these studies is presented in table 3.1. Consistent with hypotheses derived from interdependence theory, greater satisfaction level and investment size were fairly consistently associated with greater tendencies toward voice and loyalty and with lesser tendencies to engage in

TABLE 3.1   Determinants of Exit, Voice, Loyalty, and Neglect

Variable	Publication	Exit	Voice	Loyalty	Neglect
Constructiveness vs. Destructiveness Dimension		*(−)*	*(+)*	*(+)*	*(−)*
Commitment Level	Morrow, 1985	●●	●●	●●	●●
Satisfaction Level	Rusbult et al., 1982 Rusbult et al., 1986a	●●●●●	●●●●●	●●●●○	●●●●●
Investment Size	Rusbult et al., 1982 Rusbult et al., 1986a	●●●●●	●●●●○	●●●●○	●●●●○
Greater Femininity	Rusbult et al., 1986	●○○	●●●	●●●	○○○
Lesser Masculinity	Rusbult et al., 1986	●●○	●●●	●●○	●●○
Gender (Females)	Rusbult et al., 1986	●○○	●●○	●○○	●●●
Activity vs. Passivity Dimension		*(+)*	*(+)*	*(−)*	*(−)*
Quality of Alternatives	Rusbult et al., 1982 Rusbult et al., 1986a	●●●●○	○○○○○	●●●○○	●○○○○
Severity of Problem	Rusbult et al., 1986a	●●	●●	●○	○○
Internal Locus of Control	Morrow, 1985	○○	●○	●○	○○
Self-Esteem	Rusbult et al., 1987	●●●	○○○	●○○	●●○
Respondent Youth	Rusbult et al., 1986a	●	●	●	●
Respondent Education	Rusbult et al., 1986a	●	●	●	○
Respondent Income	Rusbult et al., 1986a	○	●	●	○
Duration of Relationship	Rusbult et al., 1986a	●	●	●	○

Note: Each circle represents a study; each darkened circle represents support for an effect.

exit and neglect. However, quality of alternatives influenced only two modes of response—individuals with superior alternatives were more likely to react to relationship problems with exit and were less likely to engage in loyalty.

Thus, it appears that dependence deriving from each of these three "forces"—or qualities of interdependence—translates into enhanced attempts to deal with relationship problems in a more constructive manner. Greater dependence due to high satisfaction and/or greater investments and/or poorer alternatives appears to lead individuals to deal with dissatisfaction in relatively more desirable ways, either actively attempting to solve problems (voice) or passively but hopefully waiting for conditions to improve (loyalty); highly dependent persons appear to inhibit destructive impulses, such as deliberately destroying a relationship (exit) or passively allowing a relationship to collapse (neglect).

Other Determinants of Responses to Dissatisfaction

Commitment Level. More recent research has explored the influence of additional features of relationships. For example, Morrow (1985) examined the impact of commitment level on response tendencies. Commitment level "subjectively summarizes" degree of dependence on a relationship and consists of intentions to remain with the partner as well as feelings of being "linked" to the relationship (Rusbult, 1983). Based on the above findings regarding the effects of dependence on response tendencies—and reasoning from the point of view of an interdependence analysis—it was predicted that individuals who were more committed to their relationships would be more likely to react constructively and less likely to react destructively to dissatisfying incidents. As can be seen in table 3.1, this hypothesis received strong support. Commitment was consistently positively linked with voice and loyalty and was consistently negatively related to exit and neglect.

Severity of Problem. We have also examined the impact of problem severity on each of the four responses to dissatisfaction, predicting that individuals would be more likely to engage in active responses—exit or voice—to the extent that relationship problems were more severe, or potentially more deleterious to the relationship's well-being (Morrow, 1985; Rusbult et al., 1986a). That is, we expected that greater severity would induce stronger motivation to take direct action to deal with the dissatisfying incident, either solving the problem or ending the relationship. When relationship problems were more mild, we expected that individuals would be more likely to react passively, allowing circumstances to take their own course. As can be seen in table 3.1, this hypothesis received partial support—greater problem severity indeed encouraged exit and voice while inhibiting loyalty, but severity was unrelated to tendencies to engage in neglect.

Psychological Femininity and Masculinity. This program of research also explored the effects of several individual-level dispositions, including psychological masculinity and femininity (Rusbult et al., 1986). Most sex-role researchers and theorists characterize psychological femininity as a communal orientation, one associated with greater interpersonal warmth and a stronger concern with maintaining stable, healthy interpersonal relations (cf. Bem, 1974; Berzins, Welling, & Wetter, 1978; Wiggins & Holzmuller, 1978). Accordingly, we predicted that femininity would affect response tendencies along the constructiveness/destructiveness dimension, greater femininity promoting voice and loyalty and inhibiting exit and neglect. In contrast, psychological masculinity is generally characterized as an emphasis on instrumental behaviors (e.g., career, leadership) or a tendency toward greater interpersonal dominance. Accordingly, we predicted that masculinity would affect response tendencies along the activity/passivity dimension, greater masculinity promoting exit and voice while inhibiting loyalty and neglect.

Examination of the table 3.1 summary reveals that these predictions were only partially upheld. As predicted, psychological femininity was associated with greater tendencies to react constructively, with voice and loyalty. However, femininity was not consistently related to the destructive responses, exit and neglect. Surprisingly, psychological masculinity, too, influenced response tendencies along the constructiveness/destructiveness dimension, greater masculinity being associated with stronger tendencies toward exit and neglect and weaker tendencies to engage in voice or loyalty. It is interesting that psychological masculinity is not neutral with respect to couple functioning (i.e., that it does not simply affect how "actively" individuals deal with relationship problems); rather, high masculinity appears to be downright destructive to the well-being of relationships.

Self-esteem. In a series of studies concerned with the impact of self-esteem on response tendencies (Rusbult, Morrow, & Johnson, 1987), we reasoned that individuals with strong self-esteem would have a greater sense that they are worthwhile individuals with acceptable options should their relationships end (i.e., that they have good alternatives, in a very general sense). Thus, we hypothesized that self-esteem would affect response tendencies along the activity/passivity dimension, self-esteem being positively related to exit and voice and negatively related to loyalty and neglect. This prediction was confirmed primarily for the destructive reactions (see table 3.1)—individuals with greater self-esteem were more likely to react to relationship problems with exit and were less likely to behave in a neglectful manner.

Thus, when faced with a situation that promotes a destructive reaction, people with high self-regard take direct action to terminate the relationship, thinking about or actively searching for "greener grass" elsewhere; those who feel less interpersonally secure can do nothing but quietly allow conditions to worsen. It may be that the individual considers his or her personal "worth" in reacting to problems only when the relationship itself is weak. That is, it is possible that it is primarily when structural inducements to maintain relationships are weakened that individual dispositions such as self-esteem come into play in affecting response tendencies.

Locus of Control. In two studies concerned with the relationship between locus of control and response tendencies, Morrow (1985) predicted that internality/externality would affect response tendencies along the activity/passivity dimension, with individuals who feel a greater sense of control over events in their lives exhibiting greater tendencies to actively "take control" in problem situations. That is, it was predicted that individuals possessing greater internal orientation would evidence greater tendencies to react actively to problems in their relationships (i.e., exit or voice). In contrast, externally oriented individuals were expected to engage in relatively more passive reactions to dissatisfying incidents. These predictions received only weak support. In one of Morrow's two studies, internal orientation was found to be positively correlated with voice and negatively correlated with loyalty; relationships with exit and neglect were not significant in either study (see table 3.1).

Gender. The final variable for which we advanced theoretical predictions was gender (Rusbult, Zembrodt, & Iwaniszek, 1986). There is abundant evidence in the extant literature that women and men often differ in their interpersonal behavior. Relative to men, women frequently engage in greater direct communication, exhibit a more contactful and less controlling interpersonal style, are relatively more concerned with social-emotional than instrumental aspects of their everyday lives, and engage in higher levels of intimate self-disclosure (Hendrick, 1988; Huston & Ashmore, 1986; Ickes, 1981; Reis, 1986). Therefore, we predicted that compared to men, women would engage in greater voice and loyalty and would exhibit lesser exit and neglect.

As is turns out, the only effect for which we have obtained relatively consistent support is the prediction that men tend to be more neglectful than women (see table 3.1). The second most consistent finding is that women may engage in somewhat greater voice than men. However, although our findings have taken this form whenever significant sex differences have emerged in this program of research (i.e., the above pattern has never been significantly reversed), these results tend to be rather weak and inconsistently observed.

Demographic Variables. One final set of issues is worth mentioning. In the large-scale cross-sectional survey mentioned earlier (Rusbult et al., 1986a), we also examined several demographic variables, including age, education, income, and duration of relationship. This portion of our research had two goals: First, we sought to demonstrate that our earlier findings regarding the links between response tendencies and dependence factors (i.e., satisfaction, investments, alternatives) were generalizable, applying to a diverse sample of adults involved in a more heterogeneous range of relationships. Indeed, those hypotheses were generally upheld, irrespective of what portion of the sample we examined—the relationships of married and single people, in shorter- and longer-term relationships, among better- and less-well-educated individuals, and so on. A second goal was to determine whether mean levels of each response differed as a function of these demographic variables. We found that active responding (exit or voice) was more likely among younger individuals with greater education and income who were involved in shorter-term relationships; passive responding (loyalty in particular) was more likely among older persons with lesser education and income who were involved in longer-term relationships.

The Big Picture: Interpreting the Findings to Date

In general, it appears that the key to understanding variations in response tendencies along the constructiveness/destructiveness dimension is the individual's strength of motivation to maintain or restore the relationship. That is, the broad conceptual issue in understanding the odds that an individual will engage in enhanced constructive behaviors and inhibit destructive reactions involves one "side" of dependence—the degree to which there are incentives and ties that connect the individual to a relationship, making the relationship more central to her or his life. Specifically, motivation to react constructively—with voice or loyalty—appears to be greater to the degree that commitment is strong, satisfaction is high, investment size is great, and the individual is more psychologically feminine and less masculine. Destructive reactions—exit or neglect—are more probable under conditions of low commitment, low prior satisfaction, or low investments and among individuals with greater psychological masculinity. In addition, there is some evidence that destructive motivation is greater among men, at least for neglect reactions.

It is more difficult to identify the underlying construct that accounts for variations in response tendencies along the activity/passivity dimension. However, the primary construct may well be related to another aspect of dependency, "felt efficacy"—the sense of having the power and wherewithal to take action. For example, active reactions—exit and voice—are more probable among individuals who have efficacy in the sense that they possess good alternatives (exit only); feel pressure to take direct action because of greater problem severity; have an internal, "take charge" orientation (voice only); have greater self-esteem, or believe that they are worthwhile, desirable individuals (exit only); have greater education; and have low "exit" costs due to their youth and brevity of involvement. Passive loyalty and neglect reactions are more probable among individuals who are low in efficacy, or "weak" in that they possess relatively poor alternatives (loyalty only); have low pressure to take direct action because of low problem severity (loyalty only); have generally low self-esteem (neglect only); are externally oriented (loyalty only); have less education (loyalty only); and have high "exit" costs due to greater age and greater relationship duration (loyalty only). Also, it should be clear that we have been a great deal more successful at identifying variables that predict response differences along the constructiveness/destructiveness dimension than along the activity/passivity dimension.

CONSEQUENCES OF EXIT, VOICE, LOYALTY, AND NEGLECT

Do exit, voice, loyalty, and neglect responses indeed affect relationships in the manner predicted earlier? That is, do voice and loyalty yield constructive outcomes for relationships, and do exit and neglect yield correspondingly destructive outcomes? In addition to exploring the determinants of each mode of response to dissatisfaction, we have also assessed the consequences of exit, voice, loyalty, and neglect, exploring the impact of each of the four behaviors on distress and nondistress in dating relationships

(Rusbult et al., 1986b). Information regarding each of the four responses was obtained from both members of ongoing dating relationships, using both structured self-report and coded open-ended measures of response tendencies. Couple distress/nondistress was operationalized using information regarding several constructs—commitment and satisfaction, love and liking for the partner, and perceived effectiveness of couple problem-solving behaviors.

UNILATERAL RESPONSE TENDENCIES: A "GOOD MANNERS" MODEL

Examining the impact of individual-level responses—each partner's tendency to unilaterally engage in each response (i.e., ignoring the partner's mode of response)—we found that whereas variations in destructive responses (exit and neglect) substantially influenced couple distress/nondistress, variations in constructive responses (voice and loyalty) had little impact on couple functioning (see figure 3.2). That is, exit and neglect hurt relationships

Figure 3.2: Impact of individual's unilateral responses on couple functioning

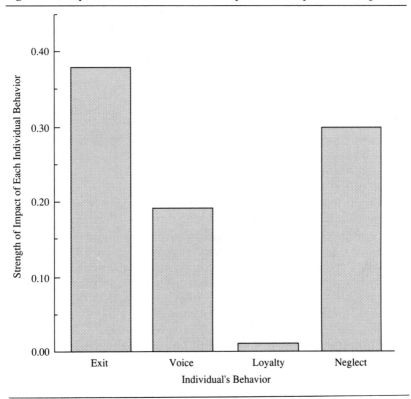

Figure 3.3: Impact of individual's reactions to partner behaviors on couple functioning

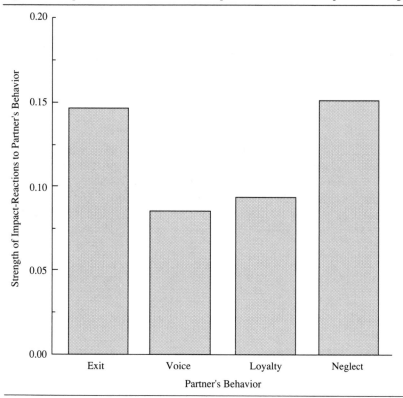

more than voice and loyalty help relationships. These findings suggest a "good manners" model: Scrupulously avoiding destructive acts appears to be more important to overall relationship functioning than is attempting to maximize constructive behaviors.

These findings are consistent with the extant research on marital distress and nondistress: Compared to nondistressed couples, distressed couples exhibit more negative problem-solving acts, deliver more negative reinforcements and engage in fewer joint recreational activities, emit higher rates of verbal and nonverbal negative behavior, are more reciprocally negative and coercive, engage in more frequent and intense negative communications, and express more hostility and rejection (Birchler & Webb, 1977; Birchler et al., 1975; Gottman et al., 1976; Hahlweg et al., 1984; Koren, Carlton, & Shaw, 1980; Markman, 1979, 1981; Raush, Barry, Hertel, & Swain, 1974). Indeed, Montgomery (1988) noted that "research addressing this question suggests that it is less important to exchange positive behaviors than it is to *not* exchange negative behaviors" (p. 345).

Interdependent Patterns of Response: Accommodation

Unfortunately, partners do *not* consistently maintain good manners. Partners eventually—and sometimes chronically—engage in potentially destructive acts. Accordingly, we also explored the impact of interdependent patterns of response (e.g., if a partner engages in neglect, what impact does it have when the individual responds to the partner with voice?). We found that variations in reactions to constructive partner behaviors were only weakly related to couple functioning (see figure 3.3): When the partner had engaged in voice or loyalty, individual responses did not predict couple functioning. However, variations in reactions to destructive partner behaviors had much to do with couple functioning: When the partner engaged in exit or neglect, couple functioning was enhanced when the individual "bit the bullet" and reacted with voice or loyalty, inhibiting impulses toward exit or neglect.

These findings, too, are consistent with the marital literature, which consistently demonstrates that in comparison to nondistressed couples, distressed couples evidence greater reciprocity of negative affect, communications, and behavior (Billings, 1979; Gottman, Markman, & Notarius, 1977; Greenshaft, 1980; Margolin & Wampold, 1981; Raush et al., 1974; Schaap, 1984; Wills, Weiss, & Patterson, 1974). For example, consider an individual who returns home at the end of the day and interrupts the partner's attempts at affectionate conversation with "Just leave me alone, I've had a hellish day." Retorting "You're a jerk" is unlikely to improve conditions; it is far more adaptive for the partner to inhibit the impulse to meet fire with fire, instead calmly letting the incident roll off his or her back or asking, "Would you like to talk about your day, darling?"

Given that the manner in which individuals react when their partners have behaved badly has much to do with couple functioning, it may be particularly fruitful to conduct further research on this phenomenon, a pattern of interdependent responding that we have termed "accommodation." Specifically, accommodation refers to an individual's willingness, when a partner has engaged in a potentially destructive behavior (exit or neglect), to (a) inhibit tendencies to react destructively in turn (inhibit exit and neglect); and (b) instead engage in enhanced constructive reactions (react with voice and loyalty). Unfortunately, whereas prior research has fairly consistently demonstrated that the tendency to accommodate—"to sidetrack or diminish negative affect cycles"—is associated with lower couple distress, little of this work has attempted to explore *why* partners behave as they do. That is, this research has tended to *describe* differences between distressed and nondistressed couples, rather than identify the critical causes of response tendencies or the dynamics by which accommodation comes about.

Accommodation Processes

Accommodation and Transformation of Motivation

In light of the importance of accommodation to healthy couple functioning, how can we develop a theoretical account of accommodative behavior? According to interdependence theory, it is important to commence by understanding the fundamental structure of the accommodative situation (Kelley & Thibaut, 1978). That is, in typical accommodative situations, what is the nature of the interdependence between partners? In this regard, the interdependence theory analysis of the given and the effective matrices (i.e., the given and effective "situations") is an important theoretical distinction. The *given matrix* represents partners' fundamental, "primitive" feelings about various joint outcomes; that is, the given matrix represents self-centered preferences for various joint behaviors, or the fundamental structure of the situation itself. Given the relatively pervasive tendency to experience negative emotions (e.g., anger, fear, sadness) when we are treated with a lack of consideration, we propose that the impulsive reaction to a destructive act often may be to react in kind; when a partner engages in a destructive act, the primitive impulse is to behave destructively in turn (e.g., "I'm hurt and angry, and I don't relish behaving well under these circumstances").

However, the given matrix does not necessarily represent individuals' actual behavioral choices. The *effective matrix* represents feelings about joint outcomes at the time the individual actually reacts to a given situation, and represents a transformation of the given matrix. Transformations are the product of the individual's thoughts and feelings about the partner and their relationship, long-term goals, enduring dispositions, and implicit or explicit norms. Thus, although a partner's destructive act may be hurtful and seem unjustified, and although one's fundamental, primitive impulse may be to react destructively in turn, on deeper consideration the individual may transform the given situation, producing an effective situation in which greater value is attached to reacting constructively (e.g., "For the good of our relationship, and because I love you, I'm willing to bite the bullet this time"). In lay language, the individual may decide that reacting constructively seems like a good idea, that it seems like the right thing to do.

We conducted two studies to determine whether this is an accurate characterization of the accommodative situation—to demonstrate that the individual's fundamental, self-centered inclination frequently (although not necessarily "absolutely") is to react destructively to a partner's potentially destructive act (Rusbult et al., 1991). Of course, it is exceedingly difficult to gain empirical access to an individual's "primitive" feelings, and it is at least equally difficult to demonstrate the existence of transformation of motivation. In our research, we adopted two strategies to demonstrate the quality and form of the given matrix.

In one study, we induced some subjects to set aside the concerns that normally influence social behavior—concern for the partner's feelings, the future of the relationship, and their public image or self-concept—and to behave as they earnestly wished to behave. In short, we asked subjects to report their honest, reflexive response preferences. Consistent with predictions, compared to subjects who expressed their response preferences under conditions of normal social concern, preferences under conditions of reduced social concern were less accommodative (see figure 3.4)—when a partner had engaged in a potentially destructive act, subjects with reduced social concern were less willing to react with voice and loyalty and were far more likely to engage in exit or neglect.

In a second study, we presented subjects with identical social situations and varied the stated level of their interdependence with a partner (e.g., acquaintances, casual dates, regular dates, seriously involved), assessing resultant differences in response preferences. That is, subjects were confronted with identical social situations and were induced to adopt different transformation-relevant motivation with regard to that situation. Consistent with an interdependence analysis, desire to accommodate was significantly lower among less interdependent partners—when the partner engaged in a potentially destructive act, subjects in more interdependent relationships were more likely to engage in voice and loyalty and were much less likely to engage in exit or

Figure 3.4: Impact of level of social concern on willingness to accommodate

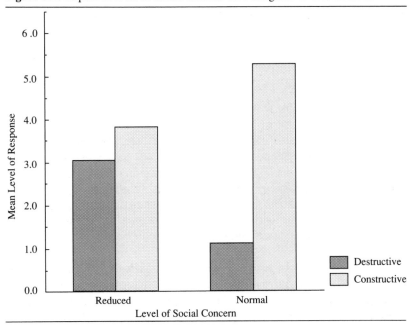

Figure 3.5: Impact of level of interdependence on willingness to accommodate

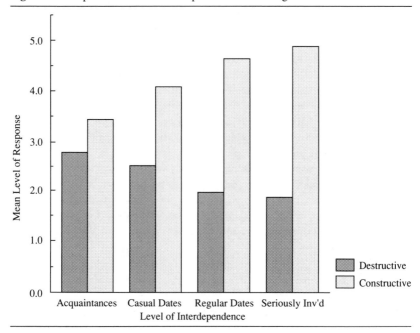

neglect (see figure 3.5). These results are consistent with the claim that individuals are to some degree fundamentally disinclined to accommodate.

Predicting Willingness to Accommodate

Given that willingness to accommodate appears to be greater to the extent that people feel inclined to engage in pro-relationship transformation of motivation (e.g., sometimes to put the needs of the relationship before their own needs), what sorts of factors are likely to induce pro-relationship transformations—what sorts of factors are associated with willingness to accommodate? We began by conducting three cross-sectional survey studies of college-age dating relationships (Rusbult et al., 1991). Two of the studies included both structured and open-ended measures of accommodation, and the third included only structured measures. In addition to measuring accommodation, each study measured some subset of the variables listed in table 3.2.

We examined four broad categories of variables: "happiness" factors (i.e., how positive/negative are the individual's feelings about the partner and their relationship?); "involvement" factors (i.e., how important, or "central," is the relationship to the individual's well-being?); "self-centeredness" factors (i.e., to what degree is the individual oriented toward his or her own, versus the partner's, well-being?); and "dependence" factors (i.e., to what degree is the individual dependent on the partner and their relationship?). Table 3.2 presents results separately for the structured and open-ended measures, and separately for destructive reactions (exit plus neglect) and constructive reactions (voice plus loyalty).

Six of the seven features of relationships we examined consistently "behaved" as predicted. Tendencies to accommodate were greater in relationships with greater commitment level (i.e., does the individual intend to maintain the relationship, and does she or he feel "attached" to it?), greater satisfaction level (i.e., does the individual love the partner and have positive feelings about their relationship?), poorer quality alternatives (i.e., how

TABLE 3.2   Correlations Between Relationship-Level and Individual-Level Predictors and Destructive and Constructive Reactions to Partners' Potentially Destructive Behavior

	Destructive Reactions		Constructive Reactions	
	Structured Measures	Open-Ended Measures	Structured Measures	Open-Ended Measures
Happiness Factors				
Satisfaction Level	−.48**	−.34**	.16**	.35**
Comparison Level	−.17**	−.18**	.04	.19**
Dependence Factors				
Commitment Level	−.50**	−.37**	.14**	.33**
Quality of Alternatives	.27**	.29**	−.07	−.24**
Investment Size	−.30**	−.21**	.11*	.19**
Normative Support	−.31**	−.17**	.09*	.18**
Global Self-Esteem	.01	.09	−.08	−.10
Social Self-Esteem	.02	.07	−.07	−.03
Importance Factors				
Centrality of Relationship	−.36**	−.39**	.15**	.34**
Psychological Femininity	−.28**	−.30**	.21**	.28**
Psychological Masculinity	.15+	.14+	−.09	−.17*
Self-Centeredness Factors				
Partner Perspective-Taking	−.29**	−	.29**	−
General Perspective-Taking	−.11	−	.27**	−
General Empathic Concern	−.12	−	.06	−
Cognitive Rigidity	.11	−	.01	−
Machiavellianism	.11	−	−.11	−

Note: Table values are zero-order *r*'s between each predictor variable and each measure of accommodation.
** *p* < .01
 * *p* < .05
 + *p* < .10

attractive is the best available alternative to the current relationship?), greater investment size (i.e., are there numerous or sizable investments linked to the relationship?), greater normative support (i.e., do people who are important to the individual support continuing the relationship?), and greater centrality of relationship (i.e., is the relationship central to what brings meaning to the individual's life?). However, greater comparison level (i.e., high expectations regarding relationship quality) was generally associated with greater, rather than lesser, willingness to accommodate, contrary to predictions.

In contrast, fewer of the individual-level variables we examined consistently "behaved" as predicted. Tendencies to accommodate were consistently greater among individuals with greater psychological femininity and greater tendencies toward partner perspective-taking (i.e., tendencies to take the partner's point of view in problem situations). We obtained moderate support for the prediction that accommodation would be greater among women and among individuals with lesser psychological masculinity and greater general perspective-taking tendencies. Finally, we obtained no support for a link between accommodation and global or social self-esteem, general empathic concern, cognitive rigidity, or Machiavellianism. Thus, these studies revealed generally good support for predictions concerning the effects of relationship-level variables but revealed somewhat weaker support for predictions involving individual-level dispositions.

Commitment as the Mediator of
Willingness to Accommodate

Following an interdependence analysis, we predicted that willingness to accommodate would be largely mediated by the extent to which individuals feel committed to their relationships. Commitment is a central construct in understanding the longevity and stability of relationships. To the extent that accommodation is promoted by concern for the long-term well-being of a relationship, the commitment construct should "summarize" such concerns more thoroughly than any of the other variables mentioned above. How so? First, decisions to remain in or end a relationship are most directly and powerfully predicted by feelings of commitment (Rusbult, 1983). Also, commitment has been shown to be associated with satisfaction, perceived quality of alternatives, magnitude of investments, centrality of relationship, and normative support for a relationship (Lin & Rusbult, 1991; Rusbult, 1980). In short, commitment is empirically related to most of the features of relationships discussed earlier and should accordingly encompass many or most of the concerns that are said to promote pro-relationship transformation of motivation.

Using data from the three cross-sectional survey studies mentioned above (Rusbult et al., 1991), we performed causal modeling analyses (cf.

Reis, 1982) to assess the plausibility of a model wherein subjective commitment is assumed to directly mediate willingness to accommodate and other features of relationships are assumed to mediate the effects of individual dispositions on both commitment and accommodation. The results of these analyses are summarized in figure 3.6. Variables that directly relate to a criterion are linked to that criterion with a direct path. For relationships with accommodation, we display the average standardized regression coefficients across all four measures of accommodation.

Consistent with predictions derived from interdependence theory, commitment largely mediates willingness to accommodate. Many of the variables we examined affected accommodation primarily through their relationship with commitment—that is, most of our predictor variables accounted for substantially less variance in accommodation once the variance attributable to commitment was accounted for. However, some predictors continued to exert

Figure 3.6: Links between individual-level variables, features of relationships, feelings of commitment, and willingness to accommodate: Summary of causal modeling results

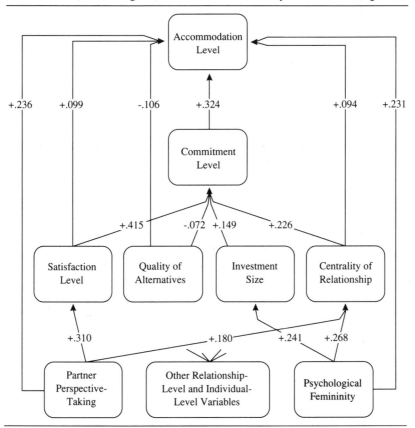

direct effects on accommodation, as can be seen in figure 3.6. Three features of relationships exerted direct effects above and beyond the mediating role of commitment—satisfaction level, quality of alternatives, and centrality of relationship. Also, two individual dispositions exerted direct effects above and beyond the variance accounted for by their links with commitment and other features of relationships—partner perspective-taking and psychological femininity.

APPLICATIONS TO THE STUDY OF ORGANIZATIONAL BEHAVIOR

As mentioned earlier, the exit-voice-loyalty-neglect typology has been applied to the study of social domains other than close relationships. For example, Lowery and his colleagues (Lowery, Lyons, & DeHoog, in press; Lyons & Lowery, 1986, 1989) have utilized this model as a means of understanding the nature and causes of citizens' reactions to dissatisfaction in the political domain. In this context, the four categories include such behaviors as the following:

Exit—leaving or contemplating leaving the jurisdiction ("voting with your feet"); opting for privatized alternatives to government services

Voice—contacting public officials; doing campaign work or making campaign contributions; discussing political issues; participating in public demonstrations; participating in neighborhood groups

Loyalty—voting; speaking well of the community; showing support for the system by attending public functions

Neglect—nonvoting; feeling that city hall has no impact on one's life; distrust of public officials

The exit-voice-loyalty-neglect typology has also been employed in attempts to understand organizational behavior—as a means of describing employee reactions to job dissatisfaction. In the context of organizations, the typology encompasses responses to dissatisfaction that have traditionally been examined in isolation from one another (as we previously noted was true of much of the work on close relationships), including such behaviors as the following:

Exit—quitting; sabotage; transferring; searching for a different job; thinking about quitting

Voice—discussing problems with a supervisor or co-workers; taking action to solve problems; suggesting solutions; seeking help from an outside agency such as a union; whistle-blowing

Loyalty—giving public and private support to the organization; waiting and hoping for improvement; wearing symbols of the organization (e.g., a pin or T-shirt); practicing good citizenship

Neglect—reduced interest or effort; chronic lateness or absences; developing negative attitudes about work; obstructionism; using company time for personal business; increased error rate

To illustrate the generalizability of several findings from the close relationships research reported earlier, several findings from our work on responses to job dissatisfaction will be reviewed. Five studies in this program of research examined the influence on exit, voice, loyalty, and neglect of variations in job satisfaction, quality of alternatives, and investment size (Farrell, Rusbult, Lin, & Bernthal, 1990; Rusbult et al., 1988; Rusbult & Lowery, 1985). Consistent with parallel hypotheses reported earlier for close relationships, we predicted that employees would be more likely to react constructively (with voice and loyalty) and less likely to react destructively (with exit and neglect) to the degree that they were satisfied with their jobs and had invested numerous or sizable resources in their jobs, and would be more likely to react actively (with exit and voice) and less likely to react passively (with loyalty and neglect) to the degree that their job alternatives were good.

These hypotheses were tested in a series of studies that employed several different methodologies—a simulation experiment, a cross-sectional survey study of industrial workers, a two-hour laboratory experiment, a two-wave panel study, and a secondary analysis of the Federal Employee Attitude Survey (conducted by the Office of Personnel Management). A meta-analysis of the results of the five studies is presented in table 3.3 (cf. Rosenthal, 1983). The table 3.3 values are z-scores corresponding to the test of significance appropriate for each study's data type (e.g., regression coefficients for studies with correlational designs; Fs for studies with experimental designs). Eleven of twelve predictions received good support: greater job satisfaction promoted voice and loyalty and inhibited exit and neglect; employees with higher-quality alternatives engaged in greater exit and voice and lower levels of neglect; and greater investment size was associated with greater voice and loyalty and lower levels of exit and neglect.

This application of our typology illustrates two assertions. The first point to be made is that the exit-voice-loyalty-neglect typology can serve a useful integrative function across a wide range of social situations. When researchers explore responses to job dissatisfaction in isolation from one another—one set of researchers exploring chronic absenteeism and another exploring job turnover and yet another exploring good citizenship behaviors— our attempts to achieve a theoretical understanding of the lawful principles

TABLE 3.3　　Impact of Job Satisfaction, Quality of Alternatives, and Investment Size on Exit, Voice, Loyalty, and Neglect Responses to Dissatisfaction: Meta-Analysis of Results

Independent Variable	Exit	Voice	Loyalty	Neglect
Job Satisfaction Effects				
Study 1: Simulation Experiment	−7.46**	1.99*	6.88**	−1.96**
Study 2: Cross-Sectional Survey Study	−10.43**	3.62**	7.61**	−2.68**
Study 3: Laboratory Experiment	−3.41**	2.03*	1.79+	−0.16
Study 4: Panel Study, Times 1 and 2	−6.10**	−1.65+	−0.82	−3.15**
Study 5: Secondary Analysis	−6.56**	6.57**	6.19**	−5.63**
Studies 1–5 Overall Effect	−15.19**	4.28**	9.68**	−6.08**
Quality of Alternatives Effects				
Study 1: Simulation Experiment	13.32**	2.37*	−3.90**	−1.02
Study 2: Cross-Sectional Survey Study	5.09**	6.23**	−0.97	−1.19
Study 3: Laboratory Experiment	4.34**	0.68	−0.31	−1.21
Study 4: Panel Study, Times 1 and 2	3.13**	2.54*	2.14*	−1.04
Study 5: Secondary Analysis	1.75+	2.94**	2.39*	−1.47
Studies 1–5 Overall Effect	12.36**	6.60**	−0.29	−2.65**
Investment Size Effects				
Study 1: Simulation Experiment	−2.04*	1.06	2.38*	−0.74
Study 2: Cross-Sectional Survey Study	−2.59**	1.13	1.19	−2.68**
Study 3: Laboratory Experiment	0.04	0.29	0.29	−2.31*
Study 4: Panel Study, Times 1 and 2	1.00	2.41*	3.29**	0.27
Study 5: Secondary Analysis	−2.99**	3.73*	2.64**	−4.18**
Studies 1–5 Overall Effect	−2.95**	3.86**	4.38**	−4.31**

Note: Table values are z-scores from a meta-analysis.
** $p < .01$, two-tailed test
 * $p < .05$, two-tailed test
 + $p < .10$, two-tailed test

that govern a particular domain are impeded. Certainly, work on each of the individual responses to work problems is important in its own right, promoting our understanding of the particular reaction under consideration. However, such an approach does little to bring the "big picture" into focus. The existence of a general typology such as the current one can do much to further our theoretical understanding of important social phenomena.

The second point to be made is that many of the hypotheses examined in this program of research appear to be fairly generalizable phenomena, applying to at least two relatively diverse domains of social behavior. It is easy to stress the claim that different forms of social behavior follow fundamentally different social "rules" (cf. Clark & Mills, 1979; Clark, Mills, & Powell, 1986; Deutsch, 1975)—it seems obvious on the face of it that there are important differences between the employee-organization relationship and the relationship between two lovers. And certainly, we do not wish to claim that people behave at work precisely as they behave with their loved ones. However, we *do* wish to emphasize that certain broad regularities apply equally to a wide range of social phenomena and that one of the goals of the social sciences should be to uncover such lawful processes.

SUMMARY

Directions for Future Research

At present, we are extending this work in several respects. In the research program on exit, voice, loyalty, and neglect in close relationships, we are: attempting to identify variables that more powerfully predict response tendencies along the activity versus passivity dimension; exploring individuals' perceptions of the intent and consequences of their partners' actions, to determine whether passive reactions are perceived differently from active responses (e.g., as less constructive and impactful); and preparing to study cross-situational consistency in responses, to determine whether individuals exhibit consistency in response tendencies across a variety of social domains (e.g., with lovers, with friends or siblings, at work). In our research on exit, voice, loyalty, and neglect in organizational settings, we are exploring the impact of normative support and job centrality on response tendencies and utilizing panel designs to better understand the precise nature of the causal links between so-called predictors (e.g., job satisfaction and job commitment) and so-called criteria (i.e., the four responses to dissatisfaction). Finally, we are extending our research on accommodative behavior in several respects, by examining the impact of accommodation, especially nonmutual accommodation, on individual partners (i.e., does nonmutual accommodation produce deleterious effects with respect to individual self-esteem, general life satisfaction, etc.?); studying the impact of both absolute dependence and mutuality of dependence on willingness to accommodate; and exploring the manner in which newly married couples negotiate the accommodative "terrain" and learn to share (or not to share) the burden of accommodation over the course of their first few years of marriage.

Potential for Application

Can research on the exit-voice-loyalty-neglect model be used to improve the quality of marital relations and other close relationships? Researchers have consistently found that marital functioning is powerfully affected by the manner in which individuals react when their partners engage in potentially destructive acts. Indeed, one hallmark of effective couple functioning appears to be the ability to accommodate—the ability to sidetrack or diminish negative affect cycles. Most couple therapies include as part of their therapeutic approach the goal of helping couples in distressed relationships develop more adaptive mechanisms for solving problems. However, we hasten to add that such intervention strategies should take into consideration not just the consequences of such problem-solving behaviors for the couple, but also the consequences for the individual partners. For example, although high levels of accommodation may well be desirable for relationships, it is at the same time quite possible that highly nonmutual accommodation may produce stress or other deleterious consequences for the "accommodation expert." In fact, we are at present actively addressing this research question.

The exit-voice-loyalty-neglect model could also be used to develop organizational policies for promoting positive employee membership behavior and discouraging destructive reactions to job dissatisfaction. The art of developing an effective retention program lies in identifying appropriate methods of maintaining high job satisfaction and encouraging employee investment in the organization, particularly among valued employees who might otherwise be at risk of exit and/or neglect. Policy possibilities relevant to the question of job satisfaction are numerous and might include work domains such as compensation, supervision, employee autonomy, and co-worker relations. Also, intrinsic investment in the organization could be encouraged through fostering the development of organization-specific skills (e.g., specific job training) or through incentives that increase community involvement or help to link employees' families to the organization.

CONCLUSIONS

The exit-voice-loyalty-neglect typology identifies a comprehensive set of possible reactions to dissatisfaction. This chapter aimed to make three primary points about the program of research we have conducted using this typology. First, the interdependence orientation seems to be a fruitful approach in helping us identify the features of relationships and individual dispositions that affect response tendencies. The research that we have conducted to date has examined a number of variables that powerfully and reliably predict the circumstances under which each category of response is more probable. Second, it appears that at least one sequence of interdependent responding is central to understanding the consequences of the various modes of response—accommodation, an interdependent pattern in which individuals react to potentially destructive partner acts with enhanced voice and loyalty and inhibited exit and neglect. Once again, an interdependence analysis has yielded some useful insights about how and why accommodation comes about. Finally, it is hoped that the generalizability of the phenomena with which we are concerned has been illustrated by demonstrating the applicability of these ideas to understanding both close relationships and organizational behavior. We believe that the exit-voice-loyalty-neglect typology shows promise in promoting the development of a comprehensive, theory-based understanding of the manner in which individuals respond to dissatisfaction. Assuming that one essential goal of the social sciences should be to uncover the lawful processes and regularities that govern the functioning of the social world, we believe this integrative function is a worthwhile contribution to the literature.

4   Determinants of Short-Term and Long-Term Success in Mediation

Dean G. Pruitt, Robert S. Peirce, Jo M. Zubek,
Neil B. McGillicuddy, and Gary L. Welton

The study reported in this chapter investigated the antecedents of success in community mediation. Mediation is a procedure for resolving conflict in which a third party works with the disputants to help them find an agreement. Community mediation provides this procedure to people who are experiencing conflict in ordinary interpersonal relationships—with neighbors, friends, relatives, spouses, former spouses, landlords, tenants, and so on. Community mediation is a growth industry in our country (see Roehl & Cook, 1985). More than 250 mediation centers have been established in the last ten years, holding more than two hundred thousand hearings each year (Ray, 1986). Cases come from many sources, including judges, district attorneys, legal aid, court clerks, police, social workers, consumer protection agencies, and self-referrals. Many of these centers have become allied with courts, which regularly refer cases to them. The mediators who hear these cases usually are trained volunteers from the ranks of school teachers, students, homemakers, and so forth.

Most cases handled by community mediation centers involve a complaint made by one party against another. This is also the way most court cases start (Felstiner, Abel, & Sarat, 1980). In mediation, the party making the complaint is called the "complainant," and the party complained against is called the "respondent."

A typical hearing in these centers starts with the mediator explaining the procedure and assuring the disputants that he or she is neutral and that the hearing will be confidential. Then the disputants get a chance to "ventilate," that is, to tell their stories, one after the other. After that, the issues are analyzed, alternatives are developed, and the disputants hopefully reach a decision. Caucusing (separate meetings between the mediator and each disputant) is common, but not inevitable, after the ventilation period. If and when a decision is made, the mediator writes it out for the disputants to sign. The resulting document ordinarily has the force of a contract.

Evaluation studies have been done on this kind of hearing, with generally positive results. Settlements are reached in most hearings, user satisfaction is high, and there are high rates of compliance with the agreements made (Kressel & Pruitt, 1989; Roehl & Cook, 1985), despite the fact that the relationships between the disputants are often quite distressed.

RATIONALE FOR THE STUDY

Our study distinguished between short-term and long-term success. "Short-term success" meant reaching an agreement that achieved both parties' goals and satisfied both parties. "Long-term success" was defined as compliance with the agreement, improved relations between the parties, and the absence of further problems in the relationship—as assessed four to eight months after the hearing.

Antecedents of Short-Term Success

Our thinking about short-term success was influenced by the literature on integrative bargaining (Pruitt, 1981; Walton & McKersie, 1965), which is the process leading to high mutual goal achievement (high joint benefit). Walton and McKersie (1965) argue that the best route to mutual goal achievement is through joint problem solving. This involves a candid exchange of information about values and priorities, leading to a common definition of the problem and a collective effort to solve it. Evidence favoring this assertion has been found in laboratory studies of bargaining showing that exchange of information about values and priorities is associated with high joint benefit (Pruitt, 1981; Pruitt & Carnevale, 1982).

Earlier laboratory studies of negotiation also showed that contentious (distributive) tactics—those designed to elicit concessions from the other side—are associated with low joint benefit (Pruitt, 1981; Pruitt & Carnevale, 1982). Examples of such tactics are positional commitments and threats. Such tactics are incompatible with joint problem solving for both user and target. Users of contentious tactics ordinarily commit themselves rigidly to a single position and hence lack the flexibility needed for problem solving. Targets of contentious tactics are likely to lose their trust in the users, diminishing their willingness to provide the information about values and priorities that is necessary for joint problem solving (Kimmel, Pruitt, Magenau, Konar-Goldband, & Carnevale, 1980). The present study provided an opportunity to test these laboratory-based results in a field setting.

It was only a small jump to the further hypothesis that hostile behavior—

anger, sarcasm, denouncement of the opponent—is also incompatible with joint problem solving and hence with the development of joint benefit. This hypothesis has received weak support in a study of labor-management mediation by Hiltrop (1989).

We also looked at two variables we assumed would affect the processes just enumerated. One was a history of escalation prior to the hearing, which we assumed would encourage hostile and contentious behavior and diminish problem solving, thus eroding short-term success. The other was the presence of intangible issues on one side or both sides. Intangible issues are nonsubstantive elements of the dispute that often underlie demands. They include ethical principles (e.g., "Thieves should not benefit from their crimes"), beliefs about one's rights (e.g., "A father has the right to see his children"), normative standards (e.g., "Parents should know the whereabouts of their children"), basic needs (e.g., "A person should feel safe at home"), and emotions based on fear and distrust (e.g., "Allowing visitation will endanger my child"). By contrast, tangible issues are the more concrete elements of a case that tend to be on the formal agenda, such as money, property, or behavior. As Lewicki and Litterer (1985) have pointed out, intangible issues tend to be deeply felt. Hence, they are likely to encourage rigid positions and hostile and contentious behavior, endangering short-term success.

In addition, we took an exploratory look at the impact of several mediator strategies on short-term success.

Antecedents of Long-Term Success

Our hypotheses about the antecedents of long-term success concerned aspects of both the agreement and the process by which it is reached. In the realm of the agreement, it can be argued that short-term success leads to long-term success. An agreement that satisfies both parties' goals will produce greater compliance, an improved relationship, and fewer new problems. The argument for this hypothesis is very straightforward (see Pruitt & Rubin, 1986). People comply with agreements that satisfy their goals, and they are pleased with and reluctant to disrupt rewarding relationships. An implication of this hypothesis is that the antecedents of short-term success mentioned earlier should be predictive of long-term success.

In the realm of process, joint problem solving during the mediation hearing can be reasonably assumed to lead to long-term success. The argument here is that joint problem solving helps open communication channels between the parties, making it easier for them to solve their future problems. One reason for this may be the enhanced trust that results from "symbolic communication by one party through which it acknowledge[s] a deeply felt claim of its opponent" (Kelman & Cohen, 1979, 295). This hypothesis is supported by evidence from the marital therapy literature that training in communication and problem solving improves relations between spouses (Jacobson, 1984; Jacobson & Follette, 1985; Johnson & Greenberg, 1985).

Other hypotheses about the impact of the mediation process were derived from procedural justice theory and research (see Lind & Tyler, 1988). One was that disputant perceptions that fair procedures were used in their hearing would lead to long-term success. This hypothesis was based on research showing that people who feel that an authority (a judge, policeman, or boss) has used fair procedures in making a decision are especially likely to respect that authority and accept his or her decision (Alexander & Ruderman, 1987; Lind, Kurtz, Musante, Walker, & Thibaut, 1980; Tyler, 1984; Tyler & Folger, 1980). Tyler (1987b) has speculated that these findings can be extended to the long-term impact of mediation. There has been no direct test of this speculation, but indirect support can be seen in McEwen and Maiman's (1989) finding that disputants who feel they had a *good* mediation hearing and that the *agreement* was fair are especially likely to comply with the terms of that agreement.

Among the sources of perceived fairness are a sense that one was able to voice one's concerns (called "voice") and a belief that these concerns were taken into consideration by the authority (Folger, 1977; Lind, Lissak, & Conlon, 1983; Musante, Gilbert, & Thibaut, 1983; Tyler, 1987a; Tyler, Rasinski, & Spodick, 1985). Hence, we also hypothesized that long-term success would be greater in mediation hearings that had these characteristics.

In addition, we examined the impact of several types of mediator behavior on long-term success.

METHOD

Subjects

Our sample consisted of seventy-three hearings at the Dispute Settlement Center in Buffalo and the Neighborhood Justice Project in Elmira, New York. Eight additional cases were lost because either the mediator or a disputant declined to participate. Most of the cases involved people in continuing relationships: neighbors, relatives, spouses, lovers, landlords and tenants, etc. Disputes involved money, property, or behavior. The cases were either self-referred or originated in city court. There were always two parties: a complainant, the person or people bringing the complaint, and a respondent, the target of the complaint. The mediators were trained volunteers from various walks of life. Different mediators and disputants were involved in each hearing.

Procedure

Prior to the hearing, the mediator was called to seek his or her participation and to ask a few questions. On the day of the hearing, two observers were seated in the rear of the hearing room when the disputants entered. An employee of the mediation service asked the disputants whether they were willing to be observed. If all consented, the observers remained and took notes on what was said throughout the hearing, one recording disputant remarks and the other recording mediator remarks. These observers had been trained in speed writing procedures, which allowed a high degree of accuracy in transcribing the spoken material. The hearings lasted an average of seventy-five minutes.

The observers interviewed the disputants at the end of the hearing. They then worked jointly to construct a verbatim transcript of the hearing. One of them also interviewed the mediator by telephone within twenty-four hours of the hearing. The actual agreements were obtained from the mediation centers.

A follow-up telephone interview was attempted with each disputant between four and eight months after the hearing. These interviews were completed with forty-six complainants and thirty-four respondents, all that could be reached with repeated calls.

Short-term Success Measures

Short-term success was defined in three ways: whether agreement was reached, satisfaction with the agreement, and goal achievement. *Reaching agreement* was coded "1," and not doing so was coded "0." (Sixty-three of the seventy-three cases reached agreement.) *Short-term satisfaction with the agreement* was measured by a five-option question in the post-hearing interview. (This question was repeated in the follow-up interviews.)

Our measure of *goal achievement* involved coding the transcripts of the mediation hearings. A list was first made of all the issues mentioned by either disputant. The relative importance of each issue to the complainant was then rated by distributing one hundred importance points among the issues. Similar ratings were made for the respondent. Estimates were next made, on a continuous scale ranging from -1 to $+1$, of the extent to which each disputant was successful in getting what he or she wanted on each issue (when agreement had been reached, the final agreements were used in making these ratings). In the final step, a goal achievement score was created for each disputant by multiplying the importance score for each issue by the success score for that issue and summing across all the issues. The resulting measures were then added together for complainant and respondent as an index of the extent to which an integrative (win-win) solution had been achieved. Intercoder reliability correlation coefficients for complainant and respondent goal achievement scores were .95 and .93 respectively.

Goal achievement had a correlation of .36 with reaching agreement and .39 with satisfaction with the agreement ($p < .01$ for both). However these three measures could not be combined into a single index, because satisfaction with the agreement could not be defined for cases not reaching agreement.

Long-term Success Measures

Three measures of long-term success were derived from the four- to eight-months follow-up interviews. Each disputant's *compliance* was assessed by the other disputant's answer to a four-option question about whether the first party had lived up to all the terms of the agreement. The *long-term quality of the relationship* was measured for each disputant by a composite (the sum of standard scores) of that disputant's answers to questions about the quality of the current relationship and whether the relationship had improved or worsened. The *development of new problems* was measured for each disputant by a composite of that individual's answers to questions about whether new problems had arisen and whether either party had taken legal or quasi-legal action against the other. Though complainant and respondent scores were highly correlated on these three measures, their data were not combined into dyad indices because there were only twenty-six full dyads in our follow-up data and we would have been forced to discard a substantial amount of data. Instead, complainants and respondents were kept separate in all analyses involving these scores.

Since the three measures just described were highly correlated (average $r(44) = .44$ for complainants, and average $r(32) = .49$ for respondents), a *long-term success* index was also constructed by adding together standard scores for compliance and satisfaction with the relationship and subtracting standard scores for the development of new problems. This index was constructed separately for the complainants and the respondents, for the reasons given above. Coefficient alpha was .72 for long-term success from the viewpoint of our forty-six complainants and .76 for long-term success from the viewpoint of our thirty-four respondents.

Procedural Justice Measures

Three items in the posthearing interview measured aspects of procedural justice. Disputants were asked to indicate whether the *hearing was fair* (a five-point scale), whether the *true underlying problems* came out (a three-point scale that was intended to measure voice), and whether the *mediator understood* what they had said (a three-point scale).

Other Content Analysis Measures

A number of measures were derived from a general content analysis of the transcripts. The coding unit consisted of (a) everything said by one party before another party spoke, or (b) everything said within six transcribed lines when one party made an extended speech. A sieve coding method was employed, such that a particular code could be awarded only once per unit, but a unit could receive more than one code. The score used for each measure was the proportion of units that received a given code.

There were five measures of *disputant hostility* (intercoder reliabilities [r's] are given in parentheses): hostile questions (.90), sarcasm (.87), swearing and angry displays (.87), behavior put-downs (.79), and character assassination (.72). These five measures were positively correlated, average $r(71) = .38, p < .001$. Hence, they were combined by means of standard scores into a hostility index, which had a coefficient alpha of .72.

There were two measures of *contentious disputant behavior*: threats, that is, statements of harmful intentions if the other failed to cooperate (.72); and positional commitments, that is, statement of an unwillingness to move from the current demand (.75). Since these measures were positively correlated, $r(71) = .38, p < .001$, they were combined into a single index of contentious behavior, which had a coefficient alpha of .53.

A measure of *intangible issues* was devised by counting all of the nonconcrete issues (e.g., principles, judgments, rights) mentioned by either party. The intercoder reliability for this measure was uncomfortably low (.28), but the measure was included in our analyses anyway because it was related in an orderly way to many other variables. In defense of this decision, it should be noted that the two coders discussed and reached agreement on all discrepancies after the intercoder reliability was calculated. We assume that this resulted in a much more reliable measure than indicated by the reliability coefficient.

We also counted the number of *new ideas* generated by the disputants in the joint sessions.

The following categories of mediator behavior were employed in the present analysis: *displaying competence*, e.g., mentioning knowledge of the law or substantive matters pertaining to the case (.74); *reassurance* about the mediator's intent and the rules governing the hearing, such as confidentiality (.75); *efforts to keep order* during the hearing (.84); *criticism of disputant positions* (.70); *embarrassing questions* about a disputant's story or position (.66); *posing problems* to be solved (.75); *agenda suggestions* (.85); *challenging disputants* to develop new ideas (.80); *suggesting new ideas* (.88); and *requesting reactions* to ideas (.89).

Miscellaneous Measures

Joint problem solving was rated by the observers at every transition between the joint and caucus sessions and at the end of the hearing. A summary measure was created for this variable by averaging all of the ratings given during the hearing. Interobserver reliability was $r = .82$ for this measure. A validity check on this measure showed it to be highly correlated with the frequency of new ideas generated by the disputants during the joint sessions, $r(71) = .49, p < .001$.

The observers also rated *mediator empathy* (on a seven-point scale) at every transition between the joint and caucus sessions. Interobserver reliability was .71 for a summary measure based on these ratings.

Prior escalation was measured in two ways: (1) The worst prior incident mentioned during the hearing by either party was rated on a seven-point scale from extremely serious (7) to extremely mild (1). The intercoder reliability for this measure was $r = .80$. (2) Items on the posthearing mediator questionnaire asked how hostile both the complainant and the respondent had been at the beginning of the hearing. This presumably reflected their prior hostility. These items were closely related to each other, $r = .67, p < .001$, and the two of them combined were correlated with the worst incident measure, $r(71) = .47, p < .001$. Hence, a prior escalation index was constructed by summing the questionnaire measures and adding this sum to the worst-prior-incident measure by means of standard scores. This index had a coefficient alpha of .64.

RESULTS AND DISCUSSION FOR
SHORT-TERM SUCCESS

Table 4.1 presents correlations among our predictor variables and our three measures of short-term success. Virtually all correlations in this table are significant and in the expected direction. As expected, when contending and hostility were high, joint problem solving was low. Joint problem solving was associated with high success of all three kinds, while contending and hostility were associated with low success. The antecedent conditions, prior escalation and intangible issues, were associated with high contending and hostility and with low joint problem solving, as expected. They were also predictive of poor short-term outcomes, though not all of these correlations were significant. A subanalysis of the intangible-issues variable showed that the two components most closely related to the other variables shown in table 4.1 were statements of ethical principles and statements of fear and distrust.

The exploratory analysis of mediator behavior suggested that the best advice to mediators is to reconceptualize the issue structure and encourage

TABLE 4.1   Correlations among Short-Term Outcomes and Their Antecedents

	1.	2.	3.	4.	5.	6.	7.
Short-Term Outcomes							
1. Agreement							
2. Goal achievement	.36**						
3. Satisfaction	—	.39**					
Events in Hearing							
4. Joint problem solving	.47**	.33**	.27*				
5. Contending	−.42**	−.25*	−.44**	−.35**			
6. Hostility	−.31**	−.42**	−.42**	−.62**	.51**		
Antecedent Conditions							
7. Prior escalation	−.17	−.20+	−.39**	−.48**	.47**	.65**	
8. Intangible issues	−.29*	−.40**	−.41**	−.45**	.29*	.55**	.33**

+ $p < .10$
* $p < .05$
** $p < .01$

disputants to think. Posing problems to be solved was predictive of reaching agreement, $r(71) = .30$, $p < .01$; creating an agenda was related to goal achievement, $r(71) = .35$, $p < .01$; challenging disputants to generate new ideas was predictive of both reaching agreement, $r(71) = .24$, $p < .05$, and goal achievement, $r(71) = .23$, $p < .05$. Requesting disputant reactions to new suggestions was related to reaching agreement, $r(71) = .26$, $p < .05$. Similar results for agenda formation have been obtained in a labor-management setting by Carnevale, Lim, and McLaughlin (1989).

Mediator suggestions of possible solutions were also useful. The number of such suggestions made was predictive of reaching agreement, $r(71) = .39$, $p < .01$, and disputant goal achievement, $r(71) = .31$, $p < .05$. This suggests that mediators often come up with good ideas that integrate the parties' separate perspectives, which is not surprising, since they occupy a neutral middle ground.

Our data also suggest that mediators should be empathic toward disputants, listening understandingly to their statements. Mediator empathy was related to all three measures of short-term success: reaching agreement, $r(71) = .24$, $p < .05$, goal achievement, $r(71) = .20$, $p < .10$, and disputant satisfaction, $r(59) = .24$, $p < .10$. Empathy was even more highly correlated with joint problem solving, $r(71) = .40$, $p < .001$; and the partial correlations between empathy and short-term success were close to zero with joint problem solving held constant. This suggests that the impact of empathy on short-term success may have been mediated by joint problem solving.

RESULTS AND DISCUSSION FOR LONG-TERM SUCCESS

Tables 4.2 and 4.3 show correlations between our measures of long-term success (columns) and the predictor variables (rows). Table 4.2 is based on the forty-six follow-up interviews with complainants, and table 4.3 is based on the thirty-four follow-up interviews with respondents. The first column in each table reports correlations with the long-term-success index. The next three columns report correlations with the components of this index: reports about the other party's compliance, the quality of the relationship, and whether new problems have developed.

TABLE 4.2 Correlations with Long-Term Success as Reported by the Complainant

	Long-Term Success	R's[a] Compliance	Quality of Relationship	New Problems
A. Short-Term Success				
1. Agreement	.14	−.03	.18	−.15
2. C's goal achievement	−.14	−.19	.12	.02
3. R's goal achievement	.10	.02	.15	−.07
4. C's satisfaction	.12	.12	.08	−.07
5. R's satisfaction	.14	.02	.08	−.26
B. Disputant Behavior and Characteristics				
1. Prior escalation	−.42**	−.28 +	−.38**	.36*
a. Worst prior event	−.29*	−.13	−.29*	.30*
b. C's initial hostility	−.29*	−.24 +	−.24	.19
c. R's initial hostility	−.50**	−.39**	−.43**	.38**
2. Joint problem solving	.30*	.11	.41**	−.20
3. Hostility during session	−.19	−.14	−.15	.17
4. Contending during session	−.21	−.17	−.25 +	.07
5. Intangible issues	−.03	.12	−.21	.01
C. Procedural Justice				
1. C's perceived fairness	.01	−.03	.04	−.03
2. R's perceived fairness	.40**	.32*	.29*	−.36*
3. C's perception all the issues came out	.19	.11	.27 +	−.09
4. R's perception all the issues came out	.42**	.33*	.44**	−.22
5. C's perception mediator understood	.31*	.25 +	.21	−.27*
6. R's perception mediator understood	.13	.01	.23	−.09

a. C = complainant; R = respondent
+ $p < .10$
* $p < .05$
** $p < .01$

TABLE 4.3   Correlations with Long-Term Success as Reported by the Respondent

	Long-Term Success	C's[a] Compliance	Quality of Relationship	New Problems
A. Short-Term Success				
1. Agreement	−.22	−.31+	.03	.23
2. C's goal achievement	−.07	.18	.06	.04
3. R's goal achievement	.22	.08	.29+	−.17
4. C's satisfaction	−.17	−.14	.22	.05
5. R's satisfaction	.32+	.14	.35+	−.31+
B. Disputant Behavior and Characteristics				
1. Prior escalation	−.09	.09	−.18	.14
a. Worst prior event	.00	.11	.06	−.07
b. C's initial hostility	−.03	.09	−.16	.03
c. R's initial hostility	−.22	−.02	−.25	.30+
2. Joint problem solving	.06	−.03	.26	.07
3. Hostility during session	.00	.02	−.12	−.10
4. Contending during session	.05	.06	−.04	−.09
5. Intangible issues	.00	.08	−.11	−.01
C. Procedural Justice				
1. C's perceived fairness	−.26	−.25	−.08	.29+
2. R's perceived fairness	.18	.11	.14	−.21
3. C's perception all the issues came out	.01	−.11	.04	−.11
4. R's perception all the issues came out	.29+	.21	.27	−.23
5. C's perception mediator understood	−.02	−.10	−.02	.09
6. R's perception mediator understood	.12	−.04	.11	−.23

a. C = complainant; R = respondent
+ $p < .10$
* $p < .05$
** $p < .01$

Correlations with Short-term Success and Disputant Characteristics

Sections A of tables 4.2 and 4.3 show correlations between our measures of short-term and long-term success. Goal achievement and satisfaction with the agreement are reported separately for the complainant and the respondent, because these distinctions were made in the long-term-success measures. As can be seen, there were no significant correlations; in other words, there was no evidence that short-term success leads to long-term success.

This lack of a relationship becomes less surprising if we consider that we are usually dealing, in community mediation, with more or less distressed interpersonal relationships. What these people cannot do very well is work with each other; hence, they come for mediation. Our measures of short-term success reflect the quality of the solution to the issues that existed at the time of the hearing. If new issues arise subsequently—as they so often do in distressed relationships—such a solution will be irrelevant, however high its quality. This suggests that long-term success can be assured only if the hearing produces an improvement in the relationship between the parties, so that new issues are less likely to develop and can be more easily solved if they do develop.

The correlations in section B1 of table 4.2 indicate that escalation prior to the hearing was inversely related to long-term success for the complainant. As can be seen, this effect was mainly due to our measure of the respondent's prior hostility. This suggests that hostile attitudes toward the complainant tend to continue after the hearing, undermining the respondent's compliance with the agreement and encouraging the respondent to make further difficulties for the complainant.

The correlations in row B2 partly support our first process hypothesis. Joint problem solving during the hearing was predictive of the complainant's later report of an improved relationship, and there were nonsignificant trends in the same direction for the respondent. We were concerned that this effect might be due to a third common factor of prior escalation. Hence prior escalation and joint problem solving were entered into a multiple regression analysis predicting the quality of the relationship as reported by the complainant. Our measure of prior escalation in this analysis was the respondent's initial level of hostility, because this had shown the highest correlation with long-term success. Both predictor variables showed significant effects (for prior escalation, beta $= -.33, p < .05$; for joint problem solving, beta $= .30$, $p < .05$). Hence, the third common factor interpretation was not supported.

A possible interpretation of this result is that joint problem solving improves the relationship between the parties, giving them new skills for dealing with future problems and greater faith that the other party is a reasonable person with whom they can talk.

There is a parallel between the results discussed so far and some findings in the evaluation of behavioral marital therapy. Jacobson and Follette (1985) compared two procedures: behavioral exchange, in which the couples developed contracts for improving both parties' behavior, and problem-solving training, in which the couples studied and practiced skills of discussing problems. For most couples, behavioral exchange procedures were successful only during the life of the therapy. Their effectiveness deteriorated as soon as therapy was finished, possibly because the contracts developed in therapy did not deal with new problems that emerged later on. This is analogous to our finding that good agreements do not necessarily have long-term value. Problem-solving training had more lasting value, as it also did in two other studies (Jacobson, 1984; Johnson & Greenberg, 1985). This finding is similar to our results on the enactment of problem solving.

The correlations in rows B3 to B5 show that three other antecedents of short-term success were unrelated to long-term success: hostile and contentious behavior during the hearing and the number of intangible issues. These results are heartening, since hostility and contending are a large part of many community mediation hearings and are usually viewed as troublesome by mediators. Perhaps mediators need not work as hard as they usually do to regulate and attenuate these phenomena. Indeed, hostile displays may have some limited value if they allow the respondents to believe that they got their points across or allow the mediator to diagnose respondent attitudes so as to move toward improving them.

Correlations with Procedural Justice

Section C of table 4.2 reports our findings for the three procedural justice questions that were asked the disputants immediately after the hearing. When *respondents* perceived the hearing as fair, *complainants* later reported greater long-term success of all kinds (Row C2). In addition, when respondents reported that all of the issues had come out (a measure of voice), complainants later reported success in the form of more respondent compliance and a better relationship (Row C4). Furthermore, complainants who perceived the mediator as understanding what they had said reported greater long-term success (Row C5).

A multiple regression analysis was done to test whether the findings just presented were independent of each other and whether prior escalation could account for these findings as a third common factor. The criterion variable was our long-term-success index for the complainant. The predictor variables were the three procedural justice measures that were correlated with this variable, along with a measure of escalation, the respondents' initial hostility. (The latter had a significant negative correlation with all three procedural justice measures.) Beta weights from this analysis are shown in table 4.4. The respondents' perceptions that the hearing had been fair ($p < .06$) and that all the issues had come out were still positively related to long-term success. This suggests that these effects were not spurious and that they were independent of each other. One effect disappeared—that for the complainants' perceptions that the mediator had understood what they said—suggesting that this was not an independent result.

The relationship between respondent perceptions of fairness and long-term success for the complainant accords with speculation from the procedural justice literature (Lind & Tyler, 1988; Tyler, 1987b). Respondents who

TABLE 4.4   Multiple Regression Analysis Antecedents of Long-Term Success for the Complainant

Source	Beta	p
Prior escalation (R's initial hostility)[a]	−.29	.05
R's perceived fairness	.27	.06
R's perception all the issues came out	.28	.05
C's perception mediator understood	.08	n.s.

a. C = complainant; R = respondent

thought they had received a fair hearing were more likely to comply with the agreement ($r = .32$) than those who did not, even though they were no more enamored with this agreement ($r = .05$ between perceived fairness and later endorsement of the agreement). This suggests that fair procedures locked the respondents into agreements they did not necessarily like.

Procedural justice theory is also supported by our finding of a relationship between respondent perceptions that all the issues had come out and long-term success for the complainant. Such perceptions can be viewed as a measure of voice, which has been shown to be related to perceptions of procedural fairness (Lind & Tyler, 1988). It should be noted, however, that this finding still held up with perceived fairness held constant. This suggests that we may have been measuring more than voice with this question—perhaps the extent to which information was being exchanged about the true underlying issues. Such information may help improve the relationship between the parties even if it is not reflected in the formal agreement. Thus party A may be better able to adjust to party Z if A learns that Z likes flattery and hates dogs, even if these issues are not addressed in their formal agreement.

It is important to note that these findings show correlations between *respondent* feelings immediately after the hearing and *complainant* reports of success four to eight months later. If respondents perceived that the hearing was unfair or that they did not get their points across, complainants had more problems in the long run. There are two possible interpretations of this trend. One is that we were more effective in measuring long-term success for the complainants than for the respondents. This is hard to believe, since we used exactly the same procedures and questions for both types of disputant. The other possible interpretation is that the burden of compliance fell more heavily on the respondents than the complainants, making their state of mind the main determinant of long-term success. Evidence for this position can be seen in the fact that goal achievement was substantially larger for the complainants (.29) than for the respondents (.13), $t(72) = 2.26$, $p < .05$, meaning that the respondents made deeper concessions and hence had the larger task of future compliance.

Mediator Characteristics and Behavior

The exploratory correlations with mediator behavior were unimpressive. Of the eighty-eight correlations calculated, one was significant at the .01 level, six were significant at the .05 level, and five at the .10 level. This is about what one could expect from chance alone. Hence, we did not draw any conclusions from these data.

CONCLUSIONS

One is never entirely secure in inferring causation from correlation. Nevertheless, our results suggest that prior escalation and intangible issues encourage hostility and contending and discourage joint problem solving, thereby reducing the likelihood of agreement and the extent to which the parties achieve their goals if agreement is reached. The mediator's strongest tools to counteract these tendencies involve intellectual structuring of the issues, challenging the parties to think, and developing new ideas.

The results for short-term success would be more impressive if short-term success had turned out to be predictive of long-term success. But such was not the case. In the long run, it did not seem to matter whether the parties had achieved their goals in the agreement or even whether agreement had been reached. The contracts with which most of these hearings ended seemed irrelevant to the future, a result that is reminiscent of findings on contracts in marital therapy. Perhaps these contracts became progressively inapplicable as new issues arose.

This suggests that community mediators should place less emphasis on solving current problems and more emphasis on the development of skills and attitudes necessary to solve future problems. The relationship we found between joint problem solving and long-term success supports this inference. Again there is a parallel in marital therapy, where problem-solving training has been shown to be successful.

This conclusion has possible implications for the value of caucusing. In a prior study (Welton, Pruitt, & McGillicuddy, 1988), we found that caucusing reduced hostility and increased the likelihood of developing new ideas with respect to the issues at hand. While these effects may improve short-term outcomes, our present results suggest that they are irrelevant to long-term success. Indeed, one can argue from our data that caucusing may detract from long-term success if it takes up time that would otherwise be devoted to joint problem solving. Perhaps the only way caucusing can contribute to long-term success is by improving the chances for joint problem solving in the next time period.

We also found that respondents who felt that the hearing had been fair and that they had been able to voice their concerns complied more fully and made the complainants happier with the relationship after the hearing. This suggests that earlier findings on procedural justice in court hearings, police actions, and employee evaluation (see Lind & Tyler, 1988) can be extended to mediation. Respondent attitudes played another role in our data—we found that respondents who showed the greatest initial hostility to the complainants were least likely to comply with the agreement and most likely to have an antagonistic later relationship with the complainant.

The practical implication of the results just cited is that mediators should pay special attention to respondents—hearing them out, trying to improve their attitudes toward the complainant, and bending over backward to seem fair. This is because they bear the larger burden of compliance and are more likely to create further problems in the relationship. Such a stance may be difficult because complainants tend to be more aggrieved and demanding (Castrianno, Pruitt, Nochajski, & Zubek, 1988) and hence are likely to attract more mediator attention. Yet the respondents' state of mind seems to be critical for long-term success.

How widely can these results be generalized? Do they have implications beyond community mediation settings? Our findings on the antecedents of short-term success and on procedural justice have parallels in several other literatures. Hence, they would appear to be broadly generalizable.

Two of our other findings—the lack of a relationship between short-term and long-term success and the value of joint problem solving for long-term success—have parallels in the research on marital therapy, another form of *interpersonal* peacemaking. But one wonders whether they can be generalized to *interorganizational* mediation in commercial, labor-management, or international settings. Contracts may be more meaningful in these settings than in interpersonal settings, and the quality of the relationship between the parties may be less important. Parallel research in these settings is clearly needed.

NOTE

This report is based on papers given at the 1989 conferences of the following associations: the Academy of Management, the American Psychological Association, and the International Association for Conflict Management. The research reported in this paper was supported by National Science Foundation Grants BNS8309167 and SES8520084. We wish to thank for their advice and support at many points in this project Charles Underhill, president of the Better Business Foundation of Western New York, Inc.; Judith Peter, director of the Dispute Settlement Center; Joyce Kowalewski, former executive director of the Neighborhood Justice Project; and David Rynders, executive director of the Neighborhood Justice Project. The following staff members of the two centers were also very helpful: Mary Beth Goris, James Meloon, David Polino, Brenda Ransom, and Beverly Stearns. We are also indebted for intellectual guidance and data gathering to Jill Dorfeld, Eldon K. Hutchinson, Carol Ippolito, Thomas Nochajski, Helena Syna, Michael Van Slyck, and W. Rick Fry.

5   Toward a More Balanced View of Conflict: There Is a Positive Side

Stephen Worchel, Dawna Coutant-Sassic, and Frankie Wong

Several years ago, I was invited to deliver a lecture on conflict to officials in Athens, Greece. I labored for months preparing the presentation. My plan was to discuss theories of conflict and conclude with a review of the numerous approaches for resolving conflict. Indeed, I was impressed by the efforts of psychologists and other social scientists in developing creative approaches to conflict resolution. Insightful theories focused on the importance of contact (Cook, 1979; Allport, 1954), cooperation on superordinate goals (Worchel, 1979; Sherif, Harvey, White, Hood, & Sherif, 1961), and indispensable contributions by all parties to problem solving (Aronson, Blaney, Stephan, Sikes, & Snapp, 1978). I found work on conflict and conflict resolution in social psychology (Worchel & Austin, 1986; Hewstone & Brown, 1986; Rothbart & Hallmark, 1988; Knudson, Sommers, & Golding, 1980), business (Baron, 1988; Ben-Yoav & Pruitt, 1984), clinical psychology (Gross, 1982; Miller, 1944), sociology (Bonacich, 1972; Gamson, 1975; Stouffer, 1949), and game theory (Rapoport, 1962; Schlenker & Bonoma, 1978). I felt I did a credible job representing the field and integrating theory, research, and application. Just as I was becoming lost in self-congratulations, a member of the audience raised his hand and rose to make an observation that brought me up short. He stated that he, too, was impressed with the work on conflict resolution, most of which originated in the United States. However, he wondered why most of the research was preoccupied with the *resolution* of conflict. Conflict, he observed, was a natural state that existed between people and groups, and no matter how hard social scientists tried, they would never eliminate or resolve conflict. He concluded with a few simple questions that I have been attempting to answer since that encounter. "What are the positive results of conflict? Rather than focusing on resolving conflict, why haven't social scientists devoted more attention to identifying the functions of conflict and developing programs to manage conflict to a positive end?''

An examination of the literature on conflict reveals that my Greek critic may have had a point. If we thumb through any book on interpersonal relations, group dynamics, or intergroup relations, we will find several pages devoted to conflict. In nearly every case conflict is presented as a villain, a destroyer of relationships, something to be exorcised as soon as possible lest it taint the interaction. A sample of these books (Forsyth, 1990; Brockner & Rubin, 1985; Stroebe, Kruglanski, Bar-Tal, & Hewstone, 1988; Miller & Brewer, 1984; Oskamp, 1985; Worchel & Austin, 1986; Stephan, 1985; Hewstone & Brown, 1986) reveals several pages or chapters that explain the causes of conflict, identify the *negative* effects of conflict, and discuss the means for *resolving* the conflict. This literature is almost totally devoid of any mention of the positive effects of conflict, how conflict can be managed effectively toward positive ends, or how individuals or groups can be encouraged to retain their separate identities while dealing effectively with the conflict at hand.

Given the context under which conflict is studied, it is easy to see why it has developed a negative reputation rivaled only by that of sin. The literature suggests that conflict resides at the roots of prejudice, discrimination, labor/management problems, marital discord, ethnic confrontations, and personal discomfort. Clearly conflict haunts some unsavory neighborhoods. Indeed, a strong case for guilt by association can be made. There are instances where conflict can and does lead to destruction and discomfort, where it hinders progress and accord, and where it instigates bias and unfair treatment.

But conflict has a Jekyll and Hyde personality, and we may be too quick to condemn if we see only the evil Mr. Hyde. The literature has done a fine job in exploring the sinister side of conflict. My aim in the remainder of this chapter is to balance the scales somewhat by focusing on the functions and value of conflict.

POSITIVE FUNCTIONS OF PERSONAL CONFLICT

Let me begin with a broad generalization: Conflict plays a positive role at all levels of human interaction (intrapersonal, interpersonal, and intergroup). This is not necessarily a novel observation, and there is considerable evidence to support it. Looking at intrapersonal conflict, Festinger (1957) argued that the conflict arising when individuals make decisions forces them to examine their self-concepts and to consider the objects involved in the decisions. This conflict motivates individuals to protect their self-concepts by seeking evidence to support the decisions. Although the search process is biased, this conflict may well create a better informed individual, one who is more familiar with the positive aspects of the chosen course and the negative aspects of the rejected course.

Deutsch (1973) expanded this reasoning by suggesting that conflict causes the individual to go through a self-examination process. It motivates the individual to mobilize his or her capabilities to deal with or overcome the conflict. Through these efforts the individual becomes better able to define her or his abilities and self-concept. Conflict often serves as the basis for the social comparison process (Festinger, 1954; Goethals, 1986). In this sense, intrapersonal conflict serves as both the initiator and the well of energy for self-examination and the formation of a clearer self-identity.

Conflict, too, plays a vital role in creativity. While conflict, defensiveness, and anxiety may narrow attention and hinder personal creativity (Wallach & Kogan, 1965), more recently a different view has begun to emerge. Wallace (1986) described the creative process as a reconciliation of paradoxical views and feelings within a person. Kolb & Glidden (1986) argued that the creativity of an organization can be enhanced by conflict if managers know how to direct interaction during the conflictual situation. Conflict, either intrapersonal or interpersonal, is often the spark leading to creative thinking and creative actions. In a series of studies, Nemeth and her colleagues (Nemeth & Kwan, 1985, 1987; Nemeth, 1986) found that people faced with disagreement by a minority were stimulated to divergent thinking. This thinking did not lead to an immediate adoption of the minority position, but it did lead people to reconsider the problem at hand and develop creative approaches in task performance.

Numerous theories of personality give conflict an exalted role in personal growth and the development of personality. According to Freud (1940/1949), the essence of the individual is the result of conflict between the id, ego, and superego. Jung (1942–57/1967) viewed personality as the being constructed on a foundation of conflict between opposites: masculinity/femininity, introversion/extroversion, good/evil. The well-adjusted person is the one who can incorporate these competing tendencies within the personality. The troubled person is one who attempts to avoid or ignore these competing tendencies by rigidly adopting one side of the conflicting issue. And Erickson (1963) argued that we reach true happiness only after dealing with the conflict involved in a crisis over our identity.

CONFLICT: AT THE HEART OF PASSION?

Although frequent conflict in close relationships can be the sign of a troubled relationship (Peterson, 1983), numerous investigators have shown that a relationship without conflict, or one in which conflict is avoided, can be equally troubled (Berscheid, 1983; Levinger, 1983). In an interesting analysis, Berscheid pointed out that passion quickly abandons close relationships. Romantic relationships "go flat" as emotions become muted. Conflict or some other form of interruption may raise the emotional level of the individuals and "spice up" the interaction. This view is captured in popular songs that put music to the joy and passions involved in "making up" after conflict. Thus, far from being a destroyer, a certain degree of conflict can actually invigorate relationships. In any case, it is not the conflict that is the problem, but rather the management and response to conflict that determines the health of the unit (Gottman, 1979).

In addition to giving new energy to tired relationships, conflict can serve as a "warning signal" that a relationship is headed for serious problems (Deutsch, 1973) and identify the nature of the problems. Immediate efforts that "resolve" the conflict can often have disastrous consequences, because there may be two components to this interpersonal conflict. The manifest content concerns the immediate issue at hand ("You want to go to the movies, and I want to go fishing"). There is also a latent content in many conflicts that becomes the more important issue that should be examined ("You dominate this relationship and don't pay attention to my needs"). In an insightful analysis of conflict, Filley (1975) makes the point that couples should not be too quick to jump into a conflict-*resolving* mode of behavior. Rather, their first response should be to analyze the conflict and determine the statement it is making about the relationship. Their analysis should include identifying the manifest content of the disagreement and determining whether the issues involve an opposition of means to reach a common goal or two incompatible goals. Filley argues that it is the failure to carefully analyze the conflict, rather than the existence of the conflict per se, that gets relationships into trouble. He suggests that couples are too ready to believe that their fight involves incompatible goals rather than a difference over the means of achieving a common goal.

THE PLACE OF CONFLICT IN GROUP BEHAVIOR

The Jekyll and Hyde sides of conflict are nowhere more evident than in group and intergroup relations. Conflict and its most extreme disguise, competition, have been identified as the cause of intergroup hostility (Sherif et al., 1961; Kahn & Ryen, 1972; Carnevale, Pruitt, & Seilheimer, 1981), prejudice (Allport, 1954; Rokeach, Smith, & Evans, 1960; Branthwaite & Jones, 1975; Brown & Abrahms, 1986), and discrimination (Dovidio, Mann, & Gaertner, 1989). The roots of war are often deeply embedded in conflict over territory or basic attitudes and values (Glad, 1990; Kaplan & Markus-Kaplan, 1983).

On the other hand, conflict may initiate broad and important social change (Simmel, 1955). Looking within the United States, open and sometimes violent conflict between blacks and whites served as the stepping stone for reform of nearly every facet of life including education, voting, political districting, employment, law, and even the content of textbooks and popular television programming. Similar reforms can be laid at the feet of conflict involving people of different genders, religions, ages, and sexual orientations. It is a matter of speculation whether these changes would have occurred without open confrontation. However, it is a matter of record that the confrontation was a motivating source for these changes.

Efforts to avoid or ignore conflict can have disastrous effects on group process and productivity. Groupthink may be viewed as one result of conflict avoidance. After studying historical material in which "good" groups made bad decisions, Janis (1972, 1982) suggested that groupthink can be avoided when a leader encourages some conflict. Groupthink is most likely to occur in a cohesive group with a stronger leader. Encouraging minority or deviant members to openly express their alternative viewpoints can play a very positive role in group decision making.

Conflict has often served as the elixir for conflict. Sherif et al. (1961) found that two enemies would become temporary allies if the conflict widened to include a common foe. The common-enemy approach has long been recognized by politicians as a means of consolidating their power. It is probably no accident that nations often enter into war at precisely the time when they are experiencing an increase in internal unrest (Kluckhohn, 1960; Withey & Katy, 1965; Mitchell, 1928). As Simmel (1955) points out, "One unites in order to fight." Clearly this policy of "war for the sake of internal harmony" has its drawbacks. First, it usually serves to put internal conflict on hold, rather than to present a long-term solution to the issues that initiated the conflict. Second, from a conflict-reduction standpoint, Sherif et al. (1961) point out that this policy actually broadens the scope of conflict, rather than diminishes it; now the conflict involves three parties rather than the two that were initially at odds.

ETHNOCENTRISM AND PATRIOTISM

The idea that external conflict can play a uniting role has been at the base of recent work in which I have been involved with Arnold Vedlitz, a political scientist at Texas A&M University. We draw heavily on the views of a variety of social scientists, including Landis and Boucher (1987), Greenberg, Pysczczynski, and Solomon (1986), Becker (1973), Bar-Tal (1990), and Streufert and Streufert (1986). We begin with the premise from social identity theory (Tajfel, 1982; Tajfel & Turner, 1986) that an important component of the individual's self-identity is derived from the groups to which he or she belongs. Clearly, each person belongs to a variety of groups at any one time. Two important groups at the roots of individual identity are one's nation and one's ethnic group (or groups). The nation is defined by territorial boundaries and a recognized political structure. The ethnic group is defined by the individual's ancestral roots. The ethnic group itself has no geographical boundary, although it may have an identifiable or mythical homeland. The ethnic group is often further identified by a common language and religion, a recognized history, and in some cases, shared physical characteristics. Ethnic groups often cross the boundaries of nations, and this fact may place the nation and ethnic group in conflict.

Giving the nation a central role in defining one's self-concept is at the heart of patriotism. Similarly, a reliance on the ethnic group to define personal identity, and pride in that ethnic group, are important components of ethnocentrism. The annals of political history are often written by the clash of these two "isms." The strength of the USSR lay in the patriotism that bound together people from a variety of ethnic groups, including the Russians, Latvians, Armenians, Lithuanians, and Estonians. The strain on that country was partly caused by a rise in ethnocentrism and a decline in patriotism to the USSR. Similar struggles between patriotism and ethnocentrism are currently being played out in dozens of countries, including India, Iraq, Ireland, and Sri Lanka. History is filled with other incidents.

Speculating about the conditions that give rise to patriotism and ethnocentrism presents quite a challenge. An even more formidable issue involves identifying the factors that lead individuals to emphasize the nation over the ethnic group and vice versa. With regard to the first issue, numerous scholars have postulated that a threat to one's self-esteem increases the need to identify with a larger group and incorporate this larger group into one's self-identity. The threat may be packaged in many forms, including a concern with mortality and dying (Becker, 1973, 1975), an existential crisis, or a threat to one's material possessions or means of livelihood.

There is a less clear answer to the question whether the response to these threats will create patriotism or ethnocentrism. An examination of the history of national and international conflicts does offer some direction for future study of this issue. Patriotism often increases when a *clearly identifiable force outside the nation* threatens the nation's existence, and consequently, the individual's existence. This is essentially the classic "common enemy" paradigm, and it usually involves conflict with another nation or nations. As patriotism increases and the nation prepares to meet the conflict, ethnocentrism decreases. National identity becomes a central feature of personal identity. President Bush mounted a major campaign to convince the American people that Iraq posed a direct threat to the economy of the United States. The host of yellow ribbons that decorated buildings, trees, and automobiles demonstrated the patriotism engendered by Bush's efforts.

Ethnocentrism, on the other hand, is often the response to threats that arise within the nation's boundaries. The source of these threats is generally less identifiable, as in the case of economic recession. Identity with the ethnic group is most likely to occur when individuals feel that the internal threat is not equally menacing to everyone within the nation's boundaries, and that they are the target of the threat because of the ethnic group to which they belong. Unlike the conditions that spawn patriotism, the identifiability of the source of threat and the intensity of the threat are not as important for the rise of ethnocentrism. The astute leader is the one who can recognize the dark clouds of ethnocentrism that will threaten the integrity of the nation and turn the tide by identifying a clear threat to the nation. How fortunate it was that Saddam Hussein chose to occupy Kuwait just as the United States was entering a recession with its banking industry in serious trouble!

This is not the place to examine the support for this position. My aim in raising these issues is merely to highlight the important role that conflict plays in leading people to identify with their nations or ethnic groups. Conflict motivates individuals to become concerned with their personal identities, and as a result it unites people into groups.

CONFLICT'S ROLE IN GROUP IDENTITY AND GROUP DEVELOPMENT

Let's now examine the importance of conflict from the group's standpoint. Once again the evil side of conflict can be well documented. Conflict has led to war and the buildup of frightening arsenals of weapons. Conflict over values, goals, opportunities, and materials has split apart or destroyed groups. With its dark potential, we might expect that groups would do everything possible to avoid both internal and intergroup conflict. But this is not the case. In fact, groups often incite conflict, and this conflict plays an important role in group development.

Over the last several years my students and I have observed ongoing laboratory work groups, conducted interviews with individuals involved in political movements, and examined archival research describing group development over time. Regardless of the particular group on which we focused, one point was always clear: Groups are dynamic units that change and grow, often through a set of identifiable stages. Drawing on our own observations and considerable earlier work on group development (Tuckman, 1965; Tuckman & Jensen, 1977; Bales & Strodtbeck, 1951; Dunphy, 1968; Moreland & Levine, 1988), we constructed a model of group development that was designed to describe the cyclical changes that take place in groups, and serve as a source for predicting a host of group behaviors, including conformity, minority influence, social facilitation and loafing, group productivity, the treatment of new members, and relations with out-groups. The model has been described in detail in earlier publications (Worchel, Coutant-Sassic, & Grossman, 1991; Worchel, Grossman, & Coutant-Sassic, 1992).

Basically, we found that new groups are often founded in an atmosphere of discontent and alienation. However, dissatisfaction alone does not spark the formation of a new group. *That spark is often supplied by an event, or rumor of an event, that involves conflict and confrontation with central members of the established group.* For example, the Rosa Parks incident in Montgomery, Alabama, in which a black seamstress was arrested for refusing to yield her seat on a public bus to a white rider, was a spark for the civil rights movement led by Martin Luther King, Jr. A rumor of the beating of a prisoner by prison guards precipitated the bloody Attica riots that eventually resulted in sweeping prison reform. This type of incident serves as a catalyst that brings together diverse individuals who share a dissatisfaction with the old group.

Whether the new group begins as an offshoot of a larger, established group through the process described above, or is formed without this history, the first stage of group development involves establishing a group identity. During this stage the group is very concerned with identifying its members, defining group boundaries, and ensuring loyalty of group members. Demands for conformity are high, tolerance for dissenting opinion is low, and the group adopts clear and extreme positions on issues. *Conflict is often invited with the outgroup, but internal conflict is quickly suppressed.* Intergroup conflict serves the purpose of drawing clear lines between the in-group and the out-group, and it often widens the gulf between the two groups as each adopts increasingly extreme positions in the conflict.

Once identity is established, groups turn their attention to issues of group productivity. During this period, group members define productivity goals and identify people who can help them achieve those goals. *Any conflict, external or internal, that interferes with productivity is avoided.* In fact, out-group members who possess needed skills may be invited into the group. Following this stage, groups move into a period of individuation. *Internal conflict increases as individuals strive for personal recognition and equity, and the group attempts to maintain the supremacy of the group over the individual member.* Individuals compare their skills and resources with in-group members and their rewards and outcomes with members of other out-groups. Leadership becomes diffuse and less centralized.

The stage of decay begins as members search out alternative groups where their rewards will be higher. The honesty and ability of group leaders are openly questioned. Failure is blamed on the leaders, and success is attributed to personal attributes of the members. Subgroups form and struggle for power. *The internal conflict is contrasted with efforts by the subgroups to form coalitions with out-groups.* The initial internal conflict centers on power within the group, but later the conflict involves the freedom of the subgroups to leave the group. The decay stage sets the foundation for the formation of new groups that begin anew with a quest for independence and identity.

As you can see, conflict occurs at each stage, and the conflict is the catalyst that moves the group through its stages. On the one hand, it can be argued that conflict is responsible for ultimately destroying the integrity of the group. The internal strife between subgroups and the competing desires for inclusion and independence have this effect. On the other hand, it is conflict that often pushes members to develop new groups, and conflict plays a critical role in helping define the boundaries of the new group and giving it an identity. At the extreme, we argue that some degree of intergroup conflict is necessary for the establishment and development of groups.

Much of this work is clearly speculation, but we have collected supporting data. In one study, groups of five members met for three one-hour work periods. At several points over this time, subjects were questioned about intergroup and intragroup conflict. The most interesting item involving intergroup conflict asked subjects how much they wanted to work (cooperate) with or compete against out-groups. As can be seen in figure 5.1, subjects desired competition with out-groups during the early period of the group, but this desire for intergroup conflict decreased steadily over time.

Looking at intragroup conflict, subjects were asked how much they wanted to compete or cooperate with in-group members. As figure 5.2 indicates, there was a strong desire to cooperate with in-group members during much of the group's life, but this desire gave way to a quest for intragroup competition late in the group's life.

A similar pattern of results was found when subjects were asked how comfortable they were with "internal conflict." Figure 5.3 indicates that in general they were very uncomfortable with internal conflict except toward the end of the group, where they reported being comfortable with internal conflict. One unusual finding on this question was the increase in discomfort indicated by subjects on the last measure, taken only five minutes before the group was scheduled to end. This result may be an anomaly, or it may indicate that subjects want to leave the group with good feelings. The desire to leave under an atmosphere of cooperation and good feelings may be especially

Figure 5.1: Nature of desired interaction with out-group as a function of group life

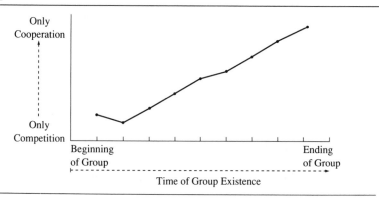

likely when subjects know that the group is scheduled to end. We may not find this pattern if subjects choose to leave a group that will continue after their departure.

A number of points can be made about these results. First, group development affects when subjects find intergroup and intragroup conflict acceptable. It is also clear that there are significant differences in the times when intergroup conflict is acceptable and when subjects are comfortable with intragroup conflict. Finally, it is also clear that subjects do not feel that conflicts are always to be avoided, or that they are always uncomfortable with competition and conflict. In fact, the data on intergroup conflict suggest that at times they will invite conflict.

More research is necessary to flesh out the model and support the position that conflict plays a critical role in the establishment of group identity.

Figure 5.2: Nature of desired interaction with in-group members as a function of group life

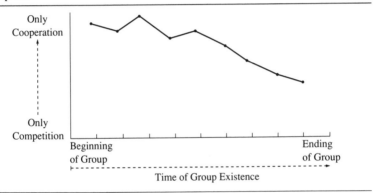

Figure 5.3: Degree of comfort with internal conflict over period of group existence

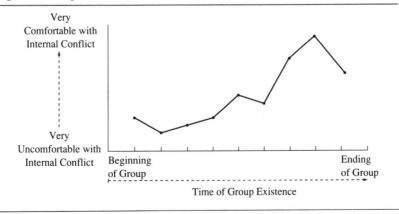

One approach that might yield some interesting results is to examine how groups respond when placed in a situation in which out-groups consistently advocate intergroup cooperation. If the model is correct, we can speculate that members of the new target group will be very uncomfortable and will, especially during the early stages of group development, behave in a way to provoke conflict and disagreement with the out-group. There is, in fact, indirect evidence that this behavior will occur. A number of studies on social identity theory involved randomly dividing people into groups and then giving them the opportunity to divide points or money between the in-group and the out-group (Tajfel, 1978; Tajfel, Flament, Billig, & Bundy, 1971). Invariably, subjects gave the lion's share of the resources to the in-group. This behavior was interpreted as an attempt to enhance the image of the in-group relative to that of the out-group. I might suggest that this blatant effort to create inequity was an attempt to provoke the out-group and invite confrontation should the two groups meet in the future. If the model is correct, the inequitable distribution of resources between groups will be most pronounced in the early life of the group and will be significantly diminished when members are aware that their group is about to disband.

Another indirect piece of evidence comes from the research on bargaining behavior. The results of several studies (Axelrod, 1984; Komorita & Barth, 1985) show that the tit-for-tat strategy of responding is most likely to result in cooperative behavior. However, constant cooperative behavior from the opponent is responded to with competitive responses; one party will take advantage of a consistently cooperative party. The standard reasoning for this behavior is that the cooperative party is viewed as weak. Indeed, this may be the case in many instances. However, I would like to suggest that the constantly cooperative opponent interferes with the other party's desire to draw boundaries, establish independence, and demonstrate strength. Competition in the face of constant cooperation may, in some cases, be used to provoke the other party to compete and engage in conflict. I would expect that the tendency to take advantage of the cooperative party will be most pronounced if the interaction involves groups, when the interaction occurs early in the group's development and/or when there exists a threat to the independence or identity of the group. These predictions are based on the premise that conflict is important and desirable in establishing group identity. Caution is in order when interpreting existing results as support of the group development position, because the previous research involved bargaining between individuals, not groups. However, it should be noted that the interactions took place when the individuals first arrived at the experiment and were unacquainted with each other. This is precisely the time when we might expect concern with establishing identity to be highest.

REDUCING DISCRIMINATION WITHOUT
SACRIFICING IDENTITY

Before closing, I'd like to address one more issue that is often at the heart of programs designed to reduce prejudice and hostility. Several investigators (Miller & Brewer, 1984; Gaertner, Mann, Murrell, & Dovidio, 1989), including myself (Worchel, 1986), have suggested that prejudice and discrimination can be reduced by eliminating or diminishing the salience of group boundaries. This position is also implied in some research espousing equal status contact (Cook, 1984; Clore, Bray, Itkin, & O'Murphy, 1978). Indeed, there is evidence that actions that blur the boundaries between groups do reduce intergroup hostility and discrimination (Gaertner et al., 1989; Gaertner, Mann, Dovidio, Murrell, & Pomare, 1990; Worchel, Axsom, Ferris, Samaha, & Schweitzer, 1978; Amir, 1976).

While I do not wish to argue with the success of this approach, I do think it has limited utility and may have inherent long-range liabilities. One major limitation is that it is often difficult, if not impossible, to reduce these group boundaries. Clear group distinctions often exist between groups (black/white, similar dress/distinctive clothing, male/female), and it is impossible to mute these distinctions. The alternative, often employed in laboratory research, is to make these distinctions unimportant or to reduce their salience. Once again, this may work toward reducing intergroup hostility over the short run. However, reducing salience between groups may result in ignoring or playing down important and valuable differences between the groups. Attempting to ignore differences between blacks and whites, Anglos and Hispanics, males and females, or Protestants and Jews may overlook important and valuable differences between the two groups. The rich heritage of ethnic or racial groups may be ignored, or valuable differences in the behavior or perspectives of males and females may be trampled, in the rush to ignore group distinctions and create "one big happy group." Eliminating conflict and prejudice may be achieved at the price of ignoring group identity.

If we view group membership as an important part of individual identity, this homogenization of groups will prove uncomfortable and threatening in the long run. The ultimate result will be that individuals will resurrect the group boundaries and invite conflict within the group at some point in time. In other words, attempts to reduce prejudice by reducing natural group distinctions will serve as short-term solutions, but their long-run success will be doubtful.

Is there another alternative? I suggest that there is. One solution is to recognize the differences, in fact, emphasize the differences. This action will protect the identity of the different groups, but it may set the stage for inviting conflict between the groups. The destructiveness of this conflict can be diminished by focusing on the ways in which the unique skills of members of the various groups can be combined to solve a common problem. This step is similar to the jigsaw approach used by Aronson and his colleagues (Aronson et al., 1978) to reduce prejudice. In this case, individuals from different racial or ethnic groups are encouraged to learn different parts of a puzzle. The puzzle can only be solved if all members learn their material and combine their unique knowledge in working on the puzzle. This approach does not necessarily diminish the integrity of the individual's group identity; it demonstrates how the independent persons can retain their identities while working on a common problem. I suggest that the approach be taken a step further by explicitly recognizing the uniqueness of the various groups and encouraging individuals to learn about the other groups and become familiar with their special history and abilities. This knowledge not only retains their unique identities, but it can be used in determining how to combine efforts most effectively as common problems arise.

Clearly, there are dangers to this approach. Groups may be motivated to perceive the weaknesses and shortcomings of the out-groups. Competition between the various groups might develop, as each attempts to demonstrate its superior talents. However, these potentially destructive tendencies can be dealt with by encouraging group members to take creative action in developing long-term plans for combining the various talents represented by the groups. The groups can be given problems, such as the jigsaw puzzle, that require the combination of the different talents and knowledge. Equal status, then, takes on a different meaning. No longer does equal status involve demonstrating that the two groups are similar. Rather, it requires that individuals see that each group can contribute to solving a common problem.

Once again, I must end a section with a call for further research. The proposed actions run counter to many approaches showing a reduction in prejudice that accompanies a reduction in the salience of group boundaries. However, we know very little about the long-range impact of this approach. It may prove problematical to ignore the salience of clear group distinctions over the long haul. The natural tendency of individuals may be to recognize these distinctions and boundaries.

A Concluding Comment

I must admit to a strong temptation to close this chapter by advocating a life of conflict and strife. My purpose has not been to blindly praise conflict and extol its virtues. I do, however, wish to avoid the opposite, and equally foolhardy, position that quickly condemns conflict as a carrier of evil. Conflict, intrapersonal, interpersonal, or intergroup, may be uncomfortable, stressful, and followed by destructive consequences. There are cases where conflict is best avoided or, at least, resolved. As my Greek critic pointed out, there is an extensive and excellent literature on all these points. That literature is both insightful and valuable for understanding and improving human interaction.

My point is that this literature covers only part of the picture. There is another side to conflict that has been less well studied. Conflict, itself, is not the smoke that signals that something is amiss within an individual or between individuals. Nor does conflict always require an immediate remedy to reduce its level. Rather, conflict is a natural and necessary part of life and social interaction. It is as likely to initiate deep and positive personal reflection as it is to result in personal distress. It is as likely to motivate growth in a relationship as it is to be a sign of a troubled relationship. And it is as likely to propel group development as it is to instigate intergroup destruction and prejudice.

Conflict itself is not the problem. Problems, however, arise as a result of unwise reactions to conflict or efforts to avoid conflict. My own research suggests that timing is a critical issue in determining the value of conflict. There are times when individuals or groups may seek out conflict and benefit by dealing with it. And there are times when conflict in certain areas will be especially stressful, beget destructive reactions, and result in a negative state. Research that studies conflict in this context will yield greater understanding and identify constructive approaches to avoiding excessive personal stress, prejudice, and discrimination.

NOTE

This chapter was written with the support of an Advanced Research Project from the Texas Coordinating Board of Higher Education. We appreciated the insightful comments of Janusz Reykowski on early drafts of the manuscript.

Part II

INTERGROUP CONFLICT

6   Intergroup Perception and
       Social Conflict

Myron Rothbart

Comprehensive reviews by Allport (1954) and by Levine and Campbell (1972) reveal a bewildering array of ideas dedicated to understanding the origin of hostility between groups. Earlier attempts to simplify this array contrasted "realistic" sources of group conflict with psychological factors, with the latter construed as primarily irrational in character (e.g., Coser, 1956; Bernard, 1957). Given the explosion of research on cognitive processes in intergroup relations in the 1970s and 1980s (e.g., see Hamilton, 1981), modern critics would have to recognize some difference between the traditional motivational theories of intergroup conflict and more recent approaches emphasizing cognitive and perceptual processes.

Motivational theories typically have posited a need to disparage out-groups, with the targets of hostility being either out-groups in general or specific out-groups that have been the objects of historical enmity. The origins of this need vary, from theory to theory, and include the draining off of aggressive energy (cf. the frustration-aggression-displacement model of Dollard, Doob, Miller, Mowrer, & Sears, 1939, and the symbolic displacement/ projection theory of Bettelheim & Janowitz, 1949), the intolerance of ambiguity that results from the repression of hostile impulses toward parents (Adorno, Frenkel-Brunswik, Levinson, & Sanford, 1950), or the esteem-enhancing function served by feeling superior to other groups (Cialdini et al., 1976; Veblen, 1902; Tajfel & Turner, 1986).

In contrast, cognitive-perceptual theories offer a second class of explanations and assume that otherwise functional thought processes exacerbate intergroup conflict by illusorily generating the perception of differences between groups (e.g., Hamilton & Gifford, 1976) or by exaggerating the apparent magnitude of small, existing differences. Cognitive-perceptual theories typically emphasize memory, categorization, and judgment as the loci of intergroup misperception.

In contrast to the first two classes of "psychological" explanations, realistic conflict theories posit real competition over limited resources as the cause of intergroup strife. And finally, real differences between groups may be the cause of dislike, since we value our own physical, linguistic, behavioral, value, or attitudinal attributes more than those different from our own. Whether this last category should be included under "realistic" or under "psychological" factors is arbitrary and a point for later discussion.

Although this taxonomy suggests four reasonably distinct contributors to intergroup conflict, even this somewhat elaborated distinction probably does more harm than good in helping us understand the nature of intergroup conflict. First, many of the differences between these approaches are more apparent than real, and second, this taxonomy implicitly suggests that the causes are mutually exclusive rather than mutually reinforcing. My goal in this chapter is to first describe some of our own work on the cognitive-perceptual aspects of intergroup relations, and to question the value of some of the distinctions outlined above. Since the earlier distinction, between realistic and psychological causes, grew out of the implicit belief that realistic factors were more palpable, stable, and potent than more ephemeral psychic processes, I will try to argue that cognitive-perceptual processes are potent, indeed, and permeate the assumptions underlying the most lethal form of intergroup conflict—our current strategy regarding the use of nuclear weapons.

Is There a Clear Distinction between Realistic Conflict Theories and Those Based on Real Group Differences?

In considering this question, it is helpful to examine Sherif's classic Robbers Cave experiment on intergroup relations, recently reissued (Sherif, Harvey, White, Hood, & Sherif, 1961/1988). In a campground setting, twenty-four eleven-year-old boys were placed into two separate groups on a quasi-random basis with first competitive, and later cooperative, experiences contrived for the two groups.

Sherif et al. found that considerable hostility could be generated by the competitive orientation, which could then be reversed by a number of consecutive cooperative experiences. According to Sherif, the competitive and cooperative experiences defined the nature of "functional relations" between the groups, which is the central concept in his theory. Before evaluating the results of this study, two points should be considered. First, the nature of the competition was primarily (although not exclusively) athletic, including the accrual of points that could later be exchanged for small prizes. Second, there was some evidence suggesting that hostility was present when each group had become aware of the other's presence in the campground, *before* the competitive interactions were defined between the groups.

The Sherif experiments permit a number of important conclusions. The first is that neither historical enmity nor the presence of significant physical, cultural, language, or religious differences are necessary conditions for establishing intergroup conflict. Because of quasi-random assignment to groups, substantial differences between the two groups were absent, as was a history of protracted conflict. Sherif wanted to conclude that "the functional relations" between groups define the nature of intergroup relations and that intergroup competition generated intergroup hostility.

There are at least two questions worth asking about the Sherif experiments. First, while there was no question that the two groups at Robbers Cave State Park were competing on the baseball field for athletic recognition, as well as for points that could later be exchanged for prizes, do we want to think of this as an instance of realistic conflict? Conflict over life and death is certainly not involved, nor is there even competition for objects that significantly affect material well-being. Whereas contemporary examples of conflict in South Africa, Northern Ireland, and the Middle East clearly involve direct competition for important geographic, economic, or political resources, the competitions for awards and prizes at Robbers Cave do not seem to be of the same character. Instead, it is very likely that these were competitions in which self-esteem and self-worth were implicated. If we accept competition over esteem as an instance of realistic conflict, is it not possible that esteem can be threatened by the existence of any attributes different from our own?

What is the dividing line between competition over important resources (realistic conflict) and less significant forms of social competition that occur over relatively trivial matters? The answer to this question blurs the distinction between external, ostensibly realistic factors generating conflict, and those that are intrapsychic in nature. Probably the earliest answer to the question came from Jonathan Swift, who, in *Gulliver's Travels,* implied that the conflict between the Protestants and the Catholics in Europe was equivalent to a war between nations that differed in their preference for breaking an egg on its large or its small side. Freud (1926/1959) later described the phenomenon in which we exaggerate the importance of negligible differences as "the narcissism of small differences."

The observations of Swift and Freud raise a second question about the Sherif findings. Since there was evidence of hostility between the two groups before the competitive nature of the intergroup relation was defined, there could be effects of "mere categorization," of being assigned to one of two arbitrary, mutually exclusive dichotomies. Such effects were clarified, to a large extent, by the work of Tajfel (Billig & Tajfel, 1973; Tajfel, 1970) and of Rabbie and Horwitz (1969). In these studies, subjects randomly assigned to one of two mutually exclusive dichotomies (for example, under- or overestimators of dots, or people who prefer Klee to Kandinsky) showed both evaluative and resource preference for members of their own social category. Thus, arbitrary differences in group assignment led to differences in intergroup perception even where there was (a) random assignment to condition, (b) no historical enmity, (c) no meaningful basis for divisions between the two group, *and* (d) no explicit competition. This work on the minimal group paradigm is consistent with the observation that hostility in the Robbers Cave experiment began even before competition was established. From the Tajfel and Rabbie and Horwitz experiments, we can argue that competition itself is not a necessary condition for conflict, but that membership in dichotomous social categories is sufficient to induce preference for the in-group.

To summarize, the distinction between realistic conflict and the existence of real group differences as contributors to intergroup conflict may reflect our need for categorization more than it does our fidelity to intergroup processes. Although competition over resources necessary for survival would clearly be an example of realistic conflict, many forms of intergroup conflict appear to be generated by competition for symbols that confirm social value or status. In addition, work using the minimal group paradigm suggests that mere categorization, in the absence of explicit competition or status concerns, is sufficient to generate bias that favors the in-group. One interpretation of the minimal group findings is that there is implicit competition for valued status, even when the basis for categorization is novel or arbitrary (Tajfel & Turner, 1986).

MOTIVATIONAL VERSUS COGNITIVE THEORIES

To pursue another of the earlier distinctions, recall that motivational theories postulated a need or motivation to disparage an out-group, whereas cognitive perceptual theories emphasize a bias in information processing and an absence of motivation to disparage the out-group. Can we clearly distinguish between these approaches on the basis of observed effects? Some of our own work on cognitive processes may be helpful in addressing this question.

In some of our earliest work on cognitive factors in stereotyping, we showed that when we make judgments about the characteristics of a group of individuals, we give disproportionate weight to the more extreme members of the category (Rothbart, Fulero, Jensen, Howard, & Birrell, 1978). Basing our argument on Kahneman and Tversky's availability heuristic, we argued that those individual members of a category who were most memorable would be disproportionately represented in our representation of that category. Subjects were presented with information about fifty men. In one experiment, the fifty men varied in physical height, with ten of the men being over six feet. In a parallel second experiment, the men varied with respect to the social desirability of behaviors they had engaged in, with ten of the men engaging in criminal activities. Within each experiment there was a "mild" and an "extreme" condition, in which the ten men possessed a moderate or extreme amount of the relevant attribute. For example, in the height experiment, the ten men were either slightly over six feet tall or significantly over six feet; in the social behavior experiment, the ten men engaged in "minor" crimes (tax evasion, vandalism) or "extreme" crimes (murder, rape). Subjects were asked to estimate the proportion of men who, in the height experiment, were over six feet tall, or who, in the social behavior experiment, engaged in criminal behavior. For both experiments, subjects gave higher estimates in the extreme than in the mild condition. Moreover, in the social behavior experiment, where it was possible to assess subjects' recall for the social behaviors, they were more likely to remember extreme than mild crimes.

These findings in themselves do not suggest that our images of other groups will be disproportionately negative, just that they may be disproportionately extreme. There is, however, other evidence to suggest that negative events are generally perceived as more deviant (more extreme) than positive events from our everyday experience (Kanouse & Hanson, 1971; Parducci, 1968). Thus, the members of a group likely to be most memorable, and also disproportionately represented, are the extreme negative members of the category. When making judgments about the in-group, negative impressions of in-group members will likely be balanced by positive information we have about in-group members, but in judgments about the out-group, where we have less information, the negative information about out-group members may predominate. Note that it is thus possible to generate unrealistically negative images of out-groups without necessarily inferring motivational processes. The work of Hamilton and his colleagues on illusory correlation (Hamilton & Gifford, 1976; Hamilton, 1981) suggests in addition that the co-occurrence of an infrequent class of individuals (e.g., members of a minority group) with infrequent behaviors (e.g., undesirable behaviors) tends to be overestimated, leading to the erroneous inference, for example, that undesirable behaviors are more likely to be associated with minority group members.

A second set of studies is more critical to the distinction between motivation and cognitive interpretations. Rothbart, Evans, and Fulero (1979) presented subjects with behavioral information about a group of fifty men, in which the perceivers' expectations about the group were varied. Our general findings were that subjects remembered best those individuals for whom they had an initial expectation. If they expected the group to be friendly, they were more likely to remember the friendly than the intelligent individuals; if they expected the group to be intelligent, they were more likely to remember the intelligent than the friendly individuals. In short, those individuals who confirmed the initial expectancy were most likely to be remembered.

Building on these findings, Howard and Rothbart (1980) went back to the minimal group paradigm used by Tajfel. College students were arbitrarily categorized as under- or overestimators of dots and then given decks of cards containing ostensive self-disclosure information about previous under- and overestimators who participated in our experiments. The self-disclosure information was in the form of statements, some of which described a subject's most favorable behaviors ("I saved money to send my parents to Hawaii") or most unfavorable behaviors ("I falsely spread nasty rumors about a roommate I disliked"). Half of the behaviors in the deck were favorable, and half unfavorable, randomly intermixed. Subjects were asked to "postdict" which behaviors were engaged in by under- or overestimators of dots (recall that the subjects themselves had been categorized as either under- or overestimators of dots). Not surprisingly, subjects were more likely to put the favorable behaviors in their own category and the unfavorable behaviors in the other category.

This provided evidence that the social categorization procedures used in the minimal group paradigm resulted in the perception that *we* are better than *they*. Reasoning from the Rothbart, Evans, and Fulero (1979) findings, if subjects are more likely to remember expected behaviors, wouldn't they be more likely to remember more negative out-group behaviors and more positive in-group behaviors? New subjects were given two decks of cards, one describing underestimator behaviors and one describing overestimator behaviors. The ratio of favorable to unfavorable behaviors was identical for both stimulus groups. The findings corroborated the predictions: For out-group behaviors, subjects were far more likely to remember unfavorable than favorable behaviors; for in-group behaviors, subjects were more likely to remember favorable than unfavorable behaviors.

One way to characterize this research is that it describes a process whereby an ephemeral categorization becomes instantiated and reinforced by selective memory for events that confirm the implicit expectations generated by the initial categorization. In other words, the relatively weak in-group bias generated by mere categorization derives strength, over time, due to the cognitive biases that selectively fill the "psychological data base" with unfavorable out-group behaviors. Examples from this biased data base would only strengthen the belief that *we* are better than *they*.

This process could be described as a self-confirmatory cognitive system that appears "determined" to derogate the out-group. To return to the question raised earlier, can we clearly distinguish between the *effects* of a motivational view in which there is a "need" to disparage the out-group, and a cognitive system, such as the one we have described, that has the same teleological characteristic of "wanting" to confirm its initial, biased expectations? Although there is a clear conceptual difference in the generative mechanisms, both systems can have the appearance of "being motivated" to disparage the out-group.

The phenomenon we have been describing is usually referred to as "ethnocentrism," as Sumner (1906) originally defined it, in which we view our own group as the standard against which other groups are judged. I would like to turn now to another line of research that is concerned not with the perceived superiority of in-group over out-group, but with the perceived homogeneity or complexity of in-group and out-group. This research suggests another set of cognitive mechanisms that can serve to perpetuate negative stereotypes of the out-group.

THE PERCEPTION OF OUT-GROUP HOMOGENEITY

Bernadette Park and I (Park & Rothbart, 1982) conducted a series of studies having to do with the perception of out-group homogeneity, a field in which there have been earlier contributions by Linville and Jones (1980) and Quattrone and Jones (1980). We asked men and women to make judgments about men and women, and found that a group was perceived as more extreme in stereotype-related attributes by judges of the other gender than by judges of the same gender. Thus, the proportion of men viewed as endorsing the item "I enjoy competitive challenges" (stereotypic of men) was judged to be higher by women than by men, while the proportion of men viewed as endorsing the item "I enjoy expressing my love for children" (counter-stereotypic of men) was judged to be lower by women than by men. The tendency for a group to be judged as more stereotypic and less counter-stereotypic by out-group than by in-group was true when judging females and when judging males.

The study I want to focus on here, however, is a bit different. In our experiment 2, men and women were asked to make judgments about men and women with different college majors. For example, women were asked to describe female dance majors and female physics majors, and, of course, men would be asked to make the same judgments. We found that women saw an enormous difference between female dance and female physics majors, but male judges did not (see figure 6.1).

In making their judgments, women would tend to ignore gender, or "femaleness," and focus on the more differentiating attribute of major (which we called "occupation" or "role"). In contrast, men making judgments about the same categories tended to focus on the less differentiated attribute, gender, and to ignore occupation or role, and saw comparatively little difference between these two categories. When we reversed the question and asked male and female subjects about male dance majors and male physics majors, we found symmetrical effects: Men saw much greater differences between these two categories than did women judges. What appears to have happened is that judges, when focusing on the out-group, use the less differentiating attribute (gender) in making their judgments, ignoring the more differentiating attribute, whereas the reverse pattern is true for making judgments about the in-group.

We found comparable effects in the domain of memory. In our experi-

Figure 6.1: Judgments about same- and opposite sex stimulus persons, where stimulus person is described by college major that is either gender stereotypic or gender counter-stereotypic

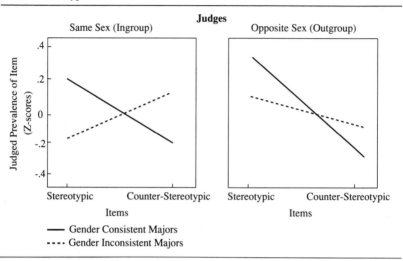

ment 4, subjects were presented with one-paragraph "news briefs," describing, for example, a person who saved a child from a burning building. The paragraphs contained information about the age, gender, and occupation of the protagonist. The stories were given on day 1 to subjects in a large introductory class, under the guise of a journalism study. Subjects were asked to judge the paragraphs on clarity, quality in writing, and so on. On day 3, we came back to the same class and asked them to try to reproduce the stories verbatim on three-by-five-inch cards. After this free recall task, they turned over the cards and were asked to specify (1) whether the protagonist in the story was male or female, and (2) the protagonist's occupation. The findings paralleled the results of experiment 2. When judging in-group or out-group members, people generally remembered gender quite well. However, memory for the more differentiating attribute of occupation was far better for same-sex (in-group) members than for other-sex (out-group) members.

In our view, this last experiment raises again some basic questions about the self-perpetuating character of stereotypes. Since subjects had difficulty remembering the differentiating information concerning out-group members, how could they develop a more realistically complex view of the out-group? Unlike other research on the perception of intragroup variability, this experiment presented the *same* information about in-group and out-group members, yet consistent with the Howard and Rothbart (1980) results, subjects did not remember equivalent information about their own and the other social category. We draw two inferences from this set of experiments. First, there will be different attributional consequences when observing a behavior associated with an in-group or out-group member. As an example, if I (as an Oregonian) read about a new cult in California, my undifferentiated view of Californians leads me to associate this event with Californians in general. But if I read about the same cult in Oregon, my highly differentiated view of Oregonians would allow me to associate the cult with some plausible subculture (e.g., counterculture communes in Southern Oregon) that is dissociated from Oregonians-in-general.

Second, we infer that it is going to be difficult to develop a more differentiated view of the out-group. If we cannot learn that members of the out-group differ in important ways (cf. Park & Rothbart's [1982] experiment 4), it will be difficult to develop a more differentiated and less homogeneous view of that social category.

But these results also raise the more general question of how we are able to change our perception of a group on the basis of experience with exemplars of the group; it is to that issue that we now turn.

CATEGORY-EXEMPLAR DYNAMICS AND THE CONTACT HYPOTHESIS

As is well known, the most prominent idea concerned with changing stereotypes is the contact hypothesis. This hypothesis exists in a number of different forms, but the most basic form states that our experience with individual members of a social category will generalize to the category as a whole. In a paper with Oliver John, we analyzed this issue of generalization and argued that there was strong reason to believe that generalization from exemplars to category would be relatively rare, rather than commonplace (Rothbart & John, 1985). Although the contact hypothesis predicts that favorable experiences with individual exemplars of a disliked category will increase that category's favorability, we argued that exemplars that are a poor fit to the category will, instead of modifying the category itself, be dismissed as atypical of the category. It is as if poor-fitting members of the category are not really members of the category at all, calling the contact hypothesis's critical assumption of generalization into question. Individual category members who are logical members of the category are not necessarily psychological members of the category. To use an anecdote from one of our papers (Rothbart & Lewis, 1988):

> There are no good women climbers. Women climbers either aren't good climbers or they aren't real women. (Anonymous climber, cited in Blum, 1980, p. 1)*

*I wish to thank Jenny Crocker and Ken Rasinski for this quote.

One would think that the criteria for being a member of the category "women" would be unambiguous, but this assumption ignores the possibility that our actual criterion for a woman is the exemplar's overall goodness-of-fit to the concept of "women," which includes stereotypic attributes as well as the physical properties that define membership in the category.

Experiments with Scott Lewis (Rothbart & Lewis, 1988) on generalization of attributes from typical and atypical exemplars and with Sriram Natarajan and Carene Davis-Stitt (Rothbart, Natarajan, & Davis-Stitt, in preparation) on memory for typical and atypical exemplars support some of the conjectures put forth by Rothbart and John (1985). In addition, Oliver John and I have been at work for a number of years on a massive longitudinal study of stereotype change to examine, among other things, the actual stability of our beliefs about a variety of social groups. One of the clearest predictions of the Rothbart and John model (certainly not unique to that model) is that the mechanism that allows us to exclude individual members of a category that are inconsistent with category attributes suggests that our stereotypes should perseverate in the face of disconfirming experiences with individual exemplars. Although we have not fully completed our analysis of the longitudinal study, we have found that over a four-year period, the average stability of the stereotypes for fourteen different social groups was .92, which is hardly a significant drop from a baseline seven-day test-retest correlation of .96 (Rothbart & John, in press).

One of the strongest conclusions of the research we have been describing is that due to a number of factors, many of which appear to be cognitive in character, we have very strong images of how in-groups and out-groups differ, even when there is rather little objective evidence to support those perceived differences. Moreover, once these perceived differences become established, we have reason to believe that they are highly stable and difficult to change.

Are the Different Classes of Explanations for Intergroup Conflict Mutually Exclusive?

It seems reasonable to view the four classes of explanation as mutually augmenting rather than mutually exclusive. One example from Rothbart and John (1985), regarding the nature of categories and category exemplars, illustrates this point. What determines the "choice" of categories that an individual person becomes associated with? We proposed that the most strongly activated social category will become "chosen," with strength of activation affected by at least two factors: (1) endogenous activation by the exemplar itself (e.g., an individual woman who is highly stereotypic of the category women will clearly activate the category), and (2) exogenous activation of a category by situational context. The idea of exogenous activation requires elaboration. To the extent that the social setting itself emphasizes, for example, "femaleness," it will activate the category "women" independently of the degree of activation provided by the exemplar itself. With a high level of exogenous activation, many individuals may become associated with the category who, under lower levels of category activation, would not be perceived in terms of that category. The implications of this idea are, in our view, important because they provide a conceptual link between the social setting and the "choice" of social categories that affect our perception of an individual.

Consider the effects of competition in intergroup settings, the power of which has been demonstrated so clearly by Sherif, Deutsch, and many others. From the Rothbart and John (1985) perspective, one way in which competition affects perception is by continual activation of the in-group/out-group dichotomy. To the extent that the out-group category is highly activated, episodes of, say, selfish behavior in an individual, which might otherwise be attributed to the idiosyncratic qualities of a particular individual, are now seen as evidence of out-group perfidy. Thus, the episode of selfish behavior is attributed to the out-group category rather than the individual category member. A recent study by Judd and Park (1988) found evidence for out-group homogeneity using the minimal group paradigm, but only in an intergroup setting where competition was present.

More generally, when we now look at the original four classes of explanation for intergroup conflict (motivational, cognitive, realistic conflict, and real group differences), two caveats seem warranted. First, it is often difficult to meaningfully distinguish among some of these classes. Second, even when one can distinguish among them, any comprehensive theory of intergroup conflict has to recognize that these processes exert influence on one another in dynamic and complex ways. In-group and out-group members exaggerate the differences between one another and disproportionately remember the unfavorable acts engaged in by the out-group. These extreme perceptions are likely to lead to antagonism, even in the absence of realistic conflict, and to the extent that one group has power over another, inequality may well be generated or accentuated, producing greater real differences between the groups and possible competition over limited resources. In other words, these four factors influence one another in a highly interactive, dynamic manner. Rather than thinking of the different causes as mutually exclusive, it would be more useful to think of them as components of a dynamic, developmental intergroup process that exacerbates, rather than reduces, intergroup conflict. We are currently trying to model this dynamic process more formally.

THE PERCEPTION OF CONFLICT REDUCTION

I would now like to describe a somewhat different set of studies concerning the question of how the parties to a conflict view the process of conflict resolution. When two groups are separated by conflict, what do they believe to be the most efficacious strategies for ameliorating that conflict? Bill Hallmark and I felt that the different assumptions we make about the nature of in-groups and out-groups might be most clearly drawn in the arena of international relations (Rothbart & Hallmark, 1988). If we look at the effect of the Japanese bombing of Pearl Harbor on American opinion and morale, we instantly recognize the outrage Americans felt at this act of aggression and the determination of the United States to defeat the Japanese. Why, then, did we assume that we could bomb the North Vietnamese into a conciliatory mood, since we knew from the Pearl Harbor experience that bombing hardens resistance to negotiation? If we ask ourselves what strategy our enemies could use that would get us to change our behavior, the answer might well be conciliation, yet if we asked what we ought to do to change our enemy's behavior, the answer is often threat. To quote from Ronald Reagan (1988):

> "The Sandinistas haven't made one concession on their own without a threat hanging over them," Reagan said in an address to the National Association of Religious Broadcasters. "The way to democracy and peace in Nicaragua is to keep the pressure on the Sandinistas."

In our research we described a hypothetical conflict between two poor nations sharing an island in the middle of a large ocean. Because of a border dispute, each group had developed weapons to protect themselves, but the same weapons were a potential threat to the security of the other side. Each nation also developed countermeasures against their opponents' weapons, and each side then viewed the opponents' countermeasures as offensive rather than defensive in character. Both sides were highly motivated to increase their own security by getting the other side to scale down its armament production. Before reading the description of the conflict, subjects were asked to imagine that they were citizens of one side or the other. After reading the scenario, subjects were asked which techniques might be most effective in getting either their own side or the other side to scale down their production of armaments. The options available to the judges ranged from highly conciliatory acts (for example, unilateral disarmament) to highly coercive acts (for example, threatening to engage in military action against the other side unless they scaled down their production of armaments). When subjects were asked how to influence their own group, they judged the most effective strategies to be conciliation rather than coercion, whereas they judged the most effective strategies for influencing the other side to be more coercive in character (see figure 6.2). Although the reader may have objected to the analogy that the United States was behaving in Vietnam in the way that Japan had behaved to the United States, the virtue of this experiment is that one can describe the two

Figure 6.2: Perceived relative effectiveness of coercion (score on first unrotated factor)

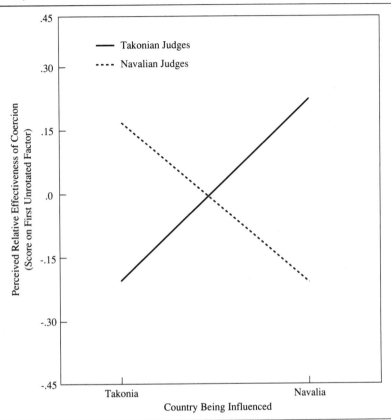

parties to the conflict in equivalent terms. In this instance, there really is no difference between the two nations. Whichever side subjects were asked to identify with was the side that they thought should be dealt with in a conciliatory manner, whereas the opponent should be dealt with more coercively.

Notice that these findings extend the asymmetries of intergroup perception to the very act of conflict reduction itself. That which motivates our own group to change its behavior is thought to be different, in some fundamental way, from that which motivates the out-group to change its behavior.

INTERGROUP PERCEPTION AND THE NUCLEAR ARMS RACE

The Rothbart and Hallmark research provides an entry for discussing the role of intergroup perception in an important real world setting:

nuclear strategy and the nuclear arms race. Although the cold war with the Soviet Union seems to be over and there is increased optimism about arms control, we should not forget that (1) the United States and Soviet Union still have approximately fifty thousand nuclear warheads pointed at one another, (2) a number of third world countries in the Middle East and elsewhere are developing nuclear weapons, (3) the United States is still deploying the mobile, MX missile (with first-strike capability), and (4) the United States continues to fund the development of a massive antimissile defense system (Strategic Defense Initiative, or SDI).

As suggested at the outset of this chapter, there has been a tendency to contrast psychological (cognitive-perceptual) factors in intergroup conflict with more realistic factors, with the implication that the former is in some ways less serious, more ephemeral, and less consequential than the latter. Since the nature of the nuclear arms race, and nuclear strategy itself, constitutes such an enormous threat to our collective survival, it would be of value to explore the role of intergroup perception in nuclear strategy. In doing so, it is essential to consider the way in which changing technology, in combination with our traditional way of thinking about war, has led us to the current dangerous impasse. Einstein's comment that the advent of the nuclear age has "changed everything except the way in which we think . . . and so we drift toward unparalleled catastrophe" appears even more profound now than when first spoken. Since World War II, the development of nuclear weapons has radically changed both the scale of destructive capability and the speed with which the destruction can be realized.

There are at least three major ways in which our current nuclear arsenal differs from earlier ones. First, the scale of destruction of a single warhead can be orders of magnitude greater than the nuclear bombs used in World War II. The bomb used at Hiroshima had the destructive equivalent of seventeen thousand tons of TNT, whereas many of the Soviet warheads contain the equivalent of twenty million tons of TNT. Second, each of the two nuclear powers (considering only the Soviet Union and the United States) has about fifteen to twenty thousand warheads available for intercontinental delivery. Third, the delivery time ranges from a maximum of about twenty-five minutes (e.g., over the North Pole) to about two minutes (if, for example, the attack is launched from a submarine off the enemy's coast). The time scale and scale of destructive capability have enormous consequences for military decision making.[1]

Consider, for example, Reagan's decision to deploy Pershing II missiles in Western Europe aimed at the Soviet Union. These weapons were placed close enough to Moscow to reduce the delivery time to about eight minutes. Since each side believes that its nuclear arsenal exists primarily to deter the other side from striking first, deterrence is meaningful only if there exists the credible possibility of retaliating after a first strike. The problem with an eight-minute delivery time is there is no time after one side launches its missiles for the other side to (a) verify the launch, and then (b) launch its own missiles before they are destroyed on the launching pad. To maintain a credible deterrent, the threatened country must adopt the policy of "launch on warning," which means launching one's own missiles first, when there is reason to *believe* the other side is considering a first strike. In short, the decision to start a nuclear war is based on what we *think* are the intentions of the other side. When we consider the intergroup relations literature on the accuracy of in-group/out-group perception, the "launch on warning" policy is, to be most generous, disastrous.

A second arena in which our strategic decisions are dysfunctional is in the Strategic Defense Initiative (SDI), more commonly known as the "Star Wars Defense." Although it has been difficult to know precisely what form the antimissile defense will take, the most prominent idea is that satellites orbiting over the enemy's territory will be able to detect a launch and destroy many of the launched missiles. Although the idea of destroying hostile missiles seems benign, the implications are not. First, the antimissile satellite has approximately ninety seconds to decide whether a launch has occurred, and whether to launch its own counterstrike, since it is crucial that the enemy missiles be destroyed before they MIRV (that is, before a single missile opens up and sends out ten or more independently targetable warheads), since the killer satellite's job becomes ten times more difficult after MIRVing. Because the counterstrike is basically equivalent to making a decision to launch a nuclear war within a ninety-second period, there is little time for human intervention in the system, and the relative weight given to a Type I error (perceiving a launch when none exists) and a Type II error (failing to recognize a true launch) errors must be preprogrammed. The question arises as to how to set the acceptable level for the two types of errors, which returns us to the question of what we think are the enemy's intentions. The software written to estimate the intentions will be based on the "software" that has already placed us next to the abyss (Parnias, 1985).

There are even more serious problems with the system, however. Most importantly, what will be the response of the other side to the deployment of SDI? We tend to act in accord with what Admiral Noel Gaylor calls "the last-move fallacy," believing that once we deploy SDI, we are once and for all secure, and that there will be no significant countermeasures by the other side. After all, why would the other side attempt to counter a purely defensive system? This, however, makes the unreasonable assumption that the other side perceives SDI in the same manner as we perceive it. But if we take the Rothbart and Hallmark (1988) results seriously and ask ourselves what we would do if the Russians deployed *their* SDI, the response would be clearer. We would view their SDI as a threat to our counterstrike (deterrent) capability, would build more missiles to overwhelm the shield, and would develop weaponry to destroy their killer satellites. And it is exactly for this reason that the effect of SDI will be to dramatically increase the number of missiles pointed at one another, which is the opposite effect of what SDI was intended to accomplish (Grossmann & Mayer-Kress, 1989; Saperstein & Mayer-Kress, 1988).

Social psychologically, there are some peculiar aspects to the assumptions underlying the logic of SDI. Whereas the ethnocentrism research suggests that we view the out-group as deficient in a number of ways, the logic of SDI imbues the out-group with a number of superior qualities, not the least of which is extraordinary charity when interpreting the motives of the out-group! Despite decades of bellicose posturing by Congress and the president, we nonetheless assume that the enemy recognizes our purely benign intentions, knowing that we would never consider using SDI for military advantage. Given that both countries tend to make their military decisions on the basis of a "worst case" scenario, the assumption that the enemy would respond to our SDI with equanimity is unwarranted.[2]

More generally, the nature of the modern nuclear arsenal raises a number of profound questions about the role of coercion and threat in international relations. Jervis (1976) suggests that the effect of military threat on inhibiting war is itself unclear. If one accepts the World War II example, the lack of military preparedness is thought to encourage aggression and provides support for a deterrence model. However, if one prefers the World War I example, a military buildup increases the likelihood of war, providing evidence for a spiral, or escalation, model. Changes in the magnitude of destruction and speed of delivery appear to shift the balance in favor of the escalation model. That is, if country A significantly increases its nuclear threat against country B, the security of both countries decreases. Whereas in the past, saber rattling may have encouraged the threatened party to withdraw, the current version of saber rattling may convince the threatened party that its very survival depends on a preemptive strike. The threatened party cannot risk delaying a response when delay threatens its own capacity to deter a strike.

The key aspect of this entire argument is that the enormous technical changes (one cannot call them "advances") that have taken place have not eliminated, but in fact have magnified, the role of perception in the decision to go to war. Given the enormous time compression resulting from the speed of modern delivery systems, and the near total destruction that can be rained on a country by a first strike, our ideas about the intentions of the enemy have become more, rather than less, central in our conduct of war.

It may be useful to end this paper with a quote from Walter Lippmann's *Public Opinion* (1922/1961), written shortly after the First World War. Lippmann was a journalist who appreciated psychology's role in social conflict, and he often used the example of Plato's Cave, in which we observe only the shadows of reality, not reality itself. Lippmann describes reality as the environment, and our perception of reality as the pseudoenvironment:

At the moment, I should like to think only about the world-wide spectacle of men acting upon their environment, moved by stimuli from their pseudoenvironments, for when full allowance has been made for deliberate fraud, political science still has to account for such facts as two nations attacking one another, each convinced that it is acting in self-defense; or two classes at war, each certain that it speaks for the common interest. They live, we are likely to say, in different worlds. More accurately, they live in the same world, but they think and feel in different ones. (P. 20)

Perception is not all there is to intergroup conflict, but we do act on our perceptions. To the extent that our perceptions do not correspond to reality, as some of the arguments made in this paper suggest, the likelihood of generating conflicts where none exists, or exacerbating the magnitude of conflicts that already exist, is disturbingly high.

NOTES

The author was supported in party by National Institutes of Mental Health Grant MH40662. Mary Rothbart, whose editorial acumen improved the style, organization, and substance of this paper, is acknowledged with gratitude.

1. Our example of the Japanese bombing of Pearl Harbor is almost quaint for a number of reasons. First, the Japanese attack failed to destroy a large portion of the United States carrier fleet, and the United States had sufficient time to develop its war industry and to successfully counterattack in the Pacific. Now, of course, no nuclear power would even bother to waste its missiles on an antiquated navy, and any response that did not occur within about fifteen minutes after the launching of a nuclear first strike by an enemy would probably never be forthcoming.

2. One justification for SDI is that even if it cannot serve as a total shield against nuclear warheads, is it not better to nonetheless be able to destroy some of the incoming weapons? Anyone who asks such a question does not realize the nature of the modern nuclear arsenal. In World War II, the Battle of Britain was won by British fighters being able to destroy even a tiny portion of the German bombers on each raid. After many raids, the number of bombers available was dramatically reduced. Exactly the opposite logic applies to the current nuclear arsenal. Even assuming that only ten thousand warheads may be launched, if 1 percent are capable of getting through, they would destroy every major city in the United States. Using Robert McNamara's estimate of two hundred megatons as more than sufficient to deter a strike (''Beyond 200 megatons, you only re-arrange the rubble''), 1 percent of the warheads could carry well beyond two thousand megatons of destruction. Even the most optimistic estimates of the effectiveness of SDI assume no more than 50 percent capability of destroying incoming missiles; given that an enemy will deploy more warheads to counteract the effects of SDI, we may actually have more warheads capable of hitting the United States than we would have without SDI.

7   Legitimacy, Status, and Dominance Behavior in Groups

Cecilia L. Ridgeway

When a group has a cooperative task or goal, the individual members are in a classic mixed-motive situation. They each have an interest in cooperating to maximize the collective task success. But they also have a competitive interest in maximizing their personal share of the rewards available in the group. Much of the conflict in task groups is produced by the interplay of these interests. Members' competitive interests are, of course, a fundamental source of conflict between members. Less obvious, but perhaps more important, is the conflict produced by the tension between, on the one hand, members' collective interests and the alliances created from them, and, on the other hand, their individual competitive interests.

One of the most important products of these mixed interests is the status hierarchy. It arises out of the interaction elicited by the mixed motives of the members. As such it represents an effective balance that members work out among their conflicting interests. It operates as a system of conflict management in addition to its other effects. Thus, an understanding of status hierarchies is fundamental to an examination of conflict within groups.

In task groups the nature of the balance of interests achieved in the status hierarchy, and, consequently, the way that conflict is managed, are shaped in turn by the dynamics of legitimacy. These normative processes created by members' cooperative interests constrain and transform competitive conflict in task groups. In order to understand the way status hierarchies direct interest-induced conflict in such groups, one must examine the legitimacy processes that structure hierarchy formation and operation.

This chapter draws on a recent program of research on legitimacy, status, and dominance in task groups (Ridgeway & Berger, 1986; Ridgeway, 1987; Ridgeway & Diekema, 1989) to examine the dynamics of legitimacy in the status processes of task groups. Specifically, this chapter considers how legitimacy dynamics affect the resolution achieved in the status hierarchy between members' mixed cooperative and competitive interests and how this in turn controls and redirects the use of dominance behavior within the status hierarchy.

When a conflict of interests occurs in a group, an effort by each interest to assert itself over the other is implied. A particularly clear behavioral form by which a representative of one interest may attempt to assert that interest over, or seek to control, another is through dominance behavior. The effectiveness of dominance behavior when it is used to assert a particular interest over another is revealing of the interests favored by a given status system. As a result, analyzing the role played by dominance behavior in a group's status hierarchy provides a sensitive barometer of the balance of conflicting interests according to which that hierarchy operates. It is for this reason that dominance behavior is a focal concern of the chapter.

The primary purpose of the chapter, then, is to provide a more thorough understanding of the role of legitimacy in status hierarchies and its impact on the management of interest-induced conflict. However, a secondary purpose is to describe the role of dominance behavior in task group status hierarchies. This conflict-oriented behavior is surprisingly interdependent with the cooperative and normative processes of legitimacy.

There are two different sets of legitimacy dynamics that will be discussed. The first and most basic establishes the effective rules by which status is granted in the group. These rules delineate the basis of the status hierarchy and the fundamental role of dominance behavior within it. The norms of the status system reflect the distinctive balance of cooperative and competitive interests by which the hierarchy functions. These initial legitimacy processes simultaneously limit the effectiveness of dominance behavior as a means of competitive status attainment and transform it into a means of social control that enforces a cooperative status system. The second set of legitimacy dynamics affects who has a right to status and influence within this status system. Consequently, it affects who has a right to exercise dominance as a control behavior and expect compliance in response. This chapter will describe three experiments that test the way legitimacy dynamics in status processes determine the effectiveness of dominance behavior.

INITIAL CONSIDERATIONS

The argument will be clearer if some basic assumptions and terms are specified in the beginning. The argument addresses groups whose members share a cooperative task that they wish to accomplish. It is limited to those of these groups that are free to construct their own status hierarchy rather than having a formal authority structure imposed on them. These assumptions encompass many common work groups such as juries, research teams, boards of advisors, and many committees and councils. A *status hierarchy* in such groups is an informal hierarchy of influence and esteem.

Another term that needs clarification is *legitimacy*. The concept is notoriously difficult to define. However, following others (Weber, 1968; Zeldith & Walker, 1984; Walker, Thomas, & Zelditch, 1986), this discussion will assume that something becomes legitimate when it becomes normative in the group and therefore subject to collective sanction when violated. Thus, efforts to gain or exercise status in a group are legitimate when they are in accord with group norms governing the status system. A given type of behavior, such as dominance behavior, is similarly legitimate when it is used in conformity with norms. Because legitimacy is based on socially enforced norms, it is an inherently collective process.

There is similarly no agreed-upon definition of dominance behavior in human groups. The term *dominance* is sometimes used simply to indicate rank in a hierarchy (Bernstein, 1980; Ellyson & Dovidio, 1985). It can also be used to indicate any assertive behavior (Harper, 1985; Mazur, 1985). However, here it will be used more narrowly to refer to a type of agonistic behavior. Drawing on what is common to several recent definitions, *dominance behavior* here will mean behavior directed toward the control of another through threat.

Legitimacy I: The Basis of Hierarchies

Dominance Hierarchies

Dominance behavior is, in some sense, the ultimate expression of individual competitive motives in a group context. It implies that a person could simply seize desired resources from other group members by threat of force. It is certainly possible to construct a hierarchy entirely on the basis of dominance behavior. The result is a classic pecking order in which individuals gain precedence over those they can out-threaten and defer to those who out-threaten them. The hierarchy is a simple stabilization of pure individual conflict.

Dominance hierarchies have important disadvantages for their participants, however. They are resource distribution hierarchies only (Ridgeway, 1984). All they do is determine who gets first choice of the available resources. They do not organize people to maximize resource production. Dominance behavior claims influence or standing in the group on the basis of threat capacity, not on the basis of contributions to task accomplishment. Consequently, dominance behavior satisfies only one side of the individual's mixed interests in a cooperative task situation. It claims a maximum share of collective resources, but does nothing to ensure that there are any collective resources available to take a share of.

Interests, Legitimacy, and Status Hierarchies

In fact, I have argued that members' collective interest in task accomplishment creates alliances of interests that normatively constrain the use of dominance behavior to claim standing in a task group (Ridgeway, 1984, 1987). These alliances of interests arise from the members' interdependence with respect to task accomplishment. They transfer the arena of members' competitive behavior to that of task performance. This is in fact a legitimacy process that establishes the fundamental basis of status in task groups. It produces a status hierarchy that is both resource producing and resource distributing. In this type of hierarchy, members' cooperative interests control or manage their competitive interests by redirecting them toward the task. A further consideration of the effects of collective interests clarifies how and why this occurs.

In a task group, the higher one's standing, the greater one's influence over task activities and, consequently, the greater one's contribution to collective success or failure. Consequently, when one member defers to another, the first member has effectively given the second increased control over collective success or failure. As status theorists (Homans, 1974; Blau, 1964; Bales, 1950) have long noted, this makes it in each member's enlightened self-interest to cooperatively defer to other members on the basis of their expected task competence. On the other hand, members' competitive interest in maximizing their personal share of rewards may sometimes outweigh their cooperative interest in deferring to those expected to perform well.

Given these conflicting possibilities, it is instructive to consider an additional set of interests involved when one member defers to another. If the winner of deference has increased control over task success, then all group members, including those who are bystanders to a given contest, have an interest in the contest's outcome. It is in the interest of bystander members that deference only be granted on the basis of inferred task competence, and they may intervene in the dyadic contest to ensure that this occurs. In other words, interdependence in task groups makes it in each member's interest that all *other* members defer on the basis of expected task competence, whatever they want for themselves. As a consequence, even if each member seeks personal dominance, each will be faced with an implicit coalition of others willing to grant deference only in proportion to apparent task competence. Thus members' collective interests create implicit alliances that constrain their competitive interests in task groups.

The process by which this occurs is in fact one of legitimacy. Emerson

(1962, 1972) has noted that group norms are properly viewed as the collective "voice" of a coalition that would stand against a member who violates them. Since interdependent collective interests in task groups create a structural likelihood of coalitions forming in support of deference to inferred task competence, these interests in effect create norms defining expectations for task performance as the appropriate basis for status in the group. These legitimating norms define the accepted rules by which the status system operates in task groups. Members enforce them by intervening against claims to status on a basis other than expected competence.

Of course members of most task groups do not usually start from scratch in defining the rules for status in their group. As socialized members of a larger society and as people who have been in task groups before, they often bring with them normative beliefs that perceived task competence is the appropriate basis for status. However, the point of this argument is that even if they did not bring such norms with them, their interdependent interests would cause them to create these norms in the group.

The legitimating norms of the status system make dominance behaviors an ineffective means of gaining influence and standing in task groups. The norms effectively shift the arena of competition and conflict among the members from raw power and dominance to perceived ability to contribute to the task. Under these norms, members' competitive interest in maximizing their share of rewards induces them to vie with one another to appear competent at the task.

Because these norms tie self-maximization to the task, the competence-based status hierarchy that emerges harnesses members' competitive interests in self-maximization to their cooperative interests in task success. This is what allows the hierarchy to be *both* resource generating and resource distributing. As such, it moderates, but does not eliminate, the tension between individuals' mixed motives in task groups.

Dominance Behavior and Social Control

While the legitimating norms of the hierarchy render dominance ineffective for attaining status, they also create a new context in which dominance behavior can be quite effective: that is, as a means of legitimate social control. It is the structural capacity to mobilize coalitional support for something that makes it normative and legitimate in a group. Coalitional support has an interesting relation to the use of dominance behavior as well.

Dominance behavior controls through threat. To be effective the threat must be credible. An individual dominator could back a threat with superior physical force, although, of course, the use of such force is usually proscribed in task groups. Even if it were not, however, the resources of force that any individual alone could command are not likely to be credible against the collective force available to an opponent operating in alliance with others. Consequently, a dominator's ability to mobilize the support of others is a major determinant of his or her capacity to credibly threaten another. This is particularly true if, as is almost always the case in task groups, the threat is to the use of social rather than physical power. Social power cannot exist without the behavioral support of others.

Because legitimacy is created by coalitional support, it gives the ability to act with collective support when acting in accord with group norms. This suggests that dominance behavior is most likely to be credible, and hence effective, when it is used legitimately in support of the normative status hierarchy. In a task group, in other words, the effective use of dominance is tied to legitimacy. It is ineffective as a means of status attainment but can be used effectively as a means of sanctioning violations of the normative system. When used as legitimate social control, dominance behavior demonstrates how task group status hierarchies enforce members' collective interests over their competitive interests when the two are in conflict.

EMPIRICAL TESTS

What is the evidence to support this analysis? There are two experiments that have tested those parts of the argument dealing with the way legitimacy processes make dominance behavior ineffective for gaining influence in a task group but useful for social control (Ridgeway, 1987; Ridgeway & Diekema, 1989). Testing the reception of dominance in turn provides some evidence of whether the normative status system of task groups does indeed organize cooperative interest to constrain and redirect individual competitive interests. The goal of the first experiment was to distinguish a set of dominance behaviors from other behaviors and show that they were indeed ineffective in achieving influence in a task group (Ridgeway, 1987).

Experiment 1

Not all assertive nonverbal behaviors reliably communicate dominance. There are a number of common nonverbal behaviors that appear to communicate confidence and competence but carry no suggestion of threat toward the other. Examples are rapid, fluent speech with a firm, factual voice tone, direct but nonstaring eye contact, a quick verbal response, a relaxed but upright posture. These have been called "task cues" because in task-oriented interaction, they are usually read as indicating confidence and competence at the task (Berger, Webster, Ridgeway, & Rosenholtz, 1986; Ridgeway, Berger, & Smith, 1985). As a result they do indeed enhance influence and status in a task group by enhancing the appearance of task competence.

Dominance behaviors, in contrast, are distinguished by the element of threat. Examples are a loud voice with a commanding tone; aggressively staring eye contact, often with lowered brows; pointing; intrusive gestures; and a tense, forward-leaning posture (Mazur et al., 1980; Keating et al., 1981; Leffler, Gillespie, & Conaty, 1982; Lee & Ofshe, 1981).

In the first experiment, these lists of behaviors were used to devise four nonverbal cue patterns, either high or low in task cues and neutral on dominance cues or dominant or submissive in dominance cues but neutral in task cues. Videotapes were then made of an actress who portrayed each pattern while delivering an identical set of arguments for a low financial award in an insurance-related jury case adapted from Nemeth and Wachtler (1974). Pretests of the videotapes confirmed that the actress had adequately displayed the four patterns of nonverbal behavior, although the high-dominance tape was also rated fairly high rather than neutral in task cues. This partial confounding of cue patterns on the high-dominance tape was less than ideal. It is important to note, however, that it biased the results against, rather than for, the hypothesis that the dominant pattern would be no more effective in gaining influence than the low-task, or submissive, pattern. Further, supporting the conceptual validity of these cue patterns, pretest subjects rated the actress as more intimidating, threatening, and demanding when she displayed the high-dominance pattern but rated her as more intelligent in the high-task pattern.

The theoretical argument about legitimacy and dominance emphasizes the reactions of group members who are bystanders to a given deference encounter or influence attempt. To capture this point, the target actress directed her arguments toward another nonverbally neutral actress, who in turn argued for a high financial award in the jury case. This put the subjects who viewed the videotape of the two contending actresses in the position of a bystander to their conflict.

To create a sense of a group, subjects were told that they and the two videotaped women were part of an "extended communication three-person group" and that they would return to the laboratory to be videotaped along with the two women they saw. To avoid the confounding effect on influence of preestablished status differences, subjects and the actresses were peers in that all were female college students aged seventeen to twenty-three. The subjects read the jury case and made an initial award judgment. Then they viewed one of the four videotapes and made a final award judgment. Again to increase group involvement, they were told that their final award would be combined with those of their videotaped groupmates and evaluated by experts on insurance cases. There were four conditions, one for each stimulus tape, with about twenty-one subjects in each for a total of eighty-three subjects.

The principal results are shown in table 7.1. Final awards were analyzed with an analysis of covariance using initial awards as the covariate. Since the target actress argued for a distinctively low award ($2,000), lower adjusted awards indicate greater influence. Planned comparisons showed as predicted

TABLE 7.1   Experiment 1: Mean awards by cue pattern

Condition Cue Pattern	1 High-Task	2 Dominant	3 Low-Task	4 Submissive
Dollar Award adjusted final[a]	$11,729.42	$13,688.76	$14,092.97	$14,525.58
Highest Acceptable Award adjusted final[a]	$15,068.96	$19,246.58	$18,084.70	$17,841.14
Lowest Acceptable Award adjusted final[a]	$7,950.99	$8,681.76	$8,643.94	$8,435.26

a. Adjusted for initial award in analysis of covariance

that the dominant target was no more influential than the submissive or low-task target ($p > .35$). Only the confident but nondominant high-task target had significantly greater influence ($p < .05$), again as expected if task group norms enforce inferred competence as the basis of influence and status. On postexperimental questionnaires, subjects rated the dominant target as significantly more dominating, intimidating, and aggressive than the high-task target, but as significantly less skilled and competent at the task than the high-task target, again as predicted. Note that the dominant target failed to gain influence and was perceived as less skilled despite moderately high task cues. Dominance not only may have failed to enhance, it may even have detracted from perceived competence and influence in these female peer groups. Ratings of how likable the targets were also showed the dominant target to be noticeably disliked compared to the others.

The pattern of these results strongly supports the theoretical argument about the ineffectiveness of dominance behavior as a means of status attainment in task groups. Along with the work of many others (Bales, 1950; Berger, Conner, & Fisek, 1974; Wood & Karten, 1986), they also support the argument that the normative, legitimate basis of status in task groups is inferred task competence.

On the other hand, this study had some important limitations. First, the subjects were all females. The theoretical argument indicates no reason why the fundamental role of dominance behavior in status attainment should be different in male and female groups. But without male comparison groups, this possibility cannot be ruled out. This is especially problematic because dominance behavior may be more gender role appropriate for males than for females.

A second limitation is that the use of videotaped stimuli to control nonverbal behavior also prevented live interaction between the bystander subject and the dominator. Would the subject also deny influence to a threatening dominator who was actually present? Also, the theoretical analysis suggests that bystander subjects should actually intervene against a person who seeks influence through dominance behavior. Would bystanders actually sanction or attack the dominator as well as deny added influence? The argument about the legitimate use of dominance behavior for social control in task groups suggests that bystanders might even direct dominance behavior back at the offending dominator. To examine these questions, a second experiment was conducted that allowed live interaction (Ridgeway & Diekema, 1989).

Experiment 2

In the second study, four person, all-male or all-female peer groups of college students discussed the same jury award case used in the first experiment. Each group consisted of two confederates and two subjects who were bystanders to the interaction between the confederates. In half the groups, the main confederate directed dominance behavior toward the other confederate in the first few moments of interaction. In the control groups, the main confederate phrased her or his opening remarks as suggestions rather than commands and engaged neutrally and normally in the group discussion. Main confederates were trained in a set of specific arguments that they presented in both neutral and dominant conditions. The main confederate argued in favor of a low ($0) award in all conditions. The second confederate always reacted neutrally regardless of condition.

There were four conditions, crossing sex of group members with the dominance or neutrality of the main confederate, and ten or eleven groups in a condition, for a total of forty-two groups and eighty-four naive subjects. As in the earlier study, subjects read the jury case individually and made an initial award judgment. They then participated in the group discussion and made a final individual judgment. Subjects were again told that their final decisions would be combined into a "group decision profile" and that they would earn extra money if these were judged of superior quality.

Interaction in the groups was videotaped, and both the confederates' and the bystanders' behavior was coded. The behaviors coded as dominant were these: dismissing another's argument out-of-hand, addressing another in a dismissive or contemptuous tone of voice, a raised or angry voice, pointing or other aggressive gestures, interruptions, and hostile posturing such as leaning forward in an intrusive manner. A check of the manipulation confirmed that the main confederates in neutral conditions were coded as showing very little dominance behavior, while those in dominant conditions showed very high dominance levels. Female confederates showed lower dominance levels than male confederates, however, but there was no interaction of gender and group type (dominant or neutral). The bystanders' (i.e., the naive subjects') behavior was coded for dominance directed toward the main confederate, dominance behavior directed toward others, and other resistance to the main confederate, including counterarguing and negative affect directed at the main confederate.

All results were analyzed by analyses of variance, with groups as the unit of analysis and the two bystanders in each group treated as a repeated measure of the group. If dominance is ineffective for gaining influence in a task group, then the influence of the dominant and neutral confederates should be similar, since they presented the same task arguments. However, bystanders should behaviorally intervene to sanction the dominant but not the neutral confederate.

Table 7.2 shows the extent to which subjects lowered their awards after exposure to the main confederate. As expected, the results showed that behaving dominantly did not enhance the confederate's actual influence compared to behaving neutrally ($p > .30$ for all award measures). In addition, dominant confederates were actually perceived on postexperimental questionnaires as marginally less influential than neutral confederates ($p = .08$). Once again, dominance was ineffective in gaining added influence, and this was true for both males and females.

Furthermore, as table 7.3 indicates, subjects did appear to intervene against dominant confederates with both resistance and dominance behaviors ($p < .0001$ for dominance and for resistance directed at the dominant vs. the neutral confederate). They did this despite the fact that dominant confederates never initiated a dominance attack on them, the bystanders. That the subjects' dominance toward these confederates was a sanction for the confederates' violation of group norms is supported by the fact that subjects virtually never directed dominance behavior toward any member of the group except the dominant confederate (table 7.3). In fact, in neutral groups, subjects almost never engaged in dominance behavior at all. On scales constructed from postexperimental questionnaire items, dominant confederates were perceived as much more dominant than neutral confederates ($p < .004$) and actually less competent at the task ($p < .006$), despite the fact that all confederates presented

TABLE 7.2   Experiment 2: Confederate influence

Condition	Male Dominance	Male Neutral	Female Dominance	Female Neutral
Mean Change				
Dollar Award	−$3,389	−$4,143	−$2,227	−$1,833
Highest Acceptable	−$1,470.59	−$3,666.67	−$2,363.64	−$2,611.11
Lowest Acceptable	−$472.22	−$2,194.44	−$1,204.55	−$500
Mean Perceived				
Influence[a]	4.47	5.30	4.36	6.00

a. influential(7)–uninfluential(1)

TABLE 7.3   Experiment 2: Bystander dominance and resistance behavior

Condition Means	Male Dominance	Male Neutral	Female Dominance	Female Neutral
Total Resistance Behaviors	19.03	6.16	12.23	3.25
Dominant Acts Directed at Confederate	12.60	1.59	7.36	0.45
Dominant Acts Directed at Others	.00	.00	.182	.00

the same arguments. Once again, the dominant confederates were noticeably disliked as well.

It is interesting that each of these results held for males and females both. There were some main effects of gender indicating lower levels of dominance behavior in female groups but no interactions of gender with group type (dominant or neutral confederate). Thus, dominance is equally ineffective for status attainment in both male and female groups.

These results show a strong pattern of support for the argument that the alliance of members' interests in task groups creates norms that make inferred task competence, not dominance, the legitimate basis for influence in task groups. This, in turn, limits the effectiveness of dominance as a means of gaining influence in task groups. It appears that the legitimated rules of status in such groups do use members' cooperative interests to constrain and redirect their competitive interests in self-maximization. In that light, it is interesting that these results also suggest that dominance behavior can and will be used by members to enforce collective concerns over competitive interests that threaten to violate the legitimate status system.

LEGITIMACY II: CANDIDATES FOR STATUS

At the beginning of the chapter, mention was made of two sets of legitimacy dynamics that affect the status hierarchies of task groups and the role of dominance behavior within them. Let us now turn to the second of these. These additional legitimacy processes affect the apparent rights that different types of people have to status and influence in task groups and, consequently, their ability to effectively use dominance behavior.

Several writers have argued that certain categories of people are viewed as more legitimate candidates for high-status positions in groups than others (Meeker & Weitzel-O'Neill, 1977; Fennell, Barchas, Cohen, McMahon, & Hildebrand, 1978; Ridgeway, 1988). Consequently, when people like this actually are in positions of high influence in task groups, they tend to be given added legitimacy and authority by the other members. This added legitimacy allows them, with the support of the group, to go beyond merely being persuasive to use controlling behaviors to direct members of the group. There is in fact evidence that substantial legitimacy is necessary for a task group leader to successfully engage in directive behavior (Eskilson & Wiley, 1976; Burke, 1968). Evidence also suggests that categories of people with low status in the larger society, such as women or minorities, often face resistance when they engage in directive influence attempts in task groups (Eagly, Makhijani, & Klonsky, 1992; Butler & Geis, 1990; Ridgeway, 1982). It is as though such people do not have sufficient legitimacy in the group to allow them to successfully wield controlling behaviors.

When high-status members do have the added legitimacy to go beyond the power of influence, the controlling behaviors they use to direct others can include dominance (e.g., commands). In this case, however, the use of dominance behavior is legitimate social control, not status attainment, and so, it should be effective in gaining compliance. Because they wield broadly legitimate authority, these high-status group members are perceived as using dominance behavior in the name of the members' collective interests to enforce that interest. In that it represents collective interests, the use of dominance by high-status members here is comparable to its use by bystander peers when they sanction a competitive violation of the performance-oriented status system.

Outside Collective Support for Status

In this analysis, as in the earlier one, collective support is the key to legitimacy. Ridgeway and Berger (1986) argue that people hold reality-based beliefs, called "referential beliefs," about the categories of people (such as whites, males, the well educated, the wealthier) that are more likely than other categories of people to hold valued status positions in society as a whole. People may not approve of such a distribution of status positions by social groups, but they believe it to be a social fact.

When people enter a task group where the members differ on one or more of these social categories (or membership in the category is task relevant), these referential beliefs are activated. People use the beliefs to form expectations about the likelihood that certain members compared to others will have high-status positions in the group. The more consistently confirming beliefs they hold that a given person will have higher status in the group than another, the more certain these expectations (Ridgeway, 1989). For instance, if one group member is a white middle-aged man and another is a young black woman, race, gender, and age beliefs will combine to create very certain expectations that the older white man will have higher status.

In fact, it is indeed quite likely that the older white man will have greater influence, since age, race, and gender are all external status character-istics in our society (Berger, Fisek, Norman, & Zelditch, 1977; Webster & Foschi, 1988). That is, widely held cultural beliefs indicate that it is more worthy in society to occupy some categories of these characteristics (e.g., male) than others (e.g., female). When a characteristic carries status value in society, research suggests that it also carries connotations of greater diffuse competence (Berger, Rosenholtz, & Zeldith, 1980). Unfortunately, for in-stance, men and whites are believed to be generally more competent than women and blacks in this society (Broverman, Vogel, Broverman, Clarkson, & Rosenkrantz, 1972; Ruble, 1983; Pugh & Wahrman, 1983; Cohen & Roper, 1972). In a task group, when members differ on a status characteristic, these beliefs lead members to anticipate greater task competence from those with higher- rather than lower-valued categories of the characteristic.

Most of the time, then, beliefs about who is likely to have high status and who is most competent will coincide. When this happens, the more certain are expectations that the person will have high status, the more likely group members are to treat that person's influence as highly legitimate. In effect, the confirming beliefs about the kinds of people who hold high status in society act like outside collective support for that person's influence in this specific group, encouraging members in the group to treat the person's authority as highly legitimate. One way group members do this is by complying with the high-status person's control behaviors in addition to accepting his or her influence. So greater legitimacy gives an influential person broader authority in the group, including the right to use dominance behavior to control others through threat. In acting as if a person's control attempts are legitimate, members in effect make them so by behaving as if they were normatively acceptable in the group.

External Status versus Skill

To understand the full implications of this second set of legitimacy dynamics, it is useful to consider how they relate to the first set. Both sets of processes have in common that they make something legitimate by creating the appearance of collective support for it, making it normative in the group. They differ in the object that they legitimate, however. The first set of processes legitimate the *rules* according to which status will be granted. The second set of legitimacy processes legitimate *candidates* for status within the group, based on the outside collective support implied by members' external status characteristics. Because external status characteristics also carry diffuse expectations for competence, the most legitimate candidates by the second set of processes are usually also the ones perceived most compe-tent at the task and therefore deserving of status by the rules legitimated in the first process.

There is one situation where these two legitimacy dynamics do not work together so smoothly, however. Occasionally a person becomes influential in a task group without being backed by consistently confirming beliefs about who holds valued status positions in the outside society. This is most likely to happen when a person low on an external status characteristic nevertheless is known to have a high degree of specific skill at the task the group confronts. For example, a husband and wife working on a family budget are in this situation when she has budgetary skill and he doesn't despite his gender-based external status advantage. The diffuse competence beliefs associated with the external status of gender combine with the contradictory specific skill information to produce aggregate perceptions of each one's competence at the group task that form the basis of influence and status within the group (Berger et al., 1977). Because of its greater relevance to the task, the specific skill information has a stronger impact, so that these aggregate perceptions favor the person with the skill advantage, who then becomes the more influential (i. e., higher status) member of the group (according to the legitimated rules of the status system). However, the person's high skill but low external status activates inconsistent beliefs about whether the person is the type who usually holds influential, high-status positions. Such inconsistent beliefs do not provide much outside collective support for that person's authority in the group (according to the second set of legitimacy dynamics).

In this situation the person should legitimately (according to the first set of processes) wield the power of persuasion. However, the person is likely to meet resistance if she or he tries to go beyond influence to exercise broader authority in the form of directive control behaviors. From an influential person like this, then, dominance behavior will be problematic. It will be less effective in gaining compliance than it would be from a person with equally high standing in the group whose authority is backed by consistent external status advantages.

Why shouldn't a high-ranking member whose influence rests on specific skill not be granted the same authority as one whose influence rests on external status? Is this a situation where the second set of legitimacy processes violate the competence-oriented rules legitimated by the first set of processes? No, it is not, as some further considerations make clear.

Exercising directive authority in a group means more than having the "best ideas," as Bales (1950) defined the task group leader. It involves taking on the additional metatask of supervising the execution of group activities. As a result, according to the legitimated rules of the status system, a high-status member should be allowed to take on this executive metatask only if he or she is perceived as competent to do so.

As sources of status in the group, specific skill and external status advantages have different implications for ability at the executive metatask of group direction. The implications of specific skill are narrow. Specific skill indicates good task ideas alone, with no suggestion of other capacities, such as executive ability. Advantages in external status characteristics, on the other hand, have very diffuse competence implications, indicating that the person will be superior not only in task ideas but in most other things, presumably including executive direction of the group. Thus, members whose high status in the group is based on consistent external status characteristics rather than specific skill information not only appear to have outside collective support for their authority; they are believed (however incorrectly) to be more broadly competent beyond the technical demands of the task itself. As a result, they are allowed the power to control through dominance and other directive means, when those whose high standing is based on skill are not.

AN EMPIRICAL TEST

Experiment 3

A third experiment was conducted to test the effects of added legitimacy on compliance with dominance behavior from a member who has high status in the group (Ridgeway, Diekema, & Johnson, 1991). Undergraduate subjects aged seventeen to twenty-two interacted in same-sex dyads in which one member was a confederate. In half of the groups the confederate was presented as a thirty-five-year-old with a master's degree, giving her or him an advantage over the subject in both age and education. These were the consistent external status groups.

In the rest of the groups, the confederate was described as being of the same age as the subject but as never having gone to college. In these inconsistent groups, subjects took a paper and pencil test purportedly measuring ability at the task they and the confederates were to work on as a group. Confederates received high scores on this test, while the subjects received only average scores. So in the inconsistent groups the confederate was low in external status (education) but high in task skill.

In all conditions, groups worked on an eighteen-trial discussion task. On each trial, subject and confederate made an initial decision, discussed the alternatives, and made a final decision. On fifteen of the eighteen trials, the confederate chose an alternative different from the subject's choice. The confederate's influence is the number of times the subject changed choices to agree with the confederate.

The argument suggests that when the most influential member of a group has the added backing of a consistent external status advantage, there will be more compliance with his or her dominance behavior than when the influential person's external statuses are inconsistent. To test this prediction, the confederate must be the most influential member of the dyad. The first nine trials were used to establish the confederate's position in the dyad. The confederate's external status or skill advantage usually ensured high influence. Only groups where the subject changed choices to agree with the confederate on the majority of the first nine trials (at least four of seven disagree trials) were included in the final analysis.

The second nine trials were the critical phase of the experiment. By this point, the confederate had become the most influential member in those groups included in the final analysis. The purpose of the critical phase was to examine whether these confederates would receive more compliance to their dominance behavior if their high-ranking position in the group was backed by a consistent external status advantage. Consequently, confederates in half of the groups accompanied their task suggestions with dominance behavior on four of the critical trials. On these trials the confederate was dismissive of the subject's choice and argument and demanded the subject's agreement in a commanding tone of voice. In the other half of the groups the confederate interacted neutrally and normally during the nine critical trials.

The final design, then, crossed sex of group members with a high-ranking confederate's consistent or inconsistent status backing and dominant or neutral behavior in a 2 × 2 × 2 format. There were approximately twenty groups in each condition with one naive subject per group for a total of 162 subjects. In addition to the collection of influence data, interaction was videotaped to validate the confederate's performance and to code behavioral evidence of the subject's compliance or resistance to the confederate during the critical phase of the experiment. Subjects also completed a postexperimental questionnaire. Manipulation checks confirmed that the dominant confederates did indeed display dramatically more dominance behaviors than the neutral confederates and that confederates in all conditions were perceived as the most influential member of their group.

While all confederates had an influence advantage over the subject in the first nine trials, the size of this advantage could vary from a mere majority to influence on all disagree trials in this phase. It was necessary to control for such differences among confederates in initial influence advantage in order to statistically equate them across conditions in their degree of high status within their dyads. Only then is it possible to make unconfounded comparisons between the compliance accorded to high status based on consistent external status advantages and that given to high status based on inconsistent skill and external status.

For these reasons, compliance data were analyzed by an analysis of covariance using the confederate's influence on the first nine trials as the covariate. Table 7.4 shows the results for subjects' compliance with the confederate on the last nine trials in terms of granting influence, making statements of an intention to agree with the confederate, and statements of an intention to disagree with the confederate. For one of the compliance measures, confederate influence, the analysis of covariance failed to meet the

TABLE 7.4   Experiment 3: Subject compliance with confederate

Condition Means	Group Gender	Condition			
		Consistent		Inconsistent	
		Neutral	Dominant	Neutral	Dominant
Confederate	Male	−0.263	0.500	−0.263	−1.000
Net Influence	Female	−0.300	0.435	0.333	0.700
Adjusted Stated	Male	10.818	14.784	14.672	14.063
Intent to Agree[a]	Female	11.858	17.311	14.401	14.626
Adjusted Stated	Male	3.322	1.004	3.964	7.046
Intent to Disagree[a]	Female	4.164	3.147	3.132	2.141

a. Statements as a percentage of total speech acts, adjusted in an analysis of covariance for confederate influence on trials 1–9.

equality of slopes assumption. Consequently, level of prior influence was controlled for this variable by simply subtracting confederate influence during trials one through nine from confederate influence during the critical phase (trials ten through eighteen), yielding a measure of net influence on which an analysis of variance was performed.

As the means and adjusted means in table 7.4 show, the predicted interaction effects occurred. In consistent external status conditions dominance behavior increased influence ($p < .04$) and stated intention to agree ($p < .05$) and decreased stated intention to disagree ($p < .04$) more than in inconsistent status conditions. These effects were stronger in male groups than in female groups but generally occurred in both. There were no three-way interaction effects for influence or stated intention to agree, indicating that the pattern did not differ significantly by sex for these variables. For stated intention to disagree, the predicted effect was strongly present in male groups, but there were no differences in female groups, yielding a significant three-way interaction.

When the influential confederate was backed by consistent external status beliefs, his or her dominance behavior generally produced more compliance from the subject. It is important to remember that in both consistent and inconsistent conditions, the confederate was the high-ranking, influential member. But in consistent conditions, the confederate was able to effectively wield directive dominance behavior as well as influence, as the confederate in the inconsistent condition could not. These results support the argument that the added legitimacy of the confederate in the consistent condition is the key to his or her effective use of dominance.

CONCLUSION

I noted at the onset that dominance behavior is usually viewed as the ultimate expression of individual competitive motives in groups. While there is an element of truth to such beliefs, the studies discussed here demonstrate how profoundly misleading they are when considered in isolation from members' cooperative interests in groups. Because the availability of allies is such an important determinant of a dominator's ability to credibly threaten another, the effective use of dominance is inherently linked to cooperative, collective processes.

The mobilization of collective support for the exercise of power is in effect the process of legitimation, of the construction and operation of a normative authority or status structure. As a result, the effective use of dominance in groups depends on the collective process of legitimation. In task groups these legitimation processes construct a status system that links individuals' competitive interests to collective interests in task success. According to the legitimated rules of this status system, an individual is subject to sanction when he or she acts on competitive interest in a manner perceived to conflict with the collective interest in task success. The result is to block individuals from effectively using dominance behavior to further their competitive interests in a greater share of the group's resources.

The legitimacy processes of task groups transform the effective use of dominance behavior from an expression of individual competition to the coercive arm of collective interests. This in turn shifts the arena of coercive conflict in the group from that between competing individuals to that between individuals and representatives of the collective interest. Dominance behavior becomes a means of social control that is most likely to be directed from high-status members toward low-status members.

Not all high-status members can employ dominance behavior with equal effectiveness, however. Given that task group hierarchies are based on perceived competence, it is ironic that members whose high status is based on specific task skill alone are less likely to be successful when they attempt to direct others through dominance. Rather, it is members whose high status is based on external status advantages that are most trusted with dominance. External status advantages seem to give a member the appearance of broader support as a representative of collective interests than do specific skills.

This analysis suggests that skilled members of status-disadvantaged groups in society, such as women and minorities, may indeed earn legitimate influence in mixed-sex or multiethnic task groups. But they may encounter resistance if they try to extend their authority to directive control behaviors such as dominance. It is as though society, once it has devalued a group of people in status worthiness, is then unwilling to trust them with coercive power to enforce the collective interest.

8 Minimizing Conflict in Organizational Settings Through Goal Alignment

Gary P. Latham

A major source of conflict within organizational settings is due to the misalignment of the goals of the employee with the goals of the organization. When goal frustration occurs among employees, the result can be a work slowdown, absenteeism, the vandalism of equipment, the deliberate lack of coordination between departments, the withholding of crucial information from peers, and even the misappropriation of funds. An example of the latter was a U.S. government official in the Reagan administration who was prosecuted for directing government funds illegally to the poor and hence earned the sobriquet "Robin Hood."

Voluntary turnover can be problematic when there is a misalignment of the entrepreneur's and the organization's goals. As Hall and Richter (1990) note, corporate vitality and renewal are often lost when "corporate misfits, blue-jeaned people in three-piece corporations," leave a pair of wing-tip shoes beside the exit door before attempting to start up their own business. The company often loses, because another agent for change is no longer present; thus it loses another source of ideas, of innovation, of energy. The employee often loses as well, because the failure rate of start-up businesses is high.

Though goal misalignment can produce conflict, this conflict is not always dysfunctional. Goal frustration may become the impetus for people developing new ideas and the technologies for implementing them. As a result, start-up businesses for manufacturing new products and marketing them may flourish. But, the implicit hypothesis of this chapter is that the goal conflict that results in dysfunctional behavior is not necessary for the occurrence of these positive outcomes. At least three human resource systems exist for anticipating the potential for conflict in organizations and channeling it constructively when it does occur. These systems are selection, performance appraisal, and training. The theory underlying the effectiveness of these three systems is goal setting (Locke & Latham, 1990a). In brief, the theory states that (a) specific hard goals lead to higher performance than do vague goals such as "Do your best" or no goals at all; (b) given goal commitment, high goals lead to higher performance than do easy goals; and (c) variables such as participation in decision making increase performance only to the extent that they lead to the setting of specific hard goals.

SUPERORDINATE GOALS

An organization's culture can be defined in terms of the values that differentiate it from other organizations (Latham & Crandall, 1991). These values can usually be crystallized in terms of a well-articulated superordinate goal. Such a goal is effective if it galvanizes people by making clear to them that what they are striving to achieve is worthwhile. For example, the goal to be a high-quality, low-cost producer communicates clearly the value one company places on quality and cost. It is doubtful, however, that this goal as stated galvanizes the people on the floor who make the product.

Frank Stronach, the chairman of the board of Magna International, Inc., the giant Canadian-based automotive parts supplier, developed a corporate constitution that serves as the cornerstone of the company's culture. The constitution is designed with the specific objective of motivating employees, attracting investors, and developing commitment and excellence in management. This constitution "defines the rights of employees and investors to participate in the company's growth while also imposing certain disciplines on management" (Magna International, 1990, 2). Among the nine points listed in the constitution is the specification of pretax profits that are to be allocated to employees (10 percent of pretax profit), to management (up to 6 percent), to research and development (7 percent), and to cultural and educational causes (up to 2 percent of pretax profit). The superordinate goals of the presidents of the respective operating units are fourfold: to (a) minimize management-labor unrest, (b) focus on customer relations, (c) ensure a profit to shareholders (on the average, 20 percent of Magna's after-tax profit is to be allocated to them), and (d) manage a given debt-to-equity ratio. These four goals serve as guideposts for the management of Magna to elicit employee participation in discussions on how best to attain them.

The value of a well-formulated superordinate goal for energizing all people, regardless of their level or position within an organization, is evident in the case of Scott Paper's Northwest Timberlands Division. In 1982, the company's senior management in Philadelphia decided to sell their timber holdings in Washington state. The company feared a dramatic decrease in employee morale and a concomitant decrease in productivity as a result of this decision. Contrary to this fear, the opposite phenomena occurred. From 1982 to 1989, when the land was finally sold, both employee morale and the division's profits remained high. Why? Ron Stoppler, the local timberlands manager, ended the announcement to his people of the company's decision to sell the land with a rallying cry: "Let's send Philadelphia a message, let's make them choke."

The formulation of this superordinate goal resulted in employee involvement groups setting proximal goals and executing strategies for "making them choke." Specifically, "making them choke" meant setting specific quarterly production goals that would either make the division so profitable that senior management would regret, and hence rescind, its decision or make the employees so productive that the buyer would hire them. Thus the superordinate goal was phrased so that it created a win-win scenario for both the employees and the company. Note that in these latter two instances, Magna and Scott Paper, the goals were truly specific, difficult, and attainable. The issue now is one of selecting people who wish to pursue these goals.

EMPLOYEE SELECTION

Realistic Job Previews

Well-articulated superordinate goals facilitate the effectiveness of job previews by screening out people whose values are in conflict with the organization's culture. A job preview differs from a movie preview in that the latter shows a potential audience the best aspects of the film in the hope that it will entice people to enter the theater to see it. A job preview also shows people the best aspects of the job, with the hope that it will entice people to apply for it; but unlike a movie preview, the latter also gives a realistic picture of the negative aspects of the job (Wanous, 1980, 1989). This is done to enhance the self-selection process. A job preview does this by giving the applicant realistic information on which to make an informed decision whether the job is appropriate for him or her.

In brief, a realistic job preview focuses on what is both positive and negative about the job, the organization, and the community in which the organization is located. This information is collected systematically from exit interviews and/or current employees. To ensure candor, the information is collected in a way that preserves the respondent's anonymity. The benefit of realistic job previews is that they can reduce employee turnover significantly because of goal alignment between the organization and its employees (Wanous, 1980, 1989).

With entry-level jobs, the realistic preview generally occurs prior to a hiring decision. It may take the form of a job posting whereby potential applicants are informed in writing of the vacancy along with the positive and negative aspects of it. With high-level positions, the job preview is usually the final step in the hiring process. Thus the applicant is informed that he or she has been awarded the position. But to prevent an escalation-of-commitment effect, whereby the applicant's effort to secure the job predisposes an acceptance of the offer, the applicant is also told that a positive decision regarding this offer will not be accepted until one or more days following the job preview. This allows the applicant time to consider whether the person-job-organization fit is appropriate. Moreover, if the decision is positive, it allows the person preparation time to consider ways of coping with the adverse aspects of the job. If the person declines the offer, it reduces the organization's subsequent costs of orienting and training a person who would likely have left the organization within twelve to eighteen months after joining it. One way to ensure that the applicant pool is sufficiently large, to ensure that there are one or more candidates whose goals are congruent with the organization's, is to engage in affirmative action.

Affirmative Action

The purpose of selection is threefold, namely, (a) to hire productive people in a (b) legally defensible manner who will be (c) in alignment with the organization's culture. These three objectives can be attained through the same three steps, namely, affirmative action, job analysis, and obtaining evidence on the validity of the hiring decision. In North America, affirmative action involves actively encouraging women and minorities to apply for the job. This step not only satisfies legal-societal concerns, but it satisfies concerns for productivity and a cultural fit, because the larger the applicant pool, the higher the probability that the "right person" can be found to do the job. Equally important is the fact that a diverse work force brings to the organization different viewpoints, which in turn increases the likelihood that the organization's culture will be dynamic and grow rather than be static and risk decline.

Job Analysis

The second step in ensuring that the "right" person is hired is to conduct a systematic job analysis. The purpose of this analysis is to identify the behavior that is critical to effective performance on the job. The outcome of this analysis can be the development of behavior observation scales, or BOS (Latham & Wexley, 1977, 1981), that specify what the person must do to be effective in the organization. Thus the BOS emanating from the job analysis helps define an organization's culture by making explicit to the employee what he or she needs to do to help the organization achieve its goals. Moreover, because the job analysis is based on their input, employees understand the rationale for engaging in these behaviors.

An example of a BOS used by a utility company is shown in figure 8.1. Because the job analysis makes clear to the applicant and the employer the behaviors valued in this organization, the resulting BOS can be incorporated into the job preview. After reading and discussing the BOS, applicants can decide whether the behaviors desired by the organization (e.g., a requirement of extensive travel) are compatible with their value systems.

Validation

Once the job analysis identifies the behaviors that are critical in a given position, a selection test can be developed to identify who will demonstrate these behaviors. If the correlation between the scores of individuals on the test and the performance appraisal of the same individuals on the job is significant, the test is valid.

The selection interview is the test procedure used most frequently by employers in North America to hire people. The interview, however, has a number of shortcomings. For example, in most interviews the questions are not the same for each applicant. This lack of structure can result in one

Figure 8.1: An Example of a Behavioral Observation Scale for Assessing a Manager's Promotion of Teamwork and Effective Working Relationships

1. Encourages and facilitates cooperation and teamwork in the section.					
Almost Never	0	1	2	4	Almost Always
2. Remembers to respond to requests without having to be reminded.					
Almost Never	0	1	2	4	Almost Always
3. Consults with employees for ideas on ways to make their jobs better.					
Almost Never	0	1	2	4	Almost Always
4. Provides resources, such as time and information, that are needed by employees to do their jobs.					
Almost Never	0	1	2	4	Almost Always
5. Rewards others by expressing appreciation for their support, pointing out good work, etc.					
Almost Never	0	1	2	4	Almost Always
6. Shares ideas, expertise, and data.					
Almost Never	0	1	2	4	Almost Always
7. Keeps staff informed.					
Almost Never	0	1	2	4	Almost Always
8. Finds ways to bring the accomplishments of the section to the attention of upper management.					
Almost Never	0	1	2	4	Almost Always
9. Supports the reasonable decisions of his or her staff.					
Almost Never	0	1	2	4	Almost Always
10. Raises concerns or problems as soon as possible with those concerned rather than waiting.					
Almost Never	0	1	2	4	Almost Always
11. Treats staff fairly; e.g., refrains from showing favoritism.					
Almost Never	0	1	2	4	Almost Always

applicant being treated unfairly relative to another (e.g., when the difficulty level of the questions varies among applicants). When the questions are the same, they often are not job related. Non-job-related questions (e.g., "Do you play sports?") not only are unlikely to predict job behavior but are likely to invite bias and stereotype error (e.g., "People who don't play sports are not team players"). When the questions are job related (e.g., "Do you like to travel?"), the desired answers are often transparent to the applicant (e.g., "I love to travel"). When the desired answers are not obvious to the applicant, they often are not obvious to the interviewers either. That is, what one interviewer concludes is an acceptable answer ("It showed assertiveness") another interviewer concludes is unacceptable ("It signaled abrasivness"). Consequently, the interobserver reliability is low. Low reliability attenuates the ability to show that a selection method is valid.

Situational Interviews

A solution to these issues is the situational interview (Latham, 1989). The theory underlying this approach to interviewing is that intentions predict behavior. In brief, the critical incident technique, or CIT (Flanagan, 1954), is used to develop the BOS described above. That is, employees are asked to specify incidents where they observed someone perform an aspect of the job well or poorly. In describing an incident, job incumbents are asked to specify the circumstances or context surrounding the incident, the exact behavior that was emitted, and how the behavior led to a desirable or undesirable outcome. These incidents, which are used to develop the BOS, are turned into "what would you do" questions.

Before the questions are used to select people, a pilot study is conducted to ensure that there is variability in the answers given by different applicants to each question. If the desired answer is not obvious, the answers from the people in the pilot group should vary, as people will state their true intentions rather than what they believe the interviewer wants to hear them say. Where variability is not the case, the question is either modified or discarded.

Unique to the situational interview is the development of a scoring guide to assist interviewers in evaluating an applicant's answers as outstanding, acceptable, or unacceptable. The development of this scoring guide can be a team-building exercise, in that it forces the organization's decision makers to articulate the company's culture. In doing so, they must confront and reconcile their differences regarding the behaviors that they want employees to exhibit on the job. The result of this exercise is high consistency, or interobserver reliability, among the interviewers who use this technique, and significant validity coefficients for applicants regardless of their race or sex (Latham, Saari, Pursell, & Campion, 1980). The outcome for the organization is a high probability that the selected applicants will be productive employees who will enhance its culture. The outcome for the employees who accept the offer is a job where the probability that they will do well is high.

An example of a situational interview question used by an organization whose culture stresses team playing is shown in figure 8.2. Like BOS, situational interviews facilitate realistic job previews, because the questions communicate to the applicant the type of situations that the job incumbent will confront in the organization.

Performance Appraisal

The Appraisal Instrument

The primary purpose of performance appraisal is to coach people so that effective performance is not only maintained but enhanced. However, before one can serve effectively as a coach, the question of what is to be coached must be addressed. The answers to this question are to be found in the results of the job analysis described previously. BOS, derived directly from the job analysis, make clear the behaviors a coach should reinforce.

Figure 8.2: An Example of a Situational Question and Scoring Guide

---

You are in charge of truck drivers in Philadelphia. Your colleague is in charge of truck drivers 800 miles away in Atlanta. Both of you report to the same person. Your salary and bonus are affected 100 percent by your costs. Your colleague is in desperate need of one of your trucks. If you say no, your costs will remain low, and your group will probably win the Golden Flyer award for the quarter. If you say yes, the Atlanta group will probably win this prestigious award, because they will make a significant profit for the company. Your boss is preaching costs, costs, costs, as well as cooperation with one's peers. Your boss has no control over accounting, who are the scorekeepers. Your boss is highly competitive. He or she rewards winners. You are just as competitive, you are a real winner!

Explain what you would do.

Record answers:

Scoring Guide
1. I would go for the award. I would explain the circumstances to my colleague and get his or her understanding. (Unacceptable answer)
3. I would get my boss's advice. (Marginally acceptable answer)
5. I would loan the truck to my colleague. I'd get recognition from my boss and my colleague that I had made a sacrifice. Then I'd explain the logic to my people. (highly acceptable answer)

Moreover, the BOS facilitate self-management by making explicit the behaviors each employee should self-reinforce.

Unfortunately, most organizations use trait-oriented rather than behaviorally oriented scales. Examples of traits commonly found on such instruments include the words *visionary, aggressive, loyal,* and so on. The resulting conflict that often occurs as a result of using trait scales is twofold. First, the U.S. courts have found appraisals that are based on such scales to reflect primarily the whim and caprice of the evaluator rather than the performance of the employee (Latham & Wexley, 1993). Second, how the evaluator defines traits is generally out of alignment with how the employee defines them. The solution to this conflict is to define traits in terms of observable job behavior. This is easily done through a job analysis such as the critical incident technique (e.g., "Exactly what did the person do to demonstrate that he/she was a visionary? Aggressive? Loyal?").

Rather than focus on observable job behavior instead of traits, many organizations have embraced a management-by-objectives philosophy where the emphasis is on the "bottom line." This too is a conflict-laden strategy. As noted over twenty years ago by John Campbell and his colleagues (Campbell, Dunnette, Lawler, & Weick, 1970), bottom-line measures are often excessive in that they are affected by factors that are beyond the control of the individual. Thus an executive in the forest products industry can be rewarded undeservedly (e.g., when the dollar drops relative to the yen, and log exports rise) or penalized unfairly (e.g., if the dollar rises relative to the yen, and log exports fall). Equally bad, bottom-line measures are often deficient for performance appraisal purposes in that they do not take into account factors for which an individual should be held accountable (e.g., evaluating a secretary primarily on typing speed ignores telephone courtesy). "That which gets measured gets done." This is because the act of measurement signals to the employee that which the organization truly values. This in turn usually affects the employee's goals. And the setting of specific goals has a direct effect on the employee's subsequent behavior (Locke & Latham, 1990a).

Of even greater concern with the sole use of bottom-line measures for performance appraisal purposes is that they make self-coaching and coaching from others difficult. This is because a bottom-line measure by itself does not indicate what a person must start doing, stop doing, or continue doing to impact it. Only a job analysis, with its identification of critical behavior, explains why a bottom-line measure is high or low. In the absence of this knowledge, a focus on the bottom line can tempt both the coach and the person being coached to engage in unethical behavior to affect it. Examples of this from both industry and athletics in the past decade are too numerous to be mentioned here. Suffice it to say that to avoid ethical and legal conflicts, and to increase the probability of a coach and an employee achieving consensus on acceptable goals, behaviorally based appraisal instruments are preferable to trait and economic measures. These three measures can be integrated, however, by conducting a job analysis that defines *traits* in terms of the observable job *behaviors* that impact an organization's *bottom line* positively.

The Appraisal Process

An inherent conflict in providing feedback to the employee is the tendency for him or her to denigrate the instrument (e.g., "You evaluated me on the wrong things") and/or the appraiser (e.g., "You are not qualified to evaluate me"). A way to obviate the former conflict has already been discussed. A behaviorally derived appraisal instrument developed from a job analysis based on employee input makes it difficult for an employee to question its relevance.

At least four processes can be put in place to minimize the second source of conflict. First, the appraisal of a person's performance should be an ongoing, informal activity rather than one that occurs at fixed intervals (e.g., quarterly or once a year). When feedback is a relatively continuous process, the formal appraisal contains no information that is new or surprising to the employee. Ongoing informal appraisals are consistent with the fact that the job of a coach is to continually let people know that what they are doing is both noticed and appreciated, so that desired behaviors are reinforced and undesirable behaviors are extinguished. However, feedback is necessary but not sufficient for increasing performance. In addition, goals must be set in relation to this feedback.

For example, engineers and scientists at Weyerhaeuser Company who were given explicit feedback on BOS had performance that was not significantly different from those in a control group. In contrast, the performance of those engineers and scientists who had specific hard goals, in addition to feedback, was significantly higher than that of people who received feedback only (Latham, Mitchell, & Dossett, 1978).

Thus a second process for minimizing conflict is to set specific goals. This is because most people believe that they are already "doing their best." The ambiguity inherent in an emphasis on "doing one's best" allows people to give themselves the benefit of the doubt in evaluating their own performance; thus a wide range of performance levels may be interpreted by them as being compatible with excellence. In contrast, specific difficult goals define explicitly at the beginning, rather than at the end of the appraisal period, what constitutes success. Setting specific goals focuses attention on the future rather than the past. Thus it is not surprising that football coaches who use goal setting with their players have better won-loss records than those coaches who use such techniques less often (Anderson & Schneiner, 1979). The use of goal setting in a performance appraisal is a key variable in bringing about performance improvement (Burke & Wilcox, 1969).

A third way to manage conflict between the appraiser and the employee is to shift the primary responsibility of coaching from the employee's formal supervisor to the employee. For example, state government unionized employees were taught skills in self-management that were effective in increasing their job attendance relative to a control group (Frayne & Latham, 1987; Latham & Frayne, 1989). Again, the core of the training was the setting of specific, difficult, but attainable goals. In brief, the employees as a group brainstormed the reasons for their absenteeism, they set goals regarding attendance, they formulated strategies for overcoming the obstacles preventing them from coming to work, they selected rewards and punishers to self-administer, and they self-monitored their job attendance.

An external observer can greatly facilitate the self-management process. Thus a fourth way of not only minimizing conflict between the appraiser and the employee, but increasing the probability that the person will set specific goals based on the feedback, is the use of peer appraisals. Peer appraisals have a number of advantages over alternatives. From a legal standpoint, judgment by one's peers is congruent with the judicial process in democratic societies. From the standpoint of validity, peer appraisals, given that they are anonymous, have been found consistently to be superior to appraisals conducted by a superior, a subordinate, or oneself (Latham, 1986). This is because peers have more information than the alternative sources on which to make an evaluation. They see the person interact with the boss, colleagues, subordinates, and customers. An additional contributing factor to the validity of peers is their plurality. Thus the different biases that exist among different employees can cancel one another out. And it is this plurality that contributes to employee acceptance of the appraisal relative to an appraisal from a single source. In those instances where peers do not see one another (e.g., salespeople in charge of different geographical regions), peer appraisals obviously should not be used.

Scott Paper Company's senior management group in Mobile, Alabama, uses peer appraisals as a team-building exercise to ensure that there is consistency in their leadership across the plant site and to continuously develop the capability for job growth in themselves and in their people. For example, the vice president and his immediate staff appraise one another's performance anonymously to ensure candor. Again, the process involves feedback and the setting of specific, difficult, attainable goals in relation to this feedback. In brief, each person is interviewed as to what he or she has observed each colleague do well, and what he or she would like to see the person start doing or stop doing that is consistent with the organization's overall goals. Feedback is given in a group setting. Each person is designated the role of coach with the responsibility of helping the others grow in their respective jobs.

Two ground rules enhance the effectiveness of peer appraisals. One rule is to focus primarily on the future rather than the past. The other is to maintain anonymity regarding the source of a particular comment that was made during the interviews. The rationale for the first ground rule is that the past cannot be changed, whereas control can be exerted over the future. Moreover, conflict is likely to occur as people recall the past from different vantage points. Conflict is less likely when the emphasis is on what one would like to see occur rather than on what displeased someone last week, last month, or last year. The rationale for the second ground rule is not only to ensure candor in the interviews, but also to prevent anyone claiming ownership of other group members' thoughts or observations.

In the feedback session, emphasis is given to discussing and emphasizing the positive behaviors that have been observed. Here discussion of the past is welcomed, so that appropriate behavior is reinforced. High-level managers are arguably less likely to receive praise than people in other employee groups, because their subordinates wish to avoid perceptions of patronization, the superior seldom sees them outside of staff meetings, and their peers are in strong competition with them for promotion. Hence a strong focus on team playing, where a structure is provided for these managers to consciously focus on one another's development, can be critical to the organization's effectiveness.

Feedback that is negative is stated in terms of what the group would like to see occur in the future. To preserve the anonymity of the author or authors of the comment, and to enhance coaching skills, each person is asked to discuss how they would change the behavior under discussion. Thus, a third ground rule that enhances the effectiveness of peer appraisals and minimizes the likelihood of conflict is to focus on the behavior rather than the person.

After receiving feedback, each person presents three to five specific goals that she or he commits to the group that she or he will achieve. These goals may be modified if the group does not believe that they are based on the feedback that was given. Once there is consensus on the appropriateness of the goals, the process concludes with a discussion of how the group can assist each individual achieve them. In this way, goal setting by each individual manager becomes a team effort. The probability that the goals will be attained is high. Included in this final step is agreement on the date for a follow-up meeting to reward one another for goal attainment, to help one another in those instances where a goal was not attained, and to agree on the setting of new goals. Thus the Mobile Division prides itself on being the "leader in leadership" in the Scott Paper Company.

Training

The discussion thus far in this chapter has dealt primarily with ways of minimizing unnecessary conflict by anticipating its sources. The purpose of training is to bring about enduring changes in employee behavior

(Wexley & Latham, 1991). This section discusses training programs that are designed to teach people how to deal effectively with conflict when it occurs.

Behavior Modeling

An effective training technique for bringing about a relatively permanent change in an employee's behavior is behavior modeling (Burke & Day, 1986). This technique is based on Bandura's (1986) social cognitive theory, which states in part that people emulate behavior that they observe to be instrumental in attaining goals they wish to achieve. Thus this training employs a videotaped model whose status is not so high as to be intimidating to the trainee nor so low that trainees would not view the person as someone to model themselves after. The behaviors the model exhibits are made salient to the trainee by presenting them before and after a role play in the form of learning points (e.g., "Restate the complaint to ensure you heard it correctly"). The learning points are developed on the basis of the job analysis described earlier.

When the videotape ends, the trainees discuss what the model did well and ways they themselves might have dealt with the situation appropriately. Trainees, two at a time, then role-play before the group a situation that is specific to their own job. Feedback from fellow trainees is given on the effectiveness of each role play. The "homework assignment" is to apply what was learned in training to the job. The trainees return to the training class a week later and discuss what went well and what could have been done even better. The result of this training for supervisors of unionized employees at Weyerhaeuser Company was performance that was superior to those in a control group on both measures of learning and performance on the job (Latham & Saari, 1979).

Union-Management Relations

The goal-setting process can be designed to enable labor and management to work together to jointly set and achieve end states of mutual interest to both parties. The process takes place outside, and is hence independent of, the formal bargaining arena. The implicit objective is to increase understanding by both parties of the thinking, feelings, and behavior of both sides and to set and achieve goals that enhance the organization's effectiveness and that would be difficult to achieve by either party alone.

In setting goals, a neutral party is used to facilitate communication between management and labor, so that mutually acceptable solutions can emerge from their discussion. When meeting with representatives of only labor or only management, the role of the facilitator is to listen, with the intent of understanding and better communicating the concerns and perspectives to the other party.

The process of finding mutually acceptable goals for the two parties to work together to attain allows them to discover ways of influencing each other positively, by exploring what each party needs and what each party can therefore offer the other to induce reciprocation. It would be naive, however, to believe that conflict could be resolved if only management and labor would communicate clearly and frequently with the aim of increasing an understanding of one another. It would also be naive to believe that conflict would disappear if the individuals involved merely knew one another as human beings with similar goals and concerns.

The purpose of the goal-setting process is to create the conditions necessary for bringing about a specific type of interaction, namely, one characterized by an in-depth analysis of the conflict, exploration of mutual perspectives, generation of new ideas, and joint problem solving. Creative problem solving in this setting is a search for ways of redefining, fractionating, and transcending conflicts so that win-win solutions, which leave both parties better off, can be discovered.

The essence of the conflict between management and labor is not unlike that described by Kelman (see chapter 14) in his work with Israelis and Palestinians. Differences in the goals, perceptions, and identity concerns of the leaders in the two respective groups find expression in collective orientations and become translated into formal and informal policies. Conflict resolution thus requires changes in individual attitudes as a means for, and as an accompaniment of, changes in policy and action. Thus, the goal-setting process is designed to promote system-level changes (e. g., changes in hiring practices, use of outside contractors, layoff procedures) by way of changes in the perceptions and attitudes of influential individuals on the plant site.

In work that is currently ongoing at Scott Paper Company's Winslow plant, the leadership in five union locals interviewed me and recommended to management hiring me to lead a goal-setting process. Only the union can fire me; only management pays my consulting fees. This decision was reached jointly by management and labor, prior to my retention as a resource, to ensure that the consultant would be equally committed to the viewpoints of both parties. Thus the consultant who sees things only through the eyes of the union will not get paid; conversely, if the person views issues only from management's perspective, he or she will not be employed.

I am assisted by one representative from labor and another from management. These two people were selected jointly by the leadership of the five locals, and the general manager and his staff, on the criteria of trustworthiness, integrity, and credibility. Such a balanced resource team is superior to a neutral "disinterested" party or parties in that the team is sensitive to the nuances of both management and labor, it is alert to the cultural and social dimensions of conflicts, and it is sympathetic to the emotional and symbolic issues at stake.

The goal-setting process is similar to the peer appraisal described earlier in this chapter. The union representatives are asked the following three questions: (1) What is management doing well? (2) What would you like to see them start doing, stop doing, or consider doing differently? (3) What would you be willing to do to help them? The same three questions are asked of management relative to the union.

The feedback session takes place in an integrated group setting. Goals are subsequently set jointly, based on this feedback. Training is given to the two parties in an integrated group setting on how to reinforce one another's behavior effectively and how to deal with behavior that one person or group sees as inappropriate on the part of another.

Steering group meetings are held monthly or bimonthly to review goal progress and to set new goals. Consistent with the opening theme in this chapter, the two parties spent several months together developing a superordinate goal that they have termed a "blueprint for organizational effectiveness." This blueprint spells out principles for giving recognition and rewards, training and developing the work force, providing job security, and defining appropriate management and union leadership behavior. Task forces are formed to propose strategies for union-management steering committee approval or suggestions for revision. A by-product of the formation of the task forces is an increase in the involvement of the plant site's work force in setting and working toward goals. The ultimate objective of the goal-setting process in this particular organization is to make the plant cost-effective in a way that enhances the dignity, respect, and development of the employee, and to simultaneously transform a marginally profitable organization into one that is highly profitable.

The results after three years of work are encouraging. First, the leadership in management and labor have learned that there is someone to talk to on the other side and, more importantly, that there is something to talk about. This discovery is not trivial in a conflict that is based on a strike that occurred a decade ago where the aftermath has been an "us versus them" mentality. Second, the participants have gained insight into one another's perspective, fundamental concerns, priorities, areas of flexibility, and psychological and structural constraints. For example, work effectiveness for management means cost reduction through job enrichment by allowing operators to perform minor maintenance work and by empowering them to enhance their job skills and thus increase their marketability. In contrast, work effectiveness for the maintenance union means operators crossing union jurisdictional lines, which means the loss of work and the potential loss of jobs to its members. Thus the jointly developed blueprint represents a common vision of a future that is highly desired by both management and labor, but it does not necessarily mean that they accept the other's strategy for attaining it.

A fundamental source of the conflict between management and labor is the clash in values between collectivism, which labor embraces, and the values of individualism, which management embraces. Thus the union locals advocate in-group integrity, whereas management emphasizes the value of allowing individuals to maximize their capability. The unions believe that only they have a true interest in the work force of this particular division as they focus on promoting the welfare of the group. They perceive management as focusing primarily on promoting their own personal careers. Evidence they cite to support this perception is the actual number of plant general managers, as well as key staff members, who have been transferred to other geographical locations of the company: "We stay; they go" is a perception that is exacerbated by the union's values of harmony, accommodation, acquiescence, and relationship building within and between union memberships versus the values espoused by management for autonomy, self-reliance, independence, and risk taking, and the unspoken value for mobility. In short, the collectivists view only themselves as promoting the welfare of the group; the individualists view only themselves as strongly concerned with developing, and hence valuing, the individual. Thus it is not surprising that a primary objective of each manager in the division is "capability development" of the hourly worker; it is also not surprising that the individual hourly worker views this "altruism" as a threat to his or her value system, a threat to the very integrity of the union, by singling out and hence separating the person from his or her group.

In stark contrast to this viewpoint, the individualists believe that they are paying the collectivists the ultimate compliment when they argue the need to bring down all barriers between management and labor so that "we are one team." Individualists are not prone to recognizing differences between in-groups and out-groups (Triandis, McCusker, & Hui, 1990). Their emphasis is on teamwork where feelings of "we-they" are abolished. This perspective, and the viewpoint underlying it, is an anathema to the unions, who see a sharp contrast between in-group (union) and out-group members (management). When there is conflict between the union's and an individual member's goals, collectivists believe the union's goals should prevail. Thus, to truly remove all barriers between what they view as in-group and out-group members, let alone with members of management, whom they see as transient individuals, is clearly incompatible with their value system. For management to argue strongly that union jurisdictional lines should be ignored in favor of work effectiveness and the development of the individual is consistent with their value system. It is, nevertheless, viewed by labor as a direct assault on their core values.

Within this framework, care is taken in steering group meetings to ensure that the values espoused by one group do not presuppose the rejection of the values of the other. The formulation of primary goals and strategies for making the blueprint a reality has allowed both parties to engage in a variety of exchanges that test each other's sincerity and readiness for creating a cooperative work climate. Such discoveries are slowly breaking down the assumption that cooperation is possible only if the other side undergoes conversion and abandons its own ideology. Thus task forces have successfully developed acceptable ways for management and labor to give public recognition to one another. For example, a jointly developed job security plan regarding layoff procedures has been implemented, and principles defining appropriate management-union leadership behavior have been accepted. The focus now is on ways of improving the organization's financial situation.

Conclusions

Consistent with the other chapters in this book, this chapter has focused on conflict reduction. But the underlying theme has been on ways of gaining organizational commitment through the alignment of the organization's goals with the goals of its employees. This commitment can be achieved as follows:

1. Establish superordinate goals that clearly define the organization's culture, that is, the values that differentiate it from other organizations.
2. Communicate the superordinate goals to applicants through a realistic job preview. This allows people to make a decision as to whether the organization's values are compatible with their own.
3. Engage in affirmative action in order to increase the applicant pool. The larger the applicant pool, the higher the probability that people will be found whose goals are compatible with the organization.
4. Conduct a job analysis by employees, for employees, that defines what one must do to show commitment to the organization's goals.
5. Evaluate people on that which they have control over—their behavior.
6. Use situational interviews to identify people who are predisposed to demonstrate the behaviors identified through the job analysis as critical to effective performance in the organization.
7. Once the person is hired, provide ongoing informal coaching to reinforce desired behavior.
8. Strengthen the one-on-one coaching process with the use of peer appraisals that focus on teamwork in helping each person achieve difficult but attainable goals.
9. Use behavior-modeling training to teach people the skills they need to attain their goals.

10. To improve union-management relations, use the setting of mutually acceptable goals as a means of gaining management and labor's commitment to enhancing the organization's effectiveness.

NOTE

I wish to acknowledge the helpful editorial comments from my colleagues at the University of Toronto, Martin Evans, Dan Ondrack, and Glen Whyte, and from Jerry Ballas, Roy Barry, and Tom Czepiel, Scott Paper Company. Preparation of this article was facilitated by a grant from the Social Sciences and Humanities Research Council of Canada.

9   The Symbolic Politics of Opposition to Bilingual Education

David O. Sears and Leonie Huddy

Language issues have been at the core of political divisions between groups in a wide variety of contexts (Edwards, 1985). In Canada, French-English linguistic antipathies were partially resolved through the proclamation of official bilingualism, but in Quebec, much tension remains about any public use of English (Williams, 1984). Gaelic is the official language in Ireland, though not widely used, and is enjoying a renaissance in Northern Ireland as a symbol of Catholic resistance to British rule. Anti-Soviet rebellions in such East European regions as Estonia, Lithuania, and Moldavia focused partly on the reinstitution of native languages. Language is one of the many dimensions of ethnic dispute in Sri Lanka (Dharmadasa, 1977; Horowitz, 1985). In Malaysia, there is Malay-Chinese conflict on the role of Malay as the official language (LePage, 1984). And in the United States, disputes over English as an official language antedate the Revolution and have flared up periodically ever since (Heath, 1981). In the current era it has been joined by disputes over bilingual ballots and bilingual education (Citrin, 1988; Hakuta, 1986).

We focus here on conflict over bilingual education. Increasing immigration has resulted in thousands of children entering American public schools annually with limited or no English-speaking abilities. Bilingual education programs have been developed as one response to their educational disadvantage, but they have become politically controversial. Amidst heated debate, the Reagan administration attempted to withdraw federal funding for bilingual education programs. The defeat of bilingual ballots and the passage of English-as-official-language in California referenda in 1984 and 1986 suggests substantial opposition to officially sanctioned multilingualism. The flourishing of the "English-only" movement suggests that language has once again become a highly charged political issue in the United States (Citrin, Green, Reingold, & Walters, 1990; Dyste, 1989; Marshall, 1986).

The principal beneficiaries of bilingual education are Hispanics. The political fortunes of bilingualism, like those of most programs targeted primarily for minorities, ultimately rest in the hands of the non-Hispanic majority. Moreover, the attitudes of the primary consumers of bilingual education may well have quite a different basis than those of the mainly nonconsuming majority. Both considerations lead us, in this study, to focus on non-Hispanics' attitudes toward it.

Our first purpose, then, is to determine what contributes to opposition to bilingual education among non-Hispanics. We test among four general possibilities. First, it might derive from self-interest, that is, possible negative personal experiences related to it. Second, it might stem from anti-minority and anti-immigrant attitudes. In particular, it might be perceived as providing minorities with unfair advantages ("My grandparents had to learn English, sink or swim; why shouldn't they have to?") and so evoke resentments of minorities' demands and of special treatment given to them (as in the concept of "symbolic racism"; see Kinder & Sears, 1981; McConahay, 1986; Sears, 1988). It might also evoke antagonism toward its main beneficiaries, Hispanics and new immigrants, perhaps being perceived as blocking their full assimilation (Citrin, Reingold, & Green, 1990.) Third, opposition to bilingual education might stem from political values and ideology with no manifest racial or ethnic content. Either providing special help to some children and not others or the failure to redress inequalities of background may violate basic values. Ideology and party identification, along with general opposition to government spending on domestic programs, might play a role, given that bilingual education has been a divisive partisan issue at both state and federal levels. Fourth, it could be regarded as just another nonessential educational program, perhaps like foreign language instruction, and draw opposition from those who view such non-"three-R" programs as being of low priority.[1]

SYMBOLIC POLITICS

Our second purpose is to extend the reach of a symbolic politics theory of mass political behavior. This theory has appeared in a variety of guises, mostly sharing three basic assumptions: that people acquire learned affective responses to particular symbols relatively early in life (variously placed anywhere from childhood to early adulthood); that the learned responses from those formative early experiences (which we here generically call "predispositions") persist to some degree into and throughout adult life; and that they strongly influence the adult's attitudes toward current political stimuli. The strongest of these, which we have called "symbolic predispositions," are distinguished by their special persistence over time and influence over other attitudes.[2]

These basic ideas have undergirded research on a wide variety of problems. Research on political socialization has investigated children's and adolescents' response to such symbols as the flag, the president, stigmatized racial groups, and the political parties (e.g., Easton & Dennis, 1969). This early learning presumably produces such predispositions as party identification, racial prejudices, ethnic identities, basic values, nationalism, and attachment to various symbols of the nation and regime (e.g., Campbell, Converse, Miller, & Stokes, 1960; Jennings & Niemi, 1981). And the persistence of these predispositions has been investigated in its own right (see Alwin & Krosnick, 1991; Converse, 1975; Sears, 1983).

The activation of these predispositions by political symbols in the adult's environment, and their influence over attitudes toward such symbols, have received even more research attention. A staple finding is that standing partisan predispositions are activated by policy and candidate alternatives, thereby influencing the individual's preferences (Campbell et al., 1960; Sears, Lau, Tyler, & Allen, 1980). Basic values play the same role (Feldman, 1988). In analogous fashion, racial predispositions are activated by black candidates and racial issues, and influence attitudes toward them (Kinder & Sears, 1981; Sears, Hensler, & Speer, 1979). Other basic values can be activated by symbols of injustice, inequity, or immorality, and thus produce mass protest (Sears & McConahay, 1973; Sears & Citrin, 1985; Gusfield, 1963). Long-standing antagonisms toward such groups as the Communists, Nazis, and KKK are evoked by civil liberties debates concerning them and influence support for extending them democratic rights (Sullivan, Piereson, & Marcus, 1982).

If adults' political attitudes are most strongly influenced by predispositions originating early in life, a lesser role should be played by calculations based on their adult experiences or current interests. On this point, the symbolic politics approach is quite at odds with utilitarian, rational-actor theories. These latter assume that individuals' preferences are rooted in egocentric concerns, especially those stemming from current direct personal experiences with the attitude object or from calculation of current or future self-interest (e.g., Downs, 1957; Kiewiet, 1983). When applied to racial issues, the most relevant form of self-interest is usually the personal threat posed by minorities to the individual white's well-being. Under this set of assumptions, whites might oppose busing because of personal threat, for example, because their children are having bad personal experiences with integrated schools, or because their own children might be bused to ghetto schools (Rothbart, 1976).

Numerous studies have demonstrated the greater power of symbolic predispositions than self-interest over candidate and policy preferences (for recent reviews, see Citrin & Green, 1990; Green, 1988; Sears & Funk, 1991). In particular, self-interest has proven to have disappointing effects on the general public's political attitudes in such diverse areas as racial policies and black candidacies (Sears, 1988; McConahay, 1986), presidential and congressional elections (Kinder & Kiewiet, 1979), employment policy and national health insurance (Sears et al., 1980), and spending and tax cuts (though it has had more impact in the latter case; see Sears & Citrin, 1985). These findings have provided considerable support for the symbolic politics approach.

The Role of Symbolic Meaning

The core of the symbolic politics process, then, is that standing learned predispositions are evoked by political symbols in the current informational environment. Most of the relevant research has concerned the origins, nature, and effects of these predispositions, however. Relatively little attention has been devoted to the role of the evoking symbols and their meaning. Presumably the key to that role is that any given attitude object, such as an issue, candidate, or event, can vary in meaning, because the symbols contained in the object at any given time can vary.

Such variations might affect public opinion consequentially in two different ways. First, they could influence the overall public evaluation of an attitude object and indeed have been shown to do so quite powerfully in a number of familiar contexts. Support for intervention in the Korean War was considerably greater when it was described as intended "to stop the Communist invasion of South Korea" than when it was simply described as "the war in Korea" (Mueller, 1973). Most people support domestic spending when it is described in terms of specific program areas, such as "education" or "health," but oppose it when described as "larger government" (Sears & Citrin, 1985). Most strongly oppose spending for "welfare" but support "helping the poor," "public assistance programs to the elderly and the disabled," and programs "for low-income families with dependent children," all of which constitute a major portion of welfare spending (see Sears & Citrin, 1985; Smith, 1987). Whites support "racial integration of the schools" but overwhelmingly oppose "busing" (Schuman, Steeh, & Bobo, 1985; Sears et al., 1979). Civil liberties are frequently supported in the abstract but opposed in concrete application (e.g., McClosky & Brill, 1983). And as will be seen, symbolic meaning influences the overall evaluation of bilingual education.

A second possible effect of varying symbolic meaning goes further. The psychological dynamic underlying the symbolic approach assumes that a political symbol will trigger an appropriate predisposition relatively automatically, based on pressures toward affective consistency. For example, a Communist invasion of our ally should quickly trigger anti-Communism, and a black's candidacy, racial attitudes. Much research in social psychology and political behavior indicates, however, that such consistency pressures tend to operate fairly narrowly and locally. In fact, people can live quite comfortably with distant, indirect, general, or diffuse inconsistencies (see Abelson et al.,

1968; Converse, 1964). A simple example is the widespread simultaneous support for both tax cuts and maintenance of current levels of government services (see Sears and Citrin, 1985). As a result, a "simple symbolic politics theory" would argue that any given symbol is likely to evoke only those predispositions that are cognitively quite specifically relevant to them in a template-matching sense (Sears, Huddy & Schaffer, 1986).

The central proposition of this study, then, is that the symbolic meaning of an attitude object influences which specific predisposition it evokes. This would offer one possible explanation for the main effects of meaning on the overall public evaluation of the object. One symbolic meaning might evoke a predisposition that promotes a positive evaluation (e.g., anti-Communism presumably helped boost support for the Korean War), while another might evoke a more damaging predisposition (focusing on "war" presumably was much less helpful).

At one level this proposition would seem to be at least uncontroversial and perhaps even obvious. Clearly, when very different attitude objects differ greatly in symbolic meaning, they will evoke different predispositions. For example, "busing" evokes racial attitudes more than it does liberal-conservative ideology, while the reverse holds for "national health insurance" (Sears et al., 1980). A subtler implication is that varying the symbolic meaning of a *given* attitude object may evoke a corresponding variety of predispositions. American funding of the Nicaraguan contras could have meant protection against a Soviet incursion into Central America and evoke anti-Communism. Or it could have meant "another Vietnam" and evoke antiwar attitudes.[3]

There are supportive data for this proposition. In a recent experimental study, Kinder and Sanders (1990) showed that attitudes toward affirmative action were better explained by individualistic values when affirmative action had been framed as reverse discrimination and by inegalitarian values when it had been framed as unfair advantage for minorities. In another study, Smith (1987) showed that attitudes toward helping the poor are explained better by support for redistributive actions of government than are attitudes toward welfare.

Yet the proposition that symbolic meaning influences which predisposition is evoked is certainly not universally true. Indeed, some of the very studies in which it profoundly affected the overall level of public evaluation of an attitude object showed no parallel influence on which predispositions were evoked. For example, attitudes toward both big government (widely opposed) and spending in specific service areas (widely supported) were explained by about the same mix of party identification, ideology, and racial attitudes (Sears & Citrin, 1985). Similarly, whites' attitudes in 1972 toward both "busing" (widely opposed) and federal government action to promote school integration (more evenly divided) were explained by their racial prejudices to about the same degree (Sears et al., 1979). Racial attitudes influenced opposition to affirmative action at the same high level regardless of whether it was framed as reverse discrimination or as unfair advantage (Kinder & Sanders, 1990). And racial attitudes explained evaluations of welfare and of helping the poor to the same degree (Smith, 1987).

Though inconsistent with the symbolic politics proposition in question, these latter findings fit comfortably with the traditional definition of attitudes as *generalized* dispositions to respond to an object. That view would hold that "busing" and "school integration" are so obviously racial that they evoke much the same racial attitudes despite their somewhat different symbolic meanings. In these cases the political rose is a political rose by any other name, and the public sniffs it out accordingly. By this alternate formulation, various symbolic meanings of a particular attitude object would trigger the same underlying attitudinal dimension but influence public evaluation of the object by falling at different points on that common dimension. For example, "school integration" and "busing" might both evoke the same underlying dimension of support for racial equality, but the latter may fall at a more negative point on that underlying dimension and thus be more negatively evaluated.

In short, there is evidence both for the traditional assumption that basic predispositions are quite generally evoked by a wide range of symbols and for the symbolic politics view that the meaning of an attitude object influences which specific predisposition is evoked. We turn next, therefore, to the conditions that determine one or the other outcome.

Symbols Evoking Predispositions

As a starting point, let us return to the "simple symbolic politics theory" that a particular predisposition will be evoked almost automatically in a template-matching fashion by an attitude object if object and predisposition are manifestly and consensually similar (Sears et al., 1986). For example, a black leader who forcefully advocates blacks' interests should readily elicit whites' long-standing racial attitudes, because the contents of both attitude object and predisposition are manifestly racial. At the other extreme, an attitude object should be quite unlikely to evoke a predisposition that is not at all similar to it; a proposal to ban offshore oil drilling is not likely to evoke racial attitudes.

However, this simple theory about the matching of specific symbols and predispositions does not explain why political symbols sometimes evoke predispositions that are quite dissimilar to them in a manifest semantic sense. For example, law and order issues (like defendants' rights, gun control, or permissive judges) frequently evoke racial attitudes, even though their manifest content is not explicitly racial (see Sears et al., 1980).

To take account of such cases, the simple symbolic politics principle has earlier been supplemented with the notion that attitude objects can evoke manifestly dissimilar predispositions when the individual has a cognitive schema linking the two (Sears et al., 1986). For example, many people have cognitive schemas linking crime particularly to blacks. Law-and-order issues tend to activate such schemas, thereby evoking underlying predispositions about race.

These cognitive schemas can be thought of as socially constructed cognitive links between symbol and predisposition. They are likely usually not to be wholly arbitrary, but to be based on real, though latent, connections. For example, while law-and-order issues usually do not explicitly refer to blacks, the higher crime rate among blacks and in predominantly black residential areas provides a reality basis for the linkage. As a result we refer below to ''latent'' links to describe underlying logical or reality-based linkages between symbol and predisposition that *can* be converted into cognitive schemas, whether or not they usually are.

Sometimes such latent links generate broadly consensual cognitive schemas. Then the symbol should elicit the predisposition just as automatically and universally as if the two were manifestly similar. ''Law and order'' issues presumably evoke whites' racial attitudes because so many people link them cognitively; that is, the cognitive schemas linking them are so ubiquitous. In such cases most everyone recognizes that the political rose is a political rose, and responds accordingly.

To summarize, this symbolic politics theorizing addresses the conditions under which an attitude object's symbolic meaning influences which predisposition it evokes. The key mediating factor is the nature of the cognitive match between symbolic meaning and predisposition. At one extreme, a predisposition should usually be evoked quite automatically by (1) a manifestly similar attitude object or by (2) an attitude object that is similar only at a latent level but linked to it by a consensual schema. At the other extreme, (3) a predisposition is unlikely to be evoked if it is neither manifestly similar to the attitude object nor similar to it at a latent level and linked schematically to it.

A two-dimensional taxonomy incorporating these possibilities, with examples, is presented as table 9.1. Along one dimension, the content of symbol and predisposition can be similar at a manifest semantic level, at a latent level, or neither. The other dimension focuses on the degree of social consensus about a symbol-predisposition linkage: Almost everyone may possess a given linking schema, or not (in which case the linking schemas may be much more diverse, or limited to the particularly well informed, or indeed may be absent altogether). Presumably both dimensions are continuous rather than categorical, but this simplified table perhaps conveys the essence of the idea.

The manifest-consensual, latent-consensual, and neither-nonconsensual

TABLE 9.1   Possible bases for cognitive links between political symbols and predispositions

Social Consensus on Linkage	Semantic Similarity of Symbol and Predisposition		
	Manifest Similarity	**Latent Similarity Only**	**Neither Manifest nor Latent Similarity**
Consensual	Obviously similar (black candidate/racial attitudes)	Most people have some reality-based linking schema (law and order/racial attitudes)	Pervasive schemas based on little reality drought/belief in efficacy of rain dances)
Nonconsensual	Diversity of schemas linked to different manifest features of object (Gen. Colin Powell/militarist vs. racial attitudes)	Diversity of linking schemas (abortion/pro-life vs. pro-choice attitudes)	Linkage unlikely in absence of either reality basis or social norm

Note: Entries specify linkage, with example in parentheses (political symbol/predisposition).

cells, and the examples provided of them in table 9.1 have already been discussed above. But just as central to our analysis is the latent, nonconsensual cell, in which the symbol-predisposition link has a reality basis but is not perceived in the same fashion by everyone. An example is the case of abortion: Some respond to it as a pro-life issue, bringing to bear attitudes that revolve around murder, while others respond to it as a pro-choice issue, bringing to bear attitudes about freedom of choice and civil liberties generally.[4]

Our formulation assumes that each attitude object has a constant symbolic meaning. But it can also help predict when the various symbolic meanings of a particular object will elicit different predispositions. Such "change of meaning" effects should not occur with manifest and/or consensual symbol-predisposition similarity, because then the symbol should evoke the relevant predisposition no matter how it is presented (as in the example of both "busing" and "school integration" eliciting racial attitudes). Change of meaning effects should instead be most likely to occur with latent similarity and nonconsensual linkages. In such cases, people vary in the meaning they ascribe to the political symbol, and consequently in the predisposition(s) to which they link it. Forcefully framing the issue in terms of a particular symbolic meaning could then produce consensus on its meaning (even if only momentarily), along with accompanying consensual schemas linking it to the appropriate predisposition.

The symbolic politics view yields four specific hypotheses to this point, then: (1) Self-interest and personal experience are unlikely to influence evaluations of the attitude object very strongly, but both (2) the symbolic meaning of an attitude object, and (3) basic predispositions should have significant effects on such evaluations. (4) The symbolic meaning of the object should influence the evocation of predispositions with latent, nonconsensual similarity to the object, but not of those that match its manifest and/or consensual meaning (since they should be elicited no matter how the object is framed) or those wholly dissimilar from the object (since they are unlikely to be elicited in any case).

Bilingual Education and Symbolic Politics

A symbolic politics theory should be particularly apt for understanding public response to language conflicts. It typically views the mass public as responding to political conflicts more in terms of such symbolic tender as values and status than in terms of practical and material interests (e.g., Sears et al., 1980). Much evidence points to the symbolic role of language in both the political and the social arenas as in controversies over the official status of one language versus another (Horowitz, 1985). There are other interpretations of such conflicts, to which we will return, but the symbolic politics alternative is one of the more plausible.

Bilingual education is likely to vary considerably in symbolic meaning, because there are three quite different generic types of bilingual programs. "Cultural maintenance" programs stress the development of oral and literacy skills in English, while also maintaining these skills in the mother tongue. "Transitional" programs use the native language as a medium of instruction only until sufficient English is learned to teach solely in the latter. "English as a second language" (ESL) programs use little native language, basically providing intensive instruction (immersion) in English. Even though most programs as actually implemented are mixtures of these pure types, the political controversy has revolved more around the generic types than around the mixed applications. Not surprisingly, the maintenance version has generated the most controversy, though it has in fact been implemented the least frequently (Hakuta, 1986).

The predispositions evoked by the three types of programs might well be expected to differ considerably. The cultural maintenance version, which emphasizes preservation of foreign languages over the "melting pot," should be especially likely to evoke anti-minority attitudes. On the other hand, the ESL version, seemingly a simple educational device like spelling tests, chemistry labs, or foreign language instruction, would seem more likely to evoke attitudes toward educational priorities (particularly concerning foreign language instruction). This difference might reasonably be expected to make ESL more favorably evaluated, on the average.

On the other hand, self-interest and personal experience ought, at least in principle, to be relevant to non-Hispanics' attitudes about bilingual education. The most direct personal stake in it would presumably be held by parents with school-age children who might be personally affected by bilingual education programs, who may be concerned that such programs shift resources away from their own children directly or indirectly, and/or by parents with children in schools with significant numbers of Hispanics who might be concerned that their children's English will deteriorate by mixing with native Spanish speakers who are taught partly in Spanish. Thus, the most self-interested respondents would be parents with children in public schools, especially in heavily Hispanic schools, and those with children who have been or are taking Spanish or are in a bilingual education program.

A second source of egocentric concerns might be direct personal experience with bilingualism. Experience with another language either through contact with non-English-speaking family members, in foreign language classes, or by traveling in foreign countries may lessen fears about the proliferation of inaccessible languages and so promote support for bilingual education. Direct personal experience with bilingualism was assessed in three ways: familial language background, based on having spoken another language as a child or having had parents who did; current bilingual proficiency, assessed with four items on oral and literacy skills in a second language, which yielded an additive scale (alpha $= .83$); and Spanish familiarity, based on having spoken Spanish as a child, having had Spanish-speaking parents, or currently speaking some Spanish.

Respondents living in Hispanic areas were also more likely to have direct experience with the issue. Hispanic context was measured objectively with the actual concentration of Hispanics in the respondent's county (1980 census) and subjectively with perceived neighborhood concentration and perceptions about trends in this concentration. A composite index of Hispanic context was constructed by standardizing and additively combining the objective and combined subjective indicators ($r = .51, p < .01$).

SAMPLES

The main data base was a survey of a national U.S. probability sample consisting of 1,170 interviews of non-Hispanics. The screening question was ''What do you consider your main ethnic group or nationality to be?'' This national sample covered the forty-eight-state continental United States. It was stratified by census region, within census region by state, and within state by metropolitan and nonmetropolitan areas. The interviews were apportioned to subareas according to the 1980 census count of households (proportionate to size of household). The interviewing was done by Market Opinion Research by telephone during the summer of 1983.

Bilingual education is concerned more with Spanish-speaking than with other non-English-speaking children, as it happens. Hispanics are mostly concentrated in a few areas of the nation. To ensure a sufficiently large subsample of respondents from areas with heavier Hispanic populations, oversamples of one hundred households each were drawn from (a) Miami, Florida (Dade County); (b) Los Angeles and San Diego counties, California; (c) New York City; (d) San Antonio, Texas (Bexar, Guadelope, and Comal counties). According to the census data, the oversampled counties averaged 26.3 percent Hispanic in 1980 compared to 6.4 percent nationally.[5]

Refusal rates were around 35 percent (651 refusals), and there were 115 terminations before 1,570 completed interviews were obtained. The resulting sample was stratified by sex, making it evenly divided between men (N - 786) and women (N - 784). As is usual with telephone surveys of political opinion, the sample was most demographically skewed in terms of educational level. Forty-four percent had either graduated from or completed some college, whereas the comparable 1985 census figure for non-Hispanic adults over twenty-five years of age was 33 percent. However, it closely matched census figures in household income, occupation, heads of household, age, marital status, having children at home, and racial composition (see Cardoza, Huddy, & Sears, 1984, for the details).

The non-Hispanic public was initially generally positive toward bilingual education. On every item, a majority of those expressing an opinion were favorable. For purposes of later analysis, an additive seven-item scale of support was constructed, with a potential range of $+/-$ 10.25. Each item, and therefore the scale as a whole, had a natural midpoint. The overall mean of $+2.29$ (SD = 5.08) thus reflected majority support for bilingual education, on the average.

The overall level of self-interest in the issue was not very great. Few parents in the national sample had children directly in schools with large Hispanic enrollments (11 percent in mostly Hispanic schools) or actually in bilingual education programs (12 percent). Furthermore, Hispanics were still largely absent from the daily lives of most non-Hispanics. Almost three-quarters of the national sample lived in counties with fewer than 5 percent Hispanics; about two-thirds lived in neighborhoods with at most ''a few'' Hispanics, whose ranks were not expanding. Relatively few non-Hispanics had any familiarity with Spanish (11 percent), though experiences with other language were more common. Almost half the national sample had some form of personal experience with bilingualism: 14 percent had spoken a second language as a child, 32 percent had parents who spoke another language, 24 percent were currently proficient, even if minimally, in a language other than English.

Personal Experience

The first hypothesis was that personal experiences with bilingual education, Hispanic context, personal monolingualism, and ignorance of Spanish would not be strongly related to opposition to bilingual education. At a simple bivariate level, they indeed had only weak effects. Only two personal experience variables had significant effects, and they were in opposite directions. Parents of children in bilingual programs supported them significantly more than did parents whose children have had no such direct experiences ($t(574) = -2.09$, $p < .05$), while Hispanic context was associated with significantly greater opposition to bilingual education (for objective context, $r = .14$; subjective, $r = .13$). Knowledge of Spanish and general bilingualism (either in childhood or in terms of current proficiency) were not significantly associated with support for bilingual education.

All told, these effects of self-interest and personal experience do not go far in explaining opposition to bilingual education. A regression equation considering all these variables (using the full sample) yields significant effects for Hispanic context, knowledge of Spanish, and having a child in a bilingual education program, but accounts for only 3.5 percent of the total variance. There is little evidence of a special threat experienced by parents. In fact, the strongest supporters of bilingual education are parents with children in bilingual programs.[6] In short, self-interest and direct personal experience play a relatively minor role in fueling opposition to bilingual education in either bivariate or multivariate analyses.

Symbolic Meaning

The second hypothesis was that attitudes toward bilingual education would be influenced by its symbolic meaning. The initial, spontaneous symbolic meaning of bilingual education was determined by answers to two open-ended questions: "What is your impression of what bilingual education is?" and "What language other than English comes to mind when you think of bilingual education?" On the first question, a third of the sample described it in approximately accurate terms, divided among the various types of bilingual education in current use: "Teaching foreign students in their own language" (6 percent) was considered an accurate description of the goal of linguistic maintenance; "Teaching in two languages" (16 percent) could refer either to the maintenance or transitional approaches (although it could be confused with foreign language instruction; responses included statements such as "Two languages used in the classroom" or "The teacher speaks two languages"); and teaching English to foreign students (9 percent) resembled the ESL approach. Another third were substantially inaccurate, giving vague references to multiple languages, such as bilingualism in general (18 percent) or general foreign language instruction (21 percent). And the final 29 percent were unable to describe it at all. The overwhelming majority (81 percent) accurately cited Spanish as the language other than English most likely to be involved.

In short, "bilingual education" has a variety of symbolic meanings in the non-Hispanic public. Its manifest, consensual meaning is that it concerns instruction in a foreign language, primarily Spanish; almost all perceive it in those minimal terms. Its latent meaning, perceived by a small subset of the sample, is that it serves to maintain Hispanic children's own language and culture by teaching them in Spanish as well as English. This, of course, comes closer to the core of the political debate.

The symbolic meaning of bilingual education did influence opposition to it. Considering spontaneous meaning first, the most negative opinions were held, as expected, by those perceiving it as involving the cultural maintenance of Spanish. The distinctions among different symbolic meanings significantly affected level of support, according to a one-way analysis of variance (based on the national sample and oversample combined: $F[5, 1351] = 13.58$, $p < .01$). Also, associating it with Spanish, as most did, significantly reduced support ($t [1391] = 3.23; p < .01$).

To experimentally manipulate symbolic meaning, respondents were randomly assigned to hearing a description of one of three versions of bilingual education. In abbreviated form, they were as follows (the labels were not provided): (1) Cultural maintenance: Both English- and Spanish-speaking students would be taught all their basic subjects (reading, math, and science) in both languages, half of the time in English and half in Spanish. (2) Transitional: Spanish-speaking students would be taught their basic subjects in Spanish; then as their English improved, they would be taught less in Spanish; and finally they would switch to a regular classroom and be taught in English. (3) ESL: All students would be taught all basic subjects in English, with additional special English-language training for Spanish-speaking students.

Immediately following this vignette they were asked a series of five items about the effects of this plan, along with two questions on the likelihood of the respondent's enrolling his or her children in the program and paying more taxes to support it, yielding a seven-item additive scale. The cultural maintenance plan was liked significantly less than the other two ($F [2, 1551] = 19.23, p < .01$).

There is majority support for bilingual education programs in the non-Hispanic public, then. But programs that intend the maintenance of native cultures and languages are opposed or at best supported weakly. Those intended to teach foreign-born children to use English receive more support, even if they require some instruction in the native language.

PREDISPOSITIONS

We proposed three possible theories about the predispositional origins of opposition to bilingual education, variously emphasizing racial and ethnic biases, basic values and political orientations with no manifest racial or ethnic content, or attitudes about educational priorities.

Three measures of attitudes toward minority groups were used: a *symbolic racism* scale, measuring generalized antagonism toward minorities' demands for special treatment; an *anti-Hispanic* evaluation scale, based on feeling thermometers concerning Mexican-Americans, Cubans, and Puerto Ricans; and a four-item *nationalism* scale focused on attitudes toward the United States and immigration policy.[7]

The strongest single predictor of opposition to bilingual education is symbolic racism ($r = .37$, beta $= .34$, $p < .001$), as shown in table 9.2 (columns 1 and 2).[8] Nationalism also contributed significantly to opposition

TABLE 9.2   Opposition to bilingual education as a function of predispositions

	Bivariate Correlation	Standardized Regression Coefficients			
	1	**2**	**3**	**4**	**5**
Symbolic Predispositions					
Racial					
Symbolic racism	.37	.34**	.35**	.25**	.23**
Anti-Hispanics	.18	.07**	.12**	.06*	.02
Anti-blacks	.13		−.08*		
Nationalism	.21	.10**	.10**	.07**	.06**
Nonracial					
Inegalitarian values	.23			.06*	.05*
Hard-work values	.14			.01	.00
Party identification	.14			.00	.02
Ideology	.20			.07**	.06**
Spending Priorities					
Government spending	.27			.09**	.09**
Educational spending					
Basics	.01			−.01	−.03
Frills	.20			.06*	.02
Foreign language	.35				.27**
R²		.168	.171	.192	.259

Note: The dependent variable is premanipulation opposition to bilingual education. Entries in columns 2–5 are standardized regression coefficients where each column is a separate regression equation. All predictors are coded so that conservative position is high.
* $p<.05$
** $p<.001$

to bilingual education, though its effects were considerably weaker (note also that its scale reliability, .48, is considerably lower). Negative affect toward Hispanics, the minority group most widely perceived as demanding bilingual education, had a significant effect beyond the more generalized resentments captured in symbolic racism. And there was no comparable effect of anti-black affect (see column 3).[9] As a set, the first three of these racial attitudes accounted for a substantial 16.8 percent of the variance.

Four other symbolic predispositions are generally relevant to such political issues but have no manifest racial or ethnic content: *inegalitarian values, hard-work values, party identification,* and *political ideology.* All had significant correlations with opposition to bilingual education and both inegalitarian values and political ideology continued to have significant effects with other variables controlled (see table 9.2, column 4). However, symbolic racism remains by some distance the most powerful of the lot, and including these nonracial symbolic predispositions in the equation reduces its effects very little.

Preferences about government spending on domestic programs in particular program areas (health, welfare, etc.) are not generally assumed to have the strength and persistence of these symbolic predispositions, but are fairly strongly correlated with them and are central to contemporary partisan debate, and so should be considered in the same context. Opposition to government spending was associated with opposition to bilingual education ($r = .27$) and had a significant effect with all symbolic predispositions controlled (table 9.2, column 4). However, taken as a set, these five basic nonracial orientations did not have powerful effects relative to those of racial attitudes.

The final category concerns more proximal preferences concerning specific educational programs. Spending on math and science was supported most, and the arts (music, art, drama) and social studies, the least. On the basis of a factor analysis, we divided these into two scales: "basics" (math, science) and "frills" (the arts, social studies). As shown in table 9.2 (columns 4 and 5), bilingual education receives most opposition from those who would cut school spending on "frills" (though the value placed upon "basics" does not have a significant effect). Finally, placing a low priority on foreign language instruction strongly influenced opposition to bilingual education ($r = .35$, beta $= .27$).[10]

To summarize, opposition to bilingual education comes especially from anti-minority and anti-immigrant attitudes, as well as from more proximal preferences about educational priorities (particularly foreign language instruction). The former are dominated by symbolic racism, partly representing antagonism toward the demands of minorities in general. But it also draws opposition from antagonisms specific to the group making the demands in question (here, Hispanics). In both respects, racial attitudes are central to the process.

MATCHING PREDISPOSITIONS TO
SYMBOLIC MEANING

The fourth hypothesis, and the central feature of the study, was that the symbolic meaning of bilingual education would affect which symbolic predispositions it evoked. We begin by applying the classification of symbol-predisposition matches presented in table 9.1. There are four key categories.

The manifest content of bilingual education is concerned with foreign languages and education, and it is widely perceived as such, as seen earlier. So it would be most manifestly similar to attitudes toward foreign language instruction, which would therefore be evoked equally regardless of symbolic meaning.

Its latent content contains whatever attributes it actually possesses that are not included in its manifest content. Some of these would be consensual, appearing in the spontaneous perceptions of a majority of the public. The clearest examples are that it most often involves Spanish, and that teaching foreign languages is an educational "frill" relative to science and the "three R's" (as indicated in the spending priorities mentioned earlier). The relevant predispositions would be anti-Hispanic affect and attitudes toward spending on such frills, respectively. They too should be evoked equally regardless of symbolic meaning.

The latent but nonconsensual content consists of its real attributes not contained in its manifest content but appearing in the perceptions of discernible minorities of the public. The cultural maintenance version is the most prominent case in point: It is not part of the manifest content of bilingual education, yet is used in the classroom, is central in elite debates, and appears as a clearly articulated view of the issue in a small minority of the mass public. This depicts bilingual education as a costly liberal-Democratic social program (which would link it to ideology, party identification, and opposition to government spending) instituted in direct response to minorities' and immigrants' demands for special treatment of their children (linking it to symbolic racism and nationalism). It is based on the assumption that these children's backgrounds have disadvantaged them relative to majority children and that these children thus require otherwise unearned special help (linking it to inegalitarian and hard-work values).

Finally, some predispositions are linked to neither the manifest nor the latent meaning of the issue by even a significant subset of the public. Most were not assessed in this study, for obvious reasons. But of those that were, spending on the "basics" would seem to have the least bearing; while it could conceivably be perceived as negatively impacted by spending on bilingual education, the general public generally seems indifferent to trade-offs among spending priorities or between taxes and spending (see Sears & Citrin, 1985). It would be unlikely to be evoked by any symbolic meaning.

These hypotheses about the effects of symbol-predisposition similarity are best tested with simple bivariate correlations, since our predictors have nontrivial intercorrelations, and multivariate analyses can suppress real bivariate relationships. The data are generally confirmatory, as shown in table 9.3. The symbolic meaning of bilingual education had a major effect on the evocation of predispositions with only latent, nonconsensual similarity to it: racial attitudes, partisan preferences, and traditional social values. They correlated, on the average, .25 with opposition to cultural maintenance but only .08 with opposition to ESL. The transitional version most resembles cultural maintenance: These predispositions correlated, on the average, .23 with opposition to it.

To evaluate the significance of these differences, we carried out a series of two-way analyses of variance, with the appropriate predisposition (median

TABLE 9.3   Manifest and latent similarity: Bivariate correlations of predispositions with opposition to bilingual education

	Manipulated Symbolic Meaning		
	Cultural Maintenance	Transitional	ESL
	1	2	3
Manifest Similarity			
Foreign language spending	.24	.23	.22
Spending on "frills"	.17	.13	.12
Latent Similarity/Consensual			
Anti-Hispanic affect	.16	.22	.21
Average	.19	.19	.18
Latent Similarity/Nonconsensual			
Symbolic racism	.40	.40	.22
Nationalism	.19	.22	.09
Ideology	.21	.19	.06
Party identification	.20	.08	.00
Government spending	.33	.26	.07
Inegalitarian values	.30	.32	.22
Hard-work values	.10	.12	-.06
Average	.25	.23	.08
Neither Manifest nor Latent Similarity			
Spending on "basics"	.02	.04	.00

Note: Predispositions are keyed such that positive correlations reflect more opposition to bilingual education among conservatives.

split) and experimental condition as independent variables. The interactions were the critical terms: The latent, nonconsensual predispositions should affect opposition to bilingual education in the maintenance condition but not in ESL. And these interactions were all statistically significant or close to it.[11] These latent, nonconsensually similar predispositions, not incidentally, are at the core of the political debate over bilingual education, emphasizing the political importance of its symbolic meaning.

In contrast, the manifest or latent-consensual predispositions were evoked by all symbolic meanings at about the same level, as shown in table 9.3. Spending on foreign language instruction, spending on educational frills, and anti-Hispanic affect yielded average correlations of .19, .19, and .18 across the three conditions, respectively. And the only predisposition irrelevant to bilingual education, spending on "basics," yielded null correlations in all conditions. As would be expected, then, the interactions of condition by these four predispositions were all at chance levels: The largest F-value was 1.03.

DISCUSSION

This study was intended to examine the origins of public opinion about contemporary language conflicts as a vehicle for extending the symbolic politics approach. There were four key findings:

1. Self-interest and personal experience had relatively minor effects upon opposition to bilingual education. Non-Hispanics' opposition to it is not driven to a great extent by personal threats, either to themselves or to their children.
2. The symbolic meaning of the attitude object, bilingual education, was shown to influence evaluations of it, with cultural maintenance being opposed more than ESL. This held for both spontaneous and experimentally manipulated symbolic meaning.
3. Predispositions influenced evaluations of the attitude object. The most powerful were racial attitudes, especially symbolic racism, reflecting resentment of special treatment for minorities. This was supplemented by antagonism toward the most centrally involved minority groups, Hispanics and immigrants, and educational priorities, especially regarding foreign language instruction. Lesser but still significant effects were produced by other presumably race-neutral predispositions, such as general political conservatism, inegalitarian values, and opposition to government spending.
4. Symbolic meaning influenced which predispositions were evoked. We proposed that symbol-predisposition similarity was the key variable determining which predisposition would be evoked by a particular symbolic meaning. Accordingly, we developed a two-dimensional clas-

sification of symbol/predisposition similarities, distinguishing manifest and latent similarity, either of which could be broadly consensual throughout the population or not. Symbolic meaning most affected the evocation of predispositions linked to the issue in latent but nonconsensual fashion (such as symbolic racism, ideology, and opposition to government spending). All had much larger effects on attitudes toward cultural maintenance than on attitudes toward ESL. Manifestly and/or consensually similar predispositions (such as anti-Hispanic affect and opposition to foreign language instruction) had significant effects, but these were constant across symbolic meanings, while the one irrelevant predisposition, spending on educational "basics," had null effects in all cases.

We might note that several other studies have also found variations in symbolic meaning to influence the impact of diverse predispositions on political attitudes, though they have not explicitly used a symbolic politics framework: Kinder and Sanders (1990), regarding affirmative action; Smith (1987), regarding welfare; and Krosnick and Kinder (1990), regarding Reagan support. In analogous fashion, although not involving the evocation of attitudinal predispositions, Sears and Lau (1983) found that experimentally heightening the salience of one's self-interest increased its impact over policy and performance evaluations, and Iyengar and Kinder (1987) found that heightening the salience of particular issue areas gave them more clout over presidential performance evaluations.

Additional evidence for the central role of cognitive similarity in determining the strength of symbolic meaning effects has emerged as an incidental by-product of other studies conducted for other purposes. Sears and Lau (1983) found that varying the salience of different dimensions of self-interest affected only the impact of cognitively relevant dimensions of self-interest, and only on cognitively relevant dependent variables. Other recent studies also indicate that symbolic meaning effects are limited to cognitively relevant predictors (Kinder & Sanders, 1990) and to cognitively relevant dependent variables (Krosnick & Kinder, 1990).

These findings provide some insight into the political conditions under which manipulation of the public is most likely to occur. Such efforts should be at least fruitful on stimuli that have a clear, unambiguous, and consensual meaning. It has proven difficult, for example, to change the meaning of busing, because it is so widely viewed as a racial issue. On the other hand, manipulation should be easier on issues or candidates that lack consensual or manifest symbolism. When a new candidate, such as Michael Dukakis, comes onto the national political scene, he is something of a black box, whose profile can be molded to elicit either positive or negative underlying predispositions—though presumably within some constraints based on reality.

Presumably, controlling the public agenda is required in order to control

the symbolic meaning of an attitude object. Such control is politically consequential both in influencing overall public support for the object and in
influencing which predisposition it evokes. By manipulating the meaning of
an issue like crime, for example, as the Republican campaign did with the
"revolving door" commercials in 1988 (and the "Willie Horton" circulars),
one could manipulate the role of a powerful and damaging predisposition such
as racism. Similarly, regimes presumably can manipulate national symbols to
evoke loyalty and patriotism (Edelman, 1971; Elder & Cobb, 1983). Perhaps
most interesting are situations in which issues (or candidates) have multiple
latent meanings with no clear-cut consensus on them. Then the issue is up for
grabs, with public response dependent on the "spin" placed on it.

While we have found much support for our hypotheses about the
conditions under which predispositions are matched to political symbols,
some important gaps should be noted. We do not have a rigorous definition of
semantic similarity, for example. Nor do we have direct evidence about the
underlying process by which predispositions are evoked. Also, we have used
the concept of "schema" to explain matches based on latent similarity. There
are persuasive criticisms of this concept, such as that schemas are usually
inferred rather than measured directly, and that the schema concept is merely
"old wine in new bottles" (see Lau & Sears, 1986). However, we feel that it
offers some precision that the older and more general concepts "attitude" and
"belief system" do not, if it is applied with some circumspection and respect
for its origins and proper role. Nevertheless, we have more than a little
sympathy with such critiques and feel that fully persuasive demonstrations of
its unique value in political behavior research remain for the future.

Symbolic racism had somewhat broader effects than expected from our
symbolic politics theorizing, playing a central role even in response to ESL
(when race and ethnicity should not have been very salient). This finding
parallels those from two other studies: Racial attitudes had strong and constant
effects on evaluations of affirmative action and welfare, no matter what their
symbolic meaning (Kinder & Sanders, 1990; Smith, 1987). Whatever the
limitations of the general public in understanding the exact nature of these
issues, then, the latent linkage between their symbolic meaning and racial
attitudes is apparently sufficiently widely understood that no manifest racial
content or unusually rich cognition has been required for the linkage to be
made. And the same has evidently been true even for issues with only latent
racial content, such as crime (Sears et al., 1980) and tax cuts (Sears & Citrin,
1985).

There can be debate over the exact interpretation of the measures of
racial attitudes used in these studies and of their effects. But we would argue
that the controls on attitudes with no manifest racial content (as imposed here
in table 9.2, and analogously in the other studies cited) indicate a central role
for antagonisms specifically toward minorities (also see Sears & Kosterman,

1991).[12] This intimate relationship of anti-minority attitudes to the most basic and general of Americans' political attitudes and values, even those with no manifest racial or ethnic content, is a characteristic feature of American political life. It means that many political disputes about domestic policy will sooner or later have a racial tinge.

But why does race intrude so broadly into Americans' political attitudes? Perhaps because it has some special ability to produce consensual "code words." As a political issue it fits almost ideally the criteria for generating long-standing and powerful predispositions: For instance, it has a long political history; it has recurrently been on the public agenda; racial divisions are relatively simple, cognitively; and so on (see Sears, 1983). It is possible, then, that the racial attitudes of white Americans are so strongly learned that they intrude into issues with only latent racial content, even when these are framed in nonracial fashion.

Finally, what insight does this give us into language conflicts in general? These certainly are common enough in the world today, being at the center of many ethnic and even international conflicts. Language conflicts may be largely symbolic, without much tangible consequence for the individual's quality of life. As indicated above, these symbolic conflicts may in turn derive from racial and ethnic bias or from conflicts of basic values or ideology with little racial or ethnic content. We here certainly find evidence for the former, along with some lesser evidence of the latter. An equally important lesson, perhaps, is that the impact of such considerations depends in part on the symbolism of the issue, which can vary. The issue seems to be considerably more divisive when it elicits racial and ethnic attitudes.

Alternatively, language may be real coin in struggles for economic and social dominance between groups in competition for scarce resources. These might be directly relevant to the individual's self-interest or reflect conflict over real group interests. However, our data suggest that bilingual education is largely a symbolic issue to non-Hispanics, scarcely impinging on the realities of their daily lives. In this sense it resembles legislation to make English the official language of a city, a state, or the nation, which has usually proven to have few practical consequences even when enacted (though of course the same would not hold for some other language legislation, such as that regulating the use of English and French in Canada). We also find some evidence in other analyses (see Huddy & Sears, 1989) for a role of group conflict, but even that may be more symbolic than based on the realities of personal life and self-interest (Sears & Kinder, 1985). Sorting out that contrast remains as a challenge for the future.

In the meantime, as Citrin et al. (1990) have noted, the elite debate in the United States over language proceeds in largely symbolic terms, with the opponents of multilingualism framing the issue as a defense of American identity and the proponents arguing practical educational effects and denouncing racism and xenophobia. The present data suggest that if language conflicts are generally framed in this manner, the opponents are likely to hold the winning hand with the mass public.

APPENDIX: CONSTRUCTION OF SCALES

In general, scales were constructed by standardizing and summing the items given below, with interitem correlations given in parentheses.

Racial Attitudes

1. *Symbolic racism* (alpha = .64).
2. *Nationalism* (alpha = .48): The United States has the best government in the world (.27).* I think of myself as a citizen of the world, rather than a citizen of the United States (.28).* The government's immigration policy should be more open and less selective. (.33).* Immigrants to this country should be prepared to adopt the American way of life (.24).*
3. *Anti-Hispanic affect* (alpha = .90): Feeling thermometers on Cubans (.83); Mexican Americans (.72); Puerto Ricans (.87).

Nonracial Attitudes

1. *Inegalitarian values* (alpha = .50): If people were treated more equally in this country, we would have fewer problems.* Our society should do whatever it can to make sure that everyone has an equal opportunity to succeed.*
2. *Hard-work values* (alpha = .37): A lot of people don't get ahead because they simply don't work hard enough.* Hard work offers little guarantee of success.*

Spending

1. *Government services* (alpha = .72): Government spending on: health and medical services (.48); Social Security (.49); unemployment compensation (.56); welfare (.48).
2. *Education: basics* (alpha = .56): Spending on local school programs, math, science.
3. *Education: frills* (alpha = .33): Spending on music, art, drama, social studies.
4. *Education: foreign language* (alpha = .60): Spending on foreign language instruction; feeling about foreign language education.*

Attitudes toward Bilingual Education

1. *Premanipulation* (alpha = .83): Feeling about bilingual education? (.70)*. Spending on bilingual education (.63). Perceived effects of bilingual education: helps non-English-speaking students fit into American way of life (.69)*; teaches them to speak English (.43)*; increases their chances of finding jobs (.58)*; gives them quality education (.62)*; fewer resources available for English-speaking students (.34)*.
2. *Postmanipulation* (alpha = .84): The effects of *this plan*: fit into American way of life (.72)*; speak English (.47)*; find jobs (.63)*; quality education (.62)*; resources for English-speaking students (.42).* If this plan was introduced and you had children in the local schools, how likely would you be to enroll them in this program (.61)? Would you favor the adoption of this plan if it meant you had to pay more taxes? (.58).

NOTES

The research was supported by the National Institute of Education, and Cooperative Agreement 00-CA-80-0001. Thanks are due to Desdemona Cardoza for her collaborative assistance; to Amado Padilla, the National Center for Bilingual Education, and the Center for Advanced Study in the Behavioral Sciences for the provision of support services; and to Lawrence Bobo, Jack Citrin, Tom Jessor, Rick Kosterman, Deborah J. Stipek, and John Zaller for their helpful comments. Earlier versions of this paper were presented at the annual meetings of the American Psychological Association, New York City, 1 September 1987, and the American Political Science Association, Chicago, 4 September 1987. This paper was completed while the first author was a fellow of the John Simon Guggenheim Foundation and a fellow at the Center for Advanced Study in the Behavioral Sciences. We are grateful for financial support provided by the Guggenheim Foundation and by National Science Foundation grant #BNS87-00864.

1. Opposition to bilingual education might also derive from non-Hispanic parents' or taxpayers' perceptions of group conflict with Hispanics or immigrants. Both are addressed in a companion paper (Huddy & Sears, 1989).
2. It should be emphasized that both the timing of initial acquisition of these predispositions and the degree of their persistence over the life span are usually now treated as variables dependent on other factors, in contrast to the simple primacy-and-persistence assumptions made by early investigators (see Alwin & Krosnick, 1991; Sears, 1975, 1983).
3. Asch made the point many years ago that attitude change may result from "a change in the object of judgment, rather than in the judgment of the object" (Asch, 1940, 458).

* Four-point agree-disagree scale

4. Two cases in table 9.1 peripheral to our present concerns need be discussed only briefly. Sometimes an attitude object has multiple attributes, some of which link to one predisposition and some to another. For example, General Colin Powell is manifestly a military man, almost invariably depicted in uniform, and black. Some respond to him in terms of the former, and others in terms of the latter. And sometimes there are consensual (or at least locally consensual) links even in the absence of either manifest or reality-based latent connections; e.g., among supporters of Lyndon LaRouche, beliefs that Queen Elizabeth is a drug kingpin; beliefs in the Christian version of God in medieval Europe; or rival beliefs in national, ethnic, or tribal superiority.

5. The effects of variations in the local concentration of Hispanics are considered elsewhere in connection with more extensive tests of self-interest and group-interest theories (see Huddy & Sears, 1989).

6. Without going into detail, other analyses suggest this is not a self-selection effect (see Huddy & Sears, 1989).

7. The symbolic racism scale had an alpha of .64. It was based on three items (item-total correlations are shown in parentheses): [Should] the government in Washington make every effort to improve the social and economic position of minority groups, even if it means giving them special consideration, [or] not make any special effort to help minorities because they should help themselves? (.51); How much special consideration is being given to racial minorities right now? Too much . . . too little . . . (.51); Special measures should be taken to insure that the same percentage of Hispanics as other groups are admitted to college (reversed; .36).

8. The concept of symbolic racism has aroused some controversy (see Bobo, 1988; Kinder, 1986; Sears, 1988; Sniderman & Tetlock, 1986), and as such, it bears closer examination. It originally (see Kinder & Sears, 1981; Sears & McConahay, 1973) was defined in terms of generalized resentments about demands for special treatment by minorities and opposition to such special treatment. Two of our symbolic racism items fit the general definition well, asking about "special consideration" and making a "special effort to help" minority groups and racial minorities. The third item fits it less well, focusing on a specific policy (college admission quotas) and on Hispanics in particular rather than on minorities in general. Nevertheless, the three items all had about the same effect on opposition to bilingual education when individually substituted for the full symbolic racism scale in the basic regression equation shown in table 9.2 (column 2). The standardized coefficients were .20, .26, and .28, respectively.

9. Indeed, the sign actually reverses. This no doubt is an artifact of the collinearity of the black thermometer with the three Hispanic thermometers; the correlations range from .62 to .65.

10. These effects of predispositions are in general not compromised by correlates with demographic variables. When considered alone, the latter accounted for 5.8 percent of the total variance, and only age continued to have a significant effect (beta = −.13) when all predispositions were added to the equation.

11. For symbolic racism, $F = 4.69$, 2/1547 df, $p < .001$; nationalism, $F = 2.28$, 2/1541 df, $p < .11$; ideology, $F = 3.81$, 2/1386 df, $p < .03$; government spending, $F = 11.34$, 2/1536 df, $p < .0001$; party identification, $F = 5.32$,

2/1480 df, $p < .005$; inegalitarian values, $F = 3.68$, 2/1476 df, $p < .03$; and hard-work values, $F = 2.27$, 2/1491 df, $p < .11$.

12. The use of this analytic strategy to document a racial component in attitudes toward law and order (Sears et al., 1980) and toward California tax revolt (Sears & Citrin, 1985, 169) was apparently overlooked in some critiques (see Sniderman & Tetlock, 1986, 134; see also Kinder, 1986, 160).

10 Individual Versus Group Identification as a Factor in Intergroup Racial Conflict

James M. Jones and Kim T. Morris

Interracial conflict in the United States is as old as the country itself. In spite of this fact, the contemporary problems of racial conflict appear surprising to many observers. It is believed by some that racial conflict reached its height in the 1960s. With the passage of the Civil Rights Act of 1964 and the Voting Rights Act of 1965, the implementation of affirmative action programs as a means of implementing the Equal Employment Opportunity Commission (EEOC) mandate, and the widespread efforts to desegregate schools, neighborhoods, and corporate boardrooms, it was only a matter of time until racial strife would be a thing of the past.

It is the viewpoint of this chapter that the decline in racial strife anticipated by the events of the 1960s was out of proportion to the realities of what was accomplished by the gains represented by the civil rights legislation. Moreover, this legislation and the related "revolutions" of blacks and students suggested both greater change than really occurred and greater commonality of purpose than was the case. Perhaps most importantly, the anticipated diminution of racial conflict failed to recognize the deep-seated cultural aspects of the conflict that the legislation failed to address.

One important way in which one might understand the relative lack of success of the 1960 changes is to consider the context of the time. The fact that blacks could not eat or sleep or drink where they wanted, go to school and be educated where they wanted, even vote without unfair restrictions and intimidations, clearly showed that blacks were denied basic rights of citizenship. This was morally unacceptable to a large segment of the society, and though there was substantial resistance, efforts to change this reality generally met with widespread support. Hence, changes sought and achieved in the 1960s emanated from a moral clarity that is no longer a central feature of racial conflict in the 1990s. As a result, conflicts between blacks and whites now are not met with widespread support of the black viewpoint on the problem.

Moreover, the addition of other "disadvantaged" groups creates a political context in which distinguishing oneself and one's group from others is a way to gain political leverage that often translates into resources and opportunities. Steele (1990) describes this as a "politics of difference" that has the net effect of encouraging group distinctiveness and discouraging commonality of purpose across group boundaries.

It is also a consequence of the 1960s that the depth of cultural considerations was largely overlooked. The notion that a "color-blind" society ought to be the prevailing philosophy and goal of social programs ignores the facts of the cultural history of oppression and the consequence of this history for contemporary generations of white and black Americans. Former secretary of education William Bennett stated this point of view quite clearly a few years ago:

> People of good will disagree about the means [but] I don't think anybody disagrees about the ends . . . I think the best means to achieve the ends of a colorblind society is to proceed as if we were a colorblind society. . . . I think the best way to treat people is as if their race did not make any difference. (Sawyer, 1986, A8)

The fact is that race does make a difference. The consequences of acting as if race makes no difference when in fact it does are quite different for a black person than for a white person. Moreover, not only does race make a difference, but culture does as well. Reactions and adaptations to racism have contributed substantially to the development of attitudes, values, beliefs, and behaviors associated with black culture.

Therefore, we argue in this chapter that there are three important factors that continue to impede the development of more positive interracial relationships. The first is the relative absence of moral clarity on the desirable course of action that amelioration of the problems of inequality might take. The historical basis of racial conflict has moved from a clear violation of basic rights and freedoms of humanity and citizenship to a set of policy and action strategies that attempt to redress those historical errors. Differing opinions and beliefs about fairness, opportunity, performance, and responsibility leave the strategies for amelioration a battleground that fuels rather than dampens conflict.

Second, there now are a wider array of competing group interests. Under the aegis of "diversity," where difference is one of the most effective levers to political influence, a need for compromises has been created that requires policies, philosophies, and actions that we have not yet learned how to manage.

Third, the belief that racial problems are based on discrimination due to skin color had led us to overinterpret the extent to which the 1960s civil rights legislation has solved these problems. A good example of this overinterpretation comes from Allan Bloom's assessment in *The Closing of the American Mind* (1987):

> White and black students do not in general become friends with one another . . . . The forgetting of race in the university, which was so predicted and confidently expected when the barriers were let down, has not occurred. There is now a large Black presence in major universities . . . but they have, by and large, proved indigestible . . . . The programmatic brotherhood of the sixties did not culminate in integration but veered off toward Black separation. (P. 91)

Not only does Bloom bemoan the failure of racial integration, he blames blacks for the failure.

> I do not believe this somber situation is the fault of the white students . . . . These students have made the adjustment, without missing a beat, to a variety of religions and nationalities, the integration of Orientals and the change in women's aspirations and roles. It would take a great deal of proof to persuade me that they remain subtly racist. Although preferential treatment of blacks goes against a deep-seated conviction that equal rights belong to individuals and are color-blind, white students have been willing by and large to talk themselves into accepting affirmative action as a temporary measure on the way to equality. . . . The discriminatory laws are ancient history, and there are large numbers of blacks at universities. There is nothing more that white students can do to make great changes in their relations to black students. (P. 92)

In Bloom's mind, whites are open and accepting and blacks have rejected their overtures. Continued racial conflict is laid at the doorstep of those who have been victimized over several hundred years. The cultural consequences of racism for both blacks and whites is important here. Whites may draw upon the positive aspects of the cultural heritage that promotes freedom, equality, and opportunity, which leads to a "color-blind" solution in keeping with these principles. Blacks draw a different lesson from history and see racism as the context in which all cultural values ultimately have meaning. The racist context confers negative meaning on distinctive black attitudes, values, and behaviors. Black attitudes toward whites are bound up in feelings of survival and often are expressed in defense of their collective legitimacy and right to full participation in society on their own terms. Attempts to lessen racial strife, therefore, must recognize the different places from which members of racial groups come.

Much of the work in social psychology on intergroup conflict derives from a conception of interracial conflict in which whites are "responsible" for the conflict. As a result, it is white groups and their perceptions, attitudes, and behaviors that are targets for change. In this chapter, we will look at the implications of these strategies for reducing intergroup conflict from the perspective of one of the nondominant groups, African Americans. We raise the possibility that what appears to be an unquestionably right strategy for reducing group conflict from the white or dominant-group perspective may have some importantly different implications from the black or non-dominant-group point of view.

In the second section, we will look briefly at the historical patterns of racial conflict, pointing out the fundamental aspects of ambivalence, ambiguity, and dilemma that have accompanied this problem for several centuries. In the third section, we will consider how this pattern of ambivalence and ambiguity complicates the attempt to ameliorate inequality, and why, as a result, some proposed remedies may exacerbate rather than ameliorate conflict. In the final section, we will consider social identity theory and provisions for the acquisition of positive identity when one is an involuntary member of a nondominant group. Specifically, we raise the question of how group identification contributes to intergroup racial conflict. The result of this analysis will suggest that historical and cultural patterns of racial conflict conspire to make strategies derived from intergroup conflict theories in social psychology inapplicable or in need of significant modification when applied to a nondominant group.

HISTORICAL BASIS OF BLACK-WHITE CONFLICT

Racial conflict has been a prominent element of the social and political history of the United States. With the current focus on race-related phenomena such as campus bigotry and hate acts, disputes about the merit and appropriateness of affirmative action, widening concerns with conflict between First Amendment guarantees of free speech and Fourteenth Amendment provisions of equal protection, race has again become a central element of politics, jurisprudence, education, and business.

Over the years, the nature of racial conflict has altered from one based in the political economy of slavery to one based in the sociopolitical reasoning of the labor market and the role of education in supplying needed human resources (Wilson, 1978, 1987). The moral debate about slavery was important and significant but often constituted a sidebar to the political, economic, and legal arguments that continued to define the meaning of race in this society. The Constitution took this debate into account by defining slaves as representing three-fifths of a man for taxation purposes. In 1857, Justice Taney acknowledged the conventional wisdom of the time in the Dred Scott case by asserting the absence of Negro rights that whites were bound to respect. In 1896, *Plessy v. Ferguson* established the legitimacy of racial segregation and the structural disadvantages in educational opportunities for blacks that accompanied this sociopolitical order. With the 1954 Supreme Court decision in *Brown v. Board of Education,* racial segregation was legally, if not practically ended. With the passage of the Civil Rights Act of 1964 and the Voting Rights Act of 1965, it seemed that we were making great strides in eliminating the shackles of racial bias in the United States.

However, the foundation of racial conflict goes much deeper than the letter of the law. The fundamental conflict between the principles of freedom and equality and the historical fact of the systematic oppression and degradation of African-Americans stands as the centerpiece of continuing racial strife. Swedish sociologist Gunnar Myrdal described this conflict as ''an American dilemma'' in his book of that title analyzing race relations.

> There is a Negro problem in the United States . . . . The very presence of the Negro in America; his fate in this country through slavery, Civil War and Reconstruction; his recent career and his present status; his accommodation; his protest and his aspiration; in fact his entire biological, historical and social existence as a participant American represent . . . an anomaly in the structure of American society. (Myrdal, 1944, lxix)

DuBois captured the conflict from the black perspective in his concept of ''double-consciousness'':

> It is a peculiar sensation, this double-consciousness, this sense of always looking at one's self through the eyes of others, of measuring one's soul by the tape of a world that looks on in amused contempt and pity. One ever feels his twoness,—an American, a Negro; two warring ideals in one dark body, whose dogged strength alone keeps it from being torn asunder. . . . The history of the American Negro is the history of this strife,—this longing to attain self-conscious manhood, to merge his double self into a better and truer self. In this merging, he wishes neither of the older selves to be lost . . . . He simply wishes to make it possible for a man to be both a Negro and an American, without being cursed and spit upon by his fellows, without having the doors of Opportunity closed roughly in his face. (Pp. 214–15)

This identity conflict was given a contemporary spin by Marvin Kalb in an interview of Jesse Jackson on *Meet the Press*, during Mr. Jackson's presidential campaign in 1984.

> *Kalb:* The question [is] . . . are you a Black man who happens to be an American running for the presidency, or are you an American who happens to be a Black man running for the presidency?
> *Jackson:* Well, I'm both an American and a Black at one and the same time. I'm both of these.
> *Kalb:* What I'm trying to get at is something that addresses a question no-one seems able to grasp and that is, are your priorities deep inside yourself, to

the degree that anyone can look inside himself, those of a Black man who happens to be an American, or the reverse?
Jackson: Well I was born Black in America, I was not born American in Black! You're asking a funny kind of Catch-22 question. *My* interests are *national* interests. (Excerpted from *Meet the Press*, 13 February 1984)

The ambivalence for blacks is the continual belief that as a black American, one is not fully American, because it is somehow assumed that the goals and aspirations associated with racial-group memberships are at variance with mainstream American goals. Only by "transcending" group-based membership is it possible, it seems, to become fully American. Yet the realities of racial oppression cannot be lost, nor can the facts of an African origin that diverges in significant cultural respects from European beginnings.

The Racism Equation

Fundamental to the social history of America is racism summarized by all of the biases described above. *Webster's Twentieth International Dictionary* defines racism thus:

Racism: 1. a belief that race is the primary determinant of human traits and capacities and that racial differences produce an inherent superiority of a particular race.

By this definition, racism emanates from a feeling of "superiority." Thus, racism is predicated on the advantage enjoyed by the dominant group.[1]

In the book *Prejudice and Racism* (1972), Jones offered a somewhat more complex analysis of racism, proposing a three-part approach:

Individual racism is based on the belief in biological inferiority of another group that is socially defined on the basis of physical criteria;

institutional racism is the intentional or unintentional manipulation or acceptance of institutional practices that unfairly restrict the opportunities of a racial group;

cultural racism is the expression of superiority of one's own cultural forms, values, styles and beliefs over those of another racial group.

What is crucial to recognize is that power, control, and domination are central features of any analysis of racism. We often do not employ power concepts in our analysis, because we lack mechanisms for understanding how descriptors of attitudinal or institutional bias translate to the "ism" of race.

Because power is a basic ingredient, we must recognize that any reaction to racism will be based on the assumption that power lies behind the expression of preference or bias. So, when we talk about "reverse racism," what do we mean? Since blacks generally do not control resources that whites wish to have, blacks do not exercise power over the lives of whites. Therefore, reverse racism rarely applies to that situation. However, whites can and do exercise control over other whites, sometimes to the disadvantage of their in-group members, and this situation is at the core of the "reverse racism" charge.

To understand reactions to racism is to understand the fundamental assumption of the victims, that whites enjoy the advantage and hence

a. they will use it to gain the upper hand in all spheres of life; and
b. blacks have a right to achieve opportunities by "almost" any means necessary.

These tenets lead to mistrust of whites and fierce loyalty to blacks in public positions when they are seen as "representing" blacks in the passion play of racial combat. It also has the tendency to undermine competitiveness, to lead to wholesale rejection of patterns of behavior associated with the "enemy." Because of the mistrust, all encounters with whites may be suspect at some level. If you are too trusting of whites, you may engender suspicion among blacks. If you are too suspicious of whites, you will likely be perceived by them as "too sensitive" on the race issue.

The fact of racism is important as a legacy of the social history of the United States. Blacks and whites alike are affected by it. Several points about racism have relevance for our continued consideration of contemporary racial conflict.

1. There is a need to understand that *superiority* is fundamental to the concept of racism. Whereas we have tended to focus on anti-black attitudes in most intergroup research, understanding pro-white attitudes may be more meaningful.
2. The consequence of superiority is that self-interest is taken for granted. When feelings of superiority are not salient, there is the feeling of "giving" to or "taking care of" the needy, which further reinforces the superiority feelings from which the giving emanated.
3. Racism involves, for its victims, fundamental mistrust of whites in power and general acceptance of members of their own group in power *when they are perceived to have a positive racial group-identification*.
4. Racism varies from individual acts to a basic worldview that is instilled daily through every institution of society. Thus, reactions may be acute or chronic as one continually strives for that balance that makes it

possible to live from day to day. In a "racialist" society, one must come to terms with what it means to be in a racial group and how one will fashion a life. It means that whites enjoy the power to determine the outcomes of other racial groups, and that for blacks, gaining access to opportunity often means putting oneself in some degree of conflict with the political and sociocultural norms of one's group and the majority society.

IMPLICATIONS OF AMBIVALENCE AND RACISM FOR GROUP CONFLICT

The ambivalence felt by blacks is mirrored in whites. Irwin Katz (1981) has developed an ambivalence/amplification theory that accounts for some of the variability in white attitudes toward blacks. His theory proposes that the two principles of humanitarianism and Protestant ethic collide when it comes to attitudes toward blacks. The humanitarian-egalitarian sentiment emerges when considering the bias to which blacks have been subjected over several centuries. The Protestant ethic, however, demands individual initiative and blames failures to accomplish on inadequacies in individuals. When it comes to explaining socioeconomic inequalities, the humanitarian approach sees structural patterns of bias and supports group-based remedies, while the Protestant ethic approach cites individual weakness and rejects group-based remedies for self-help and remediation approaches.[2]

Katz and Hass (1988) conducted two experiments to show the validity of this reasoning. Subjects in the first study filled out a set of questions that measured their attitudes toward black Americans and the extent to which they endorsed the principles of the Protestant ethic (PE) and the humanitarian-egalitarian (HE) values. An example of a pro-black attitude statement was "Many whites show a real lack of understanding of the problems that blacks face." Endorsement of the statement "The root cause of most of the social and economic ills of blacks is the weakness and instability of the black family" reflects an anti-black attitude. Examples of PE items include "Most people spend too much time in unprofitable amusements" and "The person who can approach an unpleasant task with enthusiasm is the person who gets ahead." Examples of HE items include "One should be kind to all people" and "Everyone should have an equal chance and an equal say in most things." It was expected and found (see figure 10.1) that a high score on the PE scale would be associated with higher anti-black sentiments ($r = +.40$) and a high score on the HE scale would be associated with pro-black sentiments ($r = +.46$). PE did not correlate with pro-black sentiment ($r = -.14$), nor did HE correlate with anti-black sentiment ($r = -.28$).

In a second study, white subjects filled out a racial attitude scale after being *primed* by humanitarian-egalitarian or Protestant ethic values. The

Figure 10.1: Pooled product-moment correlations between value and attitude scores

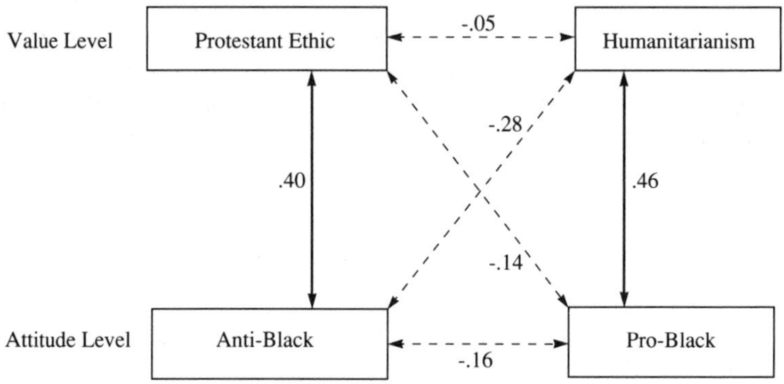

Source: Katz & Hass, 1988.

priming effect was manipulated by having subjects fill out either the HE scale or the PE scale *prior* to filling out the racial attitude scale. In a control condition, the HE and PE scales were filled out *after* the racial attitude scales. The authors sought to determine if priming subjects in humanitarian-egalitarian ideals would lead to a more positive attitude toward blacks and priming them with the PE scale would lead to a more negative attitude. As shown in table 10.1, the results confirmed this prediction. That is, when subjects filled out the HE scale first, they gave more pro-black responses on the attitude scale. When they filled out the PE scale first, they gave more anti-black responses. This finding suggests that racial attitudes are not static, but heavily influenced by the ideological or value context in which they are assessed or activated.

The historical pattern of racial conflict continues in contemporary times.

TABLE 10.1   Effect of priming scale on racial attitude scores

Measured Attitude	Priming Condition		
	HE Scale (*n* = 19)	PE Scale (*n* = 20)	Control (*n* = 20)
Pro-Black			
Mean	36.79	32.25	33.10
SD	4.13	11.56	6.94
Anti-Black			
Mean	27.79	34.05	27.70
SD	8.54	7.83	11.05

Source: Katz & Hass, 1988.

Blacks have been forced to choose between a racial and a nonracial identity as a condition for participation in society. This choice is hard and perceived to be unfair. Moreover, by forcing this choice as a condition for participation, blacks perceive the motivations of whites to be not only unfair, but an indication that racial bias continues and whites are not to be trusted. Group identity and group-based remedies seem to be the best ways to advance in this society while also maintaining some degree of protection from the individual and institutional biases that blacks face.

Whites, on the other hand, increasingly view the opportunities created by the civil rights legislation of the 1960s, and the roughly twenty years of affirmative action programs designed to enforce it, as sufficient to undo any residual structural barriers to advancement for blacks.

For example, a Gallup/*Newsweek* poll in February 1988 (*Newsweek*, 7 March 1988, 23) asked white and black respondents:

"Why do you think poor blacks have not been able to rise out of poverty? Is it mainly the fault of blacks themselves or is it the fault of society?"

	Whites	Blacks
Fault of blacks	29%	30%
Fault of society	42%	44%

"Is the federal government doing too much, too little or about the right amount to help American blacks?"

Too much	18%	5%
Too little	29%	71%
About right	36%	13%

To illustrate the ambivalence problem, note that 29 percent of whites felt blacks were at fault for their own poverty (PE sentiment), while an equal percentage felt the federal government was doing too little to help black Americans (HE). While different people expressed these views, collectively they reflect the ambivalence between individual-based notions of self-reliance and meritorious achievement and group-based notions of humanitarian aid. Note also that while the blame for poverty is evenly placed between individual and institutional reasons for both blacks and whites, the role of the federal government is viewed very differently. Over half of whites (54 percent) feel the federal government is doing either too much or just about the right amount to help blacks. On the other hand, only 18 percent of blacks hold these views. Thus, whites are about three times as likely as blacks to feel that additional federal action is unnecessary to address continued racial inequalities.

Expansion of group-based remedies is increasingly seen as not only unnecessary, but a barrier to white opportunity. Thus, one could describe the

white reaction to racial remedies as a new kind of white civil rights movement. Needless to say, the conflict is expanding, not contracting.

The bottom line of racial conflict is the manifest social, political,
economic, educational, and cultural inequalities perceived to exist between
black and white Americans. That such disparities exist is easily documented
by virtually any statistical summary chosen. What perpetuates conflict is the
reasoning that accompanies interpretations of these disparities. It is this
reasoning that is implicated in this characterization by sociologist Lawrence
Bobo (1988):

> Group conflict involves a struggle over values, or claims to status, power and
> other scarce resources in which the aims of the conflict groups are not only to
> gain the desired values, but also to affect, change or injure rivals. (Bobo, 1988,
> 91)

By definition, racism meets the conditions of group conflict described by
Bobo. Further complicating the understanding of group conflict is the way in
which symbols and ideology surface to reinforce a particular perspective or
point of view. For example, ideological hegemony ". . . exists when the ideas
of one group dominate or exert predominant influence on the major cultural
and social institutions" (Williams, 1960, 587). Willie Horton symbolized this
kind of ideological and symbolic conflict during the presidential campaign of
1988. Candidate Dukakis, from whose home state of Massachusetts Horton (a
black man) had been furloughed from prison when he raped a woman in
Maryland, argued that the incident was not a good basis for condemning the
furlough system. Candidate Bush argued the opposite, but the message that
many black and white voters picked up was that black men are dangerous!
This led to protest by blacks (and many others) but contributed to a large
victory for Bush in the election.

Thus, we have a hegemonic ideology inherent in a group defined by
racial terms and enjoying a consensus superiority. In its rudest form, this
group can simply impose its will on the subordinate group. In its more
conciliatory form, the group can impose its will selectively in the name of its
ideology. It can with relative impunity declare its adherence to principles and
traditional values, and let the system do the rest.

The real ambivalence-racism intersection comes together, as suggested,
when consideration is given to remedies for inequality. Figure 10.2 suggests
some ways in which proposed remedies can violate the basic perspectives of
each racial group and thus maintain the gap that perpetuates conflict.

It is assumed in figure 10.2 that the root problem that fuels racial
conflict is racial inequality. Since racial inequality is necessarily measured on
a group basis, and since historical patterns of racial bias are well known, it is
relatively straightforward to attribute some portion of the observed racial

disparities to patterns of group bias. This is what the group approach represents. Alternatively, one can view racial disparities, though computed on a group basis, to reflect the cumulative consequences of patterns of individual behavior. This perspective presumes that civil rights legislation of the 1960s has for the most part eliminated race-based institutional biases. Evidence of success by members of the racial group supports this view and implies that race is not a good explanation for lack of success by other members of the group. Rather, individual attributes such as effort, ability, and so forth are explanations preferred by the individual approach.

Given the differences in perception of the causes of the inequalities, it is not surprising that the remedies to the disparities take different courses. The remedy for a group-based, structural inequality must be a group-based alteration of institutional practices designed to change the race-based outcome of those practices. Affirmative action is, of course, such a remedy. By contrast, if individual ability or effort is the root cause, then carefully identifying those individuals who possess characteristics of either effort or ability is the appropriate course of action. The aggregate statistics will be improved if more members of the group are socialized, encouraged, or trained to achieve and manifest those preferred attributes.

In general, a considerably higher percentage of blacks than whites maintain a group perspective on racial inequality and argue that race-specific remedies are required. The two bases for this viewpoint rest in (1) the mistrust of whites (or of those in power, whatever their racial or ethnic character) to make decisions that will benefit blacks in the aggregate; and (2) the historical

Figure 10.2: A framework for understanding racial conflict

Perspective	Group Approach	Individual Approach
Source of Problem	Group-based structural inequalities	Individual-based deficiencies of character or effort
Proposed Remedies	Group-based decision-rules such as affirmative action (race-specific)	Individual-based decision rules such as test scores, evaluation ratings (color-blind)
Consequences	1. Violates traditional values of individualism 2. Reinforces inequality	1. Fails to recognize the cumulative inequality that leads to unfair individual competition 2. Fails to recognize continuing structural and procedural inequities and bias 3. Underestimates common affirmative actions that underlie *individual* attainments

Source: Katz & Hass, 1988.

patterns of racial disadvantage that create an unlevel playing field so that equal treatment (i.e., a color-blind approach) is inherently unequal.

By contrast, a higher percentage of whites believe that traditional American values bestow rights to individuals and that abrogation of those individual freedoms undermines the values upon which our society is based. As a result, the conflict is more difficult to resolve, because it is not simply a matter of "deserving" equality; it is a matter of achieving it. Each point of view undermines the premise of the other. Both positions are based solidly in values, practices, and beliefs that have merit. Nevertheless, the conflict between them is salient, and actions that seem to favor one viewpoint over the other seem to arouse animosity in the other side. The stakes are not only tangible in terms of resources and opportunities; they also are symbolic as a reflection of reality and the meaning attached to it.

Here is where issues become complicated. There are significant negative consequences associated with each perspective and the proposed remedies. The American tradition of individualism is violated by group-based remedies. As a result of this perceived violation of traditional and widely accepted norms, those who benefit from the practices themselves tend to be invalidated. It is often the case that when individual-merit assumptions appear to be violated, the result is a perpetuation of inequality and a perception of the beneficiaries as being less qualified. This belief sustains the original presumption of deficiency upon which the remedy was based.

Conversely, the individual-based approach fails to appreciate the continued discrimination that gives support to the group-based claims. If bias continues in the system, then a color-blind approach will systematically disadvantage members of groups against whom such discrimination is practiced. There is enough empirical evidence to support both the openness of opportunity and the race-based limitations of it. The glass is either half full or half empty, depending on your viewpoint. Thus, conflict persists, and little if any systematic headway is made.

The Role of Identification in Black Reactions to Ambivalence and Racism

Historically, racial conflict has been conceived in terms of white acts of bias against blacks. In this pattern of conflict, whites are the perpetrators and blacks the victims. Social psychological analyses of prejudice, discrimination, and racism have focused on ways to modify the attitudes and behaviors of whites.

One of the most successful approaches to intergroup racial conflict is social identity theory. The main lines of reasoning in this approach suggest that intergroup conflict is part of a general process of social categorization in which there are tendencies: (1) to categorize people into groups; (2) to accentuate the differences between members of one's own group and those of another; (3) to accentuate the similarities among members of one's own group; (4) to evaluate the characteristics of members of one's group more positively; and (5) to derive positive social identities from group membership (Tajfel & Turner, 1979; Abrams & Hogg, 1990).

This analysis has been an effective way of understanding why social categorization is so strongly linked to in-group bias. It rests principally on the dual processes of cognition and motivation (self-enhancement). Cognitive processes are responsible for the categorical judgments that, in turn, provide motivational meaning for self-referents.

One of the most salient aspects of race is its social significance. Race, according to vanden Berghe (1967), refers to a group that is "socially defined on the basis of physical criteria." Because of its physical characteristics, race is one of the most salient social perception categories into which humans are placed. In this society, as reviewed earlier in this chapter, race has carried with it significant emotional meanings.

Research has shown that reducing the salience of the group boundary (Gaertner et al., 1989) or providing individuating information (Lockesley, Hepburn, & Ortiz, 1982) reduces the tendency toward in-group bias. The reasons for this reduction lie in the reduced tendency to use categorical information (group-based) in interpersonal situations (individual-based). From the perspective of the perpetrator of conflict, this approach is reasonable. The traditional values of individualism are well served by the diminution of group boundaries and group-based social perception and identification. But what about from the perspective of the victim?

There are two problems faced by members of the victimized group. First, group identification is not only a source of positive social identity; it can be viewed as a "protective" identity. That is, the shared fate of being victimized by racism provides a core of understanding and historical experience. It serves as a rallying point around which collective efforts can be organized. The NAACP, the Urban League, and black fraternities and sororities on white campuses reflect, in part, the value of this form of common identity. From this perspective, vacating a group identity exposes one to racial bias without the protection of self-contained group boundaries from which to draw support and encouragement.

Brewer (1991) has proposed a theoretical model that offers a conceptual basis for some of the individual and group tensions in identity processes. Her optimal differentiation theory is based on the assumption that needs for uniqueness and belonging or assimilation are opposing processes—to some extent pitting personal and social identities against each other. Belonging, or deindividuation, needs are satisfied *within* groups, while distinctiveness, or uniqueness, needs are satisfied through *inter*group dynamics.

The model goes on to propose that a person is in imbalance when forced by some circumstances to be pushed too far in either direction. When the assimilation pressures are greater than optimum, distinctiveness needs are aroused and in-group focus or favoritism occurs (i.e., increased differentiation from the out-group). When uniqueness is too extreme, and isolation or loneliness is a threat, movement toward assimilation occurs. However, dissociating oneself from group membership when distinctiveness pressures are too high carries a high cost, as one risks either becoming a "solo" (an unassimilated member of a large group) or losing distinctiveness in the larger group. By this analysis, needs for distinctiveness in minority groups exacerbate intergroup rivalry and make group or social aspects of identity more salient.

The second problem derives from the "stigmatization" that accompanies racial identity. That is, how can one derive positive self-enhancement from group identification when the group is negatively valued? First of all, it will depend on whose value of the group is considered salient and relevant. If one takes a positive attitude toward a racially defined reference group, then the basic processes of Social Identity Theory would operate, and positive self-enhancement would follow from group identification. If one adopts an outsider's negative value of one's own group, and the outsider also holds power over the group, then conditions for "out-group favoritism" might be more likely. This corresponds to Pettigrew's (1964) notion of "identification with the aggressor."

It is not axiomatic that members of a stigmatized group will adopt negative identification with the group. Cross's (1991) review of the self-esteem of black children showed no systematic evidence of low personal self-esteem across a wide array of attitudes toward blacks as a group. The movement of the late 1960s toward cultural awareness created a strong tendency in blacks to value the group and behave in ways that gave meaning to that enhanced valuation.

Crocker and Major (1989) propose three ways in which members of a stigmatized group could protect their self-esteem:

a. attribute negative feedback to prejudices against their group;
b. compare their outcomes with those of the in-group instead of those of the out-group;
c. selectively devalue those dimensions on which the group fares poorly while valuing those on which the group fares well.

The desire for group-specific programs increases the salience of group identity, provides a means of gaining political leverage and meaningful resources, and maintains the group boundaries that facilitate the perceptual processes outlined by Crocker and Major.

The situation described above is different from the standard SIT context that describes a process of in-group bias that promotes social stereotyping and contributes to intergroup conflict. In this situation, membership is largely involuntary, group characteristics are highly salient visually, and they are generally evaluated negatively. Hogg, Abrams, and Patel (1987) propose three social identity processes that could occur for persons in such a situation:

1. *Social mobility*—efforts are made to move into the dominant group
2. *Social creativity*—cognitive reappraisal, designed to alter the terms of social comparison in one of the following ways:
   a. adopt new comparison dimensions (athletics, social skills)
   b. change values of existing comparative dimensions (immediate gratification becomes positive)
   c. adopt a new lower-status group for comparison
3. *Social competition*—mount a direct attack on social positions of in- and out-groups. Difficult in stable times, easier in times of turmoil.

To the extent that racial group membership is conceived on relatively immutable physical criteria, then option one, social mobility, will be perceived as less likely. To the extent that power of the dominant group is well established, social competition may similarly be seen as unlikely. Social creativity, however, contains many elements of creative cognitive processes and their behavioral consequences. Under the terms of this process, one can indeed attack the position of the dominant group on moral grounds. That was the foundation of the civil rights movement of the 1960s, and many would see it as the basic dynamic that describes the contemporary so-called politics of correctness. That is, superiority of the values of the oppressed and discriminated against elevates them and the attitudes and culture they represent to positions of authority.

The question of black identity raises the pivotal question of how an individual can integrate aspects of his or her social self, defined in generally negative terms, with the core of her or his being defined daily by experiences, thoughts, actions, and reactions of others. This question has been the focus of a persistent body of research over the past fifty years.

Clark and Clark (1939) were interested in the general question of the development of consciousness of self—that is, "awareness of self as a distinct person" (594). They were specifically concerned with how race consciousness ("consciousness of self as belonging to a specific group which is differentiated from other groups by obvious physical characteristics") developed in black children. Their studies of self-identification of line drawings of white and black boys by preschool children led them to conclude that a concrete intrinsic self has probably developed by age five. Later studies by the Clarks (Clark & Clark, 1947) suggested that while identification was well developed, emotional attachment to the group identification was rather negative, leading to a "self-hatred" characterization of black identity (cf. Kardiner & Ovesy, 1951; Pettigrew, 1964).

A number of studies have taken issue with the self-hatred thesis (cf. Cross, 1991; Banks, 1976; Baldwin, Brown & Hopkins, 1991). Our purpose here is not to debate the empirical or theoretical basis for this viewpoint, but to illustrate how individual and group identification processes interact to generate tensions for racial conflict.

A traditional self-identification view of black identity posits a positive correlation between individual and group identity. That is, if identification is high and social standing is low, then personal identity will follow from group identity and be correspondingly low. Similarly, a positive group identity is projected to enhance a positive personal identity. Proponents of the "self-hatred" thesis argue for the negative consequences of this association, while Afrocentric theorists argue for its positive effects.

However, empirical support for this notion is not easily found. Cross (1991) offers a systematic review and analysis of this literature and concludes that the empirical evidence linking personal identity with reference group orientation is flawed conceptually and methodologically. One reason for this failure is that the systematic processes outlined above may well operate (and have operated) to transform the reality of membership in a stigmatized social group into a psychologically positive one.

A significant body of empirical work in black psychology has been devoted to conceptualizing and measuring racial identity in African-Americans. Measures of black identity seek to establish the basis of group identity (a) as a basis for positive self-esteem and (b) as a means for integrating individual and group identities in a society that seems destined to maintain their separation. Baldwin and colleagues (Baldwin & Bell, 1985; Baldwin, et al., 1991) argue for the necessary correlation of individual and racial identity and seek to show this association with the African Self-Consciousness scale (ASC; Baldwin & Bell, 1985). This forty-two-item scale is answered on an eight-point Likert format from *strongly disagree* to *strongly agree*. Items reflect four elements of racial identity: (1) awareness of black identity and African heritage ("Blacks born in the United States are Black or African first, rather than American or just plain people"); (2) recognition of black survival priorities and need of institutional support for them ("Black children should be taught that they are African people at an early age"); (3) active participation in proactive development of black people ("Racial consciousness and cultural awareness based on traditional African values are necessary to the development of Black marriages and families that can contribute to the liberation and enhancement of Black people in America"); and (4) active resistance to racial oppression ("It is intelligent for Blacks in America to organize to educate and liberate themselves from white-American domination").

High scorers on the ASC are considered to be normative within a black cultural context. Needless to say, high scorers are also likely to show typical in-group bias as predicted by social identity theory.

Another major conceptual basis for black identity comes from Cross's (1970, 1979, 1991) model of *nigresence*—the process of becoming black. Attempting to explain the rise of black consciousness in the 1960s, Cross outlined a developmental sequence beginning with a *pre-encounter* phase, the starting identity that is bound to change. This starting point is the negative self- and racial identities described by the self-hatred thesis. The second stage, *encounter*, is represented as a personal experience that challenges the pre-encounter view and makes a person susceptible to a changed identity. The third stage is a two-part process of *immersion-emersion*. Immersion describes the newly acquired sense of the beauty of blackness and its superiority to what went before. Over time, however, this "discovery" gives way to a feeling of incompleteness and a desire for a broader understanding of blackness that is more flexible and open. Stages four and five reflect an achieved identity that has integrated blackness into personal identity and embraced the racial group in a positive way, but views the out-group (whites) not as enemies but as participants in the systems of oppression that must be changed. Positive self-regard, combined with openness to others and a commitment to working to make the world a better place, particularly for blacks, characterizes *internalization* (stage four) and *internalization-commitment* (stage five).

Helms and her colleagues (Helms, 1990; Parham & Helms, 1981) developed the Racial Identity Attitude Scale to measure the stages of the Cross identity model. This thirty-item scale is answered on a five-point Likert scale from *strongly disagree* to *strongly agree*. Examples of items include these:

> "I believe that Black people should learn to think and experience life in ways which are similar to White people." (Pre-encounter)

> "I find myself reading a lot of Black literature and thinking about being Black." (Encounter)

> "I believe that the world should be interpreted from a Black perspective." (Immersion-emersion)

> "I believe that because I am Black I have many strengths." (Internalization)

Studies have shown the scale to have fairly good reliability and to make interesting connections between racial identity and counseling outcomes. Pomales, Claiborn, and LaFromboise (1986) found, for example, that students scoring high on the encounter stage preferred the culturally sensitive counselor. Bradby and Helms (1990) found that internalization and encounter attitudes were positively related to client satisfaction, but pre-encounter attitudes predicted the total number of sessions the client attended. Parham and Helms (1985) showed that *both* pre-encounter and immersion attitudes (pro-white/anti-black and pro-black/anti-white, respectively) were associated with distress and feelings of inferiority. Emerging black identity, as measured by encounter attitudes, was associated with self-actualization and a reduction in feelings of inferiority and anxiety.

Marvin Kalb asked Jesse Jackson essentially if he was black *or* American. This duality dilemma creates what Jones (1991) has called a "bifurcation of self" by suggesting that black elements of identity are race-based while American aspects of identity are rooted in the individual. If one embraces the individual aspect, estrangement from the moorings of racial identity subject one to "solo" status and an "unprotected" self in a society where race matters. If one embraces the black aspect, then "belonging," or "assimilation" into mainstream America, is difficult, as Kalb implies. Choosing how one will integrate the two selves becomes a political process (Jones, 1991) of compromise and goal-relevant choices.

CONCLUSION

Because society has established that race matters, yet it promotes programs and policies that allege that it doesn't, it has created a kind of Pascal's wager for black Americans. What are the relative consequences if one acts as if race *doesn't* matter when it does; or if one acts as if race *does* matter when it doesn't? Whatever the reality of these choices, it is very difficult to willingly expose oneself to the risk of the former possibility. It is perhaps more comforting to know that with the former option, one is at least exercising some active control over consequences. It is ironic, perhaps, that the individualistic concept of personal control may be responsible for a collective understanding that inhibits reaching the common goals of a racially integrated society.

The analysis and measurement of black identity recognizes the importance of these dynamic processes for understanding black responses to interracial interaction. Sewn into the fabric of this conflict are elements of mistrust and psychological dynamics designed to protect against overt and covert acts of bias and bigotry. The strategies for reducing intergroup racial conflict have been predicated on the perspective of white perpetrators. By this analysis, reducing the salience of group identification seems to be the consensus means for reducing racial conflict. The reaction of the victim has been conditioned by these acts of bias, however, such that self-protective adaptations have created a functional group identification that goes against the consensus wisdom. Reducing conflict must be considered from both the perpetrator's and the victim's perspective. How do we create a world of diversity in which difference and similarity are both valued? Brewer (1991) provides a compelling analysis of how it could be possible in an individual case.

We are left still, however, with different political currency (Steele, 1990), particularly for those groups for whom group membership was a liability for so many years. Asking now that we forget about differences naively underestimates the degree of mistrust and the depth and nature of adaptation to adversity that has taken so many years to evolve. Perhaps in the years ahead, we will recognize that inclusion of all perspectives is a prerequisite for a solution that will be successful and lasting.

Notes

1. Note that this "superiority" orientation to racism is consistent with the findings of Brewer (1979) that in-group bias is a stronger motivation for intergroup discrimination than is out-group hostility.

2. The debate over the qualifications of Supreme Court justice nominee Clarence Thomas captures these opposing perspectives. Thomas strongly endorses the self-help, individual initiative approach and rejects group-based remedies as a means of advancing blacks. Thomas's critics argue that systemic bias makes the self-help approach limited in its ability to alter the profile of racial opportunity. The notion that a "color-blind" approach is warranted comes from a man chosen, in part, on the basis of his color.

Part III
INTERNATIONAL CONFLICT

11 American Convictions about Conflictive U.S.A.–U.S.S.R. Relations: A Case of Group Beliefs

Daniel Bar-Tal

Within the realm of intergroup relations, the purpose of the present chapter is to demonstrate that convictions about conflict may serve as group beliefs. This state has important implications for the group's life, which will be elaborated later. For an illustration of the phenomenon, a case of the conflictive relations between the United States and the Soviet Union from the recent past was selected. Although in the last five years the nature of the relationship has changed dramatically, it cannot be forgotten that since the Bolshevik Revolution in 1917, except for a short-lived supportive relationship during World War II, the conflict between the two nations was intense and total. Specifically, it is proposed that belief in the conflict between the United States and the Soviet Union was widely shared by the American public and characterized the American society.

In view of the above-stated proposal, this chapter has several objectives. First, it will introduce the concept of *group beliefs*. Second, it will explain how a conflict may be conceptualized as a belief and will provide a brief example of a specific group that formally treated the belief about the American-Soviet conflict as a group belief. Third, it will explicate the provided example and suggest that the belief in U.S.A.-U.S.S.R. conflict can be viewed as an American group belief. Fourth, the chapter will review the history of the U.S.A.-U.S.S.R. relations and American public beliefs about the conflict. Finally, it will discuss several implications derived from the present conception.

NATURE OF GROUP BELIEFS

Two of the important concepts frequently used by behavioral scientists are "belief" and "group." Though both have been studied extensively, they have rarely been related. While beliefs have been mostly examined as an intraindividual phenomenon, the traditional analysis of group processes paid relatively little attention to beliefs as a group phenomenon. Beliefs, though they do not exist apart from individuals, cannot be studied only on the individual level. Individuals who live in groups hold common beliefs that define their reality, not only as individuals, but also as group members. Such reality becomes especially important when group members become aware that they share it.

There are important differences for the group between the situations when a belief is held by one member of the group or even by all the members, who are not aware of sharing this belief, and the situations when a belief is held by all the members, or a portion of them, who are aware of the sharing. Beliefs in the former situations may be influencing the group as a whole, as, for example, when leaders affect their followers. But they do not provide a sufficient explanation for the binding element that allows group members to perceive themselves as a group, to develop collective identity, to have common traditions, and to act in a coordinated manner. As Lewin (1947) pointed out, "It seems to be impossible to predict group behavior without taking into account group goals, group standards, group values, and the way a group 'sees' its own situation and that of the other groups" (p.12).

Beliefs that are known to be shared by group members may contribute to the direction that a group behavior takes, the influence that group members exert on their leaders and vice versa, the coordination of group activities, the structure of the group, and the intensity and involvement of group members with certain beliefs. But first of all, they may have the distinctive potential for determining group identity and its boundaries.

Thus, it is suggested that just as understanding individual behavior requires knowledge and examination of personal beliefs, so too does understanding of group behavior require examination of group beliefs. Therefore, the present framework introduces the concept of group beliefs to focus on the neglected beliefs that group members are aware of sharing and to characterize them (see Bar-Tal, 1990a, for extensive analysis).

Definition of Group Beliefs

Group beliefs are convictions that group members (a) believe that they share and (b) endorse as defining their groupness. The first point pertains to any knowledge content that is the subject of the group belief, and the second pertains to specific knowledge saying that the first belief is shared by group members. Any content can become the subject of a group belief. But most frequently the contents of group beliefs pertain to group identity, history, tradition, goals, myths, values, ideology, and norms. The conviction that a belief is shared is an important element of the definition. It distinguishes between those beliefs that are considered to be uniquely personal and those beliefs that are considered to be common. Beliefs that are not perceived to be shared are called ''personal beliefs,'' whereas beliefs that are believed to be shared are called ''common beliefs.''

But not all the common beliefs become group beliefs. The second part of the definition suggests that group beliefs are those beliefs that define the essence of the group and provide the rationale for the feeling of belonging to the group. They provide the cognitive basis that unites group members into one entity. In fact, group beliefs serve as a foundation for group formation and later as the bond for group existence. ''We are exploited,'' ''Communism is the best system for human beings,'' ''Jesus is God's son,'' and ''Iraq is our enemy'' are examples of possible group beliefs.

Group beliefs are functional for human beings. There are numerous functions that they can fulfill for an individual and a group, but the two most important ones, which are implied by the definition, are *identification* and *information*. Group beliefs serve the function of identification, which is important for group existence and survival. That is, group members identify themselves with their group beliefs, see group beliefs as characterizing their group as well as their membership, and view them as defining the boundary of the group. From another perspective, since groups, in principle, try to be differentiated, group beliefs often provide a criterion for differentiation. Group beliefs draw the line between the in-group and the out-groups. They indicate that those who do not hold the group beliefs are different. In this respect, group beliefs unite group members. They define the identity of the group and serve as one of the bases that allow a categorization of individuals as group members. Groups may have one, several, or many group beliefs.

Group beliefs also have an informative function. They provide knowledge about the group. On the basis of this knowledge it is possible to structure the incoming information regarding this group. These beliefs shape the worldview of group members as a group unit. They give meaning to group reality and allow understanding of the past, the present, and the expectations of the group.

In addition, specific contents may fulfill other functions. For example, group beliefs of prejudice and delegitimization, which lead to discrimination against another group, may fulfill a function of establishing a sense of group superiority over the other group (Bar-Tal, 1989), or group beliefs indicating that the rest of the world has negative behavioral intentions toward that group help to prepare group members for the worst in their lives and enable group members to take a course of action without considering the reactions of other groups (Bar-Tal, 1986).

Four important points should be noted with regard to group beliefs. First, *the present approach places the conception of group beliefs within the subjective framework*. Group members share a group belief and have confidence in it. This belief is part of their reality, although there are probably individual differences with regard to the ascribed characteristics of group beliefs.

Second, *group beliefs differ with regard to their interrelationships with other beliefs*. Some group beliefs are related into large systems, as in the case of ideological groups. In other cases they can be interrelated into small belief systems.

Third, *the accessibility of certain group beliefs may change from time to time*. That is, although a group may have in its repertoire a long list of group beliefs, not all of them have to be accessible at the same time. Different group beliefs may appear in group members' minds in different situations, because different situations may invoke different beliefs. However, some group beliefs may be very central for defining the essence of the group and, therefore, may be more or less constantly accessible in the group members' repertoire.

Fourth, *group beliefs may change with time*. The change can take place by the addition and/or omission of beliefs or by the reformulation of the old ones. Such change reflects a process of adaptation to the changing conditions in the environment and to the changing needs of group members. The present analyzed case of American beliefs about U.S.A.-U.S.S.R. conflictive relations is an example of such change. It is recognized that the recent events in the U.S.S.R. and Eastern Europe have changed the contents of the beliefs. It is probable that the American people believe at present that the conflict with the U.S.S.R. is over. Nevertheless, for many decades the beliefs about the conflict were salient and shaped Americans' reality.

BELIEFS ABOUT CONFLICT AS GROUP BELIEFS

Conflict as a Mental Phenomenon

Conceptualization regarding beliefs about a particular conflict that functions as a group belief is based on an assumption that a conflict can be viewed as a mental phenomenon (e.g., Axelrod, 1976; Holsti, 1962; Jervis, 1976; Klar, Bar-Tal, & Kruglanski, 1988). According to Bar-Tal, Kruglanski, and Klar (1989), a conflict is defined as belief content that refers to incompatibility of goals between parties. This content of knowledge stored as a cognitive schema represents the prototype of a conflict and in principle describes its essence. Hence, a specific situation is defined to be conflictive when it is identified as one in which one's own goals are contradicted by the goals of the other party (Bar-Tal, 1990b; Bar-Tal & Geva, 1985; Bar-Tal, Klar, & Kruglanski, 1989; Kruglanski, Bar-Tal, & Klar, in press). In other words, a conflict becomes operative when a given situation is identified as such by group members according to the described prototype. Also, in most cases, in addition to holding the particular belief indicating the conflict's existence, group members usually supplement the belief with various sets of beliefs that explain and justify the background and causes of a conflict, describe its course, present acceptable solutions, and so on.

According to the conceptions presented here, Americans identified their relations with the Soviet Union as being conflictive because they believed that their goals were contradicted by the Soviets. Moreover, such beliefs served as group beliefs for specific organizations in the United States, as well as for American people in general.

Until very recently, one of the underlying bases for Americans' identification of the conflict was the perception that the Soviet communistic system is principally contradictory to the capitalistic system of the United States. Most Americans believed that both systems have difficulty coexisting, since the Soviet communistic system is inherently expansionistic, seeking dominance, threatening American religious and moral values, opposing the American social-economic order, and is inconsistent with the underlying American political ideology (Bialer, 1985; English & Halperin, 1987; Free & Cantril, 1967; Frei, 1986; Stouffer, 1966; Welch, 1970). Historically, with the exception of World War II, the Soviet Union was perceived until a few years ago as the most threatening country to the United States. Soviet past acts in Poland, Finland, the Baltic states, Iran, Greece, Berlin, East Germany, Hungary, Cuba, Czechoslovakia, Angola, Nicaragua, and Afghanistan, as well as oppressions and purges of Soviet citizens, provided unequivocal evidence regarding the contradictory goals of the Soviet Union and the United States. However, the Soviets themselves until recently continuously communicated by every medium of expression the thesis that the United States and the Soviet Union engage in an ideological, political, economic, scientific, and cultural competition (often presented as zero-sum competition)—a struggle between new and old or good and evil (e.g., Barghoorn, 1950). This information served as an important foundation for the development of the American conflict beliefs. On the basis of this information, we can understand the remark by Jules Henry (1963), who pointed out that "the most important single fact in American history since the Revolution and the Civil War is the pathogenic fear of the Soviet Union" (p. 100).

Past perception of the conflict with the U.S.S.R. should not be surprising, especially in view of the almost total rejection of Communist ideas by the American public and the prevailing feelings of threat by communism (see Stouffer, 1966). In line with the described opinions and feelings, for many years most Americans believed that the conflict was so basic that it was of zero-sum type. Only in the seventies had the idea of détente been developed, indicating that in spite of the conflicting relations reflecting the contradictory goals, the two superpowers can coexist by developing mutual understanding regarding the rules of the competition (Garthoff, 1985; Litwak, 1984; Stevenson, 1985; Ulam, 1971).

In the social-political climate regarding the U.S.A.-U.S.S.R. conflict prevailing in American society, specific groups were established whose main credo concerned this conflict. In other words, the principle group beliefs of these groups were based on the beliefs that the conflict between the United States and the U.S.S.R. was unbridgeable and basic for the American people. One example of an organization whose beliefs about the American-Soviet conflict function as group beliefs is the Committee on the Present Danger.

Committee on the Present Danger

Beliefs about the conflict between the United States and the Soviet Union defined the identity and uniqueness of the Committee on the Present Danger's members. This nonprofit, nonpartisan, educational organization was founded in November 1976 by 141 distinguished Americans from different spheres of life, including government officials, former military officers, executives, professors, writers, and so on. Later, many of the group members were appointed to the Reagan administration (see Tyroler, 1984, ix–xi).

The policy statement of the Committee on the Present Danger opens (Tyroler, 1984):

> Our country is in a period of danger, and the danger is increasing. Unless decisive steps are taken to alter the nation, and to change the course of its policy, our economic and military capacity will become inadequate to assure peace with security. (P.3)

The second part says:

> The principal threat to our nation, to world peace, and to the cause of human freedom is the Soviet drive for dominance based upon an unparalleled military buildup. (P.3)

The third part suggests that

> we must restore an allied defense posture capable of deterence at each significant level and in those theatres vital to our interest. (P.4)

Therefore, the objective of the Committee is

> to help to promote a better understanding of the main problems confronting our foreign policy based on a disciplined effort to gather the facts and a sustained discussion of their significance for our national security and survival. (P.5)

In view of these beliefs, the Committee on the Present Danger campaigned for increased U.S. defense spending and against the SALT II agreement.

The document described implies that the shared belief about the conflict between the United States and the Soviet Union was one of the bases (if not the most important one) for the establishment of the organization. Since beliefs about the conflict characterized members of this organization and united them, it served as a group belief. Thus, the acceptance of this belief was a necessary condition for becoming a member of this group. That is, the raison d'être for existence of the group was the belief about the conflict. In line with the group belief, most, if not all, of the documents published by the Committee on the Present Danger contain materials portraying the Soviet Union as a constant threat to the United States' goals. Therefore, for the group members the conflict was real and provided a challenge for the United States (see Tyroler, 1984). For example, a background document entitled "What Is the Soviet Union Up To?" suggests that

> the Soviet Union is radically different from our society. . . the Soviet Union is a country in which a ruling elite and those whom it designates live comfortably, while the remaining 250 million citizens not only have few material advantages, but are deprived of basic human liberties. . . . The attainment of the ultimate Soviet objective—a Communist world order—requires the reduction of the power, influence, and prestige of the United States, the country which the Soviet leaders perceive as the central bastion of the "capitalist" or enemy camp. They see the global conflict as a drawn-out process with the Soviet Union and America as the two principal contenders. (Tyroler 1984, 10-15)

This example demonstrates the use of the beliefs about the American-Soviet conflict as group beliefs by one organization. However, the more basic premise of this chapter is that these beliefs not only characterized specific organizations in the United States, but also served as group beliefs during many decades for the American people. This case will now be discussed at length.

THE CONFLICT BELIEF AS AMERICAN GROUP BELIEF

Sharing the Conflict Belief

Very few Americans deny that there existed a conflict between the United States and the Soviet Union. The disagreements among them may pertain to the causes of the conflict, the extent of the conflict, or its consequences. Nevertheless, in spite of these disagreements, the American-Soviet conflict was real for almost every American. These conflict beliefs developed since the establishment of the Soviet Union, following the Bolshevik Revolution in November of 1917. Thereupon, with only one short period of cooperation during World War II (1941–45), the relations between the United

States and the Soviet Union were continuously, until recently, characterized by Americans as conflictive (e.g., Cohen, 1986; English & Halperin, 1987; Filene, 1967; Free & Cantril, 1967; Frei, 1986; Gallup, 1972, 1978; Maddux, 1980; Ulam, 1971; Welch, 1970).

A study of various polls indicated that, through the years, Americans maintained their beliefs about conflictive relations with the Soviet Union. It was only during the years of cooperation against the common enemy that the beliefs somewhat changed. However, as Key (1964) indicated:

> Even in the period of our alliance with Russia during World War II popular expectations about Russian friendship did not become great. From 1942 to 1946, a series of surveys was conducted on the question, "Do you think Russia can be trusted to cooperate with us after the war is over?" The "yes" percentage never rose above 55. Fluctuations occurred in these responses, but on the whole the long-standing distrust of the Russians demonstrated an imposing stability against the pressures of wartime sentiment. (P. 55)

Following World War II, beliefs about the conflict became dominant among the American people. According to Gallup (1972), on 17–22 May 1946, 58 percent of Americans believed that Russia "is trying to build herself up to the ruling power of the world," and 71 percent disapproved of Russian policy. On 5–10 March 1948, 77 percent of Americans believed that Russia "is trying to build herself to the ruling power of the world." The percentage rose to 81 percent in November 1950. This trend continued through the years, although specific events related to American-Soviet relations affected Americans' attitudes (Gallup, 1972, 1978). Thus, between 1972 and 1976 about 83 percent constantly expressed some degree of being threatened by communism, and 85 percent expressed some concern about the Soviet Union. Similarly, between 1978 and 1981, about 85 percent of the American public believed that there is a conflict between the United States and the Soviet Union (Smith, 1983).

Still, in 1985, 53 percent of respondents from the national sample said that political differences—such as the military threat from the Soviet Union— were the first things that came to mind when they thought about the Soviet Union. The same percentage of people believed in an extreme item saying that the military threat from the Soviet Union is constantly growing and is a real immediate danger to the United States (*New York Times Magazine*, 10 November 1985).

These beliefs of the American public about the Soviet Union generally followed the lead of the various opinion leaders' sources (e.g., Erikson, Luttberg, & Tedin, 1980; Schneider, 1984). Therefore, of special importance for understanding the scope of conflict attitudes are the studies that examined the beliefs of American elites. In two extensive surveys reported by Holsti and

Rosenau (1984), data about beliefs of over 2,200 American leaders were collected in 1976 and 1980. The respondents represented every sector of American public leadership, including business executives, labor officials, educators, and clergy. The analysis of their beliefs indicates that the great majority of the American leadership believed that "the Soviet Union is generally expansionist rather than defensive in its foreign policy goals" (84 percent in 1976 and 85 percent in 1980). Moreover, while the elites differed with regard to the conception of the conflict, its scope, and so on, they agreed that it actually existed (Holsti & Rosenau, 1986).

Also, Herrmann (1985) pointed out that although the American elites may disagree with regard to Soviet motivation, they agreed that the "USSR is interested in power and seeks to improve its influence vis-à-vis the United States" (p.377). Similarly, in his analysis of the American national leaders' commitment to containment, he found that the overwhelming majority of the American elite samples of 1979 and 1982 perceived the U.S.S.R. as a threat, while the opinion differences pertained to the level of the threat and the intensity of commitment to containment (Herrmann, 1986).

The Conflict Belief as Group Belief

The basic premise presented here suggests that beliefs about the conflict between the United States and the Soviet Union served as group beliefs for the Americans. This premise implies that beliefs about the conflict were shared by Americans and that they provided one of the bases for their self-characterization. The beliefs about the U.S.–U.S.S.R. conflict served the important function of demarcating the boundaries of American people. Since these beliefs were distinctive for dividing "we" versus "they," they provided a simple definition of "we-ness" by comparison to the Soviets, who were the most salient and vivid "they."

Beliefs about the conflict allowed Americans to know who they were and who their enemy was on a simple "ideological" level. The distinction allowed one to draw one's own boundary and to delineate differences from other groups. Within this framework, the beliefs about the conflict represented the ideological disparity between the Soviet Union and the United States, without resorting to complex societal, economic or political elaborations. They provided one of the important bases for defining belongingness, since by comparison of one's own goals or values to the ones held by Soviets, Americans could emphasize their uniqueness. In this respect, the beliefs provided one of the bases for self-categorization in the process of group identity formation (Tajfel, 1978, 1982; Turner, 1987).

The goals of the Soviet Union and the United States were perceived as so contradictory that the beliefs about the conflict were held with great confidence. Moreover, since contradictory goals pertaining to moral, religious, political, and economic realms are considered as very central, the beliefs about the conflict were also considered as such. These beliefs stamped every domain of American life, dominated the public repertoire for several decades, molded the American culture, and permeated the American ethos. In fact, the beliefs about the conflict became one of the most salient features characterizing American society; as a result, these beliefs, together with other group beliefs, underlay the distinctiveness of the American people.

In heterogeneous American society, which is made up of groups from different races, religions, and ethnic origins, with a variety of values, opinions, or norms, beliefs about the United States–Soviet Union conflict are of special importance. Against the background of differences and disagreements among Americans, the widely shared beliefs about the conflict's existence provide one of the uniting forces for the American people. These beliefs served as a foundation glue that bonded Americans in unity against the Soviet threat. Much has been written about the functions of a conflict and an enemy for group life (e.g., Coser, 1956; Finlay, Holsti, & Fagen, 1967; North, Koch, & Zinnes, 1960; Volkan, 1985). It is beyond the scope of the present paper to review this literature. It is recognized, however, that the beliefs about the American-Soviet conflict, in addition to helping crystallize identification as group beliefs, served also other important functions such as increasing cohesiveness, pressuring to conform, allowing self-righteousness, enhancing group esteem, heightening morale, mobilizing group members' energy, and scapegoating.

The beliefs about the presence of the Soviet-American conflict were axioms that guided the behavior of the American people. Anyone who analyzed American behavior had to grasp the breadth and depth of the beliefs about the American-Soviet conflict within American society that prevailed through many decades. The beliefs not only served as foundations for United States foreign and security policies (see, for example, Little, 1983), but also affected almost every aspect of American life. The past attempts to improve the educational system through comparisons with the Soviet system, the space race, the sport competitions, the content of American films, or even commercials indicated that the conflict beliefs had a profound influence on American behavior.

History of U.S.A.–U.S.S.R. Relations and American Public Beliefs

A review of the history of American-Soviet relations indicates that the beliefs about the conflict emerged after the Bolshevik Revolution in 1917. Subsequently, although American-Soviet relations have had their ups and downs, the beliefs about the conflict have persisted almost continuously until recently, with a brief interim during 1941–45.

From the beginning of the revolution in November 1917, American beliefs about the Soviet Union were generally negative. The nationalization of land, industry, and banks, and especially the Brest-Litovsk Treaty between Russians and Germany, which led to Russian withdrawal from the war, were disapproved by the Americans. As Filene (1967) writes:

> The fact that the Bolsheviks preached a form of revolutionary socialism was in itself a sufficient sin for those Americans who, during the summer of 1917, were becoming used to damning and imprisoning domestic anti-war socialists, anarchists, and just plain radicals. The Bolsheviks' frankly-avowed goal of withdrawing Russia from the war set most of the American public unhesitatingly against them. The indictment, filled with labels such as "escaped murderers" and "hysterical, criminal, and impatient socialist fanatics" grew in volume and venom through the autumn. (P. 21)

Of special importance to the formation of the beliefs about conflict were Soviet pronouncements about the inevitability of worldwide Communist revolution as well as stated intentions to promote it. These actions contributed to the "Red Scare" that swept the United States in 1919 and 1920. In line with this negative climate, President Wilson did not recognize the Soviet Union. With the eruption of the Domestic War, the American public favored armed intervention with growing enthusiasm. Between the summer of 1918 and spring of 1920, American soldiers were part of the intervention act to fight the Bolsheviks (Maddox, 1977). Filene (1967) points out that the nonrecognition of the Soviet government was a natural and almost unquestioned aspect of the national climate. Later, the original hostility toward the Bolsheviks became modified, partly by a decline in interest, partly by a surge of sympathy for the Russian people during the famine of 1921-23, and primarily by the turn toward capitalism signaled by Lenin's introduction of the New Economic Policy. In the late twenties, an antichurch campaign in the U.S.S.R. revived some of the animosity; however, many of the liberal intelligentsia were attracted by the new experiments of the Soviet society. This mood led to the recognition of the U.S.S.R. by President Roosevelt in 1933.

The United States' relations with the Soviet Union in the years 1933–41 were more or less stable, without any dramatic developments. The American public, which accepted President Roosevelt's recognition relatively favorably, reacted with varying disapproval to the internal events in the Soviet Union and with total rejection of the Soviet-German pact in 1939 as well as expansion toward the West and the Finnish war. The following conclusion by Maddux (1980), in a study about American-Soviet relations, describes the American public opinion during the years 1933–41:

> The first eight years of America's formal relations with the Soviet Union did not dissolve the hostilities and suspicions of the past. Ironically, recognition

brought only a brief interlude of friendly relations, and officials on both sides soon returned to traditional suspicions and bitter disagreements. (P. 162)

Following the German invasion of the Soviet Union and the Japanese attack on Pearl Harbor, the United States and the Soviet Union developed strong cooperative relations in an attempt to defeat the threatening enemy. The years 1941–45 were the only years of American-Soviet cooperation and friendly relations that affected American public opinion (see Small, 1974) until the recent events. In these years, the American public expressed relatively favorable attitudes about the Soviet Union (e.g., Levering, 1976).

The cooperative relations dissolved almost immediately following the end of World War II and deteriorated quickly to the lowest point of confrontation in the period called the "cold war." The cold war began during the Truman administration, following Soviet attempts to occupy Iran, to penetrate Greece and Turkey, and to absorb eight Eastern European countries into the Soviet orbit (Caldwell, 1981; Gaddis, 1972; Larson, 1985; Stoessinger, 1979; Ulam, 1971). For the next two dozen years, American-Soviet relations were characterized by almost constant confrontation in various global sites and continuous attempts at mutual delegitimization through various communication channels. The negative perceptions of the Soviet Union by the American public and the strength of the beliefs about the conflict peaked during this period. The Soviet Union was perceived as the greatest enemy, with the desire to conquer the world (Buckley, 1978).

Although 1955 (the spirit of Geneva), 1959 (the spirit of Camp David), and 1963–64 (post-missile-crisis relaxation) were periods of easing tension, only during the administration of President Nixon was a formal conception of détente formalized. According to the American government, détente implied a guarantee of peace and security through peaceful coexistence and the maintenance of stability, in spite of basic ideological disagreement. The purpose of détente was to ease the tension between the two superpowers. Indeed, whenever the two countries initiated direct talks, signed agreements, and exchanged visitors, American public opinion showed support for these steps and diminished negative attitudes (e.g., Caldwell & Diebold, 1981; Garthoff, 1985; Litwak, 1984).

President Carter focused the conflict with the Soviet Union on human rights issues (Garthoff, 1985). But with the invasion of Afghanistan, the tension between the United States and the U.S.S.R. increased, and the American public reacted with negative outbursts. The election of Reagan signaled additional change. Reagan sought to "get tough with the Soviets" by rebuilding the American arsenal. Until 1987, the rhetoric of the Reagan administration established an atmosphere of salient conflict (Stevenson, 1985). The INF agreement between the United States and the Soviet Union, as well as the summit meeting between the leaders in November 1987 in Washington, eased again the tension between the two superpowers, and the American public reacted accordingly.

Since 1987 relations with the Soviet Union went through a dramatic change. The changes in Gorbachev's policies, including the relinquishing of domination over the Eastern European countries, introduction of some democratic principles into the Soviet political system, gradual return to some capitalistic bases of the economy, and most important a change of policy toward the Western world, including the United States, have had a significant effect on the American leadership and public. The cold war and the conflict between the United States and the U.S.S.R. came to an end, at least for the present period.

This review indicates that the accessibility of beliefs about the conflict and their strength depends greatly on the American people's perception of the events (see Quester, 1978). At times of confrontations, as for example during the cold war, missile crisis, or Afghanistan invasion, these beliefs became accessible. They then became widely expressed and central. At other times, when cooperation, agreements, or détente were the focus, their centrality diminished. At the latter times, beliefs about the conflict were less widely expressed (see Gallup, 1972, 1978), but these periods were infrequent and brief. In the history of American-Soviet relations, the prevailing information up to the last five years indicated that the Soviet Union was an adversary in serious and direct conflict with the United States. The information from the Soviet Union about their internal affairs (e.g., collectivization of Russian farmers, purges of the Communist party members, extensive use of prison camps and firing squads against innocent people), as well as information about the Soviet military threat, expansion, and brutality in various parts of the world, maintained the conflict beliefs of the American public for nearly seven decades.

DISSEMINATION OF THE CONFLICT BELIEFS

The beliefs about the conflict with the Soviet Union were imparted to the American public and maintained by the various political, educational, and cultural institutions. They were readily available and constantly emphasized. Since the Bolshevik Revolution in 1917, and especially since the beginning of the cold war, the beliefs about the conflict were systematically and continuously transmitted to the public by many epistemic sources through all the available channels of communication. This process indicates that the beliefs were widely spread and were one of the central themes of the American ethos.

First, all of the American presidents since 1917 maintained and expressed, with some differences, beliefs about the conflict with the Soviet Union (see Bowie, 1984; Grayson, 1978). For example, President Hoover referred to the

Bolsheviks as people who resort "to terror, bloodshed, and murder." President Roosevelt "abhorred the indiscriminate killings of thousands of innocent victims" in Russia and perceived the Soviet Union as a dictatorship. President Truman believed that the Soviet Union "exploits misery and suffering for the extension" of its own power. President Eisenhower suggested that the Soviet Union was a threat because it strove to expand as an "empire spanning two continents, from Aachen to Vladivostok." Similarly, President Kennedy perceived the direct Soviet threat as demonstrated by the "Soviet military buildup on the island of Cuba." President Johnson believed that the "two nations will undoubtedly have commitments that will conflict." President Nixon indicated that "intransigence remains the cardinal feature of the Soviet system." President Carter pointed out that the competition between the United States and the Soviet Union was "still critical." President Reagan believed that the Soviet Union was an "evil empire" whose objective was to expand its dominance. On 8 March 1983, he said:

> They are the focus of evil in the modern world. [It is a mistake] to ignore the facts of history and the aggressive impulses of an evil empire, to simply call the arms race a giant misunderstanding and thereby remove yourself from the struggle between right and wrong, good and evil.

Although various administrations differed to some extent with regard to the style, themes, and focus of these beliefs, they constantly expressed them. For example, Frei (1986) provides an extensive analysis by Reagan administration officials of American beliefs about the Soviet Union (see also, Talbott, 1984). According to these beliefs, the conflict was based on the nature of the two contradictory political-economic-social systems and especially on the expansionistic, power-seeking, and intransigent motives of the Soviet Union. Frei quotes several administration officials, including General Lewis Allen, chief of staff of the air force:

> When official American spokesmen have their potential adversary and American-Soviet relationships in mind, they often tend to think in terms of a dichotomy: on this side there is the "free world" or the "cause of freedom"; on the other side is Soviet power, "slavery" and "oppression". The dichotomy is seen as a fundamental contradiction of ideas, an inextricable difference of "views of the right of men and nation", leading to a "protracted conflict" between the United States and the Soviet Union. (Frei, 1986, 120)

Caspar Weinberger, the former secretary of defense, expressed his realization of "a clear recognition that we face adversaries with serious long-term goals incompatible with our own" (Frei, 1986, 125). The secretary of the air force, Verne Orr, suggested:

It is a classic confrontation between radically different systems: individual
liberty contrasted with repression; free enterprise versus a command economy;
national self-determination as opposed to Russian imperial hegemony. It is a
contest which we cannot wish away. (Frei, 1986, 120).

The beliefs about the American-Soviet conflict were also shared by the
academic experts who wrote about them. Welch (1970) examined images of
the Soviet foreign policy held by the academic community. He analyzed
twenty-two books written in the years 1959-68 by twenty-one authors from
academia. The analysis found that the books differed with regard to images of
the Soviet Union that they project. Welch identified three types of images: *The
ultra hard image, the hard image,* and *the mixed image.* Nevertheless,
although the three categories differed in evaluations and prognosis, all of them
perceived Soviet conduct as conflictive rather than peaceable, and all fell into
the upper half of the dimension defined as ''hardness.'' That is, even the most
moderate images presented the Soviet Union as a medium-level threat, protectively
expansive, and mixedly immoral. These same findings were presented by Frei
(1986). He found that although the American academic experts, by contrast to
the government officials, expressed differential beliefs about the Soviet Union, their prevailing view portrayed the Soviet Union as being expansionistic
and as having goals contradictory to those of the United States. On this basis,
the conflict was perceived as inevitable. The disagreements among the American experts occurred mostly in their analyses of Soviet motivations, conflict
antecedents, strategies, and tactics for tension reduction.

In another study, Singer (1964) analyzed issues of *The New York Times,
Department of State Bulletin,* and *Foreign Affairs* between 1957 and 1960
with regard to expressed foreign policy beliefs. The content analysis showed
that the authors of the articles perceived the conflict in terms of differing
ideologies or contradictory social systems and in terms of struggle between
two centers of power. In addition, the analysis showed that in almost all of the
writings, Americans agreed that long-range Soviet goals pertained either to
world domination or to retaining and expanding their sphere of influence (over
90 percent). Of special interest is an examination of Soviet studies in American universities by Dallin (1973). He pointed out that they mostly propagated
a negative view of the Soviet system, the Russian people, and the state.

The beliefs about the American-Soviet conflictive relations not only
were expressed by political leaders or academic experts, but also were widely
presented by society's other institutions. It was frequently observed that the
American-Soviet conflict deeply permeated the American ethos. Every channel of American culture, including television, newspapers, magazines, popular literature, schoolbooks, and even toys, expressed until recently the belief
in conflict with the Soviets. All of these institutions crusaded against U.S.S.R.

threats and presented the Russians, and especially the Soviet system, in a negative way (see Bialer, 1985; Cohen, 1986; English & Halperin, 1987; Stein, 1982). The commonly presented themes in American culture described the Soviet Union as striving for dominance in all parts of the world, with the commitment to destroy capitalism and democratic political institutions. It was further portrayed as oppressive, a troublemaker, without respect for human life or human rights, totalitarian, aggressive, expansionistic, authoritarian, militaristic, deceptive, adventuristic, offensive, and violent. The Russians often were stereotyped as primitive, devious, cruel, manipulative, dogmatic, immature, untrustful, or capricious (Bronfenbrenner, 1961; Dallin, 1973; Frei, 1986; White, 1984; Ugolnik, 1983).

The mass media presented a mainly negative picture of the Soviet Union and emphasized its conflicting relations with the United States. The news usually focused on events that not only had negative implications for American-Soviet relations, but also expressed a threatening view of the Soviet Union. The contradictory goals of the United States and the Soviet Union in different parts of the globe (Angola, Afghanistan, Nicaragua, South Africa, the Middle East, Poland, or Cambodia) and even at the negotiation table exemplified the conflicting relations of the two countries to the American public.

This trend appeared almost from the early days of the Soviet Union up to 1988. With the withdrawal of the Russians from World War I, the newspapers began to propagate beliefs about conflicting relations between the United States and the Soviet Union. *The New York Times*, for example, warned of the Red Peril and suggested that possible Soviet invasions in Europe and Asia were imminent (see Lippmann & Menz, 1920). Dormann (1983), who extensively analyzed American mass media coverage of the Soviet Union in November 1982 concluded that

> throughout the hundreds of thousands of words printed and broadcast following Brezhnev's death, and to a lesser degree in the treatment of the MX controversy, the media's interpretation of Soviet history, behavior and intentions was unrelentingly negative. The emphasis was on a bone-deep current of darkness.... For the most part ... the media have helped to make crisis a permanent aspect of the American consciousness, and to create a garrison state of mind. (Pp. 67, 69)

The ABC series *Amerika*, shown during the month of February 1987, was one of the extreme examples of the mass media products that reflected the conflicting view of the American-Soviet relations. This television production depicted what life in the United States would be like under Soviet occupation. It described food riots, gulags, grade-school brainwashing, and mass killings of rebellious farm squatters. The portrayal of the Russians as enemies was presented also in children's television programs. For example, episodes of *Greatest American Hero* or *Dukes of Hazard* showed Russians as enemies to be chased. Even some television commercials (e.g., for RC Cola, Wendy's, Meisterbrau, and Miller) ridiculed the Soviet political system. For example, the dumpy Soviet fashion model in the Wendy's ad has only one drab outfit in the collection she displays. The RC Cola ad shows a rustic cabin where peasants dance before a fireplace and toast each other with contraband cola until the door swings open revealing two KGB agents.

The American film industry reflects the political climate of Soviet-American relations. With the exception of the cooperative period 1941-45, whenever American films have referred to the Soviet Union, it has mainly been in negative ways. Fyne (1985) described the Soviet theme in American films and noted that the first anti-Soviet films appeared right after the Bolshevik Revolution (*A Sammy in Siberia*, 1919; *Bavu*, 1923). Between 1927 and 1941, there were dozens of films made that depicted the Soviet Union in a pejorative way (e.g., *Red Salute, Espionage, Tovarich*, or *Comrade X*). Similarly, Cogley (1956), who reviewed the theme of anticommunism in movies between 1939 and 1954, pointed out that after the signing of the German-Soviet Pact in 1939, Hollywood introduced several comedies in which Communists and their ideas were ridiculed. Later, this theme disappeared and then reappeared after World War II. Cogley notes that between 1947 and 1954 about thirty-five to forty anti-Communist movies were produced. In these movies a Communist threat from the Soviet Union was a major implication (e.g., *Ninotchka, Iron Curtain, The Red Menace, Walk East on Beacon*).

Recent analyses show that American movies continued to provide support for the beliefs about conflictive relations between the United States and the Soviet Union (e.g., Hann, 1983; Perkovich, 1987; Roffman & Pardy, 1981). Movies such as *Red Dawn, Rambo, Invasion USA, Rocky IV*, or *White Nights*, to name only a few, presented negative images of the Soviet Union. The Russians were described mostly as dogmatic, cruel, ruthless, or cold-blooded. Moreover, the movies presented a threatening picture of the Soviet Union—as expansionistic, brutal, and unreliable. For example, the film *Red Dawn*, released in the summer of 1984, described an invasion by Soviet, Cuban, and Nicaraguan troops who take over the western United States, shoot up a school, murder townspeople, and take men into a concentration camp. Also, the film *Rambo* described an American superfighter who goes into Vietnam to search for American POWs. He is caught, interrogated, and tortured by a sadistic Russian officer who speaks with a German accent.

The same themes can be found in popular literature. Various fiction and nonfiction books focus on the conflictive American-Soviet relations and use them as either a main plot or a background in the story. A book by Tom Clancy, *Red Storm Rising*, published in 1986, is an example of how American fiction literature spread and maintained beliefs about the Soviet Union. The book described a Soviet attack on Western European countries as a possible scenario for World War III.

In sum, the presented analysis, without providing any value or validity judgment, attempted to shed a new light on American beliefs about the conflictive relations between the United States and the Soviet Union that prevailed for a long time. The analysis presented them as group beliefs because they were widely shared and characterized a uniqueness of the American people. The final part of this chapter discusses implications of the proposed group belief conception.

IMPLICATIONS

The proposed conception implies that group beliefs, as all beliefs, exist in the individual's mind. Groups, organizations, or societies do not hold beliefs collectively—only individual members in the aggregate groups hold beliefs. But the present conception describes a widely recognized phenomenon that group members share beliefs and these beliefs may be viewed as defining the uniqueness of that group. Moreover, the presented approach suggests that group beliefs are more than a mere sum of group members' personal beliefs. Sharing of a belief by group members, and a recognition that this characterizes them, provides group beliefs with distinguished properties.

First of all, group beliefs serve as a basis for group identity. They provide a common basis with which individuals can identify and through which they can define their membership in the group. All the self-defined groups must have group beliefs, and a necessary condition for a formation of such a group is formulation of group beliefs. That is, in order for group members to feel that they have something in common that distinguishes them from outgroups, they need to have group beliefs.

In the analyzed case, American group beliefs about the conflict with the Soviet Union characterized this society and underlay one of its common features. This was one of the defining characteristics of American society. It served as a uniting belief that drew the boundary of belongingness.

Secondly, group beliefs tend to arouse high confidence in their content. The perception of group members that a group belief is shared and characterizes them causes the belief to have high validity. The recognition that a belief is shared by group members reduces subjective feelings of uncertainty and increases the perceived validity of this belief (see Festinger, 1954; Jones & Gerard, 1967). Therefore, group beliefs are usually considered by group members as facts, truths, or verities. One consequence of holding group beliefs with high confidence is their relative freezing in the group members' repertoire. Group beliefs do not change easily, since freezing implies closure. That is, group members do not easily entertain alternative hypotheses to group beliefs, but tend to collect information that validates them. The change of group beliefs is of special difficulty, when they are central. The centrality of group beliefs indicates their importance for the group's life. Central group beliefs may become part of the group's culture and tradition, and then they are especially enduring.

For many years Americans had confidence in their beliefs about conflict with the Soviet Union. Although they differed with regard to ascribed central- ity to these beliefs, they widely shared them. These beliefs defined the reality for the great majority of the American public. They were maintained for a long time and were one of the ingredients of the American ethos. Only when unequivocal information showed that the conflict had come to an end did American people change their beliefs.

Third, group beliefs provide group members with special powers. The mere perception that group members share group beliefs indicates strength. Converse (1964) suggested in his classic analysis of beliefs that the number of people associated with a particular belief system is an important factor in a political system.

> Claims to numbers are of some modest continuing importance in democratic systems for the legitimacy they confer upon demand; and much more sporadically, claims to numbers become important in nondemocratic systems as threats of potential coercion. (P. 207)

In addition, the power of group beliefs is derived from the perception of unity and commonality that may characterize group members who are aware of sharing beliefs. Knowledge that group members share a given belief expresses a unity of the group and indicates common fate. Group members derive strength out of this knowledge.

One consequence of these feelings of strength is that group beliefs may serve as a basis for demands, desires, or goals of group members. Leaders of the group usually take into consideration the group's beliefs when they make decisions that affect the group's life. Because they are aware that group members share a belief and are influenced by the belief in their group behavior, leaders pay special attention to group beliefs. Group beliefs reflect the direction that group members desire to take in their behavior. Therefore, leaders frequently make decisions regarding group behavior that correspond to group beliefs.

In the case discussed here, there was a strong relationship between the beliefs of the American public and the beliefs of American leaders. American leaders depend on the public to be elected, but at the same time, the public allows trusted leaders to deviate somewhat from the group beliefs, contingent on the circumstances of the situation. The beliefs about the conflict between the United States and the Soviet Union were firmly held by the elites and the public. These beliefs were among the dominating themes of American poli- tics. On the one hand, the public supported a firm stand against the Soviet

Union, and on the other hand, the leaders recognized the conflict and confirmed their commitment to American goals. It is very clear that although the presidents of the United States since 1917 until President Bush differed with regard to the way they emphasized the conflict with the Soviet Union, the style of their policy, or even its specific themes, they all shared the beliefs about the conflict.

Fourth, group beliefs may determine the attitudes and behaviors of an out-group toward the group. Group beliefs are important information for out-groups about any given group. They characterize the group and may imply even the behavior that the group may engage in. Group beliefs may indicate possible goals, ideology, values, history, norms, or characteristics of the group. This information enables acquaintanceship with the group and in turn influences the type of intergroup relations that may develop.

There is no doubt that the Soviets realized that the beliefs about the conflict were deeply rooted in the American public. They knew that American goals were contradicted by their goals, and the conflict was a reality for both groups. This information stamped every type and level of American-Soviet relations.

Finally, if one believes that group members act according to their beliefs, then group beliefs should be considered as an important source of understanding group behavior. As Krech, Crutchfield, and Ballachey (1962) suggested:

> Man acts upon his ideas. His irrational acts no less than his rational acts are guided by what he thinks, what he believes, what he anticipates. However bizarre the behavior of men, tribes or nations may appear to an outsider, to the men, to the tribes, to the nations, their behavior makes sense in terms of their own world view. (P. 17)

Group beliefs provide the cognitive basis to many group behaviors. They may serve as reasons, goals, explanations, or justifications for group behavior. In other words, group beliefs may function as guiding forces for a group and, therefore, may determine the direction, intensity, and persistence of group behavior. This is one of the most important implications of group beliefs.

American group beliefs about the conflict with the Soviet Union played an important part in shaping American behavior. Anyone who wants to understand American policy in the past, either foreign or internal, must take into account these beliefs. Decisions about spending, the budget, trade, international relations, and many other matters were greatly affected by the beliefs about the conflict (see, for example, Little, 1983).

CONCLUSIONS

The analyzed case of American beliefs about the conflict with the Soviet Union in the recent past serves as an example for other possible cases. It is possible that also in Israel, Iran, or Iraq, beliefs about conflict are part of group beliefs and have significant influences on group behavior. Each of the other cases could be studied within the framework of group beliefs.

Group belief conception provides cognitive and social perspectives to the study of a group. The existence of a group is a social reality for group members. Group beliefs provide the basis that allows group members to view the group as a social reality. The group, then, is a product not only of structural characteristics, environment, situational conditions, motivational tendencies, or social influence, but also of personal cognitive processes. These processes determine the essence of the group, since group beliefs provide the contents that serve as a basis for group formation and group maintenance. It is important, therefore, that behavioral scientists study the contents of group beliefs and the process through which group members acquire them, become aware of sharing them, and are affected by them in their behavior.

NOTE

I would like to express my thanks to Michael Berbaum and Richard Herrmann, who provided valuable comments on the earlier draft of this chapter.

12 Resolving Large-Scale Political Conflict: The Case of the Round Table Negotiations in Poland

Janusz Reykowski

INTRODUCTION

Psychologists have made various attempts at contributing to a solution of large-scale political conflicts (LSPCs) that involve large masses of people (nations, mass movements, religions, etc.) and issues of power—power of control over forms of social life. After all, such conflicts, like all other conflicts between humans, are mediated by psychological processes; one may expect, therefore, that psychological intervention should have a major impact upon their course. There is extensive knowledge about conflicts and conflict resolution accumulated by psychologists (see, for example, Deutsch, 1973; Pruitt, 1986; Worchel, 1979). And psychologists have developed, already, a number of strategies of dealing with human conflicts. The strategies were tailored to conflicts of a small scale—for small groups and dyads. Would it be possible to apply them to conflicts of a larger scale?

The answer to this question is not very clear. Until now, the role of psychology in the solution of LSPCs was not at all significant—it can't be said that psychological endeavors met with success as far as the conflicts are concerned.

There are, in fact, two major approaches to this issue. One consists in development of some cognitive tools for analysis of conflict situations and strategies that might aid in its solution. The task of application of these strategies remains in the hands of leaders of the parties in conflict. A good example of this approach is the GRIT strategy proposed by Osgood (1963).

There is, also, another approach assuming a direct psychological intervention in conflict. Such an intervention consists in application of the procedures that were developed by psychologists for dealing with interpersonal conflicts and were effective in case of dyads or small groups. For example, Doob (1987) tried to contribute to solution of conflict in the Horn of Africa, in

Ireland, and in Cyprus by means of application of T-groups techniques "to persons of good will" who can ". . . spread the word to officials . . . and other influential individuals" (pp. 15–16). One can have, however, some doubts about the feasibility of this approach. In the case of conflict in small groups the participants of the training are the main target of intervention. Thus, the success of intervention (i.e., the changes in perception and attitudes of adversaries) may result in immediate alteration of the conflict. But in the case of LSPCs, the situation is different.

The improvement of relations between participants in a T-group representing two sides in conflict has no direct bearing on the conflict itself. It is assumed, however, that the changes produced by the T-group procedure can be disseminated among the members of the societies involved in conflict, which should lead to a gradual reduction in conflict. But as Germans say, "Hier ist der hund begrabe" (Here the dog is buried, meaning "This is the main obstacle"). Are there, really, good reasons to expect that changes evoked in very small groups of people will, in fact, affect societies at large—will they reach their respective leaders and elites?

As a matter of fact the chances look rather scanty. On the basis of the theory of social impact (Latane, 1981), one may expect that an impact of a particular source decreases rapidly as the size of a target group increases and as the distance between the source and the target becomes larger. Since the participants in the T-group represent a very tiny part of the conflict-ridden societies, and the social distance between them and various significant parts of the society varies from close to very remote, one may not count upon their effectiveness in disseminating the idea of reconciliation—especially if one considers that the participants themselves are not highly influential public figures. The small crowd assembled for training is not likely to extend a pressure powerful enough to change the orientations of large groups of people possessed by hate and inclined to fight. To the contrary, since the individuals coming home after the successful training experience have little chance of obtaining support in their ordinary environment, the newly acquired orientation is likely to fade away. This in fact did happen. Doob (1987), describing the results of postappraisal of Ireland and Horn of Africa seminars, writes: "Some participants in both projects could not be located, a few were afraid to see us, and of course their memories of the experience grew dim" (p. 24).

The main weakness of the whole approach seems to originate from a lack of appreciation of the major differences between a small-scale interpersonal conflict and a LSPC. The latter is closely interwoven with social and political factors. These factors must be considered if effective strategies of intervention are going to be developed. In order to accomplish this, a deeper understanding of the specific dynamics of LSPCs is necessary. However, psychological knowledge about conflicts of this kind is rather scarce.

In this chapter I will present some of my observations concerning the mechanisms of LSPCs and conditions of their resolution. They are based upon an analysis of a concrete case—the case of Poland, where at the beginning of 1989 a political agreement had been reached between two staunch enemies: the ruling coalition (which included the ruling party, PUWP, and its allies) and the political opposition, gathered under the banners of "Solidarity," that was challenging the existing system. The observations were being made from the position of a participant observer. Due to a historical accident, I found myself in the middle of the development process of the political agreement. Taking an active part in the process, I had an opportunity to observe its mechanisms.

THE CHARACTERISTICS OF THE CONFLICT

The Main Antagonists

I should begin my account with the identification of the two sides of the conflict. In most cases it is rather easy to define the sides of the conflict—one can easily say, for example, that it is Acme and Bolt (Deutsch, 1973) or Hatfields and McCoys (Austin & Worchel, 1979) who are fighting each other. But in the case of a LSPC, the problem is more complicated, since the definition of the adversaries is an issue in itself. As far as Poland is concerned, one side tended to describe the adversaries as "society versus the regime [government]" (implying that the entire nation, united under the banners of the opposition, is fighting against the narrow group of the rulers), while the other side claimed that it was a conflict between "prosocialistic and procapitalistic forces" (meaning that the ruling coalition defends the principles of socialism attacked by proponents of international capitalism). In a more passionate mood the conflict was also described as a struggle between champions of democracy and defenders of a totalitarian regime or between legal authority and subversive forces. Let me, however, choose more neutral names for the adversaries: I will describe them as "social movement (Solidarity) versus state organization (the Communist party)."

It should be stressed, however, that the simple answer to the question about who is fighting with whom is, in the case of a LSPC, misleading. In fact, the group identities and boundaries are changing; the groups are heterogeneous; and last, but not least, they are "submerged" in the large masses of bystanders—wherefrom they can recruit supporters and fans. And in some situations the bystanders play the decisive role in the conflict—they decide who wins.

The meaning of this point may become clearer if we consider the following example: In 1981 there were about ten million members of the Solidarity union, while in 1989, after legalization of Solidarity, only two million belonged to it. This has, of course, some bearings on the definition of the two sides in conflict. While in 1981 Solidarity comprised the major portion of society, eight years later it was only a rather small part of it; at the same time its rival, the official trade union called "OPZZ," had as many as 6 million members.

One should not be misled by these figures. Solidarity, in spite of the reduction of its membership, was politically very powerful. But it is obvious that the definition of the sides in conflict had to be revised between 1981 and 1989 due to the changes in the behavior of bystanders.

Bystanders, to be sure, are not neutral judges. Their interests are affected by the outcomes of the battle. They have their own desires, hopes, and biases. This should be seriously taken into consideration in any analysis of the dynamics of a LSPC.

Complexity of the Groups' Structures

The dynamics of the LSPC depend in large degree on a complex interplay of different forces within each side. With respect to the Solidarity movement, one should take into account the relationships between different strata of the organization (the leadership, the high-prestige intellectual elite, medium-level activists, the rank and file), between various interest groups (miners, teachers, shipyard workers, etc.), and between groups advocating different political strategies (hardliners advocating confrontation, e.g., so-called "Fighting Solidarity" vs. moderates surrounding Lech Walesa). In the state system the internal structure was more complex, but as far as dynamics of conflict are concerned, the most important difference regarded political strategy: It was the difference between reformists favoring an agreement with Solidarity and conservatives (named "the concrete") who wanted to suppress it.

The chances of finding a peaceful solution to the conflict were associated, first of all, with the relative strength of moderates versus hardliners in both groups. The balance between these two orientations was a very delicate matter and, in fact, very fragile. It should be stressed that all attempts at intervention in conflict must take into account this balance and avoid anything that might destabilize it. Otherwise intervention may end up with a disaster.

Issues

In every conflict there are many issues that divide its sides. But usually there are some that play the most important role. With regard to Poland it was the abolishment of political monopoly.

The political system in Poland, as in other so-called Communist countries,[1] was based, as you probably know, on the principle of the leading role of the (Communist) party. The party functioned as the framework of the state organization. In fact, it was not a party in the ordinary sense of the word—the word *party* implies that it is a part of something, in other words, there should be other parts of the same thing. But there were none. The party controlled and ran everything: economy, culture, education, mass media, health care, and science. In many spheres of life the control was rather superficial or illusory. In its early stages the party fostered the major tasks of industrialization and social advancement of the lowest classes in the society. But in the last fifteen years that was no longer the case. And the party's control was gradually diminishing. However, the most important fact was that the party had lost its original capability for mobilization of the masses and facilitation of social development.

The regime also faced a growing opposition. The opposition had at least two sources. One was political. For many people the autocratic, monocentric system was incompatible with their conception of justice and legitimacy. The people who had strong convictions concerning democratic government, civil rights, and political participation tended to reject the system. Such convictions are most typical for people with higher levels of education (see Kohn, 1969; Kohn & Schooler, 1983; Alwin, 1989). Hence, democratic ideas were the most common among the intelligentsia and well-educated workers from big industrial centers.

It should be acknowledged that as a result of the social changes in Poland these social groups increased in size substantially (e.g., in 1945 there were in Poland about eighty thousand people with college educations and about three hundred thousand with high school educations; in 1980 the respective figures were 1.4 million and 5.5 million). The higher level of education should contribute to the increase in popularity of democratic ideas. This in fact did happen. For instance, data from the early seventies showed that in response to a question about the characteristics "of a good social system," people tended to choose items related to social justice and social security (first rank); 71 percent to 84 percent[2] of respondents gave the answer that a good society "provides equal chances for everybody." The second ranked item with an approval of 58 percent to 62 percent was that the society "provides good life conditions for all citizens." The political values ("freedom of speech," "to have influence on government") were located on the third and fourth places and chosen by less than half of respondents (Nowak, 1976). But in the late eighties there was a major change in the attitudes of Polish society: "Free speech" was chosen as necessary by 70 percent of respondents (Koralewicz & Ziolkowski, in press). It can be added that there were marked social differences in approval of opinion concerning limitations of "free speech." Such limitations were approved by 28 percent of respondents with basic education, 25 percent with a trade school education, 15 percent of high school level, and 10 percent with college education.

There was also another source of opposition to Communist party rule in Poland—namely, deep dissatisfaction with its record in the socioeconomic domain. The protracted economic crisis and several futile attempts at over-coming it resulted in deterioration (in an absolute and a relative sense) of living conditions of the majority. No wonder that the majority withdrew their support for the system.[3]

The opposition against the system took the form of a social movement fighting for independence—Solidarity became the symbol and the leading force in combat against monopoly. Its immediate goal in the late eighties was to achieve an independent legal existence. And this very goal amounted to breaking the monopoly. It meant, therefore, a radical change in the system of political power.

It should be added that there were, at the same time, other important issues that divided the two sides. They differed in traditions (Solidarity stressed its affinity with the prewar Polish state, accusing its opponent of renouncing the real Polish heritage), in conceptions of national sovereignty, and in their approaches to the Catholic church. Thus, Solidarity in its own eyes represented the democratic, Polish-national, Catholic ethos challenging the state, which it described as authoritarian, atheistic, and dependent on foreign power (i.e., on the traditional Polish enemy—the Soviet Union).

Looking closely at the nature of the conflict and its main issues, one has to come to the conclusion that the interests and orientations of the two sides were opposite, especially if one takes into account that the very existence of Solidarity had to undermine the basis of political power of the ruling party. In other words, the situation in Poland at that time could be described both in terms of realistic conflict theory (which explains it as a result of competition over limited resources—in this case over power) and at the same time in symbolic and psychological terms (Rothbart, 1990). One might expect, there-fore, that a violent confrontation was inevitable. But events took a different course. Instead of escalation of conflict, both sides sat at the negotiation table (a round one) and found a satisfactory solution. The negotiations ended with an agreement about changes in the political system and defined the main steps on the road to this change. Why and how was it possible?

PRECONDITIONS OF THE NEGOTIATIONS

There were some factors that predisposed both sides to search for a peaceful solution of the conflict—to negotiations.

As far as the "state system" was concerned, its leadership had a clear appreciation of the seriousness of the crisis that wasted the country. It had experienced futile attempts at reforming the economic system—the reforms failed because they lacked sufficient support from the society; each radical program ended with social unrest. It was also evident for many people in power that the system produced large-scale alienation among the most valua-ble segments of the society—among the intelligentsia and many workers who challenged its legitimacy. Moreover, it turned out that support for the opposition against the system did not disappear. Although it tended to diminish during the first few years after the installation of martial law (in December 1981), by the end of the eighties the trend changed—the strength of opposition slowly increased. The following data from public opinion polls illustrate this point. For example, liking for Lech Walesa (Solidarity leader) was declared by 45 percent of respondents in 1985,[4] 32 percent in 1986, 20 percent in 1987, 38 percent in 1988, and 85 percent in 1989.[5] (For General Jaruzelski the respective figures are 71 percent, 70 percent, 63 percent, 49 percent, and 44 percent;[6] Centrum Badania Opinii Spolecznej, 1989). The opinion that activity of the political opposition (including Solidarity) was in the best interests of society was declared by 21 percent of respondents in 1985, 16 percent in 1986, 16 percent in 1987, 37 percent in 1988, and 84 percent in 1989.

One should not expect support for the opposition to be a transitory phenomenon. Looking back on the last three decades, it is quite clear that in the long run it will increase rather than decline. But the most pressing issue was the situation among youth. Youth were deeply disillusioned about the system. The post-martial-law generation—people in their early twenties who did not have an experience of defeat—was very militant. Young people were the major force of two waves of strikes that passed through Poland in 1988.

The leaders of the opposition (Solidarity) had their lesson, too. They realized that the ruling party had at its disposal the effective means of power. They already knew that underestimation of these means would bring about disastrous consequences. They also were aware of limited support in society for their actions. Although there were many sympathizers with Solidarity in society, few of those would follow its call for practical engagement. The leaders probably had sensed that their popularity in the public was quite low.

In 1988 both sides understood that the country was heading toward disaster.

As we look at this picture, it becomes obvious that predispositions to negotiations arose from at least two sources: the appreciation by both sides of the limits of their power and the realization of grave consequences of maintaining the conflict situation. Of course, an important aspect here was timing—both sides realized this at the same time.

It should be acknowledged, however, that the description of the situation presented above cannot be interpreted as the only one possible, as one that every rational person must accept as the truth. I myself want to claim that it is as close to objectivity as possible, but it is rather obvious that the situation can be interpreted in other ways, as well. There were, in fact, other interpretations around. For example, one of them, the "incompetent leaders" interpretation, explained the situation as the result of poor leadership of the party; it ensues that once the leadership is improved, the situation in Poland must also improve substantially. Another interpretation was based upon an assumption of the "inevitable collapse of Communism." On this view, no concessions were necessary—one just had to wait until the entire system disappears "on the junkpile of history."

The two latter interpretations differed from the former in one critical point. While the former facilitated negotiations, the latter hindered them. It means that the basic precondition of initiation of the negotiating process is a particular kind of construal of the existing situation (Ross, 1990). An important aspect of this construal was perception of the conflict, by both sides, as not being a "zero-sum" game (Bilig, 1976).

It should be noted that many conflict situations between large groups can persist over a long time, when people stick to construals that sustain the conflicts. One example, described by Bar-Tal, is that beliefs of Arabs and Israelis about each other and about their situation in the world contribute to prolongation of the violent conflict between these two nations.

Most probably these were not the only determinants of inclination to peaceful solution of the conflict. There were also other factors that played an important role. One of them was the attitude of restraint manifested by both sides during the most intensive phases of the conflict. Solidarity remained faithful to its pledge to avoid using violent means in political struggle, and the government made serious efforts to minimize hardships related to the installation of martial law. Attitudes of restraint were an important predisposition to future reconciliation.

THE NEGOTIATIONS

During 1988 some conciliatory initiatives were made by both sides. During the second wave of strikes, in August 1988, General Kiszczak, the interior minister, made, on behalf of government, the public proposal of a meeting between representatives of Solidarity and the ruling coalition at the Round Table. Secret talks, with a heavy involvement of the Catholic church, that were supposed to prepare for the negotiations, lasted for some time and after a while turned into a stalemate. Then in December the ruling party made the sudden move: It made a sweeping change in its highest leadership, recruiting new people from outside the political establishment who had a public record as advocates of radical reform based on reconciliation with the opposition (I was one of these new leaders). At the same time some of the hardliners were discharged. A few weeks later the government made the declaration that it was ready, under certain conditions, to set the ground for political pluralism, including legalization of Solidarity. This move opened the door to serious negotiations.

First Meeting

At the end of January 1989, the first encounter of the official representatives of the two sides took place—until then they were staunch enemies. There were about ten people from each side (an equal number), and the delegations were chaired by Czeslaw Kiszczak and Lech Walesa. (The Solidarity contingent included Bronislaw Geremek and Tadeusz Mazowiecki—when the old government fell, these people obtained the highest leadership positions in the country.) The delegations met in a small villa outside of Warsaw, a place named Magdalenka, and in total secret until, at the end of the meeting, about midnight, the official news agency published the official statement signed by both sides. The statement contained the information that the Round Table negotiations (the event that most Poles were awaiting for the last half year, losing hope that it would ever start) were going to be inaugurated in the next few days.

The meeting had a special ceremonial setting. Two small Mercedes buses left simultaneously, one containing the Solidarity delegation from the courtyard of Bishop Palace, the other from the courtyard of the Central Committee of the Party; they were escorted by unmarked police cars. The latter bus was first to arrive at Magdalenka, because it contained the hosts of the meeting. On the roads to Magdalenka the streetlights were shut off and special police posts secured the freeway for the buses. These steps contributed to the feeling of importance of the meeting; they conveyed the feeling that the delegations had the rank of official state representatives.

At the beginning of the meeting the atmosphere was very stiff. Apparently both sides expected some form of hostility or some traps. There were also fears that unrealistic demands from one or the other side might ruin the negotiations. But in the first few hours the mood improved, because both sides were careful not to offend the other and both made declarations that apparently met the basic expectations of the partner. That is, both sides displayed the necessary level of perspective-taking ability.[7]

Let me mention a few elements that seemed to contribute to the success of the first meeting:

- The conciliatory mood of both sides—appreciation and respect for the sensitive spots of the partner.
- Lack of any attempts at manipulation or outmaneuvering of the partner.
- Recognition of common problems that could be solved only by cooperative efforts.
- Negotiating tactics that avoided sharp confrontations. Difficult problems were postponed, and solutions of easier problems created the

common belief that there were good chances of solving the more difficult ones.

During the meeting it was possible to develop the climate of partnership. People talked together (for twelve hours), ate together, drank together, and even joked together. Toward the end of the meeting the atmosphere was quite free. A group picture was taken, and the hosts waved good-bye to the Mercedes bus departing with the Solidarity delegation. It should be noted that the meeting not only resulted in the common decision to start the Round Table negotiations immediately, but also laid the ground for development of a certain degree of mutual trust. Mutual trust is a precondition for replacement of tactics of coercion with cooperation (Deutsch, 1973; Webb & Worchel, 1986).

Organization of the Round Table Negotiations

The negotiations were conducted on three levels.

- Level one—plenary meetings of the two delegations plus some ostensibly neutral personalities. These meetings had only ceremonial functions and served as a forum of public declarations of goals and public evaluations of results. There were two such meetings, these initiating and concluding the entire negotiating process. They had a rather pompous format and were made public, directly transmitted by radio and TV.
- Level two—the main arena of the negotiating process. Three negotiating groups, so-called tables, were assembled: a table for political reform, a table for economic reform, and a table for trade unions. Each of the tables was chaired by two cochairmen who played the role of leading negotiators. I was a cochairman of the political table; my counterpart was Professor Bronislaw Geremek from Solidarity. There were about twenty persons in each team: members of the leadership of the Solidarity movement and opposition groups associated with it and members of the leadership of the ruling party, of the allied parties, representatives of government and of official unions, and members of the prestigious elite from both sides. The meetings were closed to journalists, but extensive reports about the content and results of each one were available to the public through TV, radio, and press.

    In addition to the three main tables there were also smaller negotiating groups (small tables) negotiating some specific issues. Within the political domain there were four of them; they were subordinated to the main (political) table.

- Level three—closed-door small-group meetings in Magdalenka, chaired by Walesa and Kiszczak. Their function was to deal with the most difficult problems in negotiations—the ones that slowed down the process (such as the prerogatives of the president—the new office that did not exist before;[8] the legalization of the very militant student organization supported by Solidarity; governmental decisions about closing the Gdansk shipyard—the enterprise economically unsound but famous as the cradle of the Solidarity movement; and many others). But the solutions obtained in Magdalenka were not the final ones. They had to be brought back to the tables and negotiated again in the presence of both teams. Such procedures were supposed to assure the legitimacy of the agreement and render to the public a kind of message that no secret deal was being developed.

At this moment some explanation of my role in the process is necessary. One may wonder, how would a psychologist, an academician not involved in politics, find himself in the middle of the negotiations crucial for the fate of the country?

To make a long story short, let me tell you that since 1981 I made some attempts at analyzing the political processes in Poland from a psychological perspective. I focused primarily on political conflict, trying to interpret it using psychological concepts and theories. The material for interpretation came from observation of political events, surveys of public opinion, results of sociological research, and some research of my own. In November 1981 I warned the public about upcoming confrontation; in 1982 (during martial law) together with a small group of scientists I prepared a document arguing strongly against abolishment of Solidarity—the document was presented to authorities and to some scientific communities and published, without my consent, in the West. The next years I published a number of articles (and one book) advocating political reform and reconciliation with the opposition. My point was based upon analysis of sociopsychological processes that took place in Poland. I also wrote several times to General Jaruzelski, presenting my objections to some of the policy measures intended or implemented by government and recommending a change of approach. I believed that all these activities could contribute to the development of my image as a person who might help in the task of reconstruction of the policy of government in the direction of reconciliation with Solidarity. I may add that I heard many times from politicians that the psychological perspective on sociopolitical phenomena was, for them, quite illuminating.

PSYCHOLOGICAL ASPECTS OF THE NEGOTIATIONS

Let me now describe some of the features of the negotiations that have psychological bearings and, according to my view, played a certain role in their successful conclusion.

The Concept of the Other Side

The important task of the initial stage of the negotiations was a modification of the concept of the "other side"—replacement of the concept of "enemy" with the concept of "partner."

There was a natural tendency to look at the other side as a kind of *enemy*. The governmental side tended to see the other as an impostor who was trying to take away power from the legal authority and was willing to use all available means to do so. For Solidarity the other was a kind of evil regime that grabbed power out of the society—Solidarity, as the only legitimate representative of the society, must recover a part of the power and make sure that the society's rights are respected. Thus, both sides tended to see the major goal of the negotiations as a *containment* of the adversary.

Deliberate efforts were made to change this perspective—to develop the concept of the other side as a *partner* who was interested in betterment of the situation in Poland but had a different perspective, different experience, and different image of the interests of the society. Thus, the major goal of the negotiations should be *reconciliation*.

One of the minor examples of the first success in this endeavor was elaboration of the common terminology for description of the two sides of negotiations: Instead of the former "society versus regime" or "legal authority versus illegal opposition," the awkward but neutral labels were agreed upon—"governmental coalition versus Solidarity-opposition." It was not just a question of protocol. The elimination of the affect-charged labels and introduction of the neutral ones helped to reduce tension between groups. There are research data showing that categories used for a description of social groups might contribute to misperception and augmentation of negative stereotypes (Streufert & Streufert, 1986).

The Concept of Negotiating

There were two competing approaches to negotiations: One regarded them as a situation of bargaining, the other as cooperative problem solving.

The first approach implies that one wants to get as much as possible and to give very little. It entails the negotiating tactic of setting high demands (to have a room for their reduction) and making only little promises (to have room for their increase). The results of negotiations are, therefore, an exchange of concessions. This, in fact, was the initial approach of most of the Solidarity negotiators and their supporters in the Western press. The formula was: legalization (of Solidarity) for legitimization (of government, i.e., for participation in an election that is not really free and democratic).

Efforts were made to replace this approach with another one. Some of us tried to put forth the view that it is in the best interests of the Polish society to build in Poland a democratic order, to abolish the post-Stalinist, autocratic form of government, to develop civil society. Civil society cannot be built by rulers from above, and democracy cannot be imposed. On the other hand, this process of building a new society must not destabilize the state. It means that both sides have a common task and must work together to find the best strategy for change. It should be recalled that formulation of a common goal is an important factor in overcoming an inimical relationship between groups and contributes substantially to the development of cooperative attitudes in group members (Sherif, 1977; Worchel, 1979).

Another factor that could also contribute to the gradual development of cooperative attitudes between members of negotiating teams was a very strict policy of guaranteeing an equal status for both sides. Many protocol precautions served this purpose, such as equal rights of both cochairmen of the delegations, taking turns in discussion, parity in the size of the delegations (each change has to be mutually agreed upon), and so on. There is independent evidence that equal status of groups is likely to promote cooperation between them (Worchel, 1979).

I tend to believe that cooperative philosophy eventually prevailed. The final document was formulated in the spirit of reconciliation.[9] But this conclusion can be challenged. One of the diligent observers of the negotiations, a well-known journalist of the Solidarity press (and a psychology graduate) has written a book about the negotiations that was published a year later. In the book there are no traces of this philosophy. It is written as a story about "our brave boys" who were smart and tough enough to beat ugly enemies (Gebert, 1990). Does it reflect his perception of the situation at that time, or is this the later transformation that fits the new situation that evolved afterward?

Avoiding Destructive Content

There are some issues that are likely to produce vicious arguments. One of them was an evaluation of the past. For each side the events in the past had a deep moral and personal meaning, but especially for people who had suffered from persecutions or had traumatic experiences of nasty attacks from their political opponents. An involvement in such issues could ruin the negotiations. We proposed, therefore, to adopt the norm of avoiding arguments about the past and focusing instead on the future. The norm worked more or less successfully.

Coping with Pressure Tactics and Aggression

Every now and then there were outbursts of aggression from one side or the other. My position was that this kind of aggressive display might have a snowball effect and could undermine the spirit of partnership that was slowly developing. They should be, therefore, avoided. But as a cochairman I could not directly condemn them. Public condemnation of one's own team member (or distancing from him or her) is likely to be perceived as lack of loyalty to one's group; it could be very dangerous for the morale of the group. Condemnation of aggression of the members of the opposite side amounts to involvement in conflict. My preferred reaction was to deal with the rational part of the argument while ignoring its emotional connotation. In other words, it was an attempt at changing the framework of the debate from emotional to rational.

As far as the pressure tactics are concerned, I found that it was useful to express openly and directly disagreement and discontent with them. Even sharp and tough reaction does not damage a good relationship with a partner if it is justified by the context (i.e., if the partner feels that in this particular case he or she went too far). Such reaction is even useful, because it clearly and unequivocally defines limits that should not be trespassed if negotiations are going to be successful.

Critical Moments in Negotiations

The critical moments were when the positions of the two sides concerning a particular issue were completely mutually exclusive. In such cases the negotiations tended to stumble and get stopped for hours. Sometimes it can be a small but important detail—such as, what percentage of parliamentary vote is necessary for overriding the Senate's veto: 65 percent as the ruling coalition wanted or two-thirds (67 percent) as Solidarity wanted. This small and apparently insignificant difference had (at that moment) serious political implications. It simply meant that the ruling coalition that was supposed to have 65 percent of the seats in Parliament could, or could not, pass the given legislation without the consent of Solidarity.

After extended discussion it became obvious that a solution to the problem required that one side must bow. But who? Both sides were afraid of retreat, because it amounted to losing face—a situation very dangerous for the negotiating teams.

It should be stressed that negotiating teams were under constant vigilant supervision by their respective constituencies. Solidarity's medium-level activists were very militant, always sensing weakness and softness of their negotiators. The negotiators were under constant pressure to be tougher, to get more. And the team of the ruling coalition did not have an easy life, either. The conservatives ("the concrete") were deeply suspicious. A false step could ruin the whole endeavor.

I realized that long-lasting focus on one detail produces a kind of fixation. To find a solution one must "leave the field" and take another perspective. It requires time and a change of setting. But proposals to postpone the decision met with resistance from both sides. People were saying, "There is no other solution possible, we must make a decision now." In such situations, comments about psychological traps that we all were in seemed to be helpful. The teams did agree to a postponement of the discussion. And in fact, reanalysis of the problem from another perspective outside of the negotiating room engendered the possibility of developing an idea of a compromise (in this case it was an exchange of concessions).

Looking at the negotiations from a psychological perspective, we may notice that in many respects they can be accounted for in terms of group processes. In fact, many of the characteristics of Kelman's social interaction approach to conflict resolution can be found here (Kelman & Cohen, 1979). For example, his treatment of such issues as setting, arrangement, norms, and, to some extent, definition of goals of the meetings can be applied to the Round Table negotiations.

There are also some points where the two approaches differ from each other. One of them is the role of the third party. Kelman assumes that the third party is a completely neutral side that is supposed to facilitate communication between adversaries. In case of the Round Table negotiations, the role of the third party was played by the Catholic church. It in fact contributed to initiation of the negotiations, helping in getting together representatives of both sides. But the church was not neutral. It supported Solidarity and made sure that its own interests and perspectives were duly respected. But the most important difference between Kelman's approach and ours originates from the fact that the former was primarily a psychological endeavor while the latter was a political one. The important characteristic of the Round Table negotiation process was the constant interplay between the conference rooms and the outside world. The negotiating teams had to interact with the top leadership of the respective organizations, with the representatives of various pressure groups, or state apparatus, with the collective bodies that had to ratify particular agreements, with official decision-making institutions (state council, government, parliament), and with public opinion.[10] As a matter of fact, both teams had to deal with a very dangerous accusation that the negotiations were a reconciliation between elites or a kind of a secret deal of those on the top—a deal that disregards the real feelings and real interests of the society. Of course, this criticism was a weapon of enemies of the negotiations—the fundamentalists from both sides. But one had to do everything possible to avoid the spreading of such a view.

AFTERMATH

Once the negotiations at the Round Table were concluded and the agreement signed, the political process took the new course. Its main outcome was the parliamentary election in June 1989 that brought the big success for Solidarity. As a result of it the new, non-Communist government was formed, and Solidarity very soon achieved political control over major areas of life in Polish society. The course of events was contrary to expectations of both Western political observers and Sovietologists who believed firmly that Communists would never give away their power. The changes in Poland had a triggering effect on political development in other countries belonging to the so-called Communist bloc. In half a year the bloc disintegrated altogether, and the political landscape in Poland metamorphosed entirely.

In the months after the June election the political strength of the Solidarity movement (although not the size of its membership) increased rapidly. At the same time the strength of its adversary and previous partner abated. In fact, the Communist party suffered decomposition. What were the effects of these changes upon the dynamics of the conflict?

It certainly entered a new stage. The victors embarked upon a policy of annihilation of the other side, which was losing its strength very fast. The one-time giant was turned into a scapegoat. In some respects it was a kind of role reversal. While after martial law, Solidarity activists were derogated, purged from work, and sometimes imprisoned or persecuted by police, now the people of the old regime were derogated and purged (but not harassed by the police—for the time being the new regime does not have its own police; nevertheless, some Solidarity politicians request criminal investigations against some of their more prominent enemies).

At present, the major weapon of suppression of a political enemy is a form of economic measures. By passing a law that takes away the property of the party and of organizations having something to do with the old regime, the new regime finishes off its adversary.[11]

Now, one may wonder whether this policy leads, eventually, to eradication of the one side of the conflict and by this very fact amounts to its final resolution? I would doubt it. In the case of large-scale political conflict—when large groups of people are involved (hundreds of thousands, or more)—it is not very likely that such a result can be obtained. Revolutionaries of all times have had an ambition of complete liquidation of their enemies and have never fully succeeded. Instead, they sow new seeds of hostility and prepare themselves for the new generation of enemies. In fact, many people of the old regime have the feeling that they were duped by the policy of reconciliation with Solidarity. If opportunity arose, they could become soldiers of a counterrevolution.

Telling all this, I have to stress that the Mazowiecki's government did not support the policy of annihilation of the weakened adversary; it bowed, however, to the requests of its political supporters. But Mazowiecki's government found itself in trouble. Undermined by declining popular support, it became a target of the vehement attacks coming from its own political camp. After prolonged struggle the Solidarity movement split into two major groups and several smaller ones. One of these groups launched a political campaign against the government under a slogan of acceleration of political changes. It demanded a prompt presidential election ("Walesa for president"), a swift purge of people associated with the previous regime from the public, administrative, and economic life, and fast privatization. This group, transforming itself into a political party, scored the major victory: It was able to win the presidential election and install Walesa as the president of Poland. Mazowiecki's government had to step down, and its supporters were sacked from offices and publicly denounced. Some of them believe that they were under stronger attack than the Communists—former enemies of both sides.

What we are facing here is an opening of a new chapter of the political conflict in Poland. In the meantime, as far as public opinion is concerned, everybody seems to be a loser. The authority of the Catholic church, of parliament, of government, and of Solidarity has decreased—Solidarity, which in November 1989 was approved by almost 84 percent of the society, in March 1991 had only 38 percent approval. This means that political authority has eroded rather deeply, which may weaken the chances of consolidation of the democratic order in Poland (Karl & Schmitter, 1990).

FINAL REMARKS

Looking back at the process of resolving the LSPC in Poland, one may ask a question: What can this experience tell us about the role that psychology might play in conflicts of this scale?

First of all, we should not overestimate this role. It would be utterly wrong to suggest that the participation of psychologists in the negotiations has determined the course of events or that the reaching of the agreement was possible due to the profound psychological wisdom and skills of some individuals who were able to shape the whole process. In fact, I tried to convey to you my opinion that in the case of large-scale political conflict, we are dealing with an extremely complex phenomenon where economic, social, and political mechanisms are involved. But all this complexity notwithstanding, it should not be overlooked that the course of events depends to a large extent on the way people perceive a conflict and the means they use in dealing with it.

Serious obstacles to conflict resolution are located in the minds of the people involved in the conflict. Many of these obstacles were described by Ross and Stillinger (1988), who enumerated a number of strategic and psychological barriers to conflict resolution, such as intransigence, secrecy and deception, equity considerations, biased assessment (for example, loss aversion; see Kahneman & Tversky, 1984), reactive devaluation of compromises and concessions offered by the other side (Stillinger, Epelbaum, Kettner, & Ross, 1990), and several others. It could be noticed that many, if not all, of the barriers were present in the conflict between Solidarity and the government.

What are the factors that contribute to overcoming these barriers? On the basis of the experience of the Round Table negotiations, I suggest that the main precondition for the peaceful solution of the conflict was a development of a specific state of mind—*an orientation toward cooperative solution of existing differences.* This *nonconfrontational* orientation became dominant among the leadership of both sides, among political elites, and in society at large.

Psychology can contribute to development of this nonconfrontational orientation by a variety of means. First of all, it can do it by influencing the public communication process; psychologists taking part in the public exchange of views may help the general public to reinterpret the conflict situation as a non-zero-sum game. They can also point out various psychological traps that interfere with finding a peaceful solution to the conflict. Their role can be, in this case, similar to the role of clinicians who analyze conflict situations with their clients, helping them in changing their perspectives. But to do so effectively, psychologists must be well aware of all the political, historical, economic, and symbolic concomitants of the conflict.

Psychologists can also have a direct role in negotiations. As participants they can reinforce cooperative attitudes, having a keen awareness of all the psychological factors that operate during the negotiation process.

A very important role in developing a nonconfrontational orientation is played by leaders who can create and propagate a particular kind of interpretation of a conflict situation. Leaders are classified, very often, as hardliners and moderates, depending on the kind of interpretation of the conflict situation that they espouse. It is commonly assumed that being a hardliner or a moderate is a stable characteristic of a person. Such an orientation can be, in some people, a function of their mentality (or, if you prefer, their personality); the so-called tender-minded people may prefer rather peaceful solutions to group conflicts, while the tough-minded are inclined to use force (Eysenck & Wilson, 1978). But in most people it is a kind of set that can be changed. Psychologists can provide arguments that might influence the form of thinking of the members of the elite.

Psychology as a science, and psychologists as specialists, can contribute to the formation of the public's and elites' perception of a conflict and to developing procedures that increase the probability of its peaceful solution. An important precondition for doing it effectively is an extensive knowledge of the factors that promote and sustain the problem-solving nonconfrontational orientation in society and among political elites. If we could better understand where, when, and how such an orientation arises, what contributes to its dissemination, and what can stop and limit it, we would be in a better position for developing feasible plans for promoting it, and, by the same token, we could contribute more effectively to solution of the conflicts.

NOTES

1. There are some people who argue against this label.

2. Depending on the social group.

3. It should be kept in mind that support for the system was, for a number of reasons, always very fragile and unstable.

4. All data are from the end of the respective years (December or November).

5. In the last survey the question was "Do you think that activities of the given person are in the best interests of our society?"

6. In the middle of 1989 Jaruzelski's scores were much lower—36 percent in May.

7. On the perspective-taking ability, see Hoffman (1989).

8. The office of president existed in Poland before the Second World War but was abolished in the fifties.

9. The spirit of reconciliation and cooperation did not last very long. A few months later the conflict moved to another stage.

10. It should be recognized that "the parties to negotiations, among continuing groups or organizations, are never a monolith. Attention to the conflicting interests and internal governance is essential" (Dunlop, 1983).

11. There was an intensive political and moral argument around this issue. Members of the former opposition claimed that the Communist party accumulated large wealth while being in power and that this gives its successor unfair advantage over the other political movements and parties. But it was also pointed out that oppositional movements, especially Solidarity, were heavily supported from abroad, which is also an unfair advantage in political action.

13   Yin-Yang Theory and Conflicts

Zhou Dun Ren

One of the cosmological conceptions in ancient China, as advocated by Chinese thinkers and philosophers, is complementariness as represented by yin and yang. Although its origin is still obscure, this concept can be traced back to the third century B.C., when China was in the period of Warring States. According to this theory, two elements or forces—yin and yang—make up all aspects and phenomena in life, both physical and spiritual. Yin will be found wherever there is yang, and vice versa. The yin side is complementary to the yang side, and the opposite is also true. Yin and yang form a Supreme Ultimate, the Harmony.

It takes two elements to make a conflict. Although three or more elements may also be involved, only two elements are required for conflict to ensue. The fundamental structural pattern of any conflict is A versus B.

In the present analysis, any conflict must be one between yin versus yang. The impedance to the resolution of a conflict often comes from the fact that one conflicting element fails to recognize the existence and the right to existence of the other element. The absoluteness of one element in prevailing over or replacing the other element is contrary to the principle of coexistence between yin and yang. When the conflicting elements (e.g., people or institutions) lose sight of the whole that is made up of the coexisting elements, there will not be any harmony possible. Just as it takes two to tango, so it takes two to form harmony. How many times in human history has a group tried to deny the existence of its opposite, and how many times has it failed? When the existence of one group is absolutely denied by its opposite, the group doing the denying is lost as well. This is more easily accepted theoretically, of course, than psychologically.

In ancient China, the yin-yang principle of coexistence was derived from observing the harmony of nature. This is a very interesting way to look at life and the world, compared to the view put forth by Charles Darwin many centuries later. Darwin did notice the interdependence of certain living creatures, but the core of his theory focused on the survival of the fittest (i.e., the existence or perpetuation of one species often at the expense of others). This notion has been referred to as the "animal instinct" underlying human behavior, about which we could learn much more if we were to relate it to the complementarity principle underlying yin and yang. This fundamental difference often escapes people's attention, for political, economic, and social reasons. Nonetheless, one cannot deny the very basic law of nature, namely, the coexistence of conflicting forces.

Yin-yang, however, entails more than coexistence. Coexistence can be static, whereas yin and yang will change dynamically; by the waning of one, there comes the waxing of the other. Mere coexistence itself does not imply dynamics, whereas complementariness can. Yin and yang allow dynamic changes to take place. The speed of change may depend on a variety of factors, but the change is absolute and always works toward the opposite pole of the yin-yang continuum.

This leads to my second point, namely, that there is no absolute victory or ultimate triumph. Victory today paves the way for defeat tomorrow. The quicker the victory, the quicker the defeat. Following maximum waxing—whatever costs it may entail—there occurs the start of waning. The ancient Chinese philosopher Lao Tsu had a famous saying: Peril is accompanied by luck, and luck is accompanied by peril. This is taken as the law of nature, and the law is evident in what happens in nature. This idea applies to human societies as well. Despite intellectual growth on our part, the promise of immediate gains and instant satisfaction often prevents people from seeing the shallow deceptiveness of victory.

One point philosopher Lao Tsu argues very strongly may seem irrational to some. He says the yin that looks weak, soft, feminine, and lowly is, in actuality, hard, masculine, and high. He cites the example of water and rock; as hard and strong as a rock is, it "gives in" to water, which is soft and weak. In nature, many things that are soft, weak, feminine, and lowly outlast those that are strong, hard, masculine, and high. In traditional Chinese martial arts, for example, the better boxer appears slow and weak, soft and feminine. Every fast move exposes the boxer's intentions and hampers the smooth transition to the next necessary move. It consumes more energy. More often than not, the faster boxer, if he uses sheer force and speed, gets hit harder after a number of fast offensive moves, allowing the defensive boxer an opportunity to deal a decisive blow. When the weak and soft have prepared themselves physically as well as psychologically, they will be in a favorable position to defend themselves and eventually defeat the strong enemy. During the Warring States period, there were various small kingdoms in constant conflict with one another. The stronger ones often resorted to force to invade and annex the weaker ones. This strategy was used to encourage the weak to stand up to the strong and to stop the strong from bullying the weak.

The central idea of Lao Tsu, however, is not winning or defeating. The idea is to follow the law of nature, to seek and find harmony. Given the dichotomy of yin and yang, and given the dynamics between yin and yang, harmony can be viewed as a compromise between yin and yang. When one accepts the yin-yang pattern in conflict, compromise is obvious and necessary, even though it is usually difficult to achieve harmony. There should be a constant readjustment of the compromises to the changing circumstances from both sides. Nature does this constantly. Why should human beings not follow the same course of action, given that they are part of nature? The law of nature favors harmony. A person who wishes to be happy and live long has to strive in harmony. A nation that wishes to be peaceful and prosperous has to strive in harmony, too.

14   Coalitions Across Conflict Lines: The Interplay of Conflicts Within and Between the Israeli and Palestinian Communities

Herbert C. Kelman

For some years now, my colleagues and I have been evolving an unofficial third-party approach to the resolution of intense, protracted conflicts between identity groups at the international and intercommunal levels. Within that category, I have worked extensively on the Arab-Israeli conflict, with primary emphasis on the Israeli-Palestinian component of that conflict. I have also done work over the years on the conflict between the Greek and Turkish communities in Cyprus and have followed other protracted identity conflicts around the world.

THE RELATIONSHIP BETWEEN INTERGROUP AND INTRAGROUP CONFLICT

A typical feature of the conflicts that we have explored is that the *intergroup* conflict tends to be exacerbated and perpetuated by *intragroup* conflicts: by internal conflicts within each of the two contending parties. Even when there is growing interest on both sides in finding a way out of the conflict, movement toward negotiations is hampered by conflicts between the "doves" and the "hawks"—or the "moderates" and "extremists"—within each community. These terms are imprecise, but I use them as shorthand to refer to the elements favoring and the elements opposing a negotiated solution on each side. The distinction between pro-negotiation and anti-negotiation elements itself must be qualified by the observation that we are not dealing entirely with fixed groups: The composition of the pro-negotiation and anti-negotiation forces in each community fluctuates and shifts over time.

Both the doves on the two sides and the hawks on the two sides have common interests. The two sets of doves share a fundamental interest in promoting negotiations, whereas the two sets of hawks share an interest in blocking negotiations. Doves and hawks differ, however, in the ease with which they can pursue their respective common interests.

The hawks require no coordination: They help each other by simply doing what comes naturally. Thus, by engaging in provocative actions or making threatening statements, the hawks on each side support the argument of their opposite numbers that the enemy is implacable, that negotiations are dangerous and bound to be fruitless, and that the only option is to be tough and uncompromising. As a result, for example, Israeli annexationists are strengthened whenever an extremist Palestinian group commits an act of terrorism; Palestinian rejectionists, in turn, are strengthened whenever Israeli settlers appropriate more land or intimidate the local population in the occupied territories. In short, the opponents of negotiation on the two sides form what can be described as an "implicit coalition."

On the other hand, the pro-negotiation elements on the two sides find it much more difficult to pursue their common interests. Because of the psychological and political constraints under which they labor, they are likely to undermine each other's efforts to promote negotiations. They are often ambiguous in their statements of readiness to negotiate, mostly out of domestic concerns—out of fear of alienating some of their compatriots, who might consider them too soft toward the enemy and too willing to abandon the national cause. Even when they advocate negotiation, they may do so in language that the other side finds offensive or threatening. Thus, for example, Israeli doves often stress the need for Israel's withdrawal from the occupied territories because of the "demographic threat" to the Jewish state—the concern that annexation of the territories would eventually give Israel a Palestinian-Arab majority. Moderate Palestinians, on their part, make it clear that they are prepared to recognize Israel because its military superiority leaves them no other option—not because they concede the legitimacy of establishing a Jewish state in Palestine. Statements of this kind reflect the ambivalence that even the pro-negotiation elements on the two sides often feel toward the adversary: Many favor compromise out of pragmatic considerations, rather than out of acceptance of the other's national identity and national rights. A more important reason, perhaps, for the doves' preference for pragmatic arguments is their desire to maintain credibility within their own communities. They often bend over backward to persuade their constituencies that their pro-negotiation position is based on the interests of their own group rather than sympathy for the other side.

The pro-negotiation forces on each side badly need the support and cooperation of their counterparts on the other side. But, in their choice of language and actions, they are usually more sensitive to the reactions of their domestic constituencies than to the reactions of the other side. They tend to be preoccupied with how their words will sound, and how their actions will look, at home, and with the immediate political consequences of what they say and do. But these words and actions, chosen primarily for domestic consumption, may create resentment and reinforce distrust on the other side. Thus, in contrast to the hawks, when the doves on the two sides do what comes naturally, they work at cross-purposes: They tend to communicate to the other side less moderation and willingness to negotiate than they actually represent, and thus to undermine each other's argument that there is someone to talk to on the other side and something to talk about. If the two sets of doves are to be effective, therefore, in pursuing their common interest in promoting negotiations, their efforts need to be coordinated. Our approach to conflict resolution is in part designed to contribute to such coordination.

CONFLICT RESOLUTION AS COALITION BUILDING

The unofficial third-party approach to conflict resolution that my colleagues and I have been developing and applying derives from the pioneering efforts of John Burton (1969, 1979, 1984). I have used the term *interactive problem solving* to describe the approach, which finds its fullest expression in problem-solving workshops (Kelman, 1972, 1979, 1986, 1991, 1992; Kelman & Cohen, 1986).

Problem-solving workshops are intensive meetings between politically involved but entirely unofficial representatives of conflicting parties—for example, Israelis and Palestinians, or Greek and Turkish Cypriots. Workshop participants are often politically influential members of their communities. Thus, in my Israeli-Palestinian work, they have included parliamentarians, leading figures in political parties or movements, former military officers or government officials, journalists or editors specializing in the Middle East, and academic scholars who are major analysts of the conflict for their societies and some of whom have served in advisory, official, or diplomatic positions. The workshops take place under academic auspices and are facilitated by a panel of social scientists knowledgeable about international conflict, group process, and the Middle East region.

The discussions are completely private and confidential. There is no audience, no publicity, and no record, and one of the central ground rules specifies that statements made in the course of a workshop cannot be cited with attribution outside of the workshop setting. These and other features of the workshop are designed to enable and encourage workshop participants to engage in a type of communication that is usually not available to parties involved in an intense conflict relationship. The third party creates an atmosphere, establishes norms, and makes occasional interventions, all conducive to free and open discussion, in which the parties address each other, rather than third parties or their own constituencies, and in which they listen to each other in order to understand their differing perspectives. They are encouraged to deal with the conflict analytically rather than polemically—to explore the ways in which their interaction helps to exacerbate and perpetuate the conflict, rather than to assign blame to the other side while justifying their own. This analytic discussion helps the parties penetrate each other's perspective and understand each other's concerns, needs, fears, priorities, and constraints.

Once both sets of concerns are on the table and have been understood and acknowledged, the parties are encouraged to engage in a process of joint problem solving. They are asked to work together in developing new ideas for resolving the conflict in ways that would satisfy the fundamental needs and allay the existential fears of both parties. They are then asked to explore the political and psychological constraints that stand in the way of such integrative, win-win solutions and that, in fact, have prevented the parties from moving to (or staying at) the negotiating table. Again, they are asked to engage in a process of joint problem solving, designed to generate ideas for "getting from here to there." A central feature of this process is the identification of steps of mutual reassurance—in the form of acknowledgments, symbolic gestures, or confidence-building measures—that would help reduce the parties' fear of entering into negotiations whose outcome is uncertain and risky. Problem-solving workshops also contribute to mutual reassurance by helping the parties develop—again, through collaborative effort—a nonthreatening, deescalatory language and a shared vision of a desirable future.

Workshops have a dual purpose. First, they are designed to produce changes in the workshop participants themselves—changes in the form of more differentiated images of the enemy (see Kelman, 1987), greater insight into the dynamics of the conflict, and new ideas for resolving the conflict and for overcoming the barriers to a negotiated solution. These changes at the level of individual participants are a vehicle for promoting change at the policy level. Thus, a second purpose of workshops is to maximize the likelihood that the new insights, ideas, and proposals developed in the course of the workshop are fed back into the political debate and the decision-making process within each community. One of the central tasks of the third party is to structure the workshop in such a way that new insights and ideas are likely to be generated *and* to be transferred effectively to the policy process.

The composition of the workshop is crucial in this context: Great care must be taken to select participants who, on the one hand, have the interest and capacity to engage in the kind of learning process that workshops provide and, on the other hand, have the positions and credibility within their own communities that enable them to influence the thinking of political leaders, political constituencies, or the general public. It should be noted that the third party's role, though essential to the success of problem-solving workshops, is strictly a facilitative role. The critical work of generating ideas and infusing them into the political process must be done by the participants themselves. A basic assumption of our approach is that solutions emerging out of the interaction between the conflicting parties are most likely to be responsive to their needs and to engender their commitment.

It is probably clear from this brief description of our work that the Israelis and Palestinians that we have been recruiting for our workshops belong to the pro-negotiation elements within their respective communities. They are not necessarily committed ideological doves. Indeed, we seek out participants who are within the mainstream of their societies and as close as possible to the political center, in order to maximize their domestic credibility and their potential political impact. Their interest in a negotiated solution may be based on pragmatic considerations; they may be suspicious of the other side's motives; and they may be skeptical about the possibility that an acceptable agreement can actually be achieved. Still, they must have a genuine interest in ending the conflict by negotiating an acceptable compromise agreement. Otherwise, they would not choose to participate in a workshop whose express purpose it is to bring together representatives of the two sides, on an equal basis, in order to explore ways of overcoming the barriers to negotiation.

From the point of view of the intragroup conflict within each community, workshops can thus be conceived as attempts to strengthen the hands of the pro-negotiation elements on each side in their internal struggle. They are designed to increase the likelihood that politically active and influential Israelis and Palestinians who have an interest in promoting negotiations will support each other in their respective efforts and perhaps find ways of working together in a coordinated fashion in pursuit of their common interests.

If interactive problem solving is conceived in these terms, our workshops and related activities can, in effect, be described as attempts to build a coalition across the conflict lines: a coalition between a subset of Israelis and a subset of Palestinians who are interested in opening a path toward negotiation. A working relationship between these elements would conform to the description of coalitions as "temporary alliances among some subset of the involved parties" (Stevenson, Pearce, & Porter, 1985, 258). It is consistent with these authors' definition of a coalition as "an interacting group of individuals, deliberately constructed, independent of the formal structure, lacking its own internal formal structure, consisting of mutually perceived membership, issue oriented, focused on a goal or goals external to the coalition, and requiring concerted member action" (261). All of these criteria, as elaborated by Stevenson et al. (261–62), potentially apply to the group of Israelis and Palestinians gathered in a problem-solving workshop, or to the Israeli and Palestinian participants in a series of workshops conducted over a period of time.

BUILDING AN UNEASY COALITION

A distinctive feature of the coalition formed by problem-solving workshops—stemming from the fact that it cuts across a very basic conflict line—is that it constitutes, almost by definition, an uneasy coalition. Members may share important interests, goals, and even values. In fact, they may at times be more comfortable with each other than with the hawks on their own side. Yet they share with their own hawks—that is, with the very people against whom the coalition is directed—a very powerful community.

The community shared by the pro-negotiation elements with the anti-negotiation elements on their own side—by the doves with their own hawks—is, first of all, a community of *identity*, in which a central part of their self-definition is anchored. Personal identity is characteristically linked to national identity, and this link becomes even stronger when the national group is involved in an intense, protracted conflict relationship. Second, the community shared by the doves with their own hawks is a community of *long-term interest*, since their own fate is inevitably bound up with the fate of the entire community. The peace, stability, security, prosperity, and integrity of the national community have a significant impact on the personal well-being of all members, however they may feel about the current policies of their political leadership. Finally, the community shared by the doves with their own hawks is a *political* community, since this is the arena in which they must make their impact: If the pro-negotiation forces hope to exert influence on national policy, they must address themselves to the concerns, priorities, and sensitivities within that community.

Thus, a coalition across the conflict line will always be an uneasy coalition, because it can be seen as breaking up, or threatening to break up, the national community that is so important to the identity, the long-term interests, and the political effectiveness of each coalition partner. The relationship of the coalition members to their own national community (including the hawks on their own side) complicates the coalition work in problem-solving workshops in a number of ways:

1. It creates a concern among participants about their *self-images* as they engage in collaborative work with members of the enemy community. They need to see themselves at all times as loyal members of their own group and to avoid any moves that might make them feel like traitors. They do not want to see themselves as colluding with the enemy against their own compatriots or as somehow crossing the line to the other side. Thus, maintaining the line between self and enemy is a continuing concern in this type of coalition work.
2. The relationship to their own national community creates a concern among participants about their *credibility* at home and hence their future

political effectiveness. Though they may have no personal doubts about their loyalty to their group, they must avoid all appearances of crossing the line and colluding with the enemy. They have to be cautious at all times about statements or actions that might earn them the label *traitors*.

3. The relationship of participants to their own national community results in significant *divergences in the perspectives* of the two sets of coalition partners, since even the doves share the assumptive frameworks of their national communities. Thus, for example, Israeli doves are generally enthusiastic about the Camp David accords and the Egyptian-Israeli peace treaty, because they have brought Israel peace at least with one of its neighbors and strengthened the Israeli peace camp. By contrast, even moderate Palestinians tend to see Camp David and its aftermath as a disaster, because it produced a bilateral Egyptian-Israeli agreement at the expense of the Palestinian cause. I was struck with this divergence at a joint appearance of an Israeli and a Palestinian who are among the most forthcoming representatives of their respective communities and among the earliest proponents of a two-state solution. Both have shown great sensitivity to the needs of the other side; both have been criticized on their own sides for excessive moderation; and both advocate the same political formula for resolving the Israeli-Palestinian conflict. And yet, in their attitudes toward the Egyptian-Israeli peace agreement, they shared the divergent perspectives of their respective national communities.

4. The relationship of coalition members to their own national communities burdens their interaction in problem-solving workshops, since even committed proponents of negotiation share the *memories, concerns, fears, and sensitivities of their identity group*. When these are touched off in the course of the discussions, participants may display the anger, suspicion, and intransigence that are usually associated with their more hawkish compatriots. To paraphrase the words of an Israeli participant in one of our workshops: There is a little Menachem Begin inside each Israeli and a little George Habash inside each Palestinian. Even doves harbor ''little hawks'' that can be aroused by the experience of threat, frustration, or humiliation.

In sum, a coalition that cuts across conflict lines is by its nature an uneasy coalition, because of the powerful bonds of coalition members to the very groups that the coalition tries to transcend. The participants' concerns about felt and perceived loyalty to their own group and the divergences in their assumptions and histories—all of which stem from their bonds to their national communities—create inevitable barriers to the formation of a coalition across conflict lines and to the development of effective ways of working together. Practitioners of interactive problem solving must give systematic attention to these barriers and try to overcome them in order to achieve the goals of problem-solving workshops.

BARRIERS TO COALITION WORK

Some of the conditions that particularly hamper coalition work are mutual distrust, alienating language, and fluctuations in the political and psychological climate.

Mutual Distrust

In an intense, protracted conflict, such as that between the Israeli and Palestinian communities, profound mutual distrust is an endemic condition. The conflict is widely viewed, within each community, as a zero-sum conflict over national identity and national existence (Kelman, 1987). Historical memories and current experiences serve to reinforce the prevalent assumption that the enemy's ultimate goal is the liquidation of one's own group as a national community. The rhetoric and action of the parties are replete with efforts to deny the other's national identity, legitimacy, and even humanity. The doves on each side usually share their national communities' underlying fear of the enemy's ultimate intentions.

Workshop participants are generally individuals who have come to the conclusion that the enemy has changed or is ready to change out of pragmatic considerations: that the enemy now sees its original goals as unattainable and is therefore potentially amenable to a compromise solution. Such a view is based on a differentiation between the "dreams" and the "operational programs" (Kelman, 1978, 180–81)—or the "grand design" and the "policy" (Harkabi, 1988)—of the other side. But even those who have come to make this distinction and to accept the possibility and reality of change tend to remain apprehensive and cautious about the reliability of the changes and about the enemy's true intentions: Have they really abandoned their maximalist goals, or are they merely engaging in political maneuvers? Are their changes strategic or merely tactical? Will the moderate elements be able to neutralize the extremists on their own side and mobilize public support for a compromise solution? Will they revert to a policy based on their original dreams—to a policy of liquidation of our community—if the balance of power changes and new opportunities present themselves? Are we jeopardizing our own community, or at least opening ourselves up to the accusation of doing so, by giving credence to the enemy's professions of moderation and change?

In view of these concerns, workshop participants invariably engage in a process of testing each other's sincerity and authenticity. In a variety of ways, they try to establish whether the members of the other party recognize their basic rights and needs, whether they are genuine in their commitment to a peaceful solution, and whether they represent significant tendencies within their own communities. This testing process is a necessary and important part of the workshop interaction. It is the basis for developing a *working trust* between the two sides—a trust sufficient to allow them to proceed with the coalition work of joint analysis, interactive problem solving, and planning implementation. This working trust can be established when both sides are persuaded that they have a common interest in finding a mutually satisfactory solution, that the ideas emerging out of their interactions have some political future in the two communities, and that the representatives of the other side can exert some influence on the political debate and its outcome. Most of our workshops have been successful in achieving this working trust—probably because of the selection and self-selection of participants, the atmosphere we manage to create, and the norms that govern the interaction. In the process of mutual testing, participants have generally been persuaded that their counterparts are sincere in their interest in finding a peaceful solution and that they belong to the political mainstream of their community.[1]

The working trust among Israelis and Palestinians established in workshops and other coalition-building efforts remains tenuous, and the process of mutual testing is never complete. As the interaction proceeds within any given workshop, old suspicions may be rearoused when participants from the other side fail to live up to the (perhaps unrealistic) expectations that have been created earlier. They may demonstrate insensitivity to the adversary's concerns, or incomplete understanding of the other's situation and acceptance of the other's rights, or adherence to a set of assumptions markedly different from one's own. At times, they may deliberately make provocative statements in order to remind themselves and others that they have not switched sides in the conflict. Such experiences again bring up the question whether the others' commitment to peace is genuine and whether they can really be trusted, and a new series of tests of sincerity may be introduced.

In continuing workshops, in which the same group of participants gather for a series of meetings spread out over a period of time, mutual distrust may be rearoused by events that occur in the interim between meetings. Renewed suspicions may be generated by reports of the actions or pronouncements of one of the participants or a group of participants, which are perceived as reversals by participants on the other side. Furthermore, renewed distrust may be engendered by events on the ground that bring old fears to the fore and reinforce earlier assumptions about the other side's intentions. Such real-world developments that affect the general relationship between the two parties may complicate the larger process of coalition building, if we conceive of the coalition as including not only the participants in a particular workshop or series of workshops, but the entire array of pronegotiation elements in the two communities that have been communicating with each other over time through a range of workshops, conferences, and other forms of dialogue.

The potential effect of rearousal of old fears and suspicions on coalition work was well illustrated by recent events in the Israeli-Palestinian relationship. During the last few years, particularly since the end of 1988, a growing number of meetings had taken place between Israelis and Palestinians to discuss directly the issues in the conflict and attempt to find common ground. These meetings varied considerably; some were public and some private, and they took place in different parts of the world and in different settings. Apart from our own problem-solving workshops and similar efforts, they included a variety of conferences sponsored by political, academic, religious, and peace organizations. Not all of these meetings were well conceived and successful, but overall they contributed significantly to building a coalition across the conflict line among individuals and groups searching for a mutually satisfactory solution to the conflict. This coalition has been seriously jeopardized by the deterioration in the overall relationship between the Israeli and Palestinian communities since the spring of 1990. After the collapse of the peace initiative at that time, many factors contributed to an almost classical conflict spiral, marked by rearousal of old fears, emergence of mirror images, and escalation of hostility.

Palestinians' fears were fed, for example, by the prospects of a massive immigration of Soviet Jews to Israel and by Prime Minister Shamir's pronouncement that the large immigration required a large Israel. For Palestinians, these events brought back memories of 1948 and reinforced the fear that Israel would permanently annex whatever territory was left for a potential Palestinian state, expelling large numbers of Palestinians in the process. Israelis, in turn, took the Palestinians' hostile reaction to the Soviet immigration, accompanied by the old rhetoric about Zionist expansionism, as evidence that Palestinians still did not accept Israel's raison d'être as a Jewish state and had not abandoned their original project of destroying Israel. Thus, for Israelis too, old memories of Arab hostility to Jewish immigration and the fears associated with them were rearoused.

Subsequently, Israeli fears were reinforced by Palestinian support for Iraq during the Gulf crisis that began in August 1990 and during the Gulf war itself. Many Israelis, including some members of the peace camp, concluded that Palestinians were not genuinely committed to the two-state solution and that their professed readiness to enter into serious negotiations could not be trusted. Palestinians, on their part, were appalled by the reaction of Israelis—especially of their erstwhile coalition partners from the Israeli peace camp. They felt that these Israelis showed a lack of appreciation of the limited nature of Palestinian support for Iraq, a lack of understanding of the forces that accounted for this support (including popular frustration with the failure of the Palestinian peace initiative and the political constraints of the leadership), and a lack of sympathy for Palestinian suffering (such as the economic and psychological consequences of the extended curfew during the war). They too concluded that the other side was not serious about negotiations.

The arousal of old fears, the introduction of old rhetoric, and the return to earlier levels of mutual distrust within the two communities clearly had an effect on the evolving coalition between the pro-negotiation forces on the two sides. This effect was evident in the four workshops that we conducted between November 1990 and June 1991. It became necessary to repair the collaborative relationship that had started to evolve and to renew the working trust required for coalition work. The evidence from our own workshops and from some other projects suggests that these efforts are meeting with some success. For example, in a continuing workshop, which met for the first time in November 1990, the Israeli and Palestinian participants brought to the meeting the widespread doubts within their own communities about the existence of a viable negotiating partner on the other side. But by the time the meeting was over—and not without a considerable amount of hard work— they were persuaded that such a partner was still available and that serious negotiations were possible and worth the effort. At the second meeting of the group, which was held in June 1991—with the Gulf war intervening between the two meetings—further repair work needed to be done, but the group emerged ready to engage in collaborative problem solving.

These examples illustrate the extent to which mutual distrust—historically rooted and readily reconfirmed in protracted conflict relationships—complicates coalition building and coalition work by requiring a continuing process of mutual testing and reestablishment of working trust.

Alienating Language

A second impediment to coalition work is the parties' tendency to employ words or a manner of speaking that the other side finds irritating, patronizing, insulting, threatening, or otherwise oblivious to its sensitivities. The repeated use of such language, of course, contributes to mutual distrust. One of the valuable outcomes of problem-solving workshops is to sensitize participants to the different meanings of particular words to the two sides and to make them aware of language that sends up red flags for the other. Insofar as this learning is transferred to the political process in each community, it helps in the development of a deescalatory language and thus contributes to creating a political environment more conducive to negotiation. Within the workshop proper, the development of a mutually acceptable language facilitates communication and joint problem solving.

It is not surprising that workshop participants, despite their interest in negotiating a compromise solution, tend to use language that alienates the other side. They are members of their own national communities, sharing the assumptions, attitudes, and experiences that shape the way they speak to and about the adversary. Patronizing language, for example, derives from the nature of the power relationship between the parties; delegitimizing language is part of the rhetoric of the struggle in which the parties are engaged. Ironically, however, some of the alienating language that crops up in the communications of pro-negotiation elements on both sides, inside or outside the workshop setting, is directly linked to their very reason for adopting a pro-negotiation stance and/or their attempt to justify such a stance to themselves and others. I have already alluded to this phenomenon at the beginning of the chapter, in explaining why the pro-negotiation elements on the two sides often work at cross-purposes. Let me elaborate the point here.

Participants on both sides join the coalition primarily for their own pragmatic reasons: because they have concluded that a compromise solution is in the best interest of their own community. To be sure, there are committed doves who support, as a matter of principle, a solution that would enable the two peoples to share the land they both claim and to exercise their right to national self-determination within that land. Within the Israeli peace camp, for example, there are a number of organizations that articulate that view. But the mainstream within the peace camp—such as the Peace Now movement in Israel—bases its stance on pragmatic reasons. Even those mainstream elements, on either side, who are genuinely concerned about the rights and needs of the other, are very careful in their public statements to justify their support for a negotiated compromise in terms of self-interest. It should be recalled that we deliberately try to recruit for our workshops mainstream Israelis and Palestinians who are as close as possible to the political center. Thus, workshop participants are likely to stress pragmatic considerations in their support for negotiations.

The pragmatic focus of coalitions across conflict lines is not in itself a disadvantage. After all, it is the convergence of interests between the two conflicting parties that provides the best opportunity for resolving a protracted conflict and that makes it possible to create this kind of coalition. Yet, the heavy emphasis on self-interest introduces strains on coalition work, because some of the language that coalition members use to justify compromise to their own community may be experienced as demeaning or threatening by members of the other community.

One of the arguments frequently used by Israeli peace proponents has been the demographic danger to which I have already referred. Incorporating the occupied territories into Israel, according to this argument, would greatly increase the Palestinian-Arab population in the country, bringing it close to 40 percent immediately and—in view of the higher birthrate among Palestinians—producing an Arab majority in the not too distant future.[2] Under these circumstances, Israel would have to choose between extending full citizenship to the Palestinian population and thus undermining the Jewish character of the state, or denying them citizen rights and thus undermining the democratic character of the state. This has been a strong argument when addressed to Israeli audiences, but Palestinians find it demeaning and even racist to be described as a "demographic threat." Palestinians also tend to be resentful when Israeli doves call for an end to the occupation because it is bad for the "soul of Israel." To their ears, this argument represents a misplaced emphasis in showing greater concern for the souls of the victimizers than for the bodies of the victims. More generally, in proposing withdrawal from the occupied territories and compromise with the Palestinians, Israelis sometimes insist that they are not taking this position out of concern for the Palestinians, but out of concern for the welfare of Israel. Thus, in trying to avoid alienating their own constituencies, they use language that alienates the Palestinians, to whom such statements convey the message that even Israeli doves are indifferent to their welfare.

Palestinian moderates, in turn, alienate their Israeli counterparts when they use language that justifies their readiness for compromise strictly on pragmatic grounds. They often make a point of explaining that they accept a two-state solution, not because they consider it just, but because they have no other choice. Thus, they are responding to Israel's power, but not acknowledging its legitimacy. Israelis are not surprised by this stance, but they still find the language threatening. For them, it carries the clear implication that if the Palestinians had sufficient power, they would not accept a Palestinian state alongside of Israel but would pursue their original goal of liquidating the Jewish state. Even if they accept the sincere commitment of their Palestinian interlocutors to a two-state solution under the present circumstances, they are concerned about what would happen if there were a change in the balance of power: Can they rely on the stability and permanence of an agreement that leaves Israel's legitimacy in doubt?

In short, the pragmatic considerations that bring the parties into the coalition—and that, indeed, represent the greatest hope for peaceful resolution of the conflict—have side effects that complicate coalition work. They cause the parties to use language—often for domestic consumption, but also reflective of their own attitudes—that the other side finds dehumanizing or delegitimizing. Such language creates obstacles to constructive interaction among workshop participants, which third-party facilitators must seek to overcome, with the active collaboration of the participants themselves.

Fluctuations in the Political and Psychological Climate

Workshop participants are, of necessity, always responsive to political developments in their own communities. They pursue and evaluate their coalition work in the context of the official activities, the public moods, and the internal debates within their respective bodies politic. They tend to be particularly cautious at times of fluidity within their community, when the political leadership is engaged in a new diplomatic initiative or when the general public is caught up in a collective response to major new events. Under such circumstances, coalition members try to avoid actions that contradict, or appear to contradict, the strategies pursued by the leadership or the dominant mood of the public; that might undermine their own positions in the domestic political maneuvering; or that might convey the wrong message to the other side (by giving the impression, for example, of a split in the ranks of the moderate camp in their community).

Participants' sensitivity to the fluctuations in their own community's political and psychological climate has consequences for the reliability of their coalition work. Even those who are, in principle, committed to joint efforts with the other side in the search for a mutually satisfactory solution may at times be reluctant to engage in these efforts because of domestic considerations of the moment. Thus, they may prefer to stay away from a workshop or similar meeting at a particularly sensitive time. Or, if they do participate, they may be less forthcoming than they usually are.

The effect of domestic considerations of the moment on workshop proceedings was illustrated by two Israeli-Palestinian workshops that we conducted in the spring of 1987—about half a year before the onset of the *intifada,* the Palestinian uprising, in the occupied territories. The Palestinians in these workshops seemed interested in developing ideas for concrete actions or statements that both parties could support. The Israelis did not respond with an outright no to these overtures, but they repeatedly sidestepped them. As a matter of fact, even in the privacy of the workshop itself, the Israeli participants were clearly reluctant to endorse the concept of a Palestinian state or of negotiations with the Palestine Liberation Organization (PLO). This reluctance surprised me, because I knew that at least some of the Israeli participants had been quite open to these positions in the past. And yet, the same pattern was repeated in both workshops, which took place within three weeks of each other.

In retrospect, I came to understand this pattern in terms of events on the ground during that period. Shimon Peres, leader of the Israeli Labor party and then foreign minister, was engaged in active discussions with King Hussein of Jordan, which for a while appeared to be on the verge of success. These discussions revived the so-called Jordanian option in the Israeli political debate: the attempt to resolve the conflict over the occupied territories through an agreement with the Jordanian government rather than the Palestinian leadership. As it turned out, the effort failed, and a few months later the Jordanian option became entirely irrelevant with the onset of the Palestinian *intifada*. While the Peres-Hussein explorations were in progress, however, the pro-negotiation elements in Israel—particularly those associated with the Labor party, as the majority of the participants in the two 1987 workshops were—did not want to undermine them (or appear to be undermining them) by actively pursuing a ''Palestinian option.'' Some were probably hoping that Peres would succeed, because they were themselves more comfortable with Jordan than with the PLO as the primary negotiating partner. Others may have been convinced that Peres's effort would ultimately fail and that Israel would have to deal with the Palestinian leadership directly, but they did not want to be accused of pursuing a line that contradicted an apparently promising and attractive initiative. Either way, the Israeli participants were reluctant to push their coalition work with Palestinians forward at that time, although they were anxious to maintain the relationship with their Palestinian counterparts.

In a workshop that took place in the spring of 1988, several months after the onset of the *intifada,* the pattern was reversed. This time, the Israelis called for concerted efforts and asked the Palestinians to help them persuade the Israeli public that the Palestinian commitment to the two-state option as a permanent arrangement was genuine and that a solution to the conflict consistent with Israeli security concerns was possible. But the Palestinians were reluctant to engage in active coalition work with Israelis at that point. They were reacting to the mood of the Palestinian public during that phase of the *intifada*—a mood of defiance, coupled with anger at the Israeli authorities for their violent repression of the uprising and at the Israeli people for condoning the repression. Under the circumstances, the Palestinian participants were not inclined to cooperate with their Israeli partners, particularly since they felt that the Israeli peace camp had not been sufficiently responsive to the plight of the Palestinians in the occupied territories. They felt that it was not appropriate for Israelis to ask them for help at a time when Israelis should be helping Palestinians. Interestingly, as the workshop proceeded, and after Israeli participants acknowledged the injustice that had been done to Palestinians, the two teams did engage in joint thinking about how they could help each other promote their common interests.

In the spring of 1989, fluctuations in the climate produced another reversal of sorts. By that time, Palestinians were quite interested in working with Israelis in order to reassure them about the sincerity of Palestinian peace initiatives. On the Israeli side, however, we found some reluctance, probably related to the fact that the Israeli unity (Likud-Labor) government of that time was pursuing its own initiative: an election proposal known as the ''Rabin-Shamir plan.'' I invited several members of the Knesset (the Israeli Parliament), representing the Labor party, to a semi-public symposium that included two PLO representatives. Though they expressed great interest, they decided— apparently as a group—to decline the invitation, because they did not want to appear to be pursuing an alternative channel to the election proposal that had been initiated by Yitzchak Rabin, the defense minister and a top leader of their own party.[3] In a workshop that took place a few weeks earlier, some Israeli participants, mostly academics, expressed the view that the Rabin-Shamir election proposal was the maximum that the Israeli political system could produce at that time, and that a Palestinian initiative was needed before there could be any further movement on the Israeli side. Thus, they expressed a sense of futility regarding their own potential contribution. In effect, they were saying that there was nothing for them to do at that time to promote the coalition effort.

In sum, as these examples illustrate, the coalitions that we try to build across conflict lines are very much subject to fluctuations in the political climate and the general mood in each community. These may hamper the effective functioning of the coalition and may create a lack of synchronism in the readiness for coalition work between the two sides. This is part of the reality of this kind of coalition work, with which the third-party facilitators must be prepared to contend.

WHY THE COALITION MUST REMAIN UNEASY

Barriers to the formation and effective functioning of a coalition across conflict lines, such as mutual distrust, alienating language, and fluctuations in the political and psychological climate, directly reflect the dynamics of the larger conflict. Insofar as coalition members are bona fide representatives of their national groups—as they must be if the coalition is to achieve its goal of promoting negotiations—these barriers will inevitably restrain the work of the coalition, and it is part of the task of third-party facilitators to help overcome them.

But the barriers confronting the work of coalitions across conflict lines raise an additional complication: Not only is it difficult to overcome these barriers so that coalition work can proceed, but it may in fact be counterproductive to overcome them entirely. It may be important for the coalition to remain uneasy in order to enhance the value of what participants learn during workshops themselves and of what they can achieve upon reentry into their home communities.

Workshop Learning

Experimental research by Myron Rothbart and associates (Rothbart & John, 1985; Rothbart & Lewis, 1988) suggests that direct contact between members of conflicting groups may have a paradoxical effect on intergroup stereotypes. If it becomes apparent, in the course of direct interaction with representatives of the other group, that they do not fit one's stereotype of the group, there is a tendency to differentiate these particular individuals from their group: to perceive them as nonmembers. Since they are excluded from the category, the stereotype about the category itself can remain intact.

This process of differentiating and excluding individual members of the other group from their category could well take place in workshops in which a high degree of trust develops between the parties. Such an outcome would clearly be counterproductive, since it would forestall learning about the possibilities for negotiation and peace with the other *group,* which is of course what ultimately matters. To be persuaded that one could make peace with the particular individuals participating in the workshop would be irrelevant unless these particular individuals were seen as representative of their group or of some significant segment of the group. Thus, it is important in workshops to avoid the tendency to categorize members of the enemy camp who show a readiness for peace as not really part of their group, and thus to maintain the image of the enemy as implacable. Fortunately, the workshop setting and process are well suited to recognizing, analyzing, and counteracting such tendencies. The parties themselves are alert, within the workshop setting, to the general issue of how well participants reflect their larger communities; and the third party is always ready to call attention to the relationship between what is said or done in the workshop and what is happening outside.

An Israeli-Palestinian workshop that we conducted several years ago provides a good illustration of the way in which the tendency to recategorize individuals who contradict the stereotyped image of their group may manifest itself in the workshop setting, as well as the way in which it can be counteracted. In this workshop, as in virtually all others, participants engaged in a process of testing each other's sincerity. On this occasion, they all passed the test: The participants were convinced that their counterparts on the other side were genuinely committed to a peaceful solution and that their intentions could be trusted. This trust, however, did not extend beyond the particular individuals in the room, since the Israelis tended to see the Palestinian participants as non-PLO and the Palestinians tended to see the Israeli participants as non-Zionist. As the workshop proceeded, they began to make some important discoveries about each other. The Palestinians insisted on making it very clear that they identified closely with the PLO. The Israelis, at a later point, made it very clear that they were dedicated Zionists. Thus, the Israelis had to confront the fact that the Palestinians whom they had come to trust, at least to the extent of accepting the sincerity of their commitment to peace, were PLO loyalists; and the Palestinians had to confront the fact that the Israelis whom they had come to trust were loyal Zionists.

These discoveries made it necessary for the participants to revise their image of the PLO and the Zionist movement, respectively—changing it from the view of a movement whose only purpose is to destroy one's own group to that of a movement that has some positive goals as well and with whom it may be possible, therefore, to negotiate a mutually satisfactory solution. This is an extremely important learning experience, because it opens up the possibility of peace with one's enemies as they are—peace between nationalist, PLO-affiliated, Palestinians and Zionist Israelis—without assuming that peace becomes possible only if these enemies undergo conversion and abandon their national ideology (Kelman, 1987). It is part of the task of the third party to help make this connection, as we did in our interventions during the workshop cited here.

If this learning is to occur, it is essential for the parties to reconfirm their belongingness to their national categories: to make it clear that they are not just exceptions, but part of the mainstream of their respective communities. Rothbart and John (1985) make this point when they stress that intergroup contact is most likely to lead to attitude change if the in-group/out-group distinction remains salient, so that the disconfirming information becomes associated with the group label (pp. 101–2). This brings me back to the argument that it would be counterproductive, in coalitions across intense conflict lines, to overcome the barriers to coalition work entirely—that it is important for the coalition to remain uneasy. If the coalition became so tight and comfortable that it overshadowed the conflicting communities to which the coalition members belong, workshops would actually become less capable of achieving one of their important goals: to demonstrate the possibility of peace between the two enemy camps.

The Reentry Problem

A second and major reason why coalitions across conflict lines must remain uneasy relates to what is often called the "reentry problem" (see, for example, Kelman, 1972, and Walton, 1970). If workshops are to achieve their larger purpose, participants must be able to feed the ideas and insights they develop in the course of workshops into the political debate and the decision-making process in their home communities. Their ability to do so depends on how they are perceived when they return home. If the coalition becomes so cohesive and comfortable that the participants forget the line that divides them, their effectiveness upon reentry is likely to be diminished.

In the short run, the coalition must remain uneasy if coalition members are to maintain their credibility and hence their political effectiveness within their own groups. If they become excessively involved and identified with the coalition, they may experience a severe reentry problem, feeling alienated from and rejected by their own community. Under such circumstances, they would be hampered in the successful performance of the role of change agent within that community. Thus, part of the dialectics of the interactive problem-solving process (cf. Kelman, 1979; Kelman & Cohen, 1986) derives from the competing requirements of, on the one hand, facilitating the development of a productive coalition across conflict lines but, on the other hand, in doing so, not encouraging a coalition so tight and cohesive that members' political effectiveness at home is compromised.

In the long run, the coalition across conflict lines must remain uneasy because a stable peace and coexistence between the conflicting national groups require a *national consensus within each group* in favor of the new relationship. It is not enough, therefore, for the pro-negotiation forces to prevail over the anti-negotiation forces in their own community. They have to do so in a way that promotes the formation of a new consensus within each nation. The coalition between subsets of the two parties must therefore be viewed as a strictly temporary phenomenon. Its ultimate success depends on its ability to create a situation in which each party *as a whole* can enter into a peaceful, cooperative relationship with its former enemy. To this end, it is important that the coalition members do not become so strongly bonded to each other that they jeopardize their relationship with their own national communities.

In sum, a coalition across international conflict lines is one in which it is neither possible nor desirable to promote maximal cohesiveness. Such coalitions confront the paradox of having to work at maintaining the bonds that tie members to the very groups within their own societies that the coalition is designed to oppose.

CONCLUSION

In conclusion, I want to describe briefly the current direction of my work, which reflects the concept of building a coalition across conflict lines and also illustrates some of the complexities in building such a coalition.

Until recently, the workshops and related opportunities for interaction across conflict lines that my colleagues and I have organized over the years were all self-contained events. This is not to say that there has been a lack of continuity in these earlier efforts. A number of individuals have participated in two or more of our workshops. "Alumni" of the workshops also continue to be involved in a variety of other efforts at Israeli-Palestinian communication and collaboration, in which they draw on their earlier interactions. Moreover, our workshops have had a cumulative effect in that they have contributed to the development of a cadre of individuals within the Israeli and Palestinian intellectual and political elites who have had direct experience in communicating with their counterparts on the other side—an experience that has been mostly positive and always instructive. Through these experiences, certain new insights, sensitivities, ideas for conflict resolution, and significant items of information (including a more differentiated knowledge about the relevant actors on the other side) have entered into the political debate and have helped to create a political environment more conducive to negotiation. In all of these ways it can be said that workshop participants have been part of a loose coalition of pro-negotiation elements on the two sides that has had some impact on the political process. Because of logistical and financial constraints, however, I had never attempted to organize a "continuing workshop," in which the same group of participants would meet regularly over an extended period of time. Moreover, the political situation had not been entirely congenial to systematic longer-term efforts.

With the onset of the *intifada,* the dramatic changes in the official positions of the Palestinian movement, and the proliferation of Israeli-Palestinian meetings, I decided that it had become both possible and urgently necessary to organize such a continuing workshop. There are several unique contributions that a continuing workshop can make to the larger political process, compared to the contributions of the one-time events that we organized in the past or to most of the Israeli-Palestinian conferences organized by a variety of third parties around the world in recent years. These contributions can best be conceived as elements of a systematic process of coalition building.

1. A continuing workshop represents a *sustained* effort to address concrete issues, making it possible to push the process of conflict analysis and interactive problem solving farther and to apply it more systematically than in previous workshops.
2. The longer time period and the continuing nature of the project make it possible to go beyond the sharing of perspectives—which is in itself a significant achievement of our previous workshops—to the *joint production of creative ideas.*
3. The periodic reconvening of a continuing workshop allows for an iterative and cumulative process, based on *feedback and correction.* The participants have an opportunity to take the ideas developed in the course of a workshop back to their own communities, to gather reactions, and to return to the next meeting with proposals for strengthening, expanding, or modifying the original ideas. It is also possible for participants, within or across parties, to meet or otherwise communicate with each other between workshop sessions in order to work out some of the ideas more fully and bring the results of their efforts back to the next session.
4. Finally, a continuing workshop provides far better opportunities than a singular event to address systematically the question of *how to disseminate ideas and proposals* developed at the workshop most effectively and appropriately.

Thus, as we move toward the development of continuing workshops, our efforts manifest the process of coalition building and coalition work in more explicit and concrete ways. In doing so, we are maximizing the potential contribution of interactive problem solving to conflict resolution and providing a better test of the utility of this approach. As it happens, our first continuing workshop has been convened at a time of serious deterioration in the Israeli-Palestinian relationship, as described toward the end of the section on mutual distrust. We may also have an opportunity, therefore, to make a significant contribution to defusing the dangerously critical situation presented by the current state of the Israeli-Palestinian conflict.

As I began, in the winter of 1989-90, to formulate my proposal for a continuing workshop, I received some instructive reminders of the complexities of forming a coalition across conflict lines. In my initial statement of the idea, I ran afoul of my own admonitions about the need to preserve the uneasy character of the coalition. In my own enthusiasm, I described the continuing workshop as a joint Israeli-Palestinian working group and emphasized the generation of joint products in the form of written documents to be published over the names of both the Israeli and Palestinian participants. When I discussed the idea with several knowledgeable and politically sophisticated Palestinians, they expressed some reservations that I should have anticipated on the basis of my own analysis. They felt that the proposed "joint working group" sounded too much like a separate entity transcending the two conflicting parties; to participate in such a venture might alienate Palestinians from their own community and undermine their credibility. They were also concerned that written products might create an appearance of prenegotiation documents, setting out the parties' starting positions; such documents, they felt, should be produced by the parties themselves rather than by a joint group whose members, in any event, have not been authorized to negotiate. They did not question the value of *joint thinking* by both sides, which could transform the development of each side's negotiating positions; what they wanted to avoid was any action that might appear to be preempting their political leadership.

My guess is that Israelis would have expressed similar reservations about my original formulation of the continuing workshop. They might have differed in their emphasis, since they are in a different political situation than the Palestinians. However, they would also have been concerned about alienating themselves from their own community, and undermining their credibility and political effectiveness, by in effect joining with the enemy to make proposals to their own leadership. As it turned out, I did not test the Israeli reaction, because I immediately recognized the validity of the reservations expressed by the Palestinians. I realized that I was trying to push the coalition process too far and too fast for the comfort of the two parties, particularly since I was hoping to recruit participants close to the center of the political spectrum in each community. I therefore revised my proposal along two lines: I described the continuing workshop not so much as a joint working group, but as a forum for joint thinking and exploration of ideas, provided by the third party; and I deemphasized the development of joint written products— not ruling them out, but making it clear that there was no expectation that such products would emerge at all and, if they did, it would be only by unanimous agreement of all participants and only within the limits and at the pace that they agreed upon.

Our efforts to organize a continuing workshop, after reformulating the proposal along these more modest lines, finally bore fruit.[4] My colleague, Nadim Rouhana of Boston College, has collaborated closely with me in organizing and conducting the workshop. Two highly experienced practitioners of conflict resolution, Harold Saunders of the Kettering Foundation and C. R. Mitchell of George Mason University's Institute for Conflict Analysis and Resolution, have joined us as members of the third-party panel. We succeeded in recruiting six Israeli and six Palestinian participants—four men and two women on each side—who committed themselves to a series of three workshop meetings during the year of 1990-91. The participants are high-ranking and respected individuals in their respective societies, whose activities and positions enable them to influence public discourse and political decisions by passing on the insights and ideas gained in the workshop to political leaders and the public at large. They represent significant segments of each society and its political spectrum. All, however, are within the mainstream and fairly close to the political center of their respective communities.

Despite the deterioration of the situation in the Middle East and of the relationship between Israelis and Palestinians, and despite some serious obstacles that arose in the last minute, the first meeting of the workshop convened in November 1990. The second meeting was held in June 1991, after the deepening of the crisis in Israeli-Palestinian relations as a result of the Gulf war. The third meeting is about to take place, as of the time of this writing (August 1991). At this meeting, the group will decide how to disseminate the ideas generated over the course of this continuing workshop, and whether and how it wishes to continue its collaborative work.

As our work moves in the direction of continuing workshops, the metaphor of a coalition across conflict lines becomes increasingly appropriate. It serves as a useful conceptual handle for describing our program, for sharpening the goals of our efforts, and for making decisions about recruitment of participants and about workshop structure and process. Analysis of the special character of this kind of coalition—as one that is inevitably, and must remain, an uneasy coalition—helps to identify and deal with problems in coalition building and obstacles to the coalition work itself. The concept of coalition across conflict lines and the model of the continuing workshop demonstrate, in my view, the potentially fruitful interaction between social-psychological analysis and intervention practice.

NOTES

This chapter is a product of an action research program supported by grants from the U.S. Institute of Peace and the Ford Foundation to the Harvard Center for International Affairs. I am greatly indebted to the granting agencies and to the center for their support of my work. An earlier version of the paper was prepared for a conference on coalition dynamics and improvement, which was convened at Boston University in May 1988, to honor my late friend Robert Chin on the occasion of his retirement. I dedicate the chapter to Bob's memory, with deep appreciation for his friendship over several decades.

1. Participants are not always persuaded, however, that their counterparts on the other side represent the majority of their community or a powerful bloc within that community with the capacity to "deliver" on a compromise solution. In fact, the parties tend to differ in their claims of representativeness. Palestinian participants, in recent years, have presented themselves as part of the majority of their community. Israelis, on the other hand, have described themselves as representing a minority or at most half of the population, although many have argued that under the right circumstances their views could potentially become the majority position. These self-presentations conform with the available evidence. Readiness for a compromise in the form of a two-state solution has become the mainstream position among Palestinians, both inside the occupied territories and in the diaspora. The Israeli mainstream, however, is divided over the issue of territorial compromise and Palestinian self-determination.

2. With the prospect of a large-scale immigration of Soviet Jews to Israel, this argument has lost some of its force. If the Jewish population increased through immigration, as anticipated, the initial proportion of Arabs resulting from annexation of the occupied territories would be lower (perhaps one-third of the total population), and it would take longer for Arabs to become a majority in the country. The basic outlines of the issue, however, would remain unchanged.

3. Other Israeli political figures did participate, however, including one non-Labor member of the Knesset and two leading Labor party figures (members of the party's central committee) who were not in the Knesset. The symposium itself, and follow-ups to it, were quite constructive.

4. I am very grateful to the Nathan Cummings Foundation, the John D. and Catherine T. MacArthur Foundation, and the Rockefeller Family and Associates for funding the three meetings of the continuing workshop in 1990–91, as well as the necessary preparatory and follow-up work. I am also grateful to the Rockefeller Foundation for providing us the splendid facilities of its Bellagio Study and Conference Center for the third meeting of the workshop, in August 1991.

Contributors

Daniel Bar-Tal, Ph.D.
University of Tel-Aviv

Donald H. Baucom, Ph.D.
Department of Psychology
University of North Carolina
  at Chapel Hill

Charles K. Burnett
Department of Psychology
University of North Carolina
  at Chapel Hill

Dawna Coutant-Sassic
Department of Psychology
Texas A&M University

Norman Epstein, Ph.D.
Department of Psychology
University of Maryland

Leonie Huddy, Ph.D.
Department of Psychology
UCLA

James M. Jones, Ph.D.
Department of Psychology
University of Delaware

Herbert C. Kelman, Ph.D.
Department of Psychology
Harvard University

Gary P. Latham, Ph.D.
Faculty of Management
University of Toronto

Neil B. McGillicuddy, Ph.D.
Research Institute on Alcoholism

Kim T. Morris
Department of Psychology
University of Delaware

Robert S. Peirce
Department of Psychology
SUNY at Buffalo

Dean G. Pruitt, Ph.D.
Department of Psychology
SUNY at Buffalo

Lynn Rankin
Department of Psychology
University of North Carolina
  at Chapel Hill

Janusz Reykowski, Ph.D.
Polska Akademia Nauk
Warsaw, Poland

Cecilia L. Ridgeway, Ph.D.
Department of Sociology
Stanford University

Myron Rothbart, Ph.D.
Department of Psychology
University of Oregon

Caryl E. Rusbult, Ph.D.
Department of Psychology
University of North Carolina
  at Chapel Hill

David O. Sears, Ph.D.
Department of Psychology
UCLA

Jeffry A. Simpson, Ph.D
Department of Psychology
Texas A&M University

Gary L. Welton, Ph.D.
Department of Psychology
Tarbor College

Frankie Wong, Ph.D.
Department of Psychology
Hofstra University

Stephen Worchel, Ph.D.
Department of Psychology
Texas A&M University

D. R. Zhou, Ph.D.
Center for American Studies
Fudan University
Shanghai, China

Jo M. Zubek
Department of Psychology
SUNY at Buffalo

References

CHAPTER 1. INTRODUCTION: MULTIDISCIPLINARY PERSPECTIVES ON CONFLICT

Amir, Y. (1969). Contact hypothesis in ethnic relations. *Psychological Bulletin, 71,* 319–41.

Berscheid, E., & Campbell, B. (1981). The changing longevity of close heterosexual relationships: A commentary and forecast. In M. J. Lerner & S. C. Lerner (Eds.), *The justice motive in social behavior.* New York: Plenum.

Cooper, J., & Fazio, R. H. (1984). A new look at dissonance theory. In L. Berkowitz (Ed.), *Advances in experimental social psychology* (Vol. 17). New York: Academic Press.

Deutsch, M. (1973). *The resolution of conflict.* New Haven, CT: Yale University Press.

Dewe, P. J. (1989). Examining the nature of work stress: Individual evaluations of stressful experiences and coping. *Human Relations, 42,* 993–1013.

Hollander, E. P. (1985). Leadership and power. In G. Lindzey & E. Aronson (Eds.), *Handbook of social psychology* (3d ed., Vol. 2, 485–537). New York: Random House.

Kelley, H. H., & Thibaut, J. W. (1978). *Interpersonal relations: A theory of interdependence.* New York: Wiley.

Marney, J. (1991). Leisure time diminishing: Family, housekeeping are taking a back seat to work. *Marketing (Maclean Hunter), 96,* 19.

Meehl, P. E. (1978). Theoretical risks and tabular asterisks: Sir Karl, Sir Ronald, and the slow progress of soft psychology. *Journal of Consulting and Clinical Psychology, 46,* 806–34.

Norton, A. J., & Glick, P. C. (1976). Marital instability: Past, present, and future. *Journal of Social Issues, 32,* 5–20.

Peterson, D. R. (1983). Conflict. In H. H. Kelley, E. Berscheid, A. Christensen, J. H. Harvey, T. L. Huston, G. Levinger, E. McClintock, L. A. Peplau, & D. R. Peterson (Eds.), *Close relationships* (360–96). San Francisco: Freeman.

Rogers, C. R. (1961). *On becoming a person.* Boston: Houghton Mifflin.

Steiner, I. D. (1974). Whatever happened to the group in social psychology? *Journal of Experimental Social Psychology, 10,* 93–108.

Worchel, S., & Austin, W. (Eds.) (1986). *The psychology of intergroup relations.* Chicago: Nelson-Hall.

CHAPTER 2. CONFLICT IN MARRIAGE: A COGNITIVE/ BEHAVIORAL FORMULATION

Abramson, L. Y., Seligman, M. E. P., & Teasdale, J. (1978). Learned helplessness in humans: Critique and reformulation. *Journal of Abnormal Psychology, 87,* 49–94.

Bandura, A. (1977). *Social learning theory.* Englewood Cliffs, NJ: Prentice-Hall.

Baucom, D. H. (1976). Independent masculinity and femininity scales on the California Psychological Inventory. *Journal of Consulting and Clinical Psychology, 44,* 876.

Baucom, D. H. (1980). Independent CPI masculinity and femininity scales: Psychological correlates and a sex role typology. *Journal of Personality Assessment, 44,* 262–71.

Baucom, D. H. (1982). A comparison of behavioral contracting and problem-solving/ communications training in behavioral marital therapy. *Behavior Therapy, 13,* 162–74.

Baucom, D. H., & Adams, A. (1987). Assessing communication in marital interaction. In K. D. O'Leary (Ed.), *Assessment of marital discord* (139–82). Hillsdale, NJ: Erlbaum.

Baucom, D. H., & Aiken, P. A. (1984). Sex role identity, marital satisfaction, and response to behavioral marital therapy. *Journal of Consulting and Clinical Psychology, 52,* 438–44.

Baucom, D. H., & Epstein, N. (1990). *Cognitive-behavioral marital therapy.* New York: Brunner/Mazel.

Baucom, D. H., Epstein, N., Rankin, L. A., & Burnett, C. K. (1990, November). *New measures for assessing couples' standards.* Paper presented at the annual convention of the Association for the Advancement of Behavior Therapy, San Francisco.

Baucom, D. H., Epstein, N., Sayers, S., & Sher, T. G. (1989). The role of cognitions in marital relationships: Definitional, methodological, and conceptual issues. *Journal of Consulting and Clinical Psychology, 57,* 31–38.

Baucom, D. H., & Lester, G. W. (1986). The usefulness of cognitive restructuring as an adjunct to behavioral marital therapy. *Behavior Therapy, 17,* 385–403.

Baucom, D. H., Notarius, C. I., Burnett, C. K., & Haefner, P. (1990). Gender differences and sex-role identity in marriage. In F. D. Fincham & T. Bradbury (Eds.), *The psychology of marriage: Conceptual, empirical, and applied perspectives* (150–71). New York: Guilford Press.

Baucom, D. H., Sayers, S. L., & Duhe, A. (1989). Attributional style and attributional patterns among married couples. *Journal of Personality and Social Psychology, 56,* 596–607.

Baucom, D. H., Sayers, S. L., & Sher, T. G. (1990). Supplementing behavioral marital therapy with cognitive restructuring and emotional expressiveness training: An outcome investigation. *Journal of Consulting and Clinical Psychology, 58,* 636–45.

Baucom, D. H., Wheeler, C. M., & Bell, G. (1984, November). *Assessing the role of attributions in marital distress*. Paper presented at the annual convention of the Association for the Advancement of Behavior Therapy, Philadelphia.

Beck, A. T., Rush, A. J., Shaw, B. F., & Emery, G. (1979). *Cognitive therapy of depression*. New York: Guilford.

Bennun, I. (1985a). Behavioral marital therapy: An outcome evaluation of conjoint, group, and one spouse treatment. *Scandinavian Journal of Behaviour Therapy, 14*, 157–68.

Bennun, I. (1985b). Prediction and responsiveness in behavioral marital therapy. *Behavioural Psychotherapy, 13*, 186–201.

Billings, A. (1979). Conflict resolution in distressed and nondistressed married couples. *Journal of Consulting and Clinical Psychology, 17*, 368–76.

Birchler, G. R., Weiss, R. L., & Vincent, J. P. (1975). Multimethod analysis of social reinforcement exchange between maritally distressed and nondistressed spouse and stranger dyads. *Journal of Personality and Social Psychology, 31*, 349–60.

Bradbury, T. N., & Fincham, F. D. (1989, November). *Cognition and marital dysfunction: The role of efficacy expectations*. Paper presented at the annual meeting of the Association for the Advancement of Behavior Therapy, Washington, DC.

Bradbury, T. N., & Fincham, F. D. (1990). Attributions in marriage: Review and critique. *Psychological Bulletin, 107*, 3–33.

Burnett, C. K., Egolf, J., Solon, T. T., & Sullivan, G. (1984). *The premarital inventory profile*. Chapel Hill: Intercommunications.

Christensen, A., & Nies, D. C. (1980). The Spouse Observation Checklist: Empirical analysis and critique. *American Journal of Family Therapy, 8*, 69–79.

Christensen, A., Sullaway, M., & King, C. (1983). Systematic error in behavioral reports of dyadic interaction: Egocentric bias and content effects. *Behavioral Assessment, 5*, 131–42.

Doherty, W. J. (1981a). Cognitive processes in intimate conflict: 1. Extending attribution theory. *American Journal of Family Therapy, 9*(1), 3–13.

Doherty, W. J. (1981b). Cognitive processes in intimate conflict: 2. Efficacy and learned helplessness. *American Journal of Family Therapy, 9*(2), 35–44.

Eidelson, R. J., & Epstein, N. (1982). Cognition and relationship maladjustment: Development of a measure of dysfunctional relationship beliefs. *Journal of Consulting and Clinical Psychology, 50*, 715–20.

Ellis, A. (1976). Techniques of handling anger in marriage. *Journal of Marriage and Family Counseling, 2*, 305–16.

Ellis, A., Sichel, J. L., Yeager, R. J., DiMattia, D. J., & DiGiuseppe, R. (1989). *Rational-emotive couples therapy*. New York: Pergamon.

Elwood, R. W., & Jacobson, N. S. (1982). Spouses' agreement in reporting their behavioral interactions: A clinical replication. *Journal of Consulting and Clinical Psychology, 50*, 783–84.

Emmelkamp, P. M. G., van Linden van den Heuvell, C., Ruphan, M., Sanderman, R., Scholing, A., & Stroink, F. (1988). Cognitive and behavioral interventions: A comparative evaluation with clinically distressed couples. *Journal of Family Psychology, 1*, 365–77.

Epstein, N. (1982). Cognitive therapy with couples. *American Journal of Family Therapy, 10*(1), 5–16.

Epstein, N. (1986). Cognitive marital therapy: Multi-level assessment and intervention. *Journal of Rational-Emotive Therapy, 4*, 68–81.

Epstein, N., & Eidelson, R. J. (1981). Unrealistic beliefs of clinical couples: Their relationship to expectations, goals, and satisfaction. *American Journal of Family Therapy, 9*(4), 13–22.

Epstein, N., Jayne-Lazarus, C., & DeGiovanni, I. S. (1979). Cotrainers as models of relationships: Effects on the outcome of couples therapy. *Journal of Marital and Family Therapy, 5*, 53–60.

Epstein, N., Pretzer, J. L., & Fleming, B. (1982, November). *Cognitive therapy and communication training: Comparisons of effects with distressed couples.* Paper presented at the annual meeting of the Association for the Advancement of Behavior Therapy, Los Angeles.

Epstein, N., Pretzer, J. L., & Fleming, B. (1987). The role of cognitive appraisal in self-reports of marital communication. *Behavior Therapy, 18*, 51–69.

Fincham, F. D. (1985). Attribution processes in distressed and nondistressed couples: 2. Responsibility for marital problems. *Journal of Abnormal Psychology, 94*, 183–90.

Fincham, F. D., Beach, S. R. H., & Nelson, G. (1987). Attribution processes in distressed and nondistressed couples: 3. Causal and responsibility attributions for spouse behavior. *Cognitive Therapy and Research, 11*, 71–86.

Fincham, F. D., & Bradbury, T. N. (1987a). Cognitive processes in close relationships: An attribution-efficacy model. *Journal of Personality and Social Psychology, 53*, 1106–18.

Fincham, F. D., & Bradbury, T. N. (1987b). The impact of attributions in marriage: A longitudinal analysis. *Journal of Personality and Social Psychology, 53*, 510–17.

Floyd, F. J., & Markman, H. J. (1983). Observational biases in spouse observation: Toward a cognitive/behavioral model of marriage. *Journal of Consulting and Clinical Psychology, 51*, 450–57.

Geiss, S. K., & O'Leary, K. D. (1981). Therapist ratings of frequency and severity of marital problems: Implications for research. *Journal of Marital and Family Therapy, 7*, 515–20.

Gottman, J. (1979). *Marital interaction: Experimental investigations.* New York: Academic Press.

Gottman, J., & Krokoff, L. (1989). Marital interaction and satisfaction: A longitudinal view. *Journal of Consulting and Clinical Psychology, 57*, 47–52.

Gottman, J., & Levenson, R. (1988). The social psychophysiology of marriage. In P. Noller & M. A. Fitzpatrick (Eds.), *Perspectives on marital interaction* 182–200). Clevedon, England: Multilingual Matters.

Gottman, J., Markman, H., & Notarius, C. (1977). The topography of marital conflict: A sequential analysis of verbal and non-verbal behavior. *Journal of Marriage and the Family, 39*, 461–78.

Gottman, J., Notarius, C., Markman, H., Banks, S., Yoppi, B., & Rubin, M. E. (1976). Behavior exchange theory and marital decision making. *Journal of Personality and Social Psychology, 34*, 14–23.

Hahlweg, K., & Markman, H. J. (1988). Effectiveness of behavioral marital therapy: Empirical status of behavioral techniques in preventing and alleviating marital distress. *Journal of Consulting and Clinical Psychology, 56*, 440–47.

Hahlweg, K., Revenstorf, D., & Schindler, L. (1982). Treatment of marital distress: Comparing formats and modalities. *Advances in Behavior Research and Therapy, 4,* 57–74.

Holmes, T. H., & Rahe, R. H. (1967). The social readjustment rating scale. *Journal of Psychosomatic Research, 11,* 213–18.

Hops, H., Wills, T. A., Patterson, G. R., & Weiss, R. L. (1972). *Marital interaction coding system.* Eugene: University of Oregon, Oregon Research Institute.

Huber, C. H., & Milstein, B. (1985). Cognitive restructuring and a collaborative set in couples' work. *American Journal of Family Therapy, 13*(2), 17–27.

Jacobson, N. S. (1978). Specific and nonspecific factors in the effectiveness of a behavioral approach to the treatment of marital discord. *Journal of Consulting and Clinical Psychology, 46,* 442–52.

Jacobson, N. S., Follette, W. C., & McDonald, D. W. (1982). Reactivity to positive and negative behavior in distressed and nondistressed married couples. *Journal of Consulting and Clinical Psychology, 50,* 706–14.

Jacobson, N. S., Follette, W. C., & Revenstorf, D. (1984). Psychotherapy outcome research: Methods for reporting variability and evaluating clinical significance. *Behavior Therapy, 15,* 336–52.

Jacobson, N. S., Follette, W. C., Revenstorf, D., Baucom, D. H., Hahlweg, K., & Margolin, G. (1984). Variability in outcome and clinical significance of behavioral marital therapy: A reanalysis of outcome data. *Journal of Consulting and Clinical Psychology, 52,* 497–504.

Jacobson, N.S., & Margolin, G. (1979). *Marital therapy: Strategies based on social learning and behavior exchange principles.* New York: Brunner/Mazel.

Jacobson, N. S., Waldron, H., & Moore, D. (1980). Toward a behavioral profile of marital distress. *Journal of Consulting and Clinical Psychology, 48,* 696–703.

Johnson, S. M., & Greenberg, L. S. (1985). Differential effects of experiential and problem-solving interventions in resolving marital conflict. *Journal of Consulting and Clinical Psychology, 53,* 175–84.

Jones, M. E., & Stanton, A. L. (1988). Dysfunctional beliefs, belief similarity, and marital distress: A comparison of models. *Journal of Social and Clinical Psychology, 7,* 1–14.

Margolin, G. (1978). A multilevel approach to the assessment of communication positiveness in distressed marital couples. *International Journal of Family Counseling, 6,* 81–89.

Margolin, G. (1981). Behavior exchange in happy and unhappy marriages: A family cycle perspective. *Behavior Therapy, 12,* 329–43.

Margolin, G., & Wampold, B. E. (1981). Sequential analysis of conflict and accord in distressed and nondistressed marital partners. *Journal of Consulting and Clinical Psychology, 49,* 554–67.

Markman, H. J. (1984). The longitudinal study of couples' interactions: Implications for understanding and predicting the development of marital distress. In K. Hahlweg & N. S. Jacobson (Eds.), *Marital interaction: Analysis and modification* (253–81). New York: Guilford.

Mehlman, S. K., Baucom, D. H., & Anderson, D. (1983). Effectiveness of cotherapists versus single therapists and immediate versus delayed treatment in behavioral marital therapy. *Journal of Consulting and Clinical Psychology, 51,* 258–66.

Notarius, C. I., Benson, P. R., Sloane, D., Vanzetti, N. A., & Hornyak, L. M. (1989). Exploring the interface between perception and behavior: An analysis of marital interaction in distressed and nondistressed couples. *Behavioral Assessment, 11,* 39–64.

O'Farrell, T. J., Cutter, H. S., & Floyd, F. J. (1983). *The class on alcoholism and marriage (CALM) project: Results on marital adjustment and communication from before to after therapy* (Tech. Rep. No. 4-1). Brockton, MA: Brockton/West Roxbury Veterans Administration Medical Center.

Pretzer, J., Epstein, N., & Fleming, B. (in press). The Marital Attitude Survey: A measure of dysfunctional attributions and expectancies. *The Journal of Cognitive Psychotherapy: An International Quarterly.*

Robinson, E. A., & Price, M. G. (1980). Pleasurable behavior in marital interaction: An observational study. *Journal of Consulting and Clinical Psychology, 48,* 117–18.

Sayers, S. L., Baucom, D. H., & Sher, T. G. (1989, November). *The effects of behavioral marital therapy, cognitive restructuring, and emotional expressiveness training on couples' interaction: A sequential analysis.* Paper presented at the annual convention of the Association for the Advancement of Behavior Therapy, Washington, DC.

Sayers, S. L., & Baucom, D. H. (In press). The role of femininity and masculinity in distressed couples' communication. *Journal of Personality and Social Psychology.*

Snyder, D. K. (1979). Multidimensional assessment of marital satisfaction. *Journal of Marriage and the Family, 41,* 813–23.

Snyder, D. K. (1981). *Marital Satisfaction Inventory (MSI) manual.* Los Angeles: Western Psychological Services.

Snyder, D. K., & Regts, J. M. (1982). Factor scales for assessing marital disharmony and disaffection. *Journal of Consulting and Clinical Psychology, 50,* 736–43.

Snyder, D. K., & Wills, R. M. (1989). Behavioral versus insight-oriented marital therapy: Effects on individual and interspousal functioning. *Journal of Consulting and Clinical Psychology, 57,* 39–46.

Spanier, G. B. (1976). Measuring dyadic adjustment: New scales for assessing the quality of marriage and similar dyads. *Journal of Marriage and the Family, 38,* 15–28.

Thompson, J. S., & Snyder, D. K. (1986). Attribution theory in intimate relationships: A methodological review. *American Journal of Family Therapy, 14,* 123–38.

Vincent, J. P., Friedman, L. C., Nugent, J., & Messerly, L. (1979). Demand characteristics in observations of marital interaction. *Journal of Consulting and Clinical Psychology, 47,* 557–66.

Weiss, R. L (1984). Cognitive and behavioral measures of marital interaction. In K. Hahlweg & N. S. Jacobson (Eds.), *Marital interaction: Analysis and modification* (232–52). New York: Guilford.

Weiss, R. L., Hops, H., & Patterson, G. R. (1973). A framework for conceptualizing marital conflict, a technology for altering it, some data for evaluating it. In L. A. Hamerlynck, L. C. Handy, & E. J. Mash (Eds.), *Behavior change: Methodology, concepts, and practice* (309–42). Champaign, IL: Research Press.

Weiss, R. L., & Perry, B. A. (1983). The Spouse Observation Checklist: Development and clinical applications. In E. E. Filsinger (Ed.), *Marriage and family assessment: A sourcebook for family therapy* (65–84). Beverly Hills, CA: Sage.

CHAPTER 3. UNDERSTANDING RESPONSES TO
DISSATISFACTION IN CLOSE RELATIONSHIPS: THE
EXIT-VOICE-LOYALTY-NEGLECT MODEL

Baucom, D. H., Sayers, S. L. & Duhe, A. (1989). Attributional style and attributional patterns among married couples. *Journal of Personality and Social Psychology, 56* 596–607.

Baxter, L. A. (1984). Trajectories of relationship disengagement. *Journal of Social and Personal Relationships, 1,* 29–48.

Bem, S. L. (1974). The measurement of psychological androgyny. *Journal of Consulting and Clinical Psychology, 47,* 155–62.

Berscheid, E. (1985). Interpersonal attraction. In G. Lindzey & E. Aronson (Eds.), *Handbook of social psychology* (Vol. 2, 3d ed., 413–84). New York: Random House.

Berzins, J. I., Welling, M. A., & Wetter, R. E. (1978). A new measure of psychological androgyny based on the Personality Research Form. *Journal of Consulting and Clinical Psychology, 46* 126–38.

Billings, A. (1979). Conflict resolution in distressed and nondistressed married couples. *Journal of Consulting and Clinical Psychology, 47,* 368–76.

Birchler G. R., & Webb, L. J. (1977). Discriminating interaction behaviors in happy and unhappy marriages. *Journal of Consulting and Clinical Psychology, 45,* 494–95.

Birchler, G. R., Weiss, R. L., & Vincent, J. P. (1975). Multimethod analysis of social reinforcement exchange between maritally distressed and nondistressed spouse and stranger dyads. *Journal of Personality and Social Psychology, 31,* 349–60.

Bradbury, T. N., & Fincham, F. D. (1990). Attributions in marriage: Review and critique. *Psychological Bulletin, 107,* 3–33.

Braiker, H. B., & Kelley, H. H. (1979). Conflict in the development of close relationships. In R. L. Burgess & T. L. Huston (Eds.), *Social exchange in developing relationships* (135–68). New York: Academic Press.

Buss, D. M. (1989). Conflict between the sexes: Strategic interference and the evocation of anger and upset. *Journal of Personality and Social Psychology, 56,* 735–47.

Buunk, B. (1981). Jealousy in sexually open marriages. *Alternative Lifestyles, 4,* 357–72.

Buunk, B. (1987). Conditions that promote breakups as a consequence of extradyadic involvements. *Journal of Social and Clinical Psychology, 5,* 271–84.

Clark, M. S., & Mills, J. (1979). Interpersonal attraction in exchange and communal relationships. *Journal of Personality and Social Psychology, 37,* 12–24.

Clark, M. S., Mills, J., & Powell, M. C. (1986). Keeping track of needs in communal and exchange relationships. *Journal of Personality and Social Psychology, 51,* 333–38.

Clark, M. S., & Reis, H. T. (1988). Interpersonal processes in close relationships. *Annual Review of Psychology, 39,* 609–72.

Daly, M., & Wilson, M. (1988). Evolutionary social psychology and family homicide. *Science, 242,* 519–24.

Deutsch, M. (1975). Equity, equality, and need: What determines which value will be used as the basis of distributive justice? *Journal of Social Issues, 31,* 137–49.

Eidelson, R. J., & Epstein, N. (1982). Cognition and relationship maladjustment: Development of a measure of dysfunctional relationship beliefs. *Journal of Consulting and Clinical Psychology, 50,* 715–20.

Farrell, D., Rusbult, C. E., Lin, Y. H., & Bernthal, P. (1990). Impact of job satisfaction, investment size, and quality of alternatives on exit, voice, loyalty, and neglect responses to job dissatisfaction: A cross-lagged panel study. In L. R. Jauch & J. L. Wall (Eds.), *Best papers: Proceedings of the fiftieth annual meeting of the Academy of Management* (211–15). San Francisco: Academy of Management.

Gelles, R. J. (1980). Violence in the family: A review of research in the seventies. *Journal of Marriage and the Family, 42,* 873–85.

Gottman, J. M. (1979). *Marital interaction: Experimental investigations.* New York: Academic Press.

Gottman, J. M., Markman, H., & Notarius, C. (1977). The topography of marital conflict: A sequential analysis of verbal and nonverbal behavior. *Journal of Marriage and the Family, 39,* 461–77.

Gottman, J. M. Notarius, C., Markman, H., Bank, S., Yoppi, B., & Rubin, M. E. (1976). Behavior exchange theory and marital decision making. *Journal of Personality and Social Psychology, 34,* 14–23.

Greenshaft, J. L. (1980). Perceptual and defensive style variables in marital discord. *Social Behavior and Personality, 8,* 81–84.

Hahlweg, K., Reisner, L., Kohli, G., Vollmer, M., Schindler, L., & Revenstorf, D. (1984). Development and validity of a new system to analyze interpersonal communication. In K. Hahlweg & N. S. Jacobson (Eds.), *Marital interaction: Analysis and modification* (182–98). New York: Guilford Press.

Hendrick, C. (1988). Roles and gender in relationships. In S. Duck (Ed.), *Handbook of personal relationships: Theory, research, and interventions* (429–48). Chichester, England: Wiley.

Hirschman, A. O. (1970). *Exit, voice, and loyalty: Responses to decline in firms, organizations, and states.* Cambridge: Harvard University Press.

Holmes, J. G., & Boon, S. D. (1990). Developments in the field of close relationships: Creating foundations for intervention strategies. *Personality and Social Psychology Bulletin, 16,* 23–41.

Holtzworth-Munroe, A., & Jacobson, N. S. (1985). Causal attributions of married couples: When do they search for causes? What do they conclude when they do? *Journal of Personality and Social Psychology, 48,* 1398–1412.

Huston, T. L., & Ashmore, R. D. (1986). Women and men in personal relationships. In R. D. Ashmore & F. K. DelBoca (Eds.), *The social psychology of female-male relations.* Orlando, FL: Academic Press.

Ickes, W. (1981). Sex-role influences in dyadic interaction: A theoretical model. In C.

Mayo & N. Hanley (Eds.), *Gender and nonverbal behavior* (95–128). New York: Springer-Verlag.

Jacobson, N. S., Follette, W. C., & McDonald, D. W. (1982). Reactivity to positive and negative behavior in distressed and nondistressed married couples. *Journal of Consulting and Clinical Psychology, 50,* 706–14.

Johnson, D. J., & Rusbult, C. E. (1989). Resisting temptation: Devaluation of alternative partners as a means of maintaining commitment in close relationships. *Journal of Personality and Social Psychology, 57,* 967–80.

Kelley, H. H., Cunningham, J. D., Grisham, J. A., Lefebvre, L. M., Sink, C. R., & Yablon, G. (1978). Sex differences in comments during conflict within close heterosexual pairs. *Sex Roles, 4,* 473–92.

Kelley, H. H., & Thibaut, J. W. (1978). *Interpersonal relations: A theory of interdependence.* New York: Wiley.

Koren, P., Carlton, K., & Shaw, D. (1980). Marital conflict: Relations among behaviors, outcomes, and distress. *Journal of Consulting and Clinical Psychology, 48,* 460–68.

Levenson, R. W., & Gottman, J. M. (1985). Physiological and affective predictors of change in relationship satisfaction. *Journal of Personality and Social Psychology, 49,* 85–94.

Levinger, G. (1979). A social exchange view on the dissolution of pair relationships. In R. L. Burgess & T. L. Huston (Eds.), *Social exchange in developing relationships* (169–93). New York: Academic Press.

Levinger, G., & Moles, O. C. (Eds.) (1979). *Divorce and separation: Context, causes, and consequences.* New York: Basic Books.

Lin, Y. H. W., & Rusbult, C. E. (1991). *Extending the investment model of commitment processes: The effects of normative support, centrality of relationship, and traditional investment model variables.* Unpublished manuscript, University of North Carolina at Chapel Hill.

Lowery, D., Lyons, W. E., & DeHoog, R. H. (in press). Citizenship and community attachment in the empowered locality: A critique in the reform tradition. *Urban Affairs Quarterly.*

Lyons, W. E., & Lowery, D. (1986). The organization of political space and citizen responses to dissatisfaction in urban communities: An integrated model. *Journal of Politics, 48,* 321–46.

Lyons, W. E., & Lowery, D. (1989). Citizen responses to dissatisfaction in urban communities: A partial test of a general model. *Journal of Politics, 51,* 842–68.

Margolin, G. & Wampold, B. E. (1981). Sequential analysis of conflict and accord in distressed and nondistressed marital partners. *Journal of Consulting and Clinical Psychology, 49,* 554–67.

Markman, H. J. (1979). Application of a behavioral model of marriage in predicting relationship satisfaction of couples planning marriage. *Journal of Consulting and Clinical Psychology, 47,* 743–49.

Markman, H. J. (1981). Prediction of marital distress: A five-year follow-up. *Journal of Consulting and Clinical Psychology, 49,* 760–62.

Miller, G. R., & Parks, M. R. (1982). Communication in dissolving relationships: In S. Duck (Ed.), *Personal relationships. 4: Dissolving personal relationships* (127–54). London: Academic Press.

Montgomery, B. M. (1988). Quality communication in personal relationships. In S. W. Duck (Ed.), *Handbook of personal relationships* (343–59). Chichester, England: Wiley.

Morrow, G. D. (1985). *The impact of perception of control, problem severity, and commitment on responses to dissatisfaction in romantic involvements.* Unpublished master's thesis, University of Kentucky, Lexington.

Pruitt, D. G., & Rubin, J. Z. (1986). *Social conflict: Escalation, stalemate, and settlement.* New York: Random House.

Rahim, M. A. (1983). A measure of styles of handling interpersonal conflict. *Academy of Management Journal, 26,* 368–76.

Raush, H. L., Barry, W. A., Hertel, R. K., & Swain, M.A. (1974). *Communication, conflict, and marriage.* San Francisco: Jossey-Bass.

Reis, H. T. (1982). An introduction to the use of structural equations: Prospects and problems. In L. Wheeler (Ed.), *Review of personality and social psychology* (Vol. 3, 255–85). Beverly Hills, CA: Sage.

Reis, H. T. (1986). Gender effects in social participation: Intimacy, loneliness, and the conduct of social interaction. In R. Gilmour & S. Duck (Eds.), *The emerging field of personal relationships* (91–105). Hillsdale, NJ: Erlbaum.

Reiss, I. L., Anderson, R. E., & Sponaugle, G. C. (1980). A multivariate model of the determinants of extra-marital sexual permissiveness. *Journal of Marriage and the Family, 42,* 395–411.

Rosenthal, R. (1983). Meta-analysis: Toward a more cumulative social science. In L. Bickman (Ed.), *Applied social psychology annual* (Vol. 4, 65–93). Beverly Hills, CA: Sage.

Rusbult, C. E. (1980). Commitment and satisfaction in romantic associations: A test of the investment model. *Journal of Experimental Social Psychology, 16,* 172–86.

Rusbult, C. E. (1983). A longitudinal test of the investment model: The development (and deterioration) of satisfaction and commitment in heterosexual involvements. *Journal of Personality and Social Psychology, 45,* 101–17.

Rusbult, C. E., Farrell, D., Rogers, G., & Mainous. A. G., III (1988). Impact of exchange variables on exit, voice, loyalty, and neglect: An integrative model of responses to declining job satisfaction. *Academy of Management Journal, 31,* 599–627.

Rusbult, C. E., Johnson, D. J., & Morrow, G. D. (1986a). Determinants and consequences of exit, voice, loyalty, and neglect: Responses to dissatisfaction in adult romantic involvements. *Human Relations, 39,* 45–63.

Rusbult, C. E., Johnson, D. J., & Morrow, G. D. (1986b). Impact of couple patterns of problem solving on distress and nondistress in dating relationships. *Journal of Personality and Social Psychology, 50,* 744–53.

Rusbult, C. E., Johnson, D. J., & Morrow, G. D. (1986c). Predicting satisfaction and commitment in adult romantic involvements: An assessment of the generalizability of the investment model. *Social Psychology Quarterly, 49,* 81–89.

Rusbult, C. E., & Lowery, D. (1985). When bureaucrats get the blues: Responses to dissatisfaction among federal employees. *Journal of Applied Social Psychology, 15,* 80–103.

Rusbult, C. E., Morrow, G. D., & Johnson, D. J. (1987). Self-esteem and problem solving behavior in close relationships. *British Journal of Social Psychology, 26*, 293–303.

Rusbult, C. E., Verette, J., Whitney, G. A., Slovik, L. F., & Lipkus, I. (1991). Accommodation processes in close relationships: Theory and preliminary empirical evidence. *Journal of Personality and Social Psychology, 60*, 53–78.

Rusbult, C. E., & Zembrodt, I. M. (1983). Responses to dissatisfaction in romantic involvements: A multidimensional scaling analysis. *Journal of Experimental Social Psychology, 19*, 274–93.

Rusbult, C. E., Zembrodt, I. M., & Gunn, L. K. (1982). Exit, voice, loyalty, and neglect: Responses to dissatisfaction in romantic involvements. *Journal of Personality and Social Psychology, 43*, 1230–42.

Rusbult, C. E., Zembrodt, I. M., & Iwaniszek, J. (1986). The impact of gender and sex-role orientation on responses to dissatisfaction in close relationships. *Sex Roles, 15*, 1–20.

Schaap, C. (1984). A comparison of the interaction of distressed and nondistressed married couples in a laboratory situation: Literature survey, methodological issues, and an empirical investigation. In K. Hahlweg & N. S. Jacobson (Eds.), *Marital interaction: Analysis and modification* (133–58). New York: Guilford.

Simpson, J. A. (1987). The dissolution of romantic relationships: Factors involved in relationship stability and emotional distress. *Journal of Personality and Social Psychology, 53*, 683–92.

Snyder, D. K., & Fruchtman, L. A. (1981). Differential patterns of wife abuse: A data-based typology. *Journal of Consulting and Clinical Psychology, 49*, 878–85.

Strube, M. J. (1988). The decision to leave an abusive relationship: Empirical evidence and theoretical issues. *Psychological Bulletin, 104*, 236–50.

Thibaut, J. W., & Kelley, H. H. (1959). *The social psychology of groups*. New York: Wiley.

Wachowiak, D., & Bragg, H. (1980). Open marriage and marital adjustment. *Journal of Marriage and the Family, 42*, 57–62.

Wiggins, J. S., & Holzmuller, A. (1978). Psychological androgyny and interpersonal behavior. *Journal of Consulting and Clinical Psychology, 46*, 40–52.

Wills, T. A., Weiss, R. L., & Patterson, G. R. (1974). A behavioral analysis of the determinants of marital satisfaction. *Journal of Consulting and Clinical Psychology, 42*, 802–11.

CHAPTER 4. DETERMINANTS OF SHORT-TERM AND LONG-TERM SUCCESS IN MEDIATION

Alexander, S., & Ruderman, M. (1987). The role of procedural and distributive justice in organizational behavior. *Social Justice Research, 1*, 117–98.

Carnevale, P. J. D., Lim, R. G., & McLaughlin, M. E. (1989). Contingent mediator behavior and its effectiveness. In K. Kressel, D. G. Pruitt, & Associates, *Mediation research*. San Francisco: Jossey-Bass.

Castrianno, L. M., Pruitt, D. G., Nochajski, T. H., & Zubek, J. M. (1988, March). *Complainant-respondent differences in mediation.* Paper presented at the Eastern Psychological Association convention, Buffalo, NY.

Felstiner, W. L. F., Abel, R. L., & Sarat, A. (1980). The emergence and transformation of disputes: Naming, blaming, and claiming. *Law and Society Review, 15,* 629–54.

Folger, R. (1977). Distributive and procedural justice: Combined impact of "voice" and improvement on experienced inequity. *Journal of Personality and Social Psychology, 35,* 108–19.

Hiltrop, J. M. (1989). Factors associated with successful labor mediation. In K. Kressel, D. G. Pruitt, & Associates, *Mediation research.* San Francisco: Jossey-Bass.

Jacobson, N. S. (1984). A component analysis of behavioral marital therapy: The relative effectiveness of behavior exchange and communication/problem-solving training. *Journal of Consulting and Clinical Psychology, 52,* 295–305.

Jacobson, N. S., & Follette, W. C. (1985). Clinical significance of improvement resulting from two behavioral marital therapy components. *Behavior Therapy, 16,* 249–62.

Johnson, S. M., & Greenberg, L. C. (1985). Differential effects of experiential and problem-solving interventions in resolving marital conflict. *Journal of Consulting and Clinical Psychology, 53,* 175–84.

Kelman, H. C., & Cohen, S. P. (1979). Reduction of international conflict: An interactional approach. In W. G. Austin & S. Worchel (Eds.), *The social psychology of intergroup relations.* Belmont, CA: Wadsworth.

Kimmel, M. J., Pruitt, D. G., Magenau, J. M., Konar-Goldband, E., & Carnevale, P. J. D. (1980). Effects of trust, aspiration, and gender on negotiation tactics. *Journal of Personality and Social Psychology, 38,* 9–23.

Kressel, K., & Pruitt, D. G. (1989). Conclusions: A research perspective on the mediation of social conflict. In K. Kressel, D. G. Pruitt, & Associates, *Mediation research.* San Francisco: Jossey-Bass.

Lewicki, R. J., & Litterer, J. A. (1985). *Negotiation.* Homewood, IL: Irwin.

Lind, E. A., Kurtz, S., Musante, L., Walker, L., & Thibaut, J. W. (1980). Procedure and outcome effects on reactions to adjudicated resolutions of conflicts of interest. *Journal of Personality and Social Psychology, 39,* 643–53.

Lind, E. A., Lissak, R. I., & Conlon, D. E. (1983). Decision control and process control effects on procedural fairness judgments. *Journal of Applied Social Psychology, 13,* 338–50.

Lind, E. A., & Tyler, T. R. (1988). *The social psychology of procedural justice.* New York: Plenum Press.

McEwen, C. A., & Maiman, R. J. (1989). Mediation in small claims court: Consensual processes and outcomes. In K. Kressel, D. G. Pruitt, & Associates, *Mediation research.* San Francisco: Jossey-Bass.

Musante, L., Gilbert, M. A., & Thibaut, J. (1983). The effects of control on perceived fairness of procedures and outcomes. *Journal of Experimental Social Psychology, 19,* 223–38.

Pruitt, D. G. (1981). *Negotiation behavior.* New York: Academic.

Pruitt, D. G., & Carnevale, P. J. D. (1982). The development of integrative agreements in social conflict. In V. J. Derlega & J. Grzelak (Eds.), *Living with other people*. New York: Academic.

Pruitt. D. G., & Rubin, J. Z. (1986). *Social conflict: Escalation, stalemate, and settlement*. New York: McGraw-Hill.

Ray, L. (1986). *Dispute resolution program directory*. Washington, DC: American Bar Association.

Roehl, J. A., & Cook, R. F. (1985). Issues in mediation: Rhetoric and reality revisited. *Journal of Social Issues, 41*, 161–79.

Tyler, T. R. (1984). The role of perceived injustice in defendants' evaluations of their courtroom experience. *Law and Society Review, 18*, 51–74.

Tyler, T. R. (1987a). Conditions leading to value expressive effects in judgments of procedural justice: A test of four models. *Journal of Personality and Social Psychology, 52*, 333–44.

Tyler, T. R. (1987b). The psychology of disputant concerns in mediation. *Negotiation Journal, 3*, 367–74.

Tyler, T. R., & Folger, R. (1980). Distributional and procedural aspects of satisfaction with citizen-police encounters. *Basic and Applied Social Psychology, 1*, 281–92.

Tyler, T. R., Rasinski, K., & Spodick, N. (1985). The influence of voice on satisfaction with leaders: Exploring the meaning of process control. *Journal of Personality and Social Psychology, 48*, 72–81.

Walton, R. E., & McKersie, R. B. (1965). *A behavioral theory of labor negotiations*. New York: McGraw-Hill.

Welton, G. L., Pruitt, D. G., & McGillicuddy, N. B. (1988). The role of caucusing in community mediation. *Journal of Conflict Resolution, 32*, 181–202.

CHAPTER 5. TOWARD A MORE BALANCED VIEW OF CONFLICT: THERE IS A POSITIVE SIDE

Allport, G. W. (1954). *The nature of prejudice*. Reading, MA: Addison-Wesley.

Amir, Y. (1976). The role of intergroup contact in change of prejudice and ethnic relations. In P. A. Katy (Ed.), *Towards the elimination of racism*. New York: Pergamon.

Aronson, E., Blaney, N., Stephan, C., Sikes, J., & Snapp, M. (1978). *The jig-saw classroom*. London: Sage.

Axelrod, R. (1984). The evolution of cooperation. *In the sciences*. New York: Academy of Sciences.

Bales, R., & Strodtbeck, F. (1951). Phases in group problem solving. *Journal of Applied Social Psychology, 46*, 485–95.

Baron, R. A. (1988). Attributions and organizational conflict: The mediating role of apparent sincerity. *Organizational Behavior and Human Decision Processes, 41*, 111–27.

Bar-Tal, D. (1990). *Group beliefs: A conception for analyzing group structure, process, and behavior*. New York: Springer-Verlag.

Becker, E. (1973). *The denial of death*. New York: Free Press.

Becker, E. (1975). *Escape from evil*. New York: Free Press.

Ben-Yoav, O., & Pruitt, D. G. (1984). Accountability to constituents: A two-edged sword. *Organizing Behavior and Human Processes, 34,* 283–95.

Berscheid, E. (1983). Emotion. In H. Kelley, E. Berscheid, A. Christianson, J. Harvey, T. Huston, G. Levinger, E. McClintock, L. Peplau, & D. Peterson (Eds.), *Close relationships.* New York: W. H. Freeman.

Bonacich, P. (1972). Norms and cohesion as adaptive responses to potential conflict: An experimental study. *Sociometry, 35,* 357–75.

Branthwaite, A., & Jones, J. (1975). Fairness and discrimination: English versus Welch. *European Journal of Social Psychology, 5,* 323–38.

Brockner, J., & Rubin, J. (Eds.) (1985). *Entrapment in escalating conflicts: A social psychological analysis.* New York: Springer-Verlag.

Brown, R., & Abrahms, D. (1986). The effects of intergroup similarity and goal inter-dependence on intergroup attitudes and task performance. *Journal of Experimental Social Psychology, 22,* 78–92.

Carnevale, P. J. D., Pruitt, D. G., & Seilheimer, S. D. (1981). Looking and competing: Accountability and visual access in integrative bargaining. *Journal of Personality and Social Psychology, 40,* 111–20.

Clore, G. L., Bray, R. M., Itkin, S. M., & O'Murphy, P. (1978). Inter-racial attitudes and behavior at a summer camp. *Journal of Personality and Social Psychology, 36,* 107–16.

Cook, S. W. (1979). Social science and school desegregation: Did we mislead the Supreme Court? *Personality and Social Psychology Bulletin, 5,* 420–37.

Cook, S. W. (1984). Cooperative interaction in multiethnic contexts. In N. Miller & M. Brewer (Eds.), *Groups in contact: The psychology of desegregation.* Orlando, FL: Academic Press.

Deutsch, M. (1973). *The resolution of conflict.* New Haven: Yale University Press.

Dovidio, J. F., Mann, J., & Gaertner, S. L. (1989). Resistance to affirmative action: The implications of aversive racism. In F. A. Blanchard & F. J. Crosby (Eds.), *Affirmative action in perspective.* New York: Springer-Verlag.

Dunphy, D. C. (1968). Phases, roles, and myths in self-analytic groups. *Applied Behavioral Sciences, 4,* 195–224.

Erikson, E. H. (1963). *Childhood and society* (2d ed.). New York: Norton.

Festinger, L. (1954). A theory of social comparison processes. *Human Relations, 7,* 117–40.

Festinger, L. (1957). *A theory of cognitive dissonance.* Palo Alto, CA: Stanford University Press.

Filley, A. (1975). *Interpersonal conflict resolution.* Glenview, IL: Scott Foresman.

Forsyth, D. R. (1990). *Group dynamics* (2d ed.). Pacific Grove, CA: Brooks/Cole.

Freud, S. (1949). *An outline of psychoanalysis,* (J. Strachey, Trans.) New York: Norton. (Original work published 1940).

Gaertner, S. L., Mann, J., Dovidio, J. F., Murrell, A., & Pomare, M. (1990). How does cooperation reduce intergroup bias? *Journal of Personality and Social Psychology, 59,* 692–704.

Gaertner, S. L., Mann, J., Murrell, A., & Dovidio, J. F. (1989). Reducing intergroup bias: The benefits of recategorization. *Journal of Personality and Social Psychology, 57,* 239–49.

Gamson, W. A. (1975). *The strategy of social protest.* Chicago: Dorsey Press.

Glad, B. (1990). *Psychological dimensions of war.* Newbury Park, CA: Sage.

Goethals, G. R. (1986). Social comparison theory: Psychology from the lost and found. *Personality and Social Psychology Bulletin, 12,* 261–78.

Gottman, J. M. (1979). *Marital interaction: Experimental investigations.* New York: Academic Press.

Greenberg, J., Pyszczynski, T., & Solomon, S. (1986). The causes and consequences of a need for self-esteem: A terror management theory. In R. Baumeister (Ed.), *Public self and private self.* New York: Springer-Verlag.

Gross, M. (1982). Hypnoanalytic age regression based on Piaget's cognitive development theory. *Medical Hypnoanalysis, 3,* 73–77.

Hewstone, M. R. C., & Brown, R. J. (Eds.) (1986). *Contact and conflict in intergroup encounters.*Oxford: Blackwell.

Janis, I. L. (1972). *Victims of groupthink: A psychological study of foreign policy decisions and fiascos.* Boston: Houghton Mifflin.

Janis, I. L. (1982). *Groupthink* (2d ed.). Boston: Houghton Mifflin.

Jung, C. G. (1967). *The collected works of C. G. Jung. Vol. 13. Alchemical studies* (R. F. C. Hull, Trans.). Princeton, NJ: Princeton University Press. (Original work published 1942–57).

Kahn, A., & Ryen, A. H. (1972). Factors influencing the bias towards one's own group. *International Journal of Group Tensions, 2,* 33–50.

Kaplan, K. J., & Markus-Kaplan, M. (1983). Walls and boundaries in Arab relations with Israel: Interpersonal distancing model. *Journal of Conflict Resolution, 27,* 457–72.

Kluckhohn, C. (1960). *Mirror for man: A survey of human behavior and social attitudes.* Greenwich, CT: Fawcett World Library.

Knudson, R. M., Sommers, A. A., & Golding, S. L. (1980). Interpersonal perception and mode of resolution in marital conflict. *Journal of Personality and Social Psychology, 38,* 751–63.

Kolb, D. M., & Glidden, P. A. (1986). Getting to know your conflict options: using conflict as a creative force. *Personnel Administrator, 31,* 77–90.

Komorita, S. S., & Barth, J. M. (1985). Components of reward and social dilemmas. *Journal of Personality and Social Psychology, 48,* 364–73.

Landis, D., & Boucher, J. (1987). Themes and models of conflict. In J. Boucher, D. Landis, & K. A. Clark (Eds.), *Ethnic conflict: International perspectives.* Beverly Hills, CA: Sage.

Levinger, G. (1983). Development and change. In H. Kelley, E. Berscheid, A. Christensen, J. Harvey, T. Huston, G. Levinger, E. McClintock, L. Peplau, & D. Peterson (Eds.), *Close relationships.* New York: W. H. Freeman.

Miller, N., & Brewer, M. (Eds.) (1984). *Groups in contact: The psychology of desegregation.* Orlando, FL: Academic Press.

Miller, N. E. (1944). Experimental studies of conflict. In J. McV. Hunt (Ed.), *Personality and the behavior disorders* (Vol. 1). New York: Ronald Press.

Miller, N. E. (1948). Theory and experiment relating psychoanalytic displacement to stimulus-response generalization. *Journal of Abnormal and Social Psychology, 43,* 155–78.

Mitchell, W. C. (1928). *Business cycles: The problem and its setting.* New York: National Bureau of Economic Research.

Moreland, R. L., & Levine, J. M. (1988). Group dynamics over time: Development and socialization in small groups. In J. E. McGrath (Ed.), *The social psychology of time* (151–81). Newbury Park, CA: Sage.

Nemeth, C. J. (1986). Differential contributions of majority and minority influence. *Psychological Review, 93,* 23–32.

Nemeth, C. J., & Kwan, J. L. (1985). Originality of word associations as a function of majority vs. minority influence. *Social Psychology Quarterly, 48,* 277–82.

Nemeth, C. J., & Kwan, J. L (1987). Minority influence, divergent thinking, and detection of correct solutions. *Journal of Applied Social Psychology, 17,* 788–99.

Oskamp, S. (Ed.) (1985). *International conflict and national public policy issues.* Beverly Hills, CA: Sage

Peterson, D. R. (1983). *Conflict.* In H. Kelley, E. Berscheid, A Christensen, J. Harvey, T. Huston, G. Levinger, E. McClintock, L. Peplau, & D. Peterson (Eds.), *Close relationships.* New York: W. H. Freeman.

Rapoport, A. (1962). The use and misuse of game theory. *Scientific American, 207,* 108–18.

Rokeach, M., Smith, P. W., & Evans, R. I. (1960). Two kinds of prejudice or one? In M. Rokeach (Ed.), *The open and closed mind.* New York: Basic Books.

Rothbart, M., & Hallmark, W. (1988). Ingroup-outgroup differences in the perceived efficacy of coercion and conciliation in resolving social conflict. *Journal of Personality and Social Psychology, 55,* 248–57.

Schlenker, B. R., & Bonoma, T. V. (1978). Fun and games: The validity of games for the study of conflict. *The Journal of Conflict Resolution, 22,* 9–13.

Sherif, M., Harvey, O. J., White, B. J., Hood, W. R., & Sherif, C. W. (1961). *Intergroup conflict and cooperation. The robbers cave experiment.* Norman: University of Oklahoma.

Simmel, G. (1955). *Conflict.* New York: Free Press.

Stephan. W. (1985). Intergroup relations. In G. Lindzey & E. Aronson (Eds.), *Handbook of social psychology* (3d ed., Vol. 2). New York: Random House.

Stouffer, S. A. (1949). An analysis of conflicting social norms. *American Sociological Review, 14,* 707–17.

Streufert, S., & Streufert, S. C. (1986). The development of international conflict. In S. Worchel & W. G. Austin (Eds.), *The psychology of intergroup relations.* Chicago: Nelson-Hall.

Stroebe, W., Kruglanski, A., Bar-Tal, D., & Hewstone, M. (Eds.). (1988). *The social psychology of intergroup conflict: Theory, research, and applications.* New York: Springer-Verlag.

Tajfel, H. (1978). *Differentiation between social groups: Studies in the social psychology of intergroup relations.* London: Academic Press.

Tajfel, H. (1982). *Social identity and intergroup relations.* Cambridge: Cambridge University Press.

Tajfel, H., Flament, C., Billig, M. G., & Bundy, R. P. (1971). Social categorization and intergroup behavior. *European Journal of Social Psychology, 1,* 149–78.

Tajfel, H., & Turner, J. C. (1986). The social identity theory of intergroup behavior. In S. Worchel & W. G. Austin (Eds.), *The psychology of intergroup relations.* Chicago: Nelson-Hall.

Tuckman, B. W. (1965). Developmental sequence in small groups. *Psychological Bulletin, 63,* 384–99.

Tuckman, B. W., & Jensen, M. (1977). Stages of small group development revisited. *Group and Organizational Studies, 2,* 419–27.

Wallace, B. (1986). Creativity: Some definitions: The creative personality; the creative process; the creative classroom. *Gifted Education International, 4,* 68–73.

Wallach, M. A., & Kogan, N. (1965). *Modes of thinking in young children.* New York: Holt, Rinehart & Winston.

Withey, S., & Katy, D. (1965). The social psychology of human conflict. In E. B. McNeil (Ed.)., *The nature of human conflict.* Englewood Cliffs, NJ: Prentice-Hall.

Worchel, S. (1979). Intergroup cooperation. In W. Austin & S. Worchel (Eds.), *The social psychology of intergroup relations.* Monterey, CA: Brooks/Cole.

Worchel, S. (1986). The role of cooperation in reducing intergroup conflict. In S. Worchel and W. G. Austin (Eds.), *The psychology of intergroup relations* 153–76). Chicago: Nelson-Hall.

Worchel, S., & Austin, W. (Eds.) (1986). *The social psychology of intergroup relations.* Chicago: Nelson-Hall.

Worchel, S., Axsom, D., Ferris, F., Samaha, C., & Schweitzer, S. (1978). Factors determining the effect of intergroup cooperation on intergroup attraction. *Journal of Conflict Resolution, 22,* 428–39.

Worchel, S., Coutant-Sassic, D., & Grossman, M. (1991). A developmental approach to group dynamics: A model and illustrative research. In S. Worchel, W. Wood, & J. Simpson (Eds.), *Group process and productivity.* Newbury Park, CA: Sage.

Worchel, S., Grossman, M., & Coutant-Sassic, D. (In press). Minority influence in the group context: How group factors affect when the minority will be influential. In A. Mucchi-Faina & S. Moscovici (Eds.), *Minority influence.* Chicago: Nelson-Hall.

CHAPTER 6. INTERGROUP PERCEPTION AND SOCIAL CONFLICT

Adorno, T. W., Frenkel-Brunswik, E., Levinson, D. J., & Sanford, R. N. (1950). *The authoritarian personality.* New York: Harper.

Allport, G. W. (1954). *The nature of prejudice.* Cambridge, MA: Addison-Wesley.

Bernard, J. (1957). Parties and issues in conflict. *Journal of Conflict Resolution, 1,* 111–21.

Bettelheim, B., & Janowitz, M. (1949). Ethnic tolerance: A function of social and personal control. *American Journal of Sociology, 55,* 137–45.

Billig, M., & Tajfel, H. (1973). Social categorization and similarity in intergroup behavior. *European Journal of Social Psychology, 3,* 27–52.

Blum, A (1980). *Annapurna: A woman's place.* San Francisco: Sierra Club Press.

Cialdini, R. B., Borden, R. J., Thorne, A., Walker, M. R., Freeman, S., & Sloan, L. R. (1976). Basking in reflected glory: Three (football) field studies. *Journal of Personality and Social Psychology, 34,* 366–75.

Coser, L. A. (1956). *The functions of social conflict.* Glencoe, IL: Free Press.

Dollard, J., Doob, L. W., Miller, N. E., Mowrer, O. H., & Sears, R. R. (1939). *Frustration and aggression.* New Haven, CT: Yale University Press.

Freud, S. (1959). *Group psychology and the analysis of the ego.*New York: Norton. (Originally published in 1926.)

Grossmann, S., & Mayer-Kress, G. (1989). Chaos in the international arms race. *Nature, 337,* 701–4.

Hamilton, D. L. (1981). Stereotyping and intergroup behavior: Some thoughts on the cognitive approach. In D. L. Hamilton (Ed.), *Cognitive processes in stereotyping and intergroup behavior.* Hillsdale, NJ: Erlbaum.

Hamilton, D. L. & Gifford, R. K. (1976). Illusory correlation in interpersonal perception: A cognitive basis of stereotypic judgments. *Journal of Experimental Social Psychology 12,* 392–407.

Howard, J. W., & Rothbart, M. (1980). Social categorization and memory for in-group and out-group behavior. *Journal of Personality and Social Psychology, 38*(2), 301–10.

Jervis, R. (1976). *Perception and misperception in international politics.* Princeton, NJ: Princeton University Press.

Judd, C. M., & Park, B. (1988). Out-group homogeneity: Judgments of variability at the individual and group levels. *Journal of Personality and Social Psychology, 54,* 778–88.

Kanouse, D. E., & Hanson, L. R. (1971). Negativity in evaluations. In E. E. Jones, D. E. Kanouse, H. H. Kelley, R. E. Nisbett, S. Valins, & B. Weiner (Eds.), *Attribution: perceiving the causes of behavior.* Morristown, NJ: General Learning Press.

Levine, R. A., & Campbell, D. T. (1972). *Ethnocentrism: Theories of conflict, ethnic attitudes, and group behavior.* New York: Wiley.

Linville, P. W., & Jones, E. E. (1980). Polarized appraisals of out-group members. *Journal of Personality and Social Psychology, 38,* 689–703.

Lippmann, W. (1961). *Public opinion.* New York: Macmillan. (Originally published in 1922.)

Parducci, A. (1968). The relativism of absolute judgments. *Scientific American, 219,* 84–90.

Park, B., & Rothbart, M. (1982). Perception of out-group homogeneity and levels of social categorization: Memory for the subordinate attributes of in-group and out-group members. *Journal of Personality and Social Psychology, 42*(6), 1051–68.

Parnias, D. L. (1985). Software aspects of strategic defense systems. *American Scientist, 73,* 432–40. [Also printed in *Communications of the ACM,* (1985) *28,* 1326–35]

Quattrone, G. A., & Jones, E. E. (1980). The perception of variability within in-groups and out-groups: Implications for the law of small numbers. *Journal of personality and Social Psychology, 38,* 141–52.

Rabbie, J. M., & Horwitz, M. (1969). Arousal of ingroup-outgroup bias by a chance win or loss. *Journal of Personality and Social Psychology, 13*(3), 269–77.

Reagan, R. (1988). Speech to the Annual Convention of the National Assoc. of Religious Broadcasters, Feb. 1, 1988. In *Public papers of the presidents:*

Ronald Reagan, 1988 (Vol 1). Washington, DC: Office of the Federal Register, National Archives and Records Adm.

Rothbart, M., Evans, M., & Fulero, S. (1979). Recall for confirming events: Memory processes and the maintenance of social stereotypes. *Journal of Experimental Social Psychology, 15,* 343–55.

Rothbart, M., Fulero, S., Jensen, C., Howard, J., & Birrell, P. (1978). From individual to group impressions: Availability heuristics in stereotype formation. *Journal of Experimental Social Psychology, 14,* 237–55.

Rothbart, M., & Hallmark, W. (1988). In-group-out-group differences in the perceived efficacy of coercion and conciliation in resolving social conflict. *Journal of Personality and Social Psychology, 55,* 248–57.

Rothbart, M., & John, O. P. (1985). Social categorization and behavioral episodes: A cognitive analysis of the effects of intergroup contact. *Journal of Social Issues, 41,* 81–104.

Rothbart, M., & John, O. (in press). Stereotypes, prejudice, and race. In P. M. Sniderman & P. E. Tetlock (Eds.), *Prejudice, politics, and race in America.* Stanford, CA: Stanford University Press.

Rothbart, M., & Lewis, S. (1988). Inferring category attributes from exemplar attributes: Geometric shapes and social categories. *Journal of Personality and Social Psychology, 55,* 861–72.

Rothbart, M., Sruriam, N., & Davis-Stitt, C. (in prep.). *Retrieving information about typical and atypical category members.* Univ. of Oregon, Eugene.

Saperstein, A. M., & Mayer-Kress, G. (1988). A nonlinear dynamical model of the impact of SDI on the arms race. *Journal of Conflict Resolution, 32,* 636–70.

Sherif, M., Harvey, O. J., White, B. J., Hood, W. R., & Sherif, C. W. (1988). *The Robbers Cave experiment: Intergroup conflict and cooperation.* Middletown, CT: Wesleyan University Press. (Originally published in 1961.)

Sumner, W. G. (1906). *Folkways.* Boston: Ginn.

Tajfel, H. (1970). Experiments in intergroup discrimination. *Scientific American, 223* 96–102.

Tajfel, H., & Turner, J. C. (1986). The social identity theory of intergroup behavior. In S. Worchel & W. G. Austin (Eds.), *Psychology of intergroup relations* (7–24). Chicago: Nelson-Hall.

Veblen, T. (1902). *A theory of the leisure class.* New York: Macmillan.

CHAPTER 7. LEGITIMACY, STATUS, AND DOMINANCE
BEHAVIOR IN GROUPS

Bales, R. F. (1950). *Interaction process analysis: A method for the study of small groups.* Cambridge, MA: Addison-Wesley.

Berger, J., Conner, T. L., & Fisek, M. H. (1974). *Expectation states theory: A theoretical research program.* Cambridge, MA: Winthrop.

Berger, J., Fisek, M. H., Norman, R. Z., & Zelditch, M. (1977). *Social status in social interaction: An expectation states approach.* New York: Elsevier.

Berger, J., Rosenholtz, S., & Zelditch, M. (1980). Status organizing processes. *Annual Review of Sociology, 6,* 479–508.

Berger, J., Webster, M., Ridgeway, C., & Rosenholtz, S. (1986). Status cues, expectations, and behavior. In E. J. Lawler (Ed.), *Advances in group processes* (Vol. 3, 1–22). Greenwich, CT: JAI.

Bernstein, I. S. (1980). Dominance: A theoretical perspective for ethologists. In D. R. Omark, F. F. Strayer, & D. G. Freedman (Eds.), *Dominance relations*(71–84). New York: Garland.

Blau, P. (1964). *Exchange and power in social life*. New York: Wiley.

Broverman, I. K., Vogel, S. R., Broverman, D. M., Clarkson, F. E., & Rosenkrantz, P. S. (1972). Sex-role stereotypes: A current appraisal. *Journal of Social Issues, 28,* 59–78.

Burke, P. (1968). Role differentiation and the legitimation of task activity. *Sociometry, 31,* 404–11.

Butler, D., & Geis, F. L. (1990). Nonverbal affect responses to male and female leaders: Implications for leadership evaluations. *Journal of Personality and Social Psychology, 58,* 48–59.

Cohen, E. G., & Roper, S. S. (1972). Modification of interracial interaction disability: An application of status characteristics theory. *American Sociological Review, 37,* 643–57.

Eagly, A. H., Makhijani, M. G., & Klonsky, B. G. (1992). *Gender and the evaluation of leaders: A meta-analysis. Psychological Bulletin, 111,* 3–22.

Ellyson, S. L., & Dovidio, J. F. (1985). Power, dominance, and nonverbal behavior: Basic concepts and issues. In S. L. Ellyson & J. F. Dovidio (Eds.), *Power, dominance, and nonverbal behavior* (1–27). New York: Springer-Verlag.

Emerson, R. M. (1962). Power-dependence relations. *American Sociological Review, 27,* 31–41.

Emerson, R. M. (1972). Exchange theory. 2: Exchange relations and networks. In J. Berger, M. Zelditch, & B. Anderson, *Sociological theories in progress* (Vol. 2, 58–87). Boston: Houghton-Mifflin.

Eskilson, A. & Wiley, M. G. (1976). Sex composition and leadership in small groups. *Sociometry, 39,* 183–94.

Fennell, M. L., Barchas, P., Cohen, E. G., McMahon, A. M., & Hildebrand, P. (1978). An alternative perspective on sex differences in organizational settings: The process of legitimation. *Sex Roles, 4,* 589–604.

Harper, R. G. (1985). Power, dominance, and nonverbal behavior: An overview. In S. L. Ellyson & J. F. Dovidio (Eds.), *Power, dominance, and nonverbal behavior* (29–48). New York: Springer-Verlag.

Homans, G. C. (1974). *Social behavior: Its elementary forms* (2nd. ed.) New York: Harcourt Brace Jovanovich.

Keating, C. F., Mazur, A., Segall, M. H., Cysneiros, P. G., Divale, W. T., Kilbridge, J. E., Komin, S. Leahy, P., Thurman, B., & Wirsing, R. (1981). Culture and the perception of social dominance from facial expression. *Journal of Personality and Social Psychology, 40,* 615–20.

Lee, M. T., & Ofshe, R. (1981). The impact of behavioral style and status characteristics on social influence: A test of two competing theories. *Social Psychology Quarterly, 44,* 73–82.

Leffler, A., Gillespie, D. L., & Conaty, J. C. (1982). The effects of status differentiation on nonverbal behavior. *Social Psychology Quarterly, 45,* 153–61.

Mazur A. (1985). A biosocial model of status in face-to-face primate groups. *Social Forces, 64,* 377–402.

Mazur A., Rose, E., Faupel, M., Heller, J., Leen, R., & Thurman, B. (1980). Physiological aspects of communication via mutual gaze. *American Journal of Sociology, 86,* 50–74.

Meeker, B. F., & Weitzel-O'Neill, P. A. (1977). Sex roles and interpersonal behavior in task oriented groups. *American Sociological Review, 42,* 92–105.

Nemeth, C., & Wachtler, J. (1974). Creating the perception of consistency and confidence: A necessary condition for minority influence. *Sociometry, 37,* 529–40.

Pugh, M. D., & Wahrman, R. (1983). Neutralizing sexism in mixed-sex groups: Do women have to be better than men? *American Journal of Sociology, 88,* 746–62.

Ridgeway, C. L. (1982). Status in groups: The importance of motivation. *American Sociological Review, 47,* 76–88.

Ridgeway, C. L. (1984). Dominance, performance, and status in groups. In E. J. Lawler (Ed.), *Advances in group processes* (Vol. 1, 59–93). Greenwich, CT: JAI.

Ridgeway, C. L. (1987). Nonverbal behavior, dominance, and the basis of status in task groups. *American Sociological Review, 52,* 638–94.

Ridgeway, C. L. (1988). Gender differences in task groups: A status and legitimacy account. In M. Webster & M. Foschi (Eds.), *Status generalization: New theory and research* (207–31). Stanford, CA: Stanford University.

Ridgeway, C. L. (1989). Understanding legitimation in informal status orders. In J. Berger, M. Zelditch, & B. Anderson (Eds.), *Sociological theories in progress: New formulations* (131–59). Newbury Park, CA: Sage.

Ridgeway, C. L., & Berger, J. (1986). Expectations, legitimation, and dominance behavior in task groups. *American Sociological Review, 51,* 603–17.

Ridgeway, C. L., Berger, J., & Smith, L. (1985). Nonverbal cues and status: An expectation states approach. *American Journal of Sociology, 90,* 955–78.

Ridgeway, C. L., & Diekema, D. (1989). Dominance and collective hierarchy formation in male and female task groups. *American Sociological Review, 54,* 79–93.

Ridgeway, C. L., Diekema, D., & Johnson, C. (1991, August). *Status, legitimacy, and compliance in male and female groups.* Paper presented at the annual meeting of the American Sociological Association, Cincinnati, OH.

Ruble, T. (1983). Sex stereotypes: Issues of change in the 1970s. *Sex Roles, 9,* 396–402.

Walker, H. A., Thomas, G. A., & Zelditch, M. (1986). Legitimation, endorsement, and compliance. *Social Forces, 64,* 620–43.

Weber, M. (1968). *Economy and society* (G. Roth & C. Wittich, Eds., E. Fischoff, Trans.). New York: Bedminister.

Webster, M., & Foschi, M. (Eds.) (1988). *Status generalization: New theory and research.* Stanford, CA: Stanford University.

Wood, W., & Karten, S. J. (1986). Sex differences in interaction style as a product of perceived sex differences in competence. *Journal of Personality and Social Psychology, 50,* 341–47.

Zelditch, M., & Walker, H. A. (1984). Legitimacy and the stability of authority. In E. J. Lawler (Ed.)., *Advances in group processes* (Vol. 1, 1–27). Greenwich, CT: JAI.

CHAPTER 8. MINIMIZING CONFLICT IN
ORGANIZATIONAL SETTINGS THROUGH
GOAL ALIGNMENT

Anderson, C. R., & Schneiner, D. (1979). *The effects of leader motivational style on subordinate performance: The case of the collegiate football coach.* Unpublished manuscript. College of Business & Management, University of Maryland.

Bandura, A. (1986). *Social foundations of thought and action: A social-cognitive theory.* Englewood Cliffs, NJ: Prentice-Hall.

Burke, M. J., & Day, R. R. (1986). A cumulative study of the effectiveness of managerial training. *Journal of Applied Psychology, 71,* 232–46.

Burke, R. J., & Wilcox, D. S. (1969). Characteristics of effective employee performance review and developmental interviews. *Personnel Psychology, 22,* 291–305.

Campbell, J. P., Dunnette, M. D., Lawler, E. E., & Weick, K. E. (1970). *Managerial behavior, performance, and effectiveness.* New York: McGraw-Hill.

Flanagan, J. C. (1954). The critical incident technique. *Psychological Bulletin, 51,* 327–58.

Frayne, C. A., & Latham, G. P. (1987). The application of social learning theory to employee self-management of attendance. *Journal of Applied Psychology, 72,* 387–92.

Hall, D. T., & Richter, J. (1990). Career gridlock: Baby boomers hit the wall. *Academy of Management Review, 4,* 7–22.

Latham, G. P. (1986). Job performance and appraisal. In C. Cooper & I. Robertson (Eds.), *Review of industrial and organizational psychology.* Chichester, England: Wiley.

Latham, G. P. (1989). The reliability, validity, and practicality of the situational interview. In G. Ferris & R. Eder (Eds.), *The employment interview: Theory, research, and practice* (169–82). Newbury Park, CA: Sage.

Latham, G. P., & Crandall, S. (1991). Organizational and social factors affecting training effectiveness. In J. E. Morrison (Ed.), *Training for performance.* Chichester, England: Wiley.

Latham, G. P., & Frayne, C. A. (1989). Self management training for increasing job attendance: A follow-up and a replication. *Journal of Applied Psychology, 74,* 411–16.

Latham, G. P., Mitchell, T. R., & Dossett, D. L. (1978). The importance of participative goal setting and anticipated rewards on goal difficulty and job performance. *Journal of Applied Psychology, 63,* 163–71. [Summarized by *The Wharton Magazine,* Winter 1979, 10]

Latham, G. P., & Saari, L. M. (1979). The application of social learning theory to training supervisors through behavioral modeling. *Journal of Applied Psychology, 64,* 239–46.

Latham, G. P., Saari, L. M., Pursell, E. D., & Campion, M. (1980). The situational interview. *Journal of Applied Psychology, 65,* 422–27.

Latham, G. P., & Wexley, K. N. (1977). Behavioral observation scales for performance appraisal purposes. *Personnel Psychology, 30,* 255–68.

Latham G. P., & Wexley, K. N. (1993). *Increasing productivity through performance appraisal.* Reading, MA: Addison-Wesley.

Locke, E. A., & Latham, G. P. (1990a). *A theory of goal setting and task perform-ance*. Englewood Cliffs, NJ: Prentice-Hall.

Locke, E. A., & Latham, G. P. (1990b). Work motivation and satisfaction: Light at the end of the tunnel. *Psychological Science, 1,* 240–46.

Magna International, Inc. (1990). *Annual Report.* Markham, Ontario.

Triandis, H. C., McCusker, C., & Hui, C. H. (1990). Multimethod probes of individualism and collectivism. *Journal of Personality and Social Psychology, 59,* 1006–20.

Wanous, J. P. (1980). *Organizational entry: Recruitment, selection, and socialization of newcomers.* Reading, MA: Addison-Wesley.

Wanous, J. P. (1989). Installing a realistic job preview: Ten tough choices. *Personnel Psychology, 42,* 117–34.

Wexley, K. N., & Latham, G. P. (1991). *Developing and training human resources in organizations.* Glenview, IL: Scott, Foresman.

Chapter 9. The Symbolic Politics of Opposition to Bilingual Education

Abelson, R. P., Aronson, E., McGuire, W. J., Newcomb, T. M., Rosenberg, M. J., & Tannenbaum, P. H. (Eds.) (1968). *Theories of cognitive consistency: A sourcebook.* Chicago: Rand McNally.

Alwin, D. F., & Krosnick, J. A. (1991). Aging, cohorts, and the stability of socio-political orientations over the lifespan. *American Journal of Sociology, 97,* 169–95.

Asch, S. E. (1940). Studies in the principles of judgments and attitudes: 2. Determina-tion of judgments by group and by ego standards. *Journal of Social Psychology, 12,* 433–65.

Bobo, L. (1988). Group conflict, prejudice, and the paradox of contemporary racial attitudes. In P. Katz & D. Taylor (Eds.), *Eliminating racism: Profiles in controversy.* New York: Plenum.

Campbell, A., Converse, P. E., Miller, W. E., & Stokes, D. E. (1960). *The American voter.* New York: Wiley.

Cardoza, D., Huddy, L., & Sears, D. O. (1984). *The symbolic attitudes study: Public attitudes toward bilingual education.* Los Alamitos, CA: National Center for Bilingual Research.

Citrin, J. (1988). American identity and the politics of ethnicity: Public opinion in a changing society. Paper presented at the annual meeting of the International Society of Political Psychology, Secaucus, NJ.

Citrin, J., & Green, D. P. (1990). The self-interest motive in American public opinion. In S. Long (Ed.)., *Research in micropolitics* (Vol. 3, 1–28). Greenwich, CT: JAI.

Citrin, J., Green, D. P., Reingold, B., & Walters, E. P. (1990). The official English movement and the symbolic politics of language in the United States. *Western Political Quarterly, 43,* 85–108.

Citrin, J., Reingold, B., & Green, D. P. (1990). The politics of ethnic change. *Journal of Politics, 52,* 1124–54.

Converse, P. E. (1964). The nature of belief systems in mass publics. In D. E. Apter (Ed.), *Ideology and discontent* (206–61). New York: Free Press of Glencoe.

Converse, P. E. (1975). Public opinion and voting behavior. In F. I. Greenstein & N. W. Polsby (Eds.), *Handbook of political science* (Vol. 4, 75–170). Reading, MA: Addison-Wesley.

Dharmadasa, K. (1977). Nativism, diglossia, and the Sinhalese identity in the language problem in Sri Lanka. *International Journal of the Sociology of Language, 13,* 21–31.

Downs, A. (1957). *An economic theory of democracy.* New York: Harper & Row.

Dyste, C. D. (1989). Proposition 63: The California English language amendment. *Applied Linguistics, 10,* 313–30.

Easton, D., & Dennis, J. (1969). *Children in the political system: Origins of political legitimacy.* New York: McGraw-Hill.

Edelman, M. (1971). *Politics as symbolic action: Mass arousal and quiescence.* Chicago, IL: Markham.

Edwards, J. (1985). *Language, society, and identity.* Oxford: Basil Blackwell.

Elder, C. D., & Cobb, R. W. (1983). *The political uses of symbols.* New York: Longman.

Feldman, S. (1988). Structure and consistency in public opinion: The role of core beliefs and values. *American Journal of Political Science, 32,* 416–40.

Green, D. P. (1988). Self-interest, public opinion, and mass political behavior. Unpublished doctoral dissertation, University of California, Berkeley.

Gusfield, J. R. (1963). *Symbolic crusade.* Urbana: University of Illinois Press.

Hakuta, K. (1986). *Mirror of language: The debate on bilingualism.* New York: Basic Books.

Heath, S. (1981). English in our language heritage. In C. A. Ferguson & S. Heath (Eds.), *Language in the U.S.A.* Cambridge: Cambridge University Press.

Horowitz, D. L. (1985). *Ethnic groups in conflict.* Berkeley: University of California Press.

Huddy, L., & Sears, D. O. (1989). Opposition to bilingual education: Symbolic racism or realistic group conflict? Unpublished manuscript. University of California, Los Angeles.

Iyengar, S., & Kinder, D. R. (1987). *News that matters: Television and American opinion.* Chicago: University of Chicago Press.

Jennings, M. K., & Niemi, R. G. (1981). *Generations and politics.* Princeton, NJ: Princeton University Press.

Kiewiet, D. R. (1983). *Macroeconomics and micropolitics: The electoral effects of economic issues.* Chicago: University of Chicago Press.

Kinder, D. R. (1986). The continuing American dilemma: White resistance to racial change forty years after Myrdal. *Journal of Social Issues, 42,* 151–71.

Kinder, D. R., & Kiewiet, D. R. (1979). Economic discontent and political behavior: The role of personal grievances and collective economic judgments in congressional voting. *American Journal of Political Science, 23,* 495–527.

Kinder, D. R., & Sanders, L. M. (1990). Mimicking political debate with survey questions: The case of white opinion on affirmative action for blacks. *Social Cognition, 8,* 73–103.

Kinder, D. R., & Sears, D. O. (1981). Prejudice and politics: Symbolic racism versus racial threats to the good life. *Journal of Personality and Social Psychology, 40,* 414–31.

Krosnick, J. A., & Kinder, D. R. (1990). Altering the foundation of support for the president through priming. *American Political Science Review, 84,* 497–512.

Lau, R. R., & Sears, D. O. (1986). *Political cognition: The nineteenth annual Carnegie symposium on cognition.* Hillsdale, NJ: Erlbaum.

LePage, R. (1984). Retrospect and prognosis in Malaysia and Singapore. *International Journal of the Sociology of Language, 45,* 113–26.

Marshall, D. F. (1986). The question of an official language: Language rights and the English language amendment. *International Journal of the Sociology of Language, 60,* 7–75.

McClosky, H., & Brill, A. (1983). *Dimensions of tolerance.* New York: Russell Sage.

McConahay, J. B. (1986). Modern racism, ambivalence, and the modern racism scale. In J. F. Dovidio & S. L. Gaertner (Eds.), *Prejudice, discrimination, and racism* (91–126). New York: Academic Press.

Mueller, J. E. (1973). *War, presidents, and public opinion.* New York: Wiley.

Rothbart, M. (1976). Achieving racial equality: An analysis of resistance to social reform. In P. A. Katz (Ed.), *Towards the elimination of racism.* New York: Pergamon Press.

Schuman, H., Steeh, C., & Bobo, L. (1985). *Racial trends in America: Trends and interpretations.* Cambridge: Harvard University Press.

Sears, D. O. (1975). Political socialization. In F. I. Greenstein & N. W. Polsby (Eds.), *Handbook of political science* (Vol. 2, 93–153). Reading, MA: Addison-Wesley.

Sears, D. O. (1983). The persistence of early political predispositions: The roles of attitude object and life stage. In L. Wheeler & P. Shaver (Eds.), *Review of personality and social psychology* (Vol. 4, 79–116). Beverly Hills, CA: Sage.

Sears, D. O. (1988). Symbolic racism. In P. A. Katz & D. A. Taylor (Eds.), *Eliminating racism: Profiles in controversy* (53–84). New York: Plenum Press.

Sears, D. O., & Citrin, J. (1985). *Tax revolt: Something for nothing in California* (Enlarged ed.). Cambridge: Harvard University Press.

Sears, D. O., & Funk, C. L. (1991). The role of self-interest in social and political attitudes. In M. P. Zanna (Ed.), *Advances in experimental social psychology* (Vol. 24, 1–91). San Diego: Academic Press.

Sears, D. O., Hensler, C. P., & Speer, L. K. (1979). Whites' opposition to "busing": Self-interest or symbolic politics? *American Political Science Review, 73,* 369–84.

Sears, D. O., Huddy, L., & Schaffer, L. (1986). A schematic variant of symbolic politics theory, as applied to racial and gender equality. In R. R. Lau & D. O. Sears (Eds.), *Political cognition: The nineteenth annual Carnegie symposium on cognition* (159–202). Hillsdale, NJ: Erlbaum.

Sears, D. O., & Kinder, D. R. (1985). Whites' opposition to busing: on conceptualizing and operationalizing group conflict. *Journal of Personality and Social Psychology, 48,* 1141–47.

Sears, D. O., & Kosterman, R. (1991). Is it really racism? The origins and dynamics of symbolic racism. Paper presented at the annual meeting of the Midwestern Political Science Association, Chicago.

Sears, D. O., & Lau, R. R. (1983). Inducing apparently self-interested political preferences. *American Journal of Political Science, 27,* 223–52.

Sears, D. O., Lau, R. R., Tyler, T. R., & Allen, H. M., Jr. (1980). Self-interest vs. symbolic politics in policy attitudes and presidential voting. *American Political Science Review, 74,* 670–84.

Sears, D. O., & McConahay, J. B. (1973). *The politics of violence: The new urban blacks and the Watts riot.* Boston: Houghton-Mifflin.

Smith, T. W. (1987). That which we call welfare by any other name would smell sweeter: An analysis of the impact of question wording on response patterns. *Public Opinion Quarterly, 51,* 75–83.

Sniderman, P. M., & Tetlock, P. E. (1986). Symbolic racism: Problems of motive attribution in political debate. *Journal of Social Issues, 42,* 129–50.

Sullivan, J. L., Piereson, J., & Marcus, G. E. (1982). *Political tolerance and American democracy.* Chicago: University of Chicago Press.

Williams, C. (1984). More than tongue can tell: Linguistic factors in ethnic separatism. In J. Edwards (Ed.), *Linguistic minorities, policies, and pluralism.* London: Academic Press.

CHAPTER 10. INDIVIDUAL VERSUS GROUP IDENTIFICATION AS A FACTOR IN INTERGROUP RACIAL CONFLICT

Abrams, D., & Hogg, M. A. (Eds.) (1990). *Social identity theory: Constructive and critical advances.* New York: Springer-Verlag.

Baldwin, J. A., & Bell, Y. R. (1985). The African self-consciousness scale: An Africentric personality questionnaire. *Western Journal of Black Studies, 9,* 61–68.

Baldwin, J., Brown, R., & Hopkins, R. (1991). The black self-hatred-paradigm revisited: Au Africentric analysis. In R. L. Jones (Ed.) *Black-psychology* (3d ed., 141–66). Berkeley, CA: Cobb & Henry.

Banks, W. C. (1976). White preference in blacks: A paradigm in search of a phenomenon. *Psychological Bulletin, 83,* 1179–86.

Bloom, A. (1987). *The closing of the American mind.* New York: Simon & Schuster.

Bobo, L. (1988). Group conflict, prejudice and the paradox of contemporary racial attitudes. In P. Katz & B. Taylor (Eds.), *Eliminating racism: Profiles in controversy.* New York: Plenum.

Bradby, D., & Helms, J. (1990). Black racial identity attitudes and white therapist cultural sensitivity in cross-racial therapy dyads: An exploratory study. In J. E. Helms (Ed.), *Black and white racial identity: Theory, research, and practice* (165–76). New York: Greenwood Press.

Brewer, M. B. (1979). In-group bias in the minimal intergroup situation: A cognitive-motivational analysis. *Psychological Bulletin, 86,* 307–24.

Brewer, M. B. (1991). The social self: On being the same and different at the same time. *Personality and Social Psychology Bulletin, 17*(5), 475–82.

Clark, K. B., & Clark, M. P. (1939). The development of consciousness of self and the emergence of racial identification in Negro pre-school children. *Journal of Social Psychology, 10,* 591–99.

Clark, K. B., & Clark, M. P. (1947). Radical identification and preference in Negro children. In T. M. Newcomb & E. L. Hartley (Eds.), *Readings in social psychology.* New York: Holt.

Crocker, J., & Major, B. (1989). Social stigma and self-esteem: The self-protective properties of stigma. *Psychological Review, 96,* 608–30.

Cross, W. E. (1970). Negro-to-black conversion experience. *Black World, 20,* 13–27.

Cross, W. E. (1979). The Negro-to-black conversion experience: An empirical analysis. In A. W. Boykin, A. J. Anderson, & J. F. Yates (Eds.), *Research directions of black psychologists* (107–30). New York: Russell Sage Foundation.

Cross, W. E. (1991). *Shades of black: Diversity in African-American identity.* Philadelphia: Temple University Press.

DuBois, W. E. B. (1903). *Souls of black folks.* Chicago: A. C. McClurg & Co.

Helms. J. (1986). Expanding racial identity theory to cover counseling process. *Journal of Counseling Psychology, 33,* 62–64.

Helms, J. E. (Ed.) (1990). *Black and white racial identity: Theory, research, and practice.* New York: Greenwood Press.

Hogg, M. A., Abrams, D., & Patel, Y. (1987). Ethnic identity, self-esteem, and occupational aspirations of Indian and Anglo-Saxon British adolescents. *Genetic, Social, and General Psychology Monographs, 113,* 487–508.

Jones, J. M. (1972). *Prejudice and racism* Reading, MA: Addison-Wesley.

Jones, J. M. (1991). The politics of personality: Being black in America. In R. L. Jones (Ed.), *Black psychology* (3d ed., 305–18). Berkeley, CA: Cobb & Henry.

Jones, R. L. (Ed.) (1991). *Black psychology* (3rd ed.). Berkeley, CA: Cobb & Henry.

Kardiner, A., & Ovesy, L. (1951). *The mark of oppression.* New York: Norton.

Katz, I. (1981). *Stigma.* New York: McGraw-Hill.

Katz, I., & Hass, R. G. (1988). Racial ambivalence and American value conflict: Correlational and priming studies of dual cognitive structures. *Journal of Personality and Social Psychology, 55,* 893–905.

Lockesley, A., Hepburn, C., & Ortiz, U. (1982). Social stereotypes and judgments of individuals. *Journal of Experimental Social Psychology, 18,* 23–42.

Myrdal, G. (1944). *An American dilemma.* New York: McGraw-Hill.

Parham, T. A., & Helms, J. E. (1981). The influence of black students' racial identity attitudes on preference for counselor's race. *Journal of Counseling Psychology, 28,* 250–57.

Parham, T. A., & Helms, J. E. (1985). Relation of racial identity attitudes to self-actualization and affective states of black students. *Journal of Counseling Psychology, 32,* 431–40.

Pettigrew, T. E. (1964). *Profile of the Negro American.* New York: Van Nostrand Reinhold.

Pomales, J., Claiborn, C. D., & LaFramboise, T. D. (1986). Effects of black students' racial identity on perceptions of white counselors varying in cultural sensitivity. *Journal of Counseling Psychology, 33*(1), 57–61.

Sawyer, K. (1986). King scholars steal Bennett's lines. *Washington Post,* January 15, A8.

Steele, C. (1990). *The content of our characters*. New York: St. Martin's Press.

Tajfel, H., & Turner, J. C. (1979). An integrative theory of intergroup conflict. In S. Worchel & W. G. Austin (Eds.), *The social psychology of intergroup relations*. Monterey, CA: Brooks-Cole.

vanden Berghe, P. (1967). *Race and racism: A comparative perspective*. New York: Wiley.

Williams, G. (1960). Egomania in the thought of Antonio Gramsci: Some notes on interpretation. *Journal of the History of Ideas*, Oct.-Dec., 585–97.

Wilson, W. J. (1987). *The truly disadvantaged: The inner city, the underclass, and public policy*. Chicago: University of Chicago Press.

Chapter 11. American Convictions about Conflictive U.S.A.–U.S.S.R. Relations: A Case of Group Beliefs

Axelrod, R. (1976). The analysis of cognitive maps. In R. Axelrod (Ed.), *Structure of decision* (55–73). Princeton, NJ: Princeton University Press.

Barghoorn, F. C. (1950). *The Soviet image of the United States*. New York: Kernikal Press.

Bar-Tal, D. (1986). The Masada syndrome: A case of central belief. In N. Milgram (Ed.), *Stress and coping in time of war* (32–51). New York: Brunner/Mazel.

Bar-Tal, D. (1989). Delegitimization: A social psychological analysis. In D. Bar-Tal, C. Graumann, A. W. Kruglanski, & W. Stroebe (Eds.), *Stereotyping and prejudice: Changing conceptions* (169–88). New York: Springer-Verlag.

Bar-Tal, D. (1990a). *Group beliefs: A conception for analyzing group structure, processes, and behavior*. New York: Springer-Verlag.

Bar-Tal, D. (1990b). Israel-Palestinian conflict: A cognitive analysis. *International Journal of Intercultural Relations, 14,* 7–29.

Bar-Tal, D., & Geva, N. (1985). A cognitive basis of international conflicts. In S. Worchel & W. B. Austin (Eds.), *The social psychology of intergroup relations* (2d ed., 118–33). Chicago: Nelson-Hall.

Bar-Tal, D., Klar, Y., & Kruglanski, A. W. (1989). Conflict termination: An epistemological analysis of international cases. *Political Psychology, 10,* 235–55.

Bialer, S. (1985). The psychology of U.S.-Soviet relations. *Political Psychology, 6,* 263–73.

Bowie, R. R. (1984). The president and the executive branch. In J. S. Nye, Jr. (Ed.), *The making of America's Soviet policy* (63–94). New Haven, CT: Yale University Press.

Bronfenbrenner, U. (1961). The mirror image in Soviet-American relations: A social psychologist's report. *Journal of Social Issues, 27*(3), 45–56.

Buckley, G. J. (1978). American public opinion and the origins of the cold war: A speculative reassessment. *Mid-America, 60,* 35–42.

Caldwell, D. (1981). *American-Soviet relations*. Westport, CT: Greenwood Press.

Caldwell, L. T., & Diebold, W., Jr. (1981). *Soviet-American relations in the 1980s*. New York: McGraw-Hill.

Cogley, J. (1956). *Report on blacklisting. 1: Movies.* New York: Fund for the Republic.

Cohen, S. F. (1986). *Sovieticus: American perceptions and Soviet realities.* New York: Norton.

Converse, P. E. (1964). The nature of belief systems in mass publics. In D. E. Apter (Ed.), *Ideology and discontent* (206–61). New York: Free Press.

Coser, L. (1956). *The functions of social conflict.* Glencoe, IL: Free Press.

Dallin, A. (1973). Bias and blunders in American studies on the USSR. *Slavic Review, 32,* 560–76.

Dormann, W. A. (1983). The image of the Soviet Union in the American news media: Coverage of Brezhnev, Andropov, and MX. In D. M. Rubin & M. Cunningham (Eds.), *War, peace, and the news media* (44–76). Proceedings of the Conference on War, Peace, and the News Media held at New York University, 18–19 March 1983.

English, R., & Halperin, J. J. (1987). *The other side: How Soviets and Americans perceive each other.* New Brunswick, NJ: Transaction Books.

Eirkson, R. S., Luttberg, N. R., & Tedin, K. L. (1980). *American public opinion: Its origin, content, and impact* (2d ed.). New York: Wiley.

Festinger, L. (1954). A theory of social comparison processes. *Human relations, 7,* 117–40.

Filene, P. G. (1967). *Americans and the Soviet experiment, 1917–1933.* Cambridge: Harvard University Press.

Finlay, D. J., Holsti, O. R., & Fagen, R. R. (1967). *Enemies in politics.* Chicago: Rand McNally.

Free, L. A., & Cantril, H. (1967). *The political beliefs of Americans—a study of public opinion.* New Brunswick, NJ: Rutgers University Press.

Frei, D. (1986). *Perceived images: U.S. and Soviet assumptions and perceptions in disarmament.* Totowa, NJ: Rowman & Allanheld.

Fyne, R. (1985). From Hollywood to Moscow. *Literature/Film Quarterly, 13,* 194–99.

Gaddis, J. L. (1972). *The United States and the origins of the cold war 1941–1947.* New York: Columbia University Press.

Gallup, G. H. (1972). *The Gallup poll: Public opinion 1935–1971* (Vol. 1–3). New York: Random House.

Gallup, G. H. (1978). *The Gallup poll: Public opinion 1972–77* (Vol. 1–2). Wilmington, DE: Scholarly Resources.

Garthoff, R. L. (1985). *Détente and confrontation: American-Soviet relations from Nixon to Reagan.* Washington, DC: Brookings Institute.

Grayson, B. L. (Ed.) (1978). *The American image of Russia: 1917–1977.* New York: Frederick Ungar.

Hann. H. (1983, December 11). Seeing red: How Hollywood movies handle the Russians. *New York Daily News.*

Henry, J. (1963). *Culture against man.* New York: Random House.

Herrmann, R. K. (1985). American perceptions of Soviet foreign policy: reconsidering three competing perspectives. *Political Psychology, 6,* 375–411.

Herrmann, R. K. (1986). The power of perceptions in foreign-policy decision making. Do views of the Soviet Union determine the policy choices of American leaders? *American Journal of Political Science, 30,* 841–75.

Holsti, O. R. (1962). The belief system and national images. *Journal of Conflict Resolution, 6,* 244–52.

Holsti, O. R., & Rosenau, J. N. (1984). *American leadership in world affairs.* Boston: Allen & Unwin.

Holsti, O. R., & Rosenau, J. N. (1986). Consensus lost; consensus regained? Foreign policy beliefs of American leaders (1976–1980). *International Studies Quarterly, 30,* 375–409.

Jervis, R. (1976). *Perception and misperception in international politics.* Princeton, NJ: Princeton University Press.

Jones, E. E., & Gerand, H. B (1967). *Foundations of social psychology.* New York: Wiley.

Key, V. O., Jr. (1967). *Public opinion and American democracy.* New York: Knopf.

Klar, Y., Bar-Tal, D., & Kruglanski, A. W. (1988). Conflict as a cognitive schema. In W. Stroebe, A. W. Kruglanski, D. Bar-Tal, & M. Hewstone (Eds.), *The social psychology of intergroup conflict* (73–85). New York: Springer-Verlag.

Krech, D., Crutchfield, R. S., & Ballachey, E. L. (1962). *Individual in society.* New York: McGraw-Hill.

Kruglanski, A. W., Bar-Tal, D., & Klar, Y. (in press). A social cognitive theory of conflict. *Journal of Peace Research.*

Larson, D. W. (1985). *Origins of containment: A psychological explanation.* Princeton, NJ: Princeton University Press.

Levering, R. B. (1976). *American opinion and the Russian alliance, 1939–1945.* Chapel Hill: University of North Carolina Press.

Lewin, K. (1947). Frontiers in group dynamics. *Human Relations, 1,* 5–41.

Lippmann, W., & Menz, C. (1920, August 4). A test of the news. *New Republic* (a special supplement), 1–42.

Little, D. (1983). Antibolshevism and American foreign policy, 1917–1939: The diplomacy of self-delusion. *American Quarterly, 35,* 376–90.

Litwak, R. S. (1984). *Détente and the Nixon doctrine.* Cambridge: Cambridge University Press.

Maddox, R. J. (1977) *The unknown war with Russia: Wilson's Siberian intervention.* San Rafael, CA: Presidio Press.

Maddux, T. R. (1980). *Years of estrangement: American relations with the Soviet Union, 1933–1941.* Tallahassee, FL: Florida State University.

North, R. C., Koch, H. E., & Zinnes, D. A. (1960). The integrative functions of conflict. *Journal of Conflict Resolution, 4,* 356–74.

Perkovich, G. (1987, January-February). Beyond the cold war. *Nuclear Times,* 12–16, 18, 20, 41.

Quester, G. H. (1978). Origins of the cold war: Some clues from public opinion. *Political Science Quarterly, 93,* 645–63.

Roffman, P., & Pardy, J. (1981). *The Hollywood social problem film.* Bloomington: Indiana University Press.

Schneider, W. (1984). Public opinion. In J. S. Nye, Jr. (Ed.), *The making of America's Soviet policy* (11–35). New Haven, CT: Yale University Press.

Shipler, D. K. (1985, Nov. 10). How we see each other: The view from America. *The New York Times Magazine,* 33–34, 36, 40, 48, 72, 78, 80, 82–84.

Singer, J. D. (1964). Content analysis of elite articulations. *Journal of Conflict Resolutions, 8,* 424–85.

Small, M. (1974). How we learned to love the Russians: American media and the Soviet Union during World War II. *The Historian, 36,* 455–78.

Smith, T. W. (1983). American attitudes toward the Soviet Union and Communism. *Public Opinion Quarterly, 47,* 277–92.

Stein, H. F. (1982). Adversary symbiosis and complementary group dissociation: An analysis of the U.S./U.S.S.R. conflict. *International Journal of Intercultural Relations, 6,* 55–58.

Stevenson, R. W. (1985). *The rise and fall of détente.* London: Macmillan.

Stoessinger, J. G. (1979). *Crusaders and pragmatists.* New York: Norton.

Stouffer, S. A. (1966). *Communism, conformity, and civil liberties.* New York: Doubleday.

Tajfel, H. (Ed.) (1978). *Differentiation between groups.* London: Academic Press.

Tajfel, H. (Ed.). (1982). *Social identity and intergroup relations.* Cambridge: Cambridge University Press.

Talbott, S. (1984). *The Russians and Reagan.* New York: Vintage Books.

Turner, J.C. (1987). *Rediscovering the social group.* Oxford: Basil Blackwell.

Tyroler, C. (Ed.) (1984). *Alerting America: The papers of the Committee on the Present Danger.* Washington, DC: Pergamon & Brassey's.

Ugolnik, A. (1983). The godlessness within: Stereotyping the Russians. *The Christian Century, 100,* 1011–14.

Ulam, A. B. (1971). *The rivals: America and Russia since World War II.* New York: Viking Press.

Volkan, V. D. (1985). The need to have enemies and allies. A developmental approach. *Political psychology, 6,* 219–47.

Welch, W. (1970). *American images of Soviet foreign policy.* New Haven, CT: Yale University Press.

White, R. H. (1984). *Fearful warriors: A psychological profile of U.S.-Soviet relations.* New York: Free Press.

Chapter 12. Resolving Large-Scale Political Conflict: The Case of the Round Table Negotiations in Poland

Alwin, D. (1989). Social stratification, conditions of work, and parental socialization values. In N. Eisenberg, J. Reykowski, & E. Staub (Eds.), *Social and moral values.* Hillsdale, NJ: Erlbaum.

Bar-Tal, D. (n.d.). *Understanding psychological bases of the Israeli-Palestinian conflict.* Discussion paper 12. Tel Aviv: International Center for Peace in the Middle East.

Bilig, M. (1976). *Social psychology of intergroup relations.* London: Academic Press.

Centrum Badania Opinii Spolecznej (CBOS) (1989). *Popularnosc osobistosci zycia publicznego kraju w listopadzie '89.* Komunikat z badan. Warszawa.

Deutsch, M. (1973). *The resolution of conflict.* New Haven, CT: Yale University Press.

Doob, L. W. (1987). Adieu to private intervention in political conflicts. *International Journal of Group Tensions, 17.*

Dunlop, J. T. (1983). The negotiation alternative in dispute resolution. *Villanova Law Review, 29,* 1421–48.

Eysenck, H. J., & Wilson, G. D. (1978). *The psychological basis of ideology.* Baltimore, MD: University Park Press.

Gebert, K. (1990). *Mebel.* London: Aneks.

Hoffman, M. (1989). Empathy and prosocial activism. In N. Eisenberg, J. Reykowski, & E. Staub (Eds.), *Social and moral values.* Hillsdale, NJ: Erlbaum.

Kahneman, D., & Tversky, A. (1984). Choices, values, and frames. *American Psychologist, 47,* 341–50.

Karl, T. L., & Schmitter, P. C. (1990). Modes of transition in South and Central America, Southern and Eastern Europe. Paper prepared for publication. Stanford University, Dept. of Political Science.

Kelman H. C., & Cohen, S. P. (1979). Reduction of international conflict. An interactive approach. In W. Austin & S. Worchel (Eds.), *The social psychology of intergroup relations.* Monterey, CA: Brooks.

Kohn, M. L (1969). *Class and conformity: A study in values.* Homewood, IL: Dorsey Press.

Kohn, M., & Schooler, C. (1983). *Work and personality: An inquiry into impact of social stratification.* Norwood, NJ: Ablex.

Koralewicz, J., & Ziolkowski, M. (In press). *Mentalnosc Polakow.* Poznan: Nakom.

Latane, B. (1981). The psychology of social impact. *American Psychologist, 36,* 343–45.

Nowak, S. (1976). *Ciaglosc i zmiana tradycji kulturowej.* Raport. Warszawa: Uniwersytet Warszawski.

Osgood, C. (1963). *An alternative to war or surrender.* Urbana: University of Illinois Press.

Pruitt D. (1986). *Social conflict.* New York: Random House.

Ross, L. (1990). Recognizing the role of construal process. In I. Rock (Ed.), *The legacy of Solomon Asch: Essays in cognition and social psychology.* Hillsdale, NJ: Erlbaum.

Ross, L., & Stillinger, C. A. (1988). *Psychological barriers to conflict resolution.* Stanford Center on Conflict and Negotiation Working Paper No. 4. Stanford, CA: Stanford University.

Rothbart, M. (1990). Intergroup perception and social conflict. Paper presented at the International Symposium on Group Dynamics, Texas A&M University, College Station, TX.

Sherif, M. (1977). *Group conflict and cooperation: Their social psychology.* London: Routledge & Kegan Paul.

Stillinger, C. A., Epelbaum, M., Keltner, D., & Ross, L. (1990). The "reactive devaluation" barrier to conflict resolution. *Journal of Personality and Social Psychology.*

Streufert, S., & Streufert, S. (1986). The development of international conflict. In S. Worchel & W. Austin (Eds.), *Psychology of intergroup relations.* Chicago: Nelson-Hall.

Webb, W. M., & Worchel, P. (1986). Trust and distrust. In S. Worchel & W. Austin (Eds.), *Psychology of intergroup relations*. Chicago: Nelson-Hall.

Worchel, S. (1979). Cooperation and reduction of intergroup conflict. Some determining factors. In W. Austin & S. Worchel (Eds.), *The social psychology of intergroup relations*. Monterey, CA: Brooks.

CHAPTER 14. COALITIONS ACROSS CONFLICT LINES: THE INTERPLAY OF CONFLICTS WITHIN AND BETWEEN THE ISRAELI AND PALESTINIAN COMMUNITIES

Burton, J.W. (1969). *Conflict and communication: The use of controlled communication in international relations*. London: Macmillan.

Burton, J. W. (1979). *Deviance, terrorism and war: The process of solving unsolved social and political problems*. New York: St. Martin's Press.

Burton, J. W. (1984). *Global conflict: The domestic sources of international crisis*. Brighton, Sussex: Wheatsheaf.

Harkabi, Y. (1988). *Israel's fateful hour*. New York: Harper & Row.

Kelman, H. C. (1972). The problem-solving workshop in conflict resolution. In R. L. Merritt (Ed.), *Communication in international politics* (168–204). Urbana: University of Illinois Press.

Kelman, H. C. (1978). Israelis and Palestinians: Psychological prerequisites for mutual acceptance. *International Security, 3*, 162–86.

Kelman, H. C. (1979). An interactional approach to conflict resolution and its application to Israeli-Palestinian relations. *International Interactions, 6*, 99–122.

Kelman, H. C. (1986). Interactive problem solving: A social-psychological approach to conflict resolution. In W. Klassen (Ed.), *Dialogue toward interfaith understanding* (293–314). Tantur/Jerusalem: Ecumenical Institute for Theological Research.

Kelman, H. C. (1987). The political psychology of the Israeli-Palestinian conflict: How can we overcome the barriers to a negotiated solution? *Political Psychology, 8*, 347–63.

Kelman, H. C. (1991). Interactive problem solving: The uses and limits of a therapeutic model for the resolution of international conflicts. In V. D. Volkan, J. V. Montville, & D. A. Julius (Eds.), *The psychodynamics of international relationships. Vol. 2: Unofficial diplomacy at work* (145–60). Lexington, MA: Lexington Books.

Kelman, H. C. (1992). Informal mediation by the scholar/practitioner. In J. Bercovitch & J. Z. Rubin (Eds.), *Mediation in international relations: Multiple approaches to conflict management* (64–96). New York: Macmillan.

Kelman, H.C., & Cohen, S. P. (1986). Resolution of international conflict: An interactional approach. In S. Worchel & W. G. Austin (Eds.), *Psychology of intergroup relations* (2nd ed., 323–42). Chicago: Nelson-Hall.

Rothbart, M., & John, O. P. (1985). Social categorization and behavioral episodes: A cognitive analysis of the effects of intergroup contact. *Journal of Social Issues, 41*(3), 81–104.

Rothbart, M., & Lewis, S. (1988). Inferring category attributes from exemplar attributes: Geometric shapes and social categories. *Journal of Personality and Social Psychology, 55*, 861–72.

Stevenson, W. B., Pearce, J. L., & Porter, L. W. (1985). The concept of "coalition" in organization theory and research. *Academy of Management Review, 10*, 256–68.

Walton, R. E. (1970). A problem-solving workshop on border conflicts in Eastern Africa. *Journal of Applied Behavioral Science, 6*, 453–89.

Name Index

Boldface page numbers refer to authors of chapters.

Subject Index

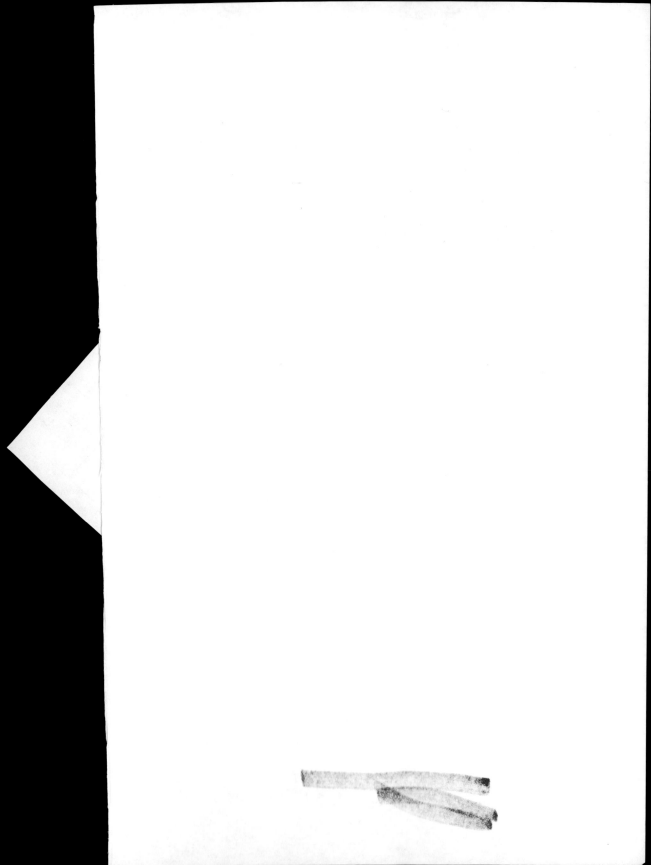

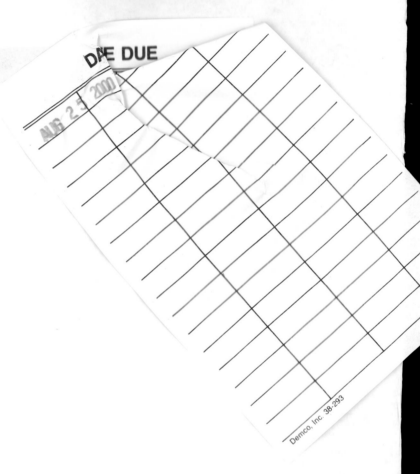